AUTHOR'S NOTE

The land itself is the primary source. I first became interested in the story of the Mad Trapper while living in Yellowknife, 1970–72. Two years of traveling out on the land and of hearing old-timers talk convinced me that there were two northern characters through whom I might come to terms with the Arctic: John Hornby and Albert Johnson. Hornby I dealt with in the novel *Snowman* (Doubleday: 1976). Johnson had to wait.

Meanwhile others were discovering Johnson, and dealing with him in one of two ways: either by giving him a criminal past before he came to the Arctic (Anderson, North), or by romanticizing him with stylized ingredients, such as an unhappy love affair (Kelley, Wiebe). Both were attempts at justification, either of the RCMP or of Johnson, and both were reductive. Several ballads, some poems, two feature-length films, and a number of television programs appeared, further romanticizing the Trapper, dramatizing the manhunt, and bringing the story more and more into the realm of folklore. None of these efforts had much influence on me.

While Johnson was being hunted down by a second-generation posse of scholars, writers, film-makers, and balladeers, I was skirmishing (1972–74) with the FBI in and around New Orleans and feeling a paranoia similar to what Johnson must have felt forty years earlier. As the FBI pursued me from the Mexican to the Canadian border, and raided the places where I hid, Albert Johnson became my conscious and visceral model.

In the summer of 1978 I retraced on foot and by canoe Johnson's probable route from his arrival at Fort

McPherson to his death on the Eagle River. The trip, for which I was well equipped, was extremely grueling, and I was laboring under none of the handicaps Johnson had labored under: a pursuing posse, no food, no shelter, and, most implacable, winter. Even in summer I found the mountains impassable and was forced to go around them.

Returning from the Yukon with the external imprint of the land, and the internal memory of having been pursued, in the fall of 1978 I took a room and started writing. The siege in the room was ended two years later when *Trapper* was finished.

The story of Albert Johnson as set forth here is factually accurate—a claim no other chronicler of the story has dared to make, though all have made use of the same source material: the extensive RCMP file in Ottawa graciously made available by RCMP historian Stanley Horrall, and the microfilmed newspaper reports in the National Archives. The newspaper articles, cables, night letters, and radiograms used in *Trapper* are all (except the one of January 16th) authentic, and have been transcribed verbatim, or edited only slightly. But while the details of the story—dates, places, names, etc.—are factually accurate, the entire story has been used here as a vehicle for a larger endeavor, and the characters, though they bear the same names as their historic counterparts, are entirely fictional. This is especially true of the main characters: Eames, Rene, Mildred Urquhart, the bishop (actually an Anglican clergyman), and, of course, Johnson. I did not know, and did not wish to know, much about these characters' backgrounds; I had ghosts of my own to exorcise. So *Trapper* is, finally, a work of fiction, and I am content to let it stand as that.

Secondary material utilized and here gratefully acknowledged includes the following. Arthurian material is from Malory, *The Morte Darthur,* ed. D. S. Brewer (Northwestern University Press, Evanston: 1973). Scriptural quotations are from *The Jerusalem Bible,* except Mildred Urquhart's recitation of *Song of Solomon* 7:6–10 (KJV). The Candlemas liturgy and the Canticle of Simeon are taken from the *Saint Andrew Daily Missal.* Mildred Urquhart's vision and King's dream of Johnson draw much of their flavor and a few of their words from the Gnostic gospels, especially *The First Apocalypse of James, The Gospel of Mary,* and *The Thunder, Perfect Mind.* Johnson's moral inventory in "The First Day" is indebted to the Buddhistic *Book of the Discipline* and *Milinda's Questions.* The bishop's birthday poem is a paraphrase of Samuel Johnson's well-known poem for Hester Thrale, and the German poems are reprinted in Gordon A. Craig, *Germany 1866–1945.* Johnson's speech to the bishop draws upon Elias Canetti's diary entries, published as *The Human Province,* and "The Third Day" is based in part on "The Strange Case of Schreber" paraphrased by Canetti in *Crowds and Power.* The Philosopher in "The Second Day" is based on material drawn from James K. Feibleman's *The New Materialism,* and in "The Eighth Day" from Werner Heisenberg's *Physics and Philosophy.* My thanks, too, to Elizabeth Hartley for notes leading to the Biochemist, to Art Turner for aeronautical advice and his dreams of Zebulon Pike, to Bryan Everitt for reading the manuscript both piecemeal and heapmeal, to Paul York for much fine art work depicting scenes in the novel and for sharing the siege in the room, to Rick Archbold of Doubleday for his sensitive editing, and, most important, to my good friend, Ed Winacott, without whom I wouldn't have taken the trip, without which I couldn't have written the book.

Finally, since it was an integral part of the writing of *Trapper,* I wish to acknowledge the music to which the various sections were written: I—Hovhaness, Symphony No. 15; II—Schönberg, String Quartets; III—Webern, Complete Works; IV—Berg, *Lulu;* V—Lutoslawski, Preludes and Fugue; VI—Stockhausen, "Inori"; VII—Shostakovich, Symphonies Nos. 4, 11, 14.

The novel *Trapper* was not written in subsidized ease or amid pleasant surroundings, but with anxiety and haste in hours stolen from a full-time job, in a cellar in Toronto where the sewer occasionally flooded.

Keswick, Ont.
Christmas 1980

PROLOGUE

Pleasant Acres Rest Home. Burnaby, British Columbia. L-shaped, ranch-style, surrounded by the split-level houses of a subdivision. A car drove up the driveway, and a young man got out. He locked the car and stood for a moment surveying the rest home's facade, the frayed palm tree and poorly tended rock garden in the middle of the driveway, the patchy grass of the untended lawn. Then he walked to and entered the main doors, proceeding to a desk in the foyer where a male orderly in white sat in a chair and a female orderly, also in white, sat on the desk itself, conversing with the male orderly.

"Excuse me. I'd like to see one of your residents, Mr. A. N. Eames."

The two orderlies quit talking. The woman on the desk twisted her body sideways to look at the visitor. She and the male orderly glanced at each other.

"I called. The lady I spoke with said I'd be able to see Mr. Eames." He waited. Neither of the orderlies answered. "I'm with the *Sun*," he added. "We're doing an article."

"Not about the Home?" said the male orderly.

"No. It's about something Mr. Eames was involved in nearly fifty years ago."

"I bet it's that Mad Trapper business," said the female to the male orderly. Then to the reporter, "He won't see you. There've been others. He won't see any of them."

1

"I'd like to try," the reporter said, and waited.

The woman clucked her tongue in her mouth, as though this were an adjunct to thinking. She was in her late thirties, but she obviously felt young at the Home. Perched on the desk, she looked young, except that the tight-fitting two-piece white uniform accentuated the spread of her buttocks. She quit clucking, and shrugged. "I'll take him," she said to the male orderly, and hopped down off the desk. "This way," she said pleasantly.

They walked along a corridor, off which were rooms on either side. The doors to most were open, revealing a single bed or twin beds, and an old man or woman, more often a woman, seated in front of a television set. At regular intervals the corridor wall was cut away to accommodate a nurses' station or a parlor room. The parlor rooms were completely open to view, and contained a sofa and several easy chairs arranged in front of a TV. Only two or three old people were sitting in them. From each room they passed the sound of the television set blared forth into the hallway.

". . . watch it, though it's on all the time," the woman was saying. "Evenings it's bingo, or cards, or TV, or church service on Sundays—the local ministers take turns coming. Now"—she held open one of two double doors which blocked the corridor; the doors were of stainless steel with a small wire net pane of thick glass— "we enter the lower intestine," she said. "That's what we call it. It's real name is 'Special Services Ward.' They couldn't call it 'Terminal,' because all of our cases here are."

"Are what?"

"Terminal."

"Oh." The reporter nodded and entered the door she held open. A sickly sweet smell assailed him. He sniffed. "Smells like a dead body," he said.

"Glycerin. Glycerin spills on the floor. In the morning, after the cleaning woman's been in, it smells of ammonia."

They proceeded along the corridor on the other side of the metal doors. The doors to each of the rooms off the corridor were of similar metal, with a small thick glass pane inset in each. All of the doors here were closed, and there was no parlor room. At the nurses' station was a register book, with slots for the names of the patient and the visitor, and the times in and out. There was no nurse in sight, but the reporter wrote in the book while his guide waited. Then they walked past the vacated nurses' station and past two more stainless steel doors.

"This is his," the orderly said. She stopped at the third metal door, and peeked through the observation pane. After a moment she drew away, and gestured for the reporter to look. "Inspector Eames of the Arctic," she said.

The old man inside was in a long bathrobe and seated, his back at a three-quarters angle to the door, in front of a television set. The set was turned off, and he appeared to be reading; a large brown book lay open on his lap. A shock of unruly white hair surmounted the thin neck, and gray stubble grizzled the gaunt sucked-in cheek and bare throat that was visible above the maroon bathrobe. The old man was wearing glasses, but due to the wire mesh in the observation window and the angle at which he was sitting it was impossible to tell whether he was in fact reading, or just dozing in his easy chair. The chair faced, past the blank TV screen, a window in the far wall. It was high and small and, like the pane in the door, not designed to be opened. There were two interior doors: one opened to a small toilet, and the other to what was probably a clothes closet. Between the two doors was a bookshelf, with a row of books on it. On the other side of the room was a cot, at the foot of the cot the easy chair in which the old man was sitting, and facing the easy chair a straight-backed chair. A bedside table stood between the cot and easy chair, with a reading lamp and some sort of game on it. The lamp was turned on, but the man in the chair did not move. Perhaps he was dozing.

"Does he ever watch TV?" asked the reporter.

"He watches a few things. Every afternoon he turns on 'The Funny Hour'—it's a great favorite around here;

he watches it, but I've never seen him laugh. Then he
watches 'Hogan's Heroes,' and 'Gomer Pyle,' and
'MASH'—that's all he ever watches, except for World
War Two documentaries, and whenever there's an old
Charlie Chan movie, he watches it. I'm sure he's seen
them all several times, and there must be at least
twenty. But mainly he reads—he's a great reader—
and plays with himself, I mean, you know"—she
laughed—"games. You see his backgammon set? He
plays by himself every night. Well, actually he plays
by himself, but he thinks he's playing *with* someone.
It's the same opponent each night. He comes supposedly
every night around eight—that's only forty-five minutes from now. Eames won't see *anyone* then."

"Let's see if he'll see me now."

She looked dubious, her hand clasping keys she had
pulled from her pocket. "If he won't," she said, glancing
up and down the vacant corridor, "I'll let you listen in.
We're not supposed to, but..." She stepped aside from
where she had been standing, revealing a small three-
pronged plug in the wall by the door. "A monitoring
device," she said. "This is a loony ward, you know—or
did you?"

"Well...no, I didn't."

"This section is. The other part's just a rest home."
She selected a key from among twenty or more on a
large key ring, and unlocked the door. "Don't tell him
you're a reporter," she said, her hand on the doorknob.
She gave it a vigorous twist, and they went in.

"Inspector Eames," she said cheerily, "are you awake?
There's a nice young man here to see you."

The old man gave a start and the book which had
lain in his lap fell to the floor. The reporter crossed
ahead of the orderly and could see as he bent down the
red lines of two recent scars from the bridge of the old
man's nose across his cheeks to his earlobes. He stooped
to retrieve the book—a large brown cloth book with an
odd title in Gothic type—and coming up with his eyes
at neck level noticed the other scar, which slit the old
man's throat from earlobe to earlobe with tiny red cross-
stitched x's. The orderly, noticing him staring at the

scars, said, "Inspector Eames had a tracheotomy earlier this year, and he came through just fine. But he still sneaks a smoke now and then, don't you, Inspector?" The old man glared at her through his glasses, the triangle of skin within the three red scars—from the bridge of his nose to his earlobes, and from ear to ear across his throat—reddening beneath the stubble of ash-colored beard. "The Inspector grows whiskers inside his mouth, too. Oh, I know all about you, Inspector. You let the night-duty orderly kiss you."

"I did not," the old man growled. "The strumpet insisted."

"She said it tickled her tongue."

"Gossipy bitch."

"The doctors, when they sewed up the Inspector, folded a flap of cheek inside his mouth, and it doesn't know it's inside," she explained merrily to the reporter as if Eames were not there. The reporter had sat down in the chair opposite Eames. Eames himself had turned his head sideways away from them both, as if they were not there, and was staring fixedly at the wall by the head of the cot. "They didn't take his voice box, though. He's still a great talker, aren't you?" She paused, waiting for Eames to say something. Eames stared at the wall and said nothing. The reporter sat staring at the cross-stitched necklace of scar. The orderly stood over both of them, arms akimbo, the palms of her hands firmly planted on her hips. "And a great reader. What were you reading, Inspector?" She picked up the book the reporter had retrieved from the floor and read from its spine: *"Secretum Secretorum.* Where did you get this? He's a deep one," she said to the reporter. "He has friends, don't you, Inspector? Did your friend bring you this? I see it's from the library." She opened the book. "My, my," she said, clucking her tongue while turning the pages at random. "Can you read this, Inspector?"

The reporter's gaze followed the old man's, to a spot on the wall, then wandered about the room, scrutinizing the metal door from inside, the washbasin and towel rack, the clothes closet door, the bookshelf. He cricked his neck slightly to see better the titles of the books on the shelf: *Life and Times of Zebulon Pike;* Malory, *The Morte Darthur;* Cruttwell, *History of the Great War;* Fuller, *The Second World War;* Bullock, *Hitler;* and one whose title he could not decipher. The orderly was still turning pages.

"He's very particular about his books, rereads those same few over and over, and when he gets a new one in his head...last week I had to find a novel for him, The Un-something, *The Unnamable.* The local library didn't have it so we had to order it from the regional library, that's in Vancouver. Do you think he rested easy till he got it? I had to call or go down every day, every day he'd ask me...There it is, there on his shelf, but he hasn't read it, have you, Inspector?" The old man continued to glare at the wall. The orderly held the book with the Gothic type title and turned the pages at random. "Listen to this," she said. "'Most beloved sone Alexandre/trust not in women/nor in theyr werkes/ nor servyces/and company not with them. For whan thy persone is betwene the armes of a woman/thou arte as a Jewell/restynge in the handes of a marchaunt/that careth not to whome it is solde. And beynge betwene her handes/is the poyson of thy welfare/and also the destruccyon of thy body. Beware therefore dere sone/of suche women/for they be venymous and deedly. For it is no newe thynge to knowe that by theyr venym many men have dyed. Thou knowest well...' Was this written for you, Inspector? Your name's Alexander...." The old man suddenly whipped out one hand and snatched the book from her grasp, sequestering it inside his bathrobe.

"Leave me alone" he yelled. His voice was tense and bitter, and his hair was white as snow, and from fear of him the young reporter jumped up from his chair and would have run for the door except that the nurse blocked his way. "Isn't it enough that I pay nine hundred a month to be a prisoner here, but the jailer has to come taunt me? And you, I know what you want—words, words, and more words!—when all the words in the world have been said and there are only curses and threats left, and lawlessness. Prick teases and word

hoards. Not a man left, not a woman worth knowing."
He rose shakily from his chair as he spoke, holding the
book in his bathrobe. "Leave an old man alone," he said
threateningly. "Leave me alone!" he fairly screamed,
and sank down again, turning his face, which was fiery
and blanched, to the wall.

"I don't think the Inspector is at home today," the
orderly said. "His company's due any time now. Isn't it
time for your game, Inspector?" she said sweetly. The
old man sat rigid, glaring fiercely at a fixed spot on the
wall. The orderly watched him a moment, then shrugged.
"Shall we go?" she said to the reporter.

In the corridor, the orderly stood with her back to
the door, trembling slightly. Her eyes were closed and
she appeared to be counting, or mumbling words to
herself, calming herself. She opened her eyes and looked
at the reporter. "I warned you," she said. "Some days
he's like that. Other days he'll stand on the other side
of this door looking out, and he's glad to see anyone.
But when he's the way he was today…" She gave a
little shudder with her shoulders, and looked solicit-
ously at the reporter. The roots of her hair, which was
bleached blond, were brown, and there were beads of
sweat on her forehead and slick black stains around
her eyelashes where her mascara had run. The reporter,
nevertheless, looked warmly back, as if to say: 'You
have a hard job, but despite the strain of it all you are
still a beautiful woman—I can see that, anyone could
see that.' She looked shaken and frail and just like the
reporter's wife looked when she wished to be hugged.

"I have to go now," the orderly said, "but if you want
to stay"—she glanced up and down the deserted corridor—"just turn this in at the desk as you go out." She
produced from her pocket a gray plastic instrument,
with a plug at one end and a funnel at the other. It
resembled a stethoscope. One end she plugged into the
wall socket, and the other end she held. "Just put it to
your ear," she instructed, "like this." Then she handed
it to him, clasping his hand as she did so. He watched
her walk away down the corridor, and waved to her at
the far doors. Then putting the monitoring device to

one ear, and peering in through the observation pane,
he eavesdropped and spied on the old man inside—as
Eames set out his backgammon board...as Eames received his visitor...as Eames and his visitor played....

(Eames in his chair. The backgammon board on the
table between him and his visitor's chair. He carefully
lays out the checkers. He speaks as if to an opponent.)
Black, I presume. Move that stupid TV if it's in your
way. Twelve, thirteen, fourteen, fifteen—there. They're
showing the documentaries again. They'll be showing
them till the next war. New commentary, the same
films. We can watch Monte Cassino tonight. No. You
never were interested in the second one, were you? My
toss? (Eames casts the dice.) Ha-ha! Beat that, you devil!
(He places the dice on the other side of the board.) Who
would have guessed you liked backgammon? Not I. So,
I start. (Eames picks up the dice, and casts.) Five and
four. (He deliberates, then moves two white checkers.
He passes the dice to the other side, picks them up,
casts them, reads them, and moves two black checkers.)
My turn. (He casts the dice, and moves the checkers.)
I've been fiddling around with that code again, you
know, the one Murray showed me. I told you about it.
I couldn't decide whether "depart" meant subtract or
divide. It means divide. You take your name...what *is*
your name? No, just the surname. There's a book out
now that proves you're Arthur Nelson. Nelson of the
Headless Valley, the Nahanni. Six and five, very good.
A hit! You're up to your old tricks, I see, blotting my
men. It's a good defensive tactic. (Eames casts, and moves
his blotted man off the bar.) The gold teeth are the link,
and there's a photograph, not a very good one. You
know that one we took of you on the Eagle? Well, it's
on the same page with this picture of Nelson. I'll show
you the book. I don't have it here now, but I'll get it.
Doubles. Five, ten, fifteen, twenty! Your toss. It'll soon
be fifty years, fifty years. These reporters are bothering
the life out of me—bloodsuckers, the lot of them. Why
don't you grant an interview? Lay the bloody thing to
rest. Not that they care, of course; they've got to fill
space, to kill time. What else ever happened in Canada?

Cocked dice—that rarely happens. Throw again, that's the beauty of the game. Six and four, ten. I don't know, after her funeral I was never interested in looking him up. I knew she'd die first. From the code. I've worked out exactly when I'm going to die, I knew for King, for Parsons, for Riddell. You were the only one I didn't know, and I still can't be sure, because of the name. And Lazarus, of course, but that's because he was dead already and he had his name changed. You're bearing off already? One, two, three, how they suddenly leave the board, King, Millen, Hersey. Ha! There's a hit. Your man's blotted, you won't gammon me. The way it works is, say you take my name: EAMES. *E* is worth twenty-five, *A* is worth three, *M* is worth... I can't remember. Here, I've got it right here. (Eames opens the brown book to a marked page, and reads.) Take tuo names of men whych are gyven them in their birthe, if thou wille know of them tuo feghtyng to-gider or stryvying whych sale ouercome, or of tuo folkes weddede whych sale lenger liv, or of tuo folk goyng any voyage whych sale come ageyne, or of a seke man whether he sale dye or liv. Counte the name of eache of them by the letteres of the ABC and by the noumber that es on eache letter therof—they give the numerical worth of each of the letters. And whan thou hast so done departe al the hole by nene, save of them that are weddid, by sevene loke thou departe. That's the depart, which I finally figured out means divide. And by the overplus of the nene or of the sevene—that's what's left over after you divide by nine, or by seven—thou salt know by one of thise eghte reules who sale ouercome, who sale rather dye, who sale rather come ageyne. And if thou wille know of any seke... You have to go? Anyway, it works out for both EAMES and JOHNSON, if we divide by nine, there's six left over in either case. So, six against six—see, it says here— Sex and sex: the strenger sale ouercome. The stronger shall overcome, and... (Eames looks up from his book, slowly closes it, and sets it down on the boards. His shoulders slump, and he sits back in the chair. Silence.) All the men are borne off. He gammoned me. No more to bear off. I should have... I don't know.... (Eames

produces a pipe from his bathrobe pocket and charges
it with tobacco. He switches off the reading lamp. Darkness. Long pause. The striking of a single match, the
lighting of the pipe.) I'm bloody tired of this game. Fifty
years, fifty years ... (The faint red light of a pipe being
puffed.) All the rest too, King and Parsons and Riddell
and Gardlund, even Mildred—all of them. I'm the only
one now. It's a farce, it's a joke with no one but me to
laugh. Laugh, you joker, laugh! Ha-ha-ha-ha ha-ha-ha-
ha ah-ah (Coughing. Deep congested coughs. The red
light of a pipe again, fainter.) My only pleasure, my
only goddamned pleasure. The stronger shall overcome.
The strenger sale ouercome. The stronger shall overcome ... (Darkness and silence in the room.)

The reporter wondered if he should knock on the
door, or at least ask the orderly to look in on the old
man. But perhaps the old man was sleeping, perhaps
he slept sitting up with a pipe in his mouth, perhaps
this was part of his ritual, his nightly ritual, and he
would resent being disturbed. Besides, the reporter
didn't want to encounter the orderly, and he felt embarrassed by what he had heard. It was sad, somehow,
and ugly, and useless, and old—it would not fit into a
story. People didn't want to read about loony old men
in rest homes, they wanted to read what they already
knew: how Johnson, a madman, had been hunted and
killed fifty years ago, and how Eames, a good man, had
hunted and killed him. The dead were dead and the
living were living, and if once you confused the line
between them no telling where it might lead. Nothing
was certain then, nothing. It was a bum assignment....

PART ONE

The River

1

A hundred and fifty miles south of the Arctic Ocean, near the mountainous boundary of the Yukon and the Northwest Territories, the Peel River flows swiftly and strong, draining the mountains to the west, and watering the land to the east and north. A few miles downstream, where the Rat and the Husky rivers flow into the Peel, which four or five miles further on flows into the Mackenzie, all the rivers are lost in a delta of blind channels, lagoons, and backwaters which, backing up further and further each year, pry open wider and wider the mouth of the Mackenzie where it empties into the ocean. But prior to its confluence with the Mackenzie, the Peel is a broad, swift river, taking its rise in the mountains to the south and flowing northward for hundreds of miles, fed by numerous mountain streams and fresh water springs and myriad lakes and small rivers. From the air, the Peel resembles a thick brown rope twisting sinuously between the Yukon's mountain terrain and the treeless tundra of the Northwest Territories. Black spruce line the river's low cutbanks, and sandbars loom dark in its channels. The river itself is turgid and brown, lighter brown at the back eddies where clear-colored streams feed into it; and over the dark sandbars down its center the water glistens in sunlight.

In the early hours of a summer day in 1931, beneath a midnight sun in a cloudless sky, a man was rafting

down the Peel River. The raft the man stood on was
poorly constructed and not very maneuverable, but it
bobbed along at a good pace, propelled by the brisk
current. Made of three logs lashed together and guided
by a long pole, the clumsy craft was not big enough to
breach the small whirlpools the river sucked down, and
from time to time it dipped into one and was swung
completely around, nearly upsetting the man. He stood
with feet braced, legs wide apart, and holding with both
hands the pole with which he fended off deadheads,
shoved off from sandbars, and balanced himself. The
river moaned and mumbled beneath and all around
him; further off it maintained a constant and dull roar
as it waged its unrelenting war against the shore a
quarter mile distant. Wind funneled up the channel and
clashed against the current, waves slopped across the
raft and slapped his ankles, numbing him. The roar
and the clash of the river registered on his senses like
a dull toothache. His eyes were fixed on the black water
just ahead, watching for deadheads which might wreck
the raft, sandbars he might run aground on, and whirlpools which might swallow or upset him. The river with
its treacheries and deceits dominated his senses. But
he was not unaware of the cloudless sky, the Arctic sun
lolling along the horizon—never rising, never setting:
circling—of black spruce bush along the bank and gray
hills beyond, and beyond the hills the blue mountains
with their white peaks, silken and soft in the midnight
sun, impossibly distant.

A flight of ducks whirred overhead, and a sea gull
squawked at him, reminding him that he was within
a day's journey of the Arctic Ocean. Not many miles
downstream from where he now was the Peel would
pour its murky waters into the murkier waters of the
Mackenzie; but he was not going that far, as far as the
ocean, or even as far as the Mackenzie. To go that far
he would have to pass through, not only Fort Mc-
Pherson, but Aklavik as well: expose himself, twice, to
being sniffed at and barked at by packs of dogs and
followed about by troops of snotty-nosed kids, yelling,
"Hey, mister, where'd you come from? Where're you

going?" His jaw set in a grimace. Where he was heading, the Rat River country, he didn't want anyone badgering him. He was going where no one else was, where no one else wanted to be, so as to be left alone.

Alone. He glanced westward, not lifting his eyes, not needing to, at the new-risen moon. It was now, he calculated by the moon's height and shape, shortly past midnight, in early July. The sun burned low on the northern horizon, above the tree line of spruce and above the distant foothills; slightly lower, however, than the spectral moon which hung in the sky like a sickle above the far range of mountains. He was drifting downstream, with the current but against the wind, lulled by the rhythm the river imposed, to which his body and mind were attuned. But he was not insensible of the sun and moon as they jockeyed for position over the mountains: of the pale light they cast, the poor heat they gave, of himself the only man beneath a cloudless sky to navigate by them.

He was noticing them, and not watching the river, when the raft ran aground. With a thud, all motion stopped, though his body continued to move; the river continued to move, but the raft did not move with it. Lurching forward he braced himself with the pole as the raft broke apart beneath him. As the logs separated and swung out with the current, he clumsily vaulted, using the pole in his hands, onto what looked like firm ground but was mud, in which as he started to sink he began pumping his legs much faster than his feet could respond. This put him into a frenzy and he remembered that in the delta there could be quicksand and that in quicksand one had to swim. He was sunk in now over his boots, the suction increasing the harder he pulled and the choice increasingly simple: sink or swim. Grasping the pole with both hands before him, he lunged forward full length on the mud, and with his hands hooked on the pole beneath him, pulled forward with shoulders and arms like a frog until his feet bubbled up and popped free. He spread his legs then, and widened his grip on the pole, and inched along on elbows and knees, gritting his teeth and cursing the mud as

he crawled. His face was turned sideways, away from
the mud and toward the pale moon which hung, un-
sullied and thin in the sky. In the mountains there
would be no mud. His jaw clenched and unclenched as
he gasped for breath. A whorl of mosquitoes was at him,
hovering in the lee of his sprawling body, whining fre-
netically in his ears, and stinging the back of his neck
and his wrists, not his hands because they were mud-
covered. In the mountains there would be no mosquitoes. He heard from a distance dogs barking and
howling, Indian sled dogs, starved for the summer so
they would work through the winter; he pictured them
staked and on chains. The dogs were about half a mile
downstream, barking at the logs of his raft as they
clanked along shoals in the shoreline. Dogs meant Indians, Indians meant Fort McPherson. Within walking
distance. Tomorrow.

The spit became firmer the further he crawled, until
he was able to crouch on his knees, then to stand. Mosquitoes were all around him now, diving, whenever he
turned his face from the wind, into his mouth and nose
and eyes. Vaguely he waved them away and, wiping
his hands on his parka and pants, reached into a pocket
and drew out a crumpled net with the bloodstains and
black spots of squashed mosquitoes clogging its holes;
this he drew over his head and with trembling fingers
tightened and tied the drawstring. From another pocket
he pulled out wool mitts and put them on. Then he knelt
down shakily on the wet sand, patted a space for rocks
and potholes, lay down and immediately fell asleep,
with the roar of the river and the whine of mosquitoes
contending in his ears.

He awoke, the hot sun full in his face, feeling as
though he'd been savaged by dogs. His face where the
net lay across it was stippled with bugbites, his eyes
swollen nearly shut, his lips chapped and sore, and he
had a crick in his neck. When he removed his mitts to
untie the drawstring, his fingers were without feeling.
He raised himself up on his elbows and looked across
at the mountains, snow-covered and clear in the sunlight, impassive, impossibly distant. Between him and

them flowed the river, a quarter mile wide at this point, flowing as it always had flowed toward the sea it had always flowed into. Beyond the river, another mud-bank, the unbroken line of black spruce; beyond the spruce, the delta, hidden from where he now lay—of swamp and lagoons, rivers and willow bush—and beyond the delta the difficult foothills, the mosquitoey, muskeggy foothills. To reach the mountains he would have to cross all that, all that and then some, because there were always unexpected ordeals, unforeseen obstacles, pitfalls, and deadheads and quicksands which were not on the map, not even in the mind's eye. He would try to account for them all, to leave time for them all, and he would be well equipped. He touched a bulge in his pocket. The money was there still, wrapped in oilcloth, and Fort McPherson was just downstream, some shacks on a high bluff, with a trading post where he would purchase his outfit. Once equipped, and once he had entered the Rat River country, no one had any excuse, or right, to bother him. He would be quits, then. Quits. Just the mountains and him, the delta and him, the river and him, just him. Whatever happened could matter only to him, and there would be nothing personal in it. Nature was not for, or against, him. That was the way he wanted it. That was the way it would be, after McPherson.

From some spruce trees behind him a raven descended, sluggish and black, to inspect him. He lay on his back, watching the bird through the slits of his swollen eyelids: the raven extending its feet for a landing, the raven flapping its wings. The man lay perfectly still, sighting the bird through slits as through gun bunkers; while the raven, with great exertion, held back from landing, clanging iron wings about two yards above him. Suddenly the man leaped up to full stature, spread his arms wide, and yelled: "You think I'm dying, don't you? Well, I am! But not fast enough for you!" He stood laughing maniacally, while the bird flew away, croaking. Then slowly and stiffly he started to walk toward the Indian village.

2

Fort McPherson was a collection of Indian shacks, out-houses, smokehouses, and dog runs overlooking a sand-bar which in summer, as the feeder streams dried up and the river went down, became coextensive with a mud flat. The mud was disguised by scrub willow and drowned alder bushes, but it was mud nonetheless—thick, squishy mud with a thin, sun-dried crust stamped with thousands of dog tracks—and the man had to scrabble up the bank, pulling himself along the low alder branches and holding to willows that rained fluff on him like the down from torn pillows. The mountains, snow-peaked and distant, were at his back, the river below and behind him. At the top of the bank he was climbing—the same bank against which, annually, the supply barge labored to unload—a passel of children gazed down at him, neither giggling nor whispering, but silently watching. They continued to watch as he continued to climb, fascinated as by a bear. Then suddenly one broke ranks and they all ran, yelping and whooping and setting unseen dogs howling, over the crest of the hill and beyond. He paused in his climb, able to see only the shingled roofs of one or two shanties and the steep mudbank before him. He was bathed in sweat, and below the black Royal Stetson hat he always wore with the headnet depending from it, the salt from the sweat on his forehead burned his eyes fiercely. The headnet had fallen down during his climb and dangled

before his face. He shoved it up onto the brim of his hat
and regarded himself: like a man tarred and feathered,
he observed wryly; the combination of mud and willow
fluff made him look tarred and feathered. Perhaps the
children who fled had wondered if he were human? He
wondered himself. Without reaching any conclusion, he
negotiated the last twenty yards of the bank and stood
in full view of Fort McPherson.

The same huddle of shanties and outbuildings he had
spied from below, but dirtier now because he was closer.
At their best, human beings were filthy, human life a
snarling fit. Not for money would he enter one of those
shacks of suffocation, stifling and sun-baked, now facing him. Not for sex, nor for money. The children who
had watched him were now hiding behind an outhouse,
watching him still. Huskies, half-starved, lay chained
in the sun, and small dogs trotted about aimlessly. A
couple of old Indian crones, hunched over a fire in the
yard, cast him a desultory look, then went on smoking
fish. He took a path through the mud-caked weeds past
an unpainted church with a fenced-in burial plot. Each
grave, within the larger fence, had its own unpainted
picket railing around it—to keep starving dogs from
digging up corpses—and from a window of the rectory
adjoining the church he saw a pasty-faced white man
peer out at him. Behind such a man would be a fat
white wife, and behind her, probably in Dawson City
or Whitehorse, a fat English bishop. Bishop Geddes, in
Whitehorse. He walked on, having no soul to inquire
about, across the vacant lot stained brown with old
sewage and blackened with burn marks, to the other
oversized building in the village, whose facade read
"Northern Traders, Ltd." and on whose stoop several
old Indian men morosely sat. The eldest, wizened and
spry, jumped up as he pushed past and started soliciting
him in Loucheux; he caught the words "boss" and *"to-
bac,"* English and French interlarded with a spate of
garbled nonsense. He thrust past the old Loucheux and
past the screen door which stood holed and torn off at
the hinges into the dark, hot, log-floored and fur-lined

trading post, at the far end of which, behind a long counter, a white man sat on a stool, regarding him.

As abruptly as he had entered, he stopped, letting his eyes adjust to the dark interior. Above the counter and along the walls were furs: lynx, muskrat, beaver, ermine, otter, with a large bear skin and a rack with rifles chained to it dominating the back wall. Ammo would be dispensed from the counter, he judged, by the small white-skinned man, almost an albino, who sat hunched up behind it. As for grub, along the walls and off to the sides were shelves stacked with tinned foods; dry foods—rice, flour, oatmeal, tea, sugar—resided in bins that sat on the floor. But the floor space was chiefly devoted to a large woodstove, tunbellied, with a crook-neck stovepipe which ran parallel with the floor nearly the full length of the store; around this stove, he imagined, the village bucks would gather in winter—to smoke, chew, and spit between chinks in the logs. Now that his eyes had adjusted to the dim light, he could see that the floor was mottled around the woodstove.

There was a third person in the store, whom he had not noticed at first. An Indian girl, stealthy and silent, was sorting and shelving dry goods; she had stopped when he entered, and now began sorting again, though there was little difference between her presence in motion and her presence at rest. He stood at the entrance of the discolored floor, disoriented and ill at ease at being confined in a building, cataloguing quickly the items he needed, not wanting to have to return, not wanting one item more, less, or different from what he'd intended, through days and nights of privation on the raft, checking and double-checking the list in his mind over and over, to purchase and be gone. How much could a man do without, and for how long?—he asked himself that all the time. The Indian girl—not, for an Indian girl, unattractive—stealthily watched him while sorting and shelving. Her he could do without, he decided, forever; she was not on his list. His hand brushed the bulge in his pocket as he strode to the counter behind which sat the store factor.

"Ye'll be wantin' sumpin', Mr. Junson?" the Scotsman said, unmoving. "Ye ere Junson, ere ye not?"

The man, if surprised to be called by name, did not register it. "I need an outfit," he said, and reached into his parka pocket to pull out his bundle of money.

The pale Scottish factor sat like a speckled frog on his highstool, blending in with his surroundings. Only his eyes moved as he watched the man open the oilcloth, pull out the bundle, then shove the bundle of bills back in the oilcloth and the oilcloth back in his pocket. This display took only a few seconds. The man did not dwell on it.

"Show me your guns," he ordered, "plus any you haven't got out. Traps, snowshoes, pocket compass, some paraffin, a sheath knife and a long-handled ax, and who can I buy a canoe from?"

The Scotsman regarded him steadily. "Y'ere goin' trappin' then, Mr. Junson?"

"I might."

The albino turned on his stool as though to get down, but did not. "Good trappin' roon' 'ere, doon the delta, tho' prices be doon like the waher. Prime beaver, brother to this 'ere"—he touched with his fingers, pale and brown-spotted, a round beaver pelt on the wall—"'ll fetch less 'n twenty, an' muskrat's 'ardly worth the skinnin'. 'Ave a license, do ye?"

"I'll take some flour, lard, tea, sugar, and some salt, too. And bring down the guns." As the factor slowly got down off his stool, and began bringing his merchandise out, the man named Johnson stood staring intently at a large topographical map tacked to the wall and surrounded by beaver and bear skins. He could see where he was, where he wanted to go, and the river route there—on down the Peel, off at the Husky, up the Rat— he memorized.

Two hours later the man strode out of the store with everything he had asked for, plus new boots and wool socks, long leather mitts that came up over his wrists, a heavy wool shirt and wool pants, a wool toque, a sailmaker's needle, an eiderdown sleeping bag, and a light tarpaulin—to double as tent and sailcloth. Most of these items he wore, though the sun beat unremittingly down on the village and on the delta beyond. He had packed and left at the store in two large canvas backpacks 150 lbs. of flour, 10 lbs. of tea, 20 lbs. of sugar, four 5-lb. tins of lard, and a 2-lb. sack of salt, with a tin cup, a skillet, and two shallow tin pans for baking bannock. In a rucksack lined with ore sample bags he stashed ammunition for the three guns he had bought. This purchase had taken the longest, the customer holding and trying each piece the factor brought down, about twenty in all. The .30-30 was quickly selected, it had been on his list. But he had wanted an over-and-under—16- or 12-gauge, and .22: two guns in one—and the factor had none, no over-and-unders at all. In the end he chose the single-shot .22 rifle for its light weight, and the 16-gauge shotgun, a huge blunderbuss of a gun, with the intention of cutting it down. The three guns alone weighed in excess of fifty pounds; and ammunition for them—he didn't want to run short—another fifty to sixty pounds. Steel traps, Nos. 2 and 4, of which he took ten each, were another bulky item; with snare wire and toggle cable, a grapnel, and a metal file for cutting, the traps came to at least fifty pounds. The ax, which he left beside the packs, weighed another fifteen, so that all in all the complete outfit, which cost him nearly $1,300, weighed over 400 pounds. He packed it all, except the .30-30 and the ax, into the two large canvas backpacks and one rucksack. These he left at the store as he emerged blinking into the sunlight to find and buy a canoe.

The wizened old Loucheux, who had lurked in the doorway all the while he was making his purchase, was waiting for him on the steps. He fell in a few steps behind as the man named Johnson strode off in the direction of the church. Halfway across the sunburnt, oil-blackened lot separating the store from the church, Johnson turned; the old Indian, smiling and cringing like a dog, ran forward with placating gestures and gibberish, miming the actions of shooting, paddling, portaging, and pointing at the end of each ludicrous gesture to himself. Johnson stared at him with con-

tempt, and stalked off. The Indian ran after him at a
safe distance, stopping at the unpainted picket fence as
Johnson strode up to the door of the rectory and knocked.
A woman opened the door; she was dumpy and fat, but
exceedingly clean, so clean and well scrubbed that the
gobbets of fat hanging down from her arms and the
dollop of fat at her neck shone pink and slick with
sweat. She was about thirty, he judged.

"Yes?" she said.

"The rector," he said, "is he home?"

"My husband," she said, "he's home. You must be
Mr. Johnson. Bishop Geddes said you was coming." She
scrutinized him, especially his boots. At last she said,
"You can step in here. I'll get him," and leaving the
door ajar she disappeared into the house.

Johnson stood on the stoop, in the sun. Through the
open doorway he could see down the hall a carpet runner to walk on, a hallrack, a large china clock, a wall
tapestry depicting a stag, and an uncomfortable-look-
ing settee with an antimacassar draped over its back.
On the hallrack and covering both arms of the settee
were snowflake pattern lace doilies. A white cat meandered up the hallway, rubbing its tail on the door-
frames; then, seeing Johnson, it veered off into a room.
Presently a man, the same pasty-faced man Johnson
had spied through the window, came padding along the
hallway. He wore a black shirt, but no collar, and short
pants. He was about Johnson's age.

"Yes?" he said. He winced as the sun struck him full
in the face, and took a step back into shadow. "Pleased
to meet you, I'm sure. The bishop said you were coming." He extended his hand, limply. It was white like
a fish, and clammy, when Johnson gripped it, like a
fish belly.

"I need a canoe," Johnson said. "Any of the Indians
around here have one? I'll pay." He pulled out his roll
of bills, showed it, and put it back in his pocket.

The rector nodded and put up his hand. He lowered
his hand and looked vacant, still nodding his head while
looking off toward the mountains. "There was one," he
said slowly, "maybe . . ." His voice lapsed off into silence.

Johnson waited. The pasty-faced priest seemed to have forgotten he was there. "Where can I find a canoe?" he repeated. "What Indian has one?"

The rector looked vaguely at him, then past him. "Some of them have them," he said finally, "they use them to go to the fish camps. Maybe downriver," he pointed vaguely, not directly downriver, but in that general direction. "Or maybe..." He lapsed off again. "Maybe one of them has, maybe more. I'm sure I've seen some." He smiled then, and looked blandly at Johnson. Johnson stared at him for a full minute, then executed a precise about-face, and stalked away.

The Anglican priest watched him march out of the yard, the old Loucheux—who was not one of his, but RC—dogging his heels. He watched as the earth opened and swallowed them both. Then slowly, he closed the door against the bright sun, the RC's, the white man Bishop Geddes had warned him against, the mosquitoes outside, and the mountains.

Two days later Johnson was encamped on a flat overlooking the river below the village. He had had to wait two whole days for an Indian to return from his fish camp. Finally the Indian had returned and had sold him his canoe for $100. It was a seventeen-footer, with sturdy ribs and gunwales of spruce, overlaid with canvas from the trading post. Along with the canoe Johnson had got two paddles; these he had lashed in across the struts, and, after a brief sleep and a quick breakfast, he was hefting the canoe onto his shoulders to carry it to the river.

The launch site was about a quarter mile distant, along a sandbar, but over a small hump so that it was not visible from where he stood. His other gear he had already portaged down, in case of sneak thieves. No Loucheux he had seen could ferret away one of his big packs before getting caught. The canoe was lighter, around 100 pounds, but it couldn't be filched by land very handily, not even by two Indians, so he'd left it till last, it and the rucksack from which he'd removed the ammo and filled instead with the gear he'd immediately need—bannock and tea makings, tin pan and tea pail, and sugar. The tarp and the sleeping bag he'd tied onto the top of the rucksack. One gun he carried, the 16-gauge, which he'd sawed off and filed down till only the action remained, and six inches of barrel. This he carried in his parka pouch, along with some slugs, a few yards of snarewire, his mosquito headnet and mitts; in one pants pocket he carried in an oilcloth his money, diminished nearly by half, and another, more valuable item he hadn't had time to look at, and hadn't time now, but he knew it was there. In the other pants pocket resided a compass, which was also tied to his belt, alongside the sheath knife. These comprised his emergency outfit, and he carried them close to his person. In the unlikely event that anything went wrong— if he should lose his canoe, or his outfit, or both—he would be able himself to survive, winter or summer, with these few items.

The canoe he had lifted onto his knee; with a grunt he hefted it over his head, and lowered it down over his hat and the rucksack. He had attached shoulder straps to the rucksack, so that it could be carried with the canoe. The two backpacks, weighing around 150 pounds each, were enough to anchor a man to a portage, without adding a cumbersome rucksack. Besides, he liked to have his hands free. The canoe, with the paddles lashed down so that the blades sat on his shoulders, balanced perfectly; and unless there were a strong wind, in which case he would grip the handles of the lashed paddles, he could portage with both his hands free. Casting a quick glance around the campsite, and stooping with the canoe to pick up the ax, he strode off toward the river—anxious for nothing, for he had done all he needed to do: he had purchased and packed his outfit and was setting out now, fully equipped, self-sufficient, not intending to return, not needing to. Let the Indians stay put and perish, and the white men go broke or wage war—what did he care? He would be in the Rat River delta, where no one else was, where no one else wanted to be; or in the Richardson Mountains, he might be there, after a winter of trapping, after he'd made himself a fur parka and windpants, he might just decide to live there—he might even go to Alaska. He wasn't, in any event, coming back here. He was traveling west, toward the mountains, the sun on the mountains, the snow on the mountains, and the ocean beyond.

He breasted effortlessly with the canoe on his shoulders the small hill overlooking the river. There, fifty yards distant, casually seated on one of his packs, was the old Loucheux, jabbering and gesturing animatedly to the white man who stood beside him, a Mountie dressed in duty uniform: blue visor cap, brown jacket with a belted on side arm, khaki shirt and blue tie, above the blue jodhpur breeches tucked into high boots which made Mounties look fat-assed like women. But this Mountie actually was fat-assed, Johnson decided, with a yellow stripe down his breeches and a yellow band on his cap. The Indian, when he spied Johnson coming, jumped up from the pack and, as Johnson advanced, he retreated. He continued backing away before Johnson until, by the time Johnson passed the packs and the yellow-striped Mountie and flipped the canoe down to his knee, then slid it into the water, the old Loucheux had slunk off out of reach and seemed ready at any moment to break and run. With his back to the Mountie, Johnson unlashed both the paddles, eased himself out of the rucksack and stashed it under the stern, then removed his hat and splashed his face with cold water, put his hat back on and strode over to where the Mountie, a gangling six-footer with a farm boy's face, was standing and sweating profusely. Johnson, who was shorter by a couple of inches, but heavier by ten or more pounds, came right at the Mountie and, without a word or so much as a glance, stooped down and lifted the pack to his knees, shoved one arm through a shoulder strap, swung the pack onto his back, shoved the other arm through, and strode off. Before the Mountie could hinder, or stop him, he had deposited the first pack in the canoe and was back for the second.

"I see you're off downriver," the Mountie said.

Johnson hefted the pack up onto his knees, then onto his back.

"You're Johnson?" The Mountie had stepped between him and the canoe; the Mountie's hand rested
on his holstered side arm.

The shorter man, stooped forward by the weight of
the backpack, peered up at the Mountie and squinted.
The Mountie, four or five feet away, and now five or
six inches taller, stood directly between him and the
sun, which was over the mountains.

"Water's low," the Mountie commented.

Johnson made no reply.

The Mountie moved aside, but followed him to the
canoe and waited while he deposited the second pack
and tied them both in. The Indian had moved in again,
to within hearing range. When the man was finished
lashing, the Mountie, without any further palaver, as-
serted authority as he'd been trained to do, by asking
a direct, identity question, the answer of which could
be checked: "Where'd you come from?" he said.

Johnson stood slowly up and turned part way round
to face the Mountie. His motions were rigid, delayed,
and seemed deliberate responses to small, separate
commands: first the standing upright from the waist
only; then the shifting of weight to one foot, and the
half turn; then the training of his eyes on the Mountie's
wet face, then over the Mountie's left shoulder. "Down
below," he mumbled.

"Where abouts?"

Johnson did not answer immediately.

"Down the Peel," he said at last. "Whitehorse. Dawson."

During the silence that followed, the old Loucheux,
crouching almost on hands and knees, crept closer in.
Never had he heard so few words exchanged between
a Mountie and another white man. Usually the Mountie
said little while the other man spoke a great deal, explaining himself. The man with much money was not
explaining himself.

"Know anyone in Whitehorse or Dawson?" the
Mountie said.

Johnson stared hard at him for a moment, as if debating something. "The Anglican bishop," he said finally. "I know Bishop Geddes."

"Ah," said the Mountie. He seemed satisfied. "Just a routine check. Lots of fellows coming north now, what with the country in the condition it's in—no jobs, farming's poor—I grew up on a farm, near Edmonton, pretty different from here," he gestured with the hand that had been on the side arm to the river and the wilderness beyond. "They don't know what they're getting into, most of them; don't know what equipment they need, or how to use it. They've just got a grubstake, and an urge to get shut of the breadlines." He paused, giving Johnson a chance at small talk. The river mumbled and moaned, tugging at the laden canoe. The stocky man remained silent. "Well, I know you've got a good outfit, I checked with Douglas at the store. And I guess you know how to use all the gear you got." He stopped talking again, making the statement a question.

"I only got what I need," Johnson said.

Constable Edgar Millen nodded. "If you're planning to do any trapping up the Rat, you'll need to get you a license. This man over here"—he indicated the old Loucheux, who smiled vacantly—"doesn't need one. But you do." He was going to quip, as he usually did, about Indian rights, and government wrongs, and how we, meaning the RCMP, have to deal with them both; but the man had glanced at the Indian with such contempt, and was glaring at him now with such hatred, that he said in as few words as possible: "You can obtain a license at any RCMP post—Aklavik, or Arctic Red River. I'm in charge at Arctic Red," he felt compelled to add, thinking maybe it was the sun in his eyes that made Johnson look so outraged, "used to be at Aklavik." The ending felt awkward. It was Johnson's turn to say something. He watched as Johnson, who had been standing and scowling, very stiffly took hold of the gunwales and started to board. "Arctic Red's about fifty miles, Aklavik's a little further," Constable Millen added.

"Right," Johnson said through clenched teeth, and felt a haze darken his sight. He had to shove off at all costs, before he did violence; but before he shoved off he had to pick up two or three of the oil drums that littered the beach. Very stiffly he walked over to where three empties sat, very stiffly bent down and picked two of them up and carried them to the canoe while he kicked the third one in front of him. Every fiber of his body, every muscle in his face was tensed and in trauma, and he felt his lips curl and start to tremble as he boarded the canoe.

"Well, good luck." Millen waved. "And, remember, if you should need us for anything, there's no post here at McPherson, the nearest is at Arctic Red."

Johnson jerked his head slightly, but against such resistance that he felt his neck muscles seize. He could scarcely see the Mountie now, though the Mountie stood only a few feet away and in sunlight. The Mountie was waving to Johnson, with the hand that had been on his firearm. The Mountie was smiling—farm-boyish, friendly.

Johnson shoved off, so forcefully that he nearly upset the canoe. And as he swept out into the current and the mosquito net fell from his hat brim and dangled in front of his face, he could see the brown tunic and stiff visored cap of the Mountie more clearly as the shoreline receded; and as he looked back at the Mountie and the Indian standing on the sandbar, he was roaring at them like the roaring of the river, and he saw the dark stain and the crippled antennae of a squashed mosquito with a small brown spider near, and, looking beyond to the village, darkness and suffocation, and the light was darkened in the mountains behind him.

3

He continued to brood as he paddled downriver, past another big sandbar which divided the channel, and past isolated Indian shacks, fish camps, set high on the banks. The sun was bright, the river swift, the weather fine, but his mind was in turmoil as he paddled downstream, still envisioning the Mountie as he had left him, squashed and crushed, a dark stain against the duncolored sand and black spruce bush. His eyes were set straight ahead on the river before him; with his peripheral vision he saw, but only as a break in the brush-and-ink forest, the bend in the river where the Husky runs in on the left and the Peel takes a turn to the right in its final run to the Mackenzie. Here the great river is at its widest, more than a half mile across, and wind and current clash at the confluence of the two rivers, whipping up whitecaps. Instinctively, he hugged the lee shore, but the lee was the inner bend of the Peel, and he missed completely the Husky, and with it the Rat, pouring in behind a sandbar on the outer curve. He was not watching for the turnoff, even though the Indian from whom he'd bought the canoe had drawn with his moccasin toe in the dirt three lines, representing the Husky, the Rat, and the Peel, and their juncture at the first bend twelve miles downstream from McPherson; a foot further off on the ground he had drawn a fourth line, the second branch of the Husky where it entered the Peel before the Peel reached the

31

Mackenzie. With a stick the Indian had scratched an
"X" at this junction, Blake's trading post: when Johnson
passed this conspicuous landmark he would know he
had overshot the main branch of the Husky by six or
eight miles. But even the trading post, though he saw
it—perched on a bluff at the confluence of two large
rivers: how could he miss it?—he passed, paddling sin-
gle-mindedly and oblivious to the passage of time and
place, on down the Peel; until, after two more big bends
in the river, and several treacherous sandbars, he found
himself passing an Indian fish camp set on a wedge of
silt and cutbank which lay at the mouth of the Peel.
He noticed the camp because the cutbank, constantly
undermined by the current, was falling away into the
river with a thunderous crash. At first he mistook the
reverberating sounds for the blasts from a shotgun; he
thought the Mountie was shooting at him. Startled by
the noise from his sullen trance, when he saw the eroded
cutbank with the fish camp on its bluff, and how far
the sun had circled, he realized that he had come too
far.

The huge body of water he was approaching, he figured rightly, must be the Mackenzie; a full mile wide
at the Y, it resembled a sea. Once in it, he wouldn't be
able to paddle against it. The Peel, along which he was
moving toward the wider reach of the Mackenzie, was
almost beyond his power to paddle against. Not wishing
to risk broadsiding the canoe in the current, he turned
himself in the canoe. Keeping low, and gripping both
gunwales, he twisted his body around, until he knelt
facing what had been the stern, and took a deep pull
with the paddle. The canoe's drift toward the open reach
slowed; with another, then another deep pull on the
paddle, he equaled, then overcame the momentum of
the Peel's current. And as he paddled steadily forward,
he sculled between strokes toward the bank, where by
keeping to the shallows along the back eddies, he could
drive stroke by stroke the heavily laden canoe back
upstream at the pace of a walk.

This brutal, mind-numbing work he kept at for an
hour, two hours, five hours. He would train his sight

on a gravel bar which veered out in the water, or a particular tree which leaned out from the bank, and paddle mechanically toward it, until he had passed it, and then pick another. In this way he attained, in five hours, the first of the two bends downstream from Blake's trading post. He remembered now, though he had not been conscious of it at the time, that upstream from the bend he was now turning the Peel kept a fairly straight course, due south, for a distance twice the distance he had just come. He had come a third of the distance he'd lost. The effort it had cost him, had left him exhausted. Combined with that, the stiff breeze which clashed with the current was still blowing out of the north; all day it had not abated. Now, as he pulled round the bend in the river, on the inside, and saw further and further before him the long stretch of river ahead, he searched the near shore for a campsite. But the lee shore was all mud, sandbar and mud flat, for a hundred yards between him and the more solid bank of black spruce. And beneath the spruce, even if he could pole his way over the mud flat, no camping place would be found: so dense and thick the underbrush, and the spruce's rootage so knotted.

Hard ahead jutted a sandbar. In order to clear it he would have to veer out into the line of current. Instead, he paddled straight for it, and drove the canoe hard aground. Standing, one foot in the water so as not to stave the canoe, he quickly untied the tarpaulin from his rucksack. Then, lashing the two paddles together in the shape of a T, he secured the base of this makeshift spar to the bow of the canoe, inserting the blade between the seat struts and lashing it there. Then he spread the sheet against it, and fastened the sheet to the yard, and affixed a hand rope to the two bottom corners so that he could haul sail. The sheet, flapping free in the breeze, caught wind enough to rock the canoe and to force him to balance himself as he tied the hauling ropes on. Then he shoved the canoe free of the sandbar, nearly upsetting as he turned into the current and brought his square-rigged craft into the wind.

The tarp bellowed out like two cheeks, thrusting the

canoe forward, and he scudded along holding the reins
with one hand and ruddering with the other. The near
shore fell away and passed alongside at a rate fully
equal to the drift of the current, which meant he was
sailing twice that fast—the speed of the current, about
eight knots per hour, plus another eight knots per hour—
at less than half, less than a quarter the effort of paddling. He was scudding up the mainstream and middle
of the channel, the long mud flats and spruce banks
falling away on either side, and he was laughing. Far
better than paddling up, or even drifting downstream:
he was against the current, and breasting it—alert, as
he had not been when with it, when it had taken him
where it wanted; now he was riding it. He worked best,
he decided, when the odds were against him, when the
sun and the moon and the stars were darkened, as they
were now. Storm clouds; must be a storm coming. The
ozone in the air, and the freshening breeze, and the
roar of the water around him exhilarated him beyond
belief. He was sailing past a long sandbar now, to the
right, which he remembered having passed on the left,
ruddering, with his arm out, around the main spit,
though he couldn't see for the sail. It was mental to-
pography he was steering by, and he trusted it, when
he was alert, as now, implicitly. Not bothering to haul
in the sail, to sight check, he skimmed around the main
spit, cutting close as though he were in a sailboat, in
a regatta, competing. There was nothing a man could
not do, if he wanted; no place he could not go; no one
and nothing to stop him, if he had time and chance with
him, and will. He skimmed along with the wind at his
back, and his sail bellied out, up the river.

In this way he reached, in advance of the storm, the
second bend in the river and the site, at the Peel's confluence with the Husky, of Blake's trading post. A wind-
borne mist had now reached him, while a slanting rain
raced up the river to drench him as he beached the
canoe, struck sail hurriedly, quickly covered the packs
with the tarp, then ran stiffly across the sandbar and
up the main bank to the trading post's veranda.

An Englishman, about fifty, with steel-gray crew cut

and deeply lined face, wearing a wool mackinaw, was seated on the screened-in porch at a wicker table about to have tea. A native woman, but more self-assured and well-preserved than any Loucheux squaw Johnson had seen, was just coming out of the trading post door with a pot of tea in one hand and a pan of squawbread in the other; there was butter, and sugar, and marmalade on the round table in front of the trader. All this Johnson took in at a glance as he rushed up the stairs of the screened-in porch and, flinging open the screen door, stepped in. The post faced south, and the wind blew out of the north; he could see the storm-darkened river off the end of the porch, and hear the drumming of rain on the roof, but the floor of the veranda, shielded by the main structure, was dry. He stood stock still just inside the screen door, puddling. If he was in, he was in.

"Bad storm," observed the trader, his voice nearly drowned out by the drumming rain on the roof, "but we need it." The woman leaned over the table, filled one tin cup with tea, then looked up, holding the teapot over a second tin cup, waiting. "Have some tea?" asked the man without looking at him. "Millie, pour Mr. Johnson some tea. Have a seat," he offered dryly, "and some bannock." He commenced to tear a strip off the squaw-bread before him and to smear some marmalade on it. Johnson, without taking his hat off, sat down opposite the trader, heaped several spoonfuls of sugar into the hot tea and, stirring once, gulped down two or three mouthfuls. The tin cup burned his lip and the liquid his tongue, but he emptied the cup in three swallows.

"Hot," said the trader, "have some more." The woman stood near and when he put his cup out refilled it. He drank a second cup without sugar, and set the cup down. "Help yourself to some bannock," the man said. And he did; tearing off a long strip of the grease-hardened flat-bread, he stuffed his mouth full while the woman named Millie, at a sign from the trader, disappeared into the post and brought out another pan of flatbread. Then she left them, while the rain drummed hard on the roof above and spattered and ran down the screens. A fresh

damp mist pervaded the porch and made soggy the bread
that was left, while off in the forest and over the river
under a canopy of black, fast-moving cloud, a whitish
vapor drifted up and enclosed them. They could have
been, the two men, the trader and the trapper, seated
at a table on the damp veranda, enclosed by rain forest
in Madagascar, or jungle in Brazil, or Mississippi delta,
or Louisiana bayou: the Mackenzie delta closed them
in as rain forests everywhere have closed men in from
time immemorial. The rain forest around them was
impersonal, though the rivers twining through the delta
had names, and the delta took its name from the rivers:
Mackenzie, Peel, Husky, Rat. The men had names, too,
and backgrounds, but they were unimportant. Even the
woman had a name.

"Millie's not Loucheux," the trader said, as though
in answer to a question, "she's Eskimo. I was at Coppermine before, RCMP." He looked off into the white
and gray forest through the rain-spattered screen, and
very deliberately sipped his tea. "Been here eighteen,
nineteen, nearly twenty years now," he said to no one
in particular, "hardly seems possible. You sometimes
feel that way, Mr. Johnson?" he said abruptly, swiveling his neck to look Johnson straight in the eyes. The
trader's eyes were steel-gray, like his hair. "You sometimes feel it doesn't matter where you are, what you
do? But make the slightest mistake"—he slashed his
throat with his finger—"and, like that, you're a goner.
Even a little mistake, in this country. You ever feel"—
he sipped his tea—"tempted, Mr. Johnson?" He took
another sip of tea. "To make a mistake, I mean, just a
small one."

Johnson regarded him icily. "I just made one," he
said. These were the first words he'd spoken. "I missed
the Rat. It's out there, but I missed it."

A near-smile played on the older man's face. "Yes,
I watched you pass. I figured you'd be back, but I didn't
know if you'd stop. You've got a ways to go yet. This,"
he waved languidly toward the rain-spattered screen
and the storm-darkened forest beyond it, "this is the

Husky, north branch. You want the south branch—it's
a ways yet."

"I figured on taking this one. There's lots of little
feeder streams, and they all lead to the mountains. The
mountains don't shift, even if the streams do. And I've
got a compass." He pulled the compass, tied to his belt
beside the sheath knife, out of his pocket, and held it,
closed, in his hand.

The trader regarded the closed fist as though Johnson held a bird in it, and what he did with it depended
on his, the trader's, answer. "There's a big deviation,"
he said at last, "up here. A compass is pretty well useless. What you need is a guide." Johnson thrust the
compass back in his pocket, and felt the blood rush to
his stomach; he felt suddenly sleepy. The trader talked
on: "You're better off going upriver. At the next big
sandbar, that's the Husky's south branch, turn right
and the Rat's right there, about a quarter mile down,
to your left. That way you can't miss it." The trader
took the remaining piece of flatbread from the pan,
carefully broke it in half, and spread marmalade on it.
"You're welcome to wait the storm out," he said, slowly
placing the breadstuff in his mouth, and masticating
with his eyes fixed on Johnson.

The thunderheads had passed over and the rain
ceased to drum. All around now the sky was fast clearing, and weak rays of sunlight shone here and there
through the vapor which was dissipating over the forest, though clouds still hung over the river. "I won't
miss it," Johnson said. He sat for a moment, then scraped
his chair and got up. "I'll be making my move now," he
announced, and strode to the screen door.

"Anything I can do for you?" asked the trader, still
sitting.

"No, nothing. Much obliged to your missus." As he
descended the slippery bank, aware of the trader's eyes
on him, he felt lightheaded and dizzy. Food, quieting
the heat of the body. Sleep, making all things new. In
the Arctic the animals stayed awake all summer long;
but he was not an animal, and he had not slept all

winter; he was exhausted. He felt he could not go another step. Sleep he needed, desperately needed, but
even more he needed to get out of sight.

He drained the canoe of rainwater, and launched it.
Not bothering to stash the tarpaulin, and dismantling
the jerry-built mast, he paddled the canoe across the
Peel's current and, disregarding the trader's directions,
into the Husky's north branch. Here spruce trees came
down to the water, and with each stroke of his paddle
the trading post hove out of sight. He proceeded a little
ways further, not half a mile but it was the mental
distance that mattered, slanted the bow of his canoe
into the Husky's main current and with a last, bone-
weary effort crossed to the opposite bank, ran aground
in a shallow back eddy, and, without bothering to dis-
embark, fell soundly asleep in the canoe.

4

Not the next day, for days and nights were a continuum, and the difference between light and dark was not so pronounced in the Arctic as the contrast between wet and dry, storm and sun, clouded or cloudless skies; so not the next day, but later, the man awoke in the canoe, his eyes swollen and puffy, his mouth dry and agape, while in and out his nose and mouth untroubled the flies buzzed. The blackflies were out. All at once, and all over the delta, the combination of rain and cloud cover had caused their larvae to hatch; as though the blackbird of storm had brushed the forest, and burst, disintegrating into a plague of blackflies intent on harassing the man. When he fell asleep in the canoe there had been none, now there were millions: biting his wrists and his forehead, wriggling in under the sweatband of his hat and up the sleeves of his parka, trying to get in and at him. He woke with a start, snorting and spitting; with a start he sat up suddenly. Shooing away a great cloud of blackflies, he removed his hat and scratched his head. Blackflies popped like fleas between his fingertips and his scalp. "A few bugs," he mused laconically, and put his hat back on. In the midst of adjusting his headnet, he looked around him.

He was a few hundred yards up the Husky, just above where it merged with the Peel. Ahead was the Husky's north branch, a large, strong, rope-colored river, pouring down at him out of the mountains, which its banks

hid, through the flat expanse of delta which it drained.
Atop its steep mudbanks, fifteen or twenty feet high,
alder and willow and poplar, together with the myriad
shrubs and vines that throve in the hothouse delta,
formed a nearly impenetrable, dun-colored wall beneath the canopy of spruce forest. Space, perhaps, for
a man to crawl through, but not room to portage a
canoe. He pulled out his pocket compass and took a
reading on the river. It ran at this point east-west. Even
allowing for a 35° to 40° deviation from true north, until
the river turned north, as it would do, it would be leading him toward the Rat. He could follow its north branch
all the way to the Y and back down its south branch
to the Rat. He could. But he did not know how far the
Y was: with switchbacks and oxbows it might be a
hundred miles up, and as far down again; whereas the
Rat, on the other tine of the Husky, was only eight or
ten miles across—but across delta, the nearly impenetrable wall of rank growth atop and behind the high
banks, through which was scarcely a crawl space, much
less a portage. He wished now that he had a map, even
a general one, even one such as he'd seen on the wall
at the trading post at McPherson. But he hadn't. He
would have to rely on his own sense of direction, his
deviant pocket compass, and to a certain extent he would
have to proceed by the method he most detested, trial
and error. A woman's way, and one he despised because
he liked to be in control: to foresee precisely the margin
of error, to brace himself for the trial. One error he'd
already made was overshooting the Rat, and it had cost
him a day and much effort. Having determined not to
slog on up the Peel to the Rat, as trader Blake had
advised (though that was the simplest course, and the
one he would have taken had trader Blake not advised
it), he wasn't about to paddle blindly up the Husky
maybe a hundred miles out of his way, when to cut
through the delta on an east-west course would lead
him directly across to the Rat. Eight miles across the
grain, he figured; twelve miles at the most. And he
grinned in anticipation of the ordeal, dispatching—even
as he shoved the canoe off the sandbar, and began vig-

orously paddling upstream—an imaginary Johnson, his
flunky, on up the Husky to explore the longer way round.
He, the real Johnson, would keep to the river so long
as it kept to his course; when it veered north, and his
batman veered with it, he would cut through and by
sheer will and prodigious effort he would beat his imaginary patrol out.

The day was overcast and there were blackflies, but
fewer now he was out on the river. He perched his bug
net on the brim of his hat, so that it covered his ears
and the back of his neck, but not his face. Now he could
see clearly: the muddy river, the muddy banks, the
solemn spruce atop the banks brooding over the dense
wall of bush through which he would have to portage,
encumbered by nearly a quarter of a ton of gear and a
seventeen-foot-long canoe. He was in no hurry to portage, to split off from his imaginary patrol. The flunky
task force was given the more routine, the less hazard-
ous, assignment. No surprises in paddling on up the
Husky; his patrol leader would be in control and could
report, at their rendezvous on the Rat, on terrain, enemy positions and activity, and could make any map
corrections. The weather would be the same. The main
thing to be determined was which way was shorter. So
long as the Husky kept to its westerly course, he and
his double would travel upstream together. In retro-
spect this would seem pleasant; intervals between the
backbreaking work of portaging and the frustrating
task of finding one's way always seemed pleasant with
hindsight, even idyllic. Paddling, whether up or downstream, was light labor—the patrol leader should not
complain. Its rhythm lulled one, not to sleep, but to a
state of repetitive motion like channel swimming, or
marathon running. The mind disengaged and grew
numb.

The man entered now into the coma-like state of
paddling against the current. He forgot his fictive patrol and imagined himself nowhere else, not even arrived at the Rat; for the place where, when he came to
it, he would know to be his place, would look no different
from the place he was now—this river, this mudbank,

this delta. Only he would know it was different—further away from the Mountie and the Indian and trader Blake, more remote in his mind's eye—a bank, not unlike the cutbanks he passed now, but different, where a man could stand up. He peered intently at the left bank as he passed it, above the fifteen-to twenty-foot-high mud cutbank, beneath the canopy of spruce forest: nowhere in the woven, leaf-matted wall, strewn and entangled with fallen and leaning and uprooted trees and brushfalls, could he spy a way in, or through. Here and there he saw scrabble marks where a bear had attempted to climb up the bank and had failed, and, a hundred yards on, tried again. The Husky's banks and the delta beyond seemed inaccessible to all but the otters, whose slippery slides striated the banks like rifling on a gun barrel. He made a mental note that there were otters, and continued to paddle upstream.

Not at the first turn in the river, which was a slight jog to the north and then back again, but at the first major bend in the Husky—a dogleg right, with an island carved out in the socket—he discovered a stream running in from the left, and, without breaking stroke, took leave of his routine patrol and veered off up the small feeder stream. As soon as he was in it, he knew the cut across the grain would be as tough a trek as he had ever done. An arbor of cedar, S-shaped and leaning, overarched the stream completely, filtering out almost all light, so that proceeding upstream was like entering a dimly lit tunnel. Fallen trees and branches—rushwood from the mountains—obstructed the stream with logjams; and logs wedged in the crotches of the cedars above him evidenced the strength of spring runoff. Come spring, the tunnel in which now a slough of black water lay, would become a conduit choked with ice chunks and rushwood, overflowing and flooding and smashing everything with its bore. He could not sound the bottom of the murky slough with his paddle, or, when he could (near the bank, which was knotted with cedar knees and a dense tangle of willow), the mud bottom yielded to the blade of his paddle like jelly. So he could not stand up, or get out. He had to crouch in the canoe and prize a way with his paddle through brushfalls and over tree trunks, and occasionally chop a way through with the ax. When the deadfalls were firmly rooted, or wedged in logjams, he had to step out and, balancing on their slick trunks, dead-lift the canoe (which with the gear in it weighed over 500 pounds) inch by inch over. Several times during these exertions, which took all his strength, he fell in; but each time he managed to pull himself up, back onto the log, or into the canoe, and begin again the maneuver.

He had gone only a little way before he was sweating profusely. The sweat stung his eyes, which he wiped through his headnet, which was so smeared with water and sweat he could hardly see out. He could see only outlines and shadows of branches and tree trunks, flanged and protruding, between the more solid black of the water and the dark overhang of the trees. And each branch he disturbed, each logjam he broke through, burst forth with a cloud of mosquitoes like ashes from a dead fire.

He was scarcely aware of the blackflies around him, there were so many. His labored breathing, his sweating, his manual exertions while constantly having to balance, were all part of the branched and difficult ordeal of which the mosquitoes and blackflies were also a part. There was no question of resting, of catching his breath, or of turning back; he stopped once, and, hurriedly lifting his headnet, saw that the tunnel had turned so that he could no longer see where he'd come from or how far he had yet to go, and, dropping his headnet, went back to hacking and prizing, lifting and hauling, shoving, falling into the water, and pulling himself out and the canoe through. Doggedly and methodically, his motions as he became more tired becoming less forceful, more wasteful, he slogged his way up the streambed, through brushfalls, deadfalls, and mud. His only thought as he cut across was that he had not yet had to portage.

The tunnel closed and the stream petered out about three miles upstream from the Husky. It happened gradually. First the mud became sand, then the sand became pebbles, and finally the pebbles gave way to round rocks and small boulders. On these he walked, stumbling as they gave way beneath him, tracking the canoe upstream by its painter, dredging a path through the trickle of water the stream had become, pulling and dragging and lifting the bow, then the midships, then the stern, up and over and through. The mosquitoes were not so bad now, nor the underbrush so thick. Sunlight shot through the spruce trees, and the stream, as it neared its source, became progressively clearer. The man pushed his headnet onto the brim of his hat and shoved his hat back on his head, releasing his forehead from the sweatband as from a vise grip. Bent forward pulling the canoe, its painter over his shoulder, he trudged up the streambed through water that sparkled with sunlight, stopping every few steps to kick stones aside, or to drop down on his knees and splash his face and lap water like a dog. Twice he took a compass reading, then trudged on, pleased with himself to be getting through without having to portage.

He reached the place, finally, where the stream disappeared underground. Spear grass and fern fronds marked the spot, and past the spongy sphagnum and horsetail through which he waded and dragged the canoe, a dense growth of willows concealed the spring's source. He plunged thigh-deep through the tangle of branches, dragging the laden canoe after him, and came churning out the other side into a stagnant lagoon, about an acre in size, surrounded on all sides except the slot through which he had entered by a jungle of shrubs and saplings, stickers and creepers, leaning and fallen and uprooted trees and brushfalls, the branches steamy with dampness and decomposition beneath the canopy of spruce forest. It was the end of his tracking, the beginning of the portage. Wearily he climbed into the canoe and, draping the headnet over his face, and thrusting his hands in his pockets, fell fast asleep.

He awoke feeling as though he'd been beaten by rods. Both arms were numb, the nerves pinched, and it took him a moment to locate the cause of the pain radiating from his shoulder blades to his thumbs: his back, where the canoe strut had pressed against it, was sore and the muscles were swollen. He moved, and felt languorous. It would take him some time to get moving, to get the blood running, the muscles warmed up. Two days out of McPherson—or was it three?—and his body was starting to harden; a week more of bloodletting and the mosquitoes would leave him alone. He raised himself in the canoe on his elbows and lifted his headnet: there was no place on the bank to build a fire, unless he cleared one; no break in the undergrowth through which to portage, unless he swamped one out. At the prospect of portaging through the rain forest he flinched. First he would make tea—boil up. Slowly he sat up in the canoe, and clumsily picked up a paddle. Only his forearms were numb now, though his ankles ached from yesterday's stepping and balancing, stumbling and falling, over the rocks. He dipped the paddle in the water, told himself to pull it out, and did; he dipped again. By the time he had reached the pond's edge, he was sentient in all parts, except his thumbs.

Taking care not to cut himself with the ax, he hacked a small clearing at the pond's edge. Then he trenched a circle with the heel of his boot, kicked together the dry wood which lay in abundance all over the ground, and put a match to it. It burned readily, so readily that he had to stomp it and douse it. His packs he pulled up onto the bank, and boiled tea and baked bannock. After he had drunk his fill of tea, and eaten an entire bannock, he baked another bannock for the trail. Then he rested, his back against a pack which was against a tree, while the fire disintegrated into ashes, and the sun burned low behind the northern tree line. He dozed awhile, trying to remember...something about bird snares. When he opened his eyes and looked at the pond it was ghostly still with early morning mist, and two white swans were on it...he dozed again....

He awoke with a start. The sun was high and the woods were still. 'Everything will burn!' he thought with alarm, and jumped up. But when he kicked at the fire, it was cold. Then he remembered his dream, a recurring dream in which he, or someone like him, was

being driven by a cordon of men toward an enclosure.
He could not see his pursuers, but he could hear them
shouting, firing their guns, and clubbing the ground as
they came. He was part of a group of large animals who
were being driven, and he could smell the animals' fear,
hear their pursuers approaching from the rear and converging from the sides, and in the high grass ahead he
could see cluster-snares set in crush-lines toward the
enclosure—each snare a cleverly contrived device consisting of a sharpened anchor peg, daggerlike, with a
hilt to which was attached the functional noose; each
cluster of snares linked by trip wire, so that the whole
snare line, and successive series of snare lines, formed
a restrictive funnel toward the enclosure. Already the
advance animals who veered off were being ensnared,
pulling the snare wire and being slowed by it, forming
a barrier to the animals behind them who were being
forced into the slot. He was watching his footing to
avoid the snares, and running so as not to be trampled,
but he thought the whole thing a mistake. The snare
lines were too elaborate, the hunters too many, the
enclosure too large for a man-trap. Surely his being
here was a mistake. Had he blundered into a caribou
crush trap? Perhaps there were signs he had not seen,
warnings he had not heeded. Now he was here, he had
to go through it; there was no getting out, no going
back. He was into the slot now, past the snares and
ensnared animals, and on through the slot into the
fenced-in enclosure which led to the crush trap. Then
he saw, at the same time he noticed that the men had
set fire to the bush behind him, the cave—natural, or
man-made?—off to the side of the crush trap through
which the animals were being driven. And, like a fox
to a baited box trap, he, or the man in the dream who
resembled him, ran to the cave and rushed in.

The instant he entered the cave, just before he awoke,
it came to him like a blow on the back of the neck—
there had been no mistake. The slaughter and the fire
outside, the animals driven by the hunters or shadows
of hunters, by the sound of their guns or echoes, had
been the decoy; the cave, not the crush, was the trap,

and he was caught in it—held by vague enclosing lines,
tangled in a meshwork of net, with crude devices fastened to his feet and to his mouth ... suggestions of traps,
no one of which held him, but the more he struggled to
free himself, the more trap sets he triggered—treadle
traps, noose snares, nets, spring traps, steel traps, gins—
as he stumbled and groped inside the cave whose walls
and floor in the shadowy light depicted hints of animal
and human tracks. It was at this point he had awakened
alarmed, and thought 'Everything will burn!' and
jumped up and kicked the cold fire. Now he felt foolish.
He kicked the dead fire anyway. And hefting one of the
backpacks up on his knee, then fitting his arms through
the shoulder straps as he swung it onto his back, he set
off hunched forward and heavily breathing into the tangled plant mass, with one arm supporting an empty
twenty-five-gallon oil drum, and in his free hand the
ax.

The portage across to the Husky's south branch
proved to be more arduous than the tracking upstream.
Triple packing and backtracking brought the mileage
he covered to nearly fifty: three times across and three
times back over the most difficult eight miles of terrain
he had ever traversed; though some of it, as much as
half, he neither portaged nor paddled. He would get
himself set, a pack on his back and the ax in his hand,
for a long trek through dense bush, swamping and slogging and sweating and stirring up bugs, when suddenly
the portage which had scarcely begun would be ended:
he would burst through the brush to the edge of another
small pond, or come on a swale whose cover of horsetail
concealed four or five feet of water and a soft bottom;
and he would fling down the oil drum and pack he'd
only just picked up, and limpingly levitate back on the
trail he'd just broken, to port the second 150-pound pack
and two oil drums, and then the canoe and rucksack.
Throughout this seventy-five-hour marathon he neither slept, ate, nor crapped. And he encountered no
animals. Part of the time he had the canoe over his
head, and much of the rest of the time he made so much
noise hacking at vines and troublesome branches and

crashing, a pack on his back and an oil drum on his
shoulder, through the bush, that it would have to have
been a very dull animal, or a mad one, to have stood
its ground in his path. He was too concerned with getting through to give much thought to wildlife; though
at each new lagoon, he scouted waterways for signs of
mink, muskrat, and beaver, and when backtracking,
provided he was not too dizzy, he spotted set locations
for lynx, wolverine, and black bear. But this was simply
old habit. Once immersed in the delta, its traffic of
tracks and droppings, trails winding through grassy
swales, and dark passageways under overhanging banks
he instinctively scented and noticed, and marked on his
mental landscape as he trudged past. He felt with a
trapper's instinct the woods and waters around him
teeming with wildlife; several times while backtracking he noticed fresh bear spoor which had not been there
when he portaged, but the bear itself, or bears, he never
encountered, nor did he care to. The trapline that he
found himself reconnoitering as he cut across to the
Husky was a trapline he knew he would never run. The
Rat itself, once he got to it, would provide ample set
locations and fur in abundance for one man. He did not
think that he would trap the Rat out.

Four days after leaving the Husky's north branch,
three days since he had eaten or slept, he reached the
mouth of the Rat. He had had to portage through rain
forest and across creek beds, pole over lagoons and
swales, wade waist-deep through swamps and hack his
way through willow thickets to reach the Husky's south
branch. After a mile or two of drifting downstream, he
reached the confluence of the Husky with the Rat just
before the two merged with the Peel. The Peel he could
see past a giant sandbar, where five days earlier (or
was it longer?) he had swept past in a snarling fit at
having met up with the Mountie—a pet which had cost
him his morning strength and which now, with hindsight, he rued. So now he was where he might have
been nearly a week earlier: bruised and beaten and
tired. He was hungry too, but more tired than hungry,
lacking, almost, the energy to negotiate the turn from

the Husky down which he was drifting to the Rat up which he must paddle. But there were no campsites, only sandbars and mud flats, steep muddy banks and dense taiga, and the current was strong.

Wearily he positioned himself amidships, bracing his weight on one knee with the other foot forward, and paddled for all he was worth to cut the corner and avoid the channel. The roar of the rivers gave him a rush and he cut across swiftly and smoothly, then set himself to paddle up into the mouth of the Rat. It was brutal work, and he felt like a salmon struggling upstream to spawn, leaping and thrashing and thrusting itself through a rapids, or up a falls. The river was strong enough, here at its mouth, and drained such a volume of water, that its final few miles had a definite downhill cant to them. He could see, even though it was late in the day and the sun lay below the tree line, the uphill grade of the river against which he struggled, as turn after turn, and switchback after switchback, he plodded stupidly up it—against the delta it drained, the foothills it drained, the mountains it drained, against the whole network of waters the Rat gathered up and here at its mouth poured against him. But there was nothing personal in it, and never again would he have to go up it. With each paddle stroke he was putting behind him the lowlands, the flatlands, the treacheries and deceits of the men who dwelt there, both red and white, and their women, all women with their cunning and snares. With each thrust up the river he was putting behind him the pit into which all men fell, trust, and the deadfall that broke strong men's backs, greed. As he pushed stroke by stroke up the throat of the Rat, he could not see the mountains ahead or the delta below: only the steep mudbanks V-ing up on each side, rifled with otter slides; the dark overhang of spruce arching out, reflected below in the water; and the long narrow barrel of river before him, himself in the chamber of waters.

5

Thirty miles up the switchbacked and steep-banked Rat River, about fifty miles from Fort McPherson, at the extreme western limit of the Mackenzie delta and not far from the Richardson Mountains, the man chose a campsite on which he now set about building a cabin. The site was on a bluff twenty to thirty feet high, bounded on three sides by the river. He did not like being surprised, or to be come upon from a blind side; but, except for an island—and the Rat had no islands— the promontory he chose on the north bank of the river was the most protected and fortlike position the Rat offered. The site afforded an unobstructed view of the river on three sides, and the north side, from which high winds and blizzards would blow, was sheltered by uninterrupted miles of rain forest. He had to scrabble up the bank of the bluff like a bear, and portage his gear from a quarter mile downstream, where the bank was much lower, but the inaccessibility of his site was offset by its impregnability.

Not that he expected anyone. He had seen no sign of an Indian since leaving Fort McPherson. And Mounties never put themselves out. As lazy as Indians, as useless as women, and he was eighty miles off their patrol. More likely to be bothered by weasels. Both were pests. Still, he did not like being surprised, and until he could put up a cabin and set out a trapline he was exposed and had for supplies only what he had brought in: flour 150 lbs., sugar 20 lbs., tea 10 lbs., four 5-lb. tins of lard, and a 2-lb. sack of salt. He set it all out, each staple in its individual sack, the flour in three sacks of 50 lbs. each. Then he stuffed a sack each of flour, sugar, and tea, and two of the 5-lb. tins of lard, in one of the twenty-five gallon oil drums he'd carried from Fort McPherson, and pounded on the lid with the ax. Hoisting the drum onto his shoulder, he stalked off toward the spot where he'd drawn the canoe up, leaving behind the large spruce trees and entering a thicket of cottonwood trees which sprouted up nearer the water. Here, about 300 yards from his cabin site, he cut poles and lashed them together, constructing what looked like a raft; then, with the pallet of poles, about three feet by four, on his back, he climbed a white birch tree— the only large white birch in sight—and wedged the platform of poles in its crotch, and looped a rope over a high, overhanging branch. Clambering down to the ground, he tied a noose around the drum and hoisted it up until it sat on the platform; then he secured the rope to the birch trunk and stepped back to survey his stage cache.

The first permanent structure he'd built in a long time, it marked as belonging to him this bend in the river, the promontory overlooking the bend where he would build his cabin, and the delta around where he would stake out his trapline. The trees, too, which anchored the promontory against the river, the fish in the water which flowed by, the birds which flew overhead, all fur-bearing peltries within a day's march—whatever crawled, crept, or swam, flew, or walked upright, or otherwise used these woods and this waterway—all were his, his to harvest or hoard, to kill or to let live. He stood with arms akimbo surveying the stage cache, then he walked back to where the rest of his gear was, pitched his tarp and bug net for sleeping, and built a fire and boiled up.

That night he dreamed again. This dream was similar to the last one, except that the meshwork indicative of some form of net, the crude devices attached to his feet, hands, and mouth, even the vague enclosing lines

and hints of animal tracks—all were of gold; the walls
of the cave within which he was fettered and gyved
were of gold, and gold cobwebs spun by a single gold
spider festooned the cave, which he recognized on awaking as an abandoned gold mine. He sat bolt upright
beneath the bug net, rubbing his eyes to drive the cobwebs from his mind. 'Am I mad?' he thought, elated,
then said aloud: "Am I mad?" When he ceased the night
noises around him began again, strangely loud. He had
not heard them until they stopped, they had not stopped
until he spoke. "AM I MAD!" he yelled, his words re-
sonating through the subdued darkness like thunder,
commanding attention. Until now he had lived in a
coma. Sleep and awakeness, silence and sound—they
had been much the same to him. But not now. Had he
been stunned by a blow on the head, by a branch in the
forest? And now that he thought of the forest, he became
aware of it—silent, dark, its darkness transected by
shadows of trees, its silence broken by sounds. When
he listened attentively he could hear hundreds of things
in extremis, crying, crawling, chirping, sighing, rubbing
up against hundreds of other things that scarcely existed, on the confines of silence and dark, and soon
ceased. When he peered intently into the dark beyond
the tarpaulin, he could spy, through a crevasse of tree
branch, a cluster of stars in the belt of Orion, defining
his dagger, its hilt. Pale stars and pitiful insects, he
was neither, but he was like both: stumbling through
the forest with his magnificent dreams and his puny
equipment, like the ones who had passed here before
him. The last group of people, the only group who had
passed this way, were Klondikers—over a hundred of
them, more than thirty years past—dragging their boats
and their gear through the delta and up the rivers that
led to the mountains, wintering at the base of the long
line of rapids that made the upper Rat unnavigable,
starving and freezing and perishing there—120 of
them—at what old-timers called "Destruction City,"
though no one had returned there since. Maybe they'd
discovered, and been forced to abandon, a gold mine.
Maybe they'd taken refuge in a cave, the cave he had

dreamed. Maybe the cave was a glittering gold mine which he, Albert Johnson, was fated to find. "Albert Johnson," he said aloud, "ALBERT JOHNSON!" he bellowed, and hundreds of creatures throughout the dark forest were suddenly hushed and attentive. If not him, who? There was no other. From his pants pocket he pulled out the oilcloth containing his money—twenties and fifties and hundreds, and two American fives—he knew the number of bills he had, though he couldn't see what they were; he counted the bills, forty-seven, twice, and laid the packet aside. Then he took out a small pouch whose contents, weighing several ounces, gave it heft in his hand. It was dark beneath the tarpaulin and he rummaged in the rucksack for a candle. A bright light was not necessary, a taper was all he needed for verification, provided it burned faithfully. Finally he found the stub of a candle and lit it, and stuck it upright in the ground. Then with his teeth he loosened the drawstring and untied it with trembling fingers, emptying the contents of the pouch into the palm of one hand. Gold teeth, five in number, and as many small pearls lay cradled in his hand. The gold teeth gleamed and the pearls glowed dully as one by one he turned them over with his thumb, running his tongue along his own teeth as he did so, first his uppers, then his lowers—molars, bicuspids, canines, incisors, canines, bicuspids, molars, then the gums where the wisdoms were missing—his own teeth discolored by tartar and coated with plaque. One by one, he tried the gold teeth, biting them; then he put them and the pearls back in the pouch, and the pouch in his pocket. A long time he lay on his back, staring up at the shadows the candle cast on the underside of the tarpaulin; until his mind, flitting this way and that like the fitful flame, like the flame was extinguished.

The next morning he set to work building a cabin. On the site he'd already selected he trenched the outlines of a hole whose dimensions were those of a pitfall for, say, a large grizzly bear—about eight feet by twelve feet. Then he commenced digging the pit to a depth of about three feet. The day was warm, the sky was clear,

the woods around fragrant with the odor of musk, leaf
mold, and wild onion seed, and other smells of dry ripe-
ness. The sod he removed, matted with grass and small
plants, was not brittle and brisk yet; there had been
enough rain, and frost only briefly each night when the
Arctic sun prolonged its descent behind the northern
tree line. His short-handled army trenching spade
obliged him to dig stooping over; occasionally he would
encounter spruce root, which he cut with the ax, but
no rock. He worked steadily without sweating, the only
sound in the still autumn air the unhurried plink of
his shovel and the rhythm of his own breathing.

The work was not work, though it was laborious; he
dug because in the place he had chosen, a dugout was
the best kind of shelter, and a shelter was necessary
because of the winter approaching. To live elsewhere
in winter, he would have to make other arrangements,
arrangements which involved other people, and the
prospect of that was more onerous to him than the job
of building a cabin. The cabin, at least, would be his,
and in it, once his trapline was set, he would be self-
sufficient. That, somehow, was fundamental in a way
that village or city life wasn't, and fundamentally de-
sirable. To be self-sufficient, if not the aim of life, was
the precondition for considering whether or not life had
an aim; not to be self-sufficient was self-defeating. It
was a victory, of sorts, to be digging your own pitfall,
not having to dig someone else's, not having to watch
out for someone else's which had been dug for you.

By late afternoon he had finished the trench; but he
was too tired to chop trees. So he pulled all the deadwood and branches from around his campsite and piled
them into his trench, then he laid green poles across
it. With the second twenty-five-gallon oil drum on his
shoulder, he scrambled down to the river. This drum
had two puncture holes, one at each end, which he enlarged with his ax: eventually the top hole would serve
for a smokestack, the bottom for a fire hole. For now,
he filled the drum half full of water, and struggled with
it up the hill to the trench, laid the drum on its side
across the green poles, and set fire to the wood in the

trench. Within minutes he had a bonfire; by the time
he had laid his traps out, he had boiling water.

Twenty steel traps laid out on the ground, Victor
double spring Nos. 2 and 4, all of them new and coated
with wax and excessively oily. To each he attached a
short piece of snarewire, and was about to gather up
all the traps and drop them in the boiling water, when
the symmetry with which they were laid out on the
ground caught his attention. He had laid them out more
or less in two circles, one circle of traps inside the other,
with the snarewire attached to each trap at right angles
to the two circles, like spokes in a pinwheel. A sudden
whim seized him. Pulling again from his pocket the
pouch containing his precious molars and stones, he
placed in the center of the two circles the five gold teeth
in a curved line, and connecting with them the five
pearls, so that the two together formed a small mouth
in the middle of the two rings of traps. Then he stepped
outside the design and stared critically at it, walked
around and studied it from every quarter, knelt down
here and there to sight along the ground and to re-
arrange with a stick this or that trap. When he was
satisfied with their placement, he set all the traps, first
the big No. 4's in the outer trap zone, then the medium-
sized No. 2's; then, straddling the mouth at the center
of his miniature trap field, he tied a long length of
snarewire to the stick in his hand, and, tossing it outside the perimeter of his model, proceeded to pull it
toward him. The stick, drawn by the wire, approached
the trap zone and slid through the No. 4 sector un-
scathed—striking the line, as it did, between the set-
springs of two traps—but as he continued to draw the
stick toward him, it tripped a trap in the No. 2 line,
whose jaws snapped, and it was broken. A grin over-
spread the man's features as he drew the trap to him
and released the stick, then he leaned forward to reset
the trap; the stick he replaced with his metal file. The
web of traps was so arranged that the gaps between the
No. 4's in the outer ring were covered by the No. 2's
inside; the mouth, guarded by concentric rings, was

unapproachable from any angle, except from above. Its parted lips lay defined in the dust at his feet, open only to him. So would the delta, too, open her cunt to him, she would show him her cave: he need only stand where he stood, in the hub and middle of his own web, tossing out and drawing in, like a spider by its signal thread, his prey. This idle pastime occupied him throughout the afternoon and into the evening, until dark came and he had to replenish the wood on the fire and the water in the drum. Then, sated with play, he inserted in the jaws of each trap a link of trapchain, dropped all the traps in the boiling water, and lay down to sleep.

His sleep was dreamless and when he awoke the brush had burned down to coals. The poles had collapsed, and the drum fallen into the pit. There was still boiling water, however, and the traps were secured by their wires. He added more water through the fire hole, then he baked a bannock and boiled up. The sun was below the tree line, the night air was chilly, the bugs few. The spruce trees were spectral and silhouetted against the glowing coals in the trench. When he had eaten his fill of the bannock, and washed it down with hot tea, he went to sleep again.

This time he did dream. He was digging a pitfall for rats—in shape like a sunken barrel-trap, with sides sloping out from the mouth, so that the floor as he dug got progressively wider. The mouth was covered with a lattice of green poles, the floor strewn with ashes, a narrow-necked jar containing honey and maize sat on the floor where he dug. The rats jumped down, but could not get the bait from the bottle and began to devour each other. All this while he was digging, deeper and wider at the bottom, further and steeper to the mouth; more and more rats jumped in and devoured each other. He dug, but so deep and at so steep an angle that he himself couldn't get out. At last there was one rat left, a huge rat the size of the pit. There was no room for any more rats; there was no room for him. The rat turned on him, to devour him. Suddenly the rat, like a *basso profundo*, burst out singing:

"When Johnny comes marching home again,
            hurrah! hurrah!
We'll give him a hearty welcome then,
            hurrah! hurrah!"

The resonance of the rat's voice, the close trench they
were in, and the mockery of the song, terrified him....

The next day he felled ten large spruce trees, lopped
them, and cut them into log lengths. While he was
hanging his traps out to weather, he caught himself
humming the rat's tune.

The next day it rained. The traps he had hung from
tree branches rusted, and the pit filled with water and
was sodden with ashes. The blackflies came out, and
he stayed beneath his tarp and inside his bug-bar all
day, damp and cold and, toward evening, hungry. He
managed to get a fire going with birchbark, and boiled
up. Darkness came early because of the rain, the first
pitch black he had seen in the delta; he slept fitfully.

The next day was overcast, there were showers, and
no sooner did firewood dry than it got rained on again.
The traps were bright orange with rust like Japanese
lanterns hung in the trees. There was work to be done,
but he did not feel like working. Each evening the sun
was being detained longer and longer below the tree
line, the air growing chillier night after night, and only
a few torpid blackflies remained. This cycle, instead of
motivating him, depressed him. He was beginning to
grow loggy, to let the weather determine the day. And
now the nasty weather had started: days that came in
like a wolverine, and slipped away like a weasel. He
worried that he had not seen an animal since entering
the delta—not a muskrat, an otter, not even a rabbit—
though he had seen plenty of signs. But while he had
seen nothing, he himself had been seen, scented, even
tracked—of that he was certain. He was always abroad,
exposed, visible—an easy target had anyone been
hunting him. No one was, but had someone been...He
broke down his guns and checked their action; then he
cleaned and oiled and reassembled them. Between
thundershowers he notched all the logs he had cut, got

rained on while boiling up, and went to sleep soaked.

Dawn brought reprieve from the bad spell he'd been in. The Arctic sky was vivid, almost lurid, after the rain, and the air was filled with ozone; no bugs. In one day he did all the bullwork: dragged his logs to the pit's edge and stacked them on top of each other; interlocked their notched ends; chopped out a door and a window. Then he fitted the last log in place at the front, over the holes for the door and window, laid poles across for the roof, and applied a layer of sod. As evening came he stopped work to boil up. In the flickering light of a campfire he appraised his primitive shack.

It was squat, only five logs high at the front and four at the rear, but it straddled a three-foot-deep excavation. The earthwork around it—the embankment of sod, and the tunneled-out doorway—overhung by the framework of logs, gave the structure a fortresslike look; or, if he closed one eye and regarded the sod roof as the ground, it resembled a half-barrel mole trap in a mole run. The tunnel leading down to the door hole was the mole run; he was the mole. The door, which he had not built yet, would be of stout poles and would open inward; for a window he would use his first beaver skin, scraped clean of all fur and fat. In the next few days he would have to put more layers of sod on the roof, and chink the side logs with moss; before snowfall a second, retaining wall should be added to the north side. But those things he would attend to, a day at a time, a task every day, by winter. He would not waste any more time due to weather or sloth. For bad days there would be inside jobs—laying poles for the floor, installing the stove, preparing bait for the traps—on good days there was the trapline to scout, sod to be dug, wood to be cut. Much yet to do, but the structure was a beginning. Across the still clearing by the light of the fire he stared approvingly at it. He would move in tonight, even though there was only a hole for a door, and for floor the damp earth. He was weary of sleeping out, of getting rained on despite the tarp, of being on guard against vermin and pests, of continually having to define himself, assert himself, by being bodily present and active, keeping alert—as if one could guard against everything, as if one could go without rest. How much could a man do without, he wondered...and for how long? He had gone pretty much without food, certainly without meat, and was getting quite thin; his trousers had to be belted on now, and he had had to cut two new belt holes. His cheeks, too—he passed his hand vaguely over his beard—were hollow, and his eyes sunken. From time to time there were blank spots, like now, when he sat and stared at the fire. The vigilance needed to make him feel safe, exposed as he was, in the open, had required too much effort. Besides, he was tired...very tired.... Resisting the impulse to sleep where he sat, he slapped himself, hard, on the face. His face felt alien, so did his hand. His feet, too, were numb, and his mind, which had brought him this far and no further, had balked and bogged down like a pack mule. Like a man in a daze, he forced his eyes from the focus of fire to the shadows beyond, to the structure. The mass of the cabin blocked out the dark trees and formed a solid black core in the darkness. Within that core he could feel safe; the logs would enclose him, the trench would conceal him. He would be visible, vulnerable, no more. He would make sorties out, but with a base to return to; the fort would serve as his hide. Tomorrow, first thing, he would build a door, a proper door, and boil his traps in wood dye—he had spied sumac bulbs near the water—and start getting up wood, and scouting trap sets, and set snares for rabbits, and...he was tired. Slowly, without intending to, he began humming; sitting by the fire and rocking slowly back and forth, he overheard himself humming, and as soon as he recognized what the tune was, he put the words to it and began singing, mechanically and in a monotone, like a phonograph record turning more and more slowly until it ceases to turn entirely:

"When Johnny comes...marching home again...
        hurrah, hurrah...
We'll give him a...hearty welcome then...
        hurrah...hurrah...

The men will cheer...and their wives will shout...
The band...will play...and we'll all...turn out...
And we'll all...be gay...when Johnny..."

He had commenced to crawl, while singing, on hands
and knees, a phrase of the song with every halting move
forward across the shadowy clearing, from the flickering fire to the mound of earthwork, and the dark mass
looming beyond. When he reached the brow of the shack,
the song died on his lips; he stopped and gazed dully
up. Then he began his descent, hands first, into the
hollow which led, like a mole run, down through the
door hole and into the barrel-like pit. Passing through
the doorway, he paused, on hands and knees, to sniff
at the newly chopped spruce logs; then he crawled inside and lay down on the rain-sodden earth. Through
the chinks in the roof, in the blue-black sky he could
see two tiny pin-lights, eyes in the sword of the Hunter.
But for them, he was where he wanted to be, out of
sight, out of mind, in his hide. He shut his eyes, and
they disappeared. He was safe in the solid black core.

PART TWO

The Delta

1

"'People needs ratses. We needs it!'

"He hissed the same words for the eleventh time. His tongue licking and relicking his lips, his eyes glancing around the office, his hands which had wormed their way out of their mitts wiping the snot from his nose, Charlie Rat crouched at the edge of the chair while his mukluks puddled the floor. The two other Loucheux stood behind him, eyes downcast, noses distended, inhaling the warm office air. They were RC's."

Corporal Richard Wild looked up from the duty report he was reading aloud to Inspector A. N. Eames to assess what effect he was having. Inspector Eames was seated as always, elbows on his desk, head clasped in both hands, meditatively smoking the crook-shanked pipe he always smoked, with his eyes shut. Behind Eames and facing Wild, King George the Fifth stared with dead level gaze from the RCMP office portrait. Corporal Wild, who three winters ago had played Puck in Western Ontario U.'s production of *A Midsummer Night's Dream,* tried to put more verve in his voice. Rolling forward onto the balls of his feet in his black duty boots, he declaimed:

"'We needs it!' Charlie Rat insisted. The words hung like Scripture, solemn and round, in the heated air of the office. He was Father Gireaux's lay reader, it was expected of him to speak up."

Corporal Wild glanced again at the Inspector, whose

unsleeping eyes were half open now behind a curtain
of smoke. He read on:

"Millen hadn't looked up yet from behind the desk
where he sat. He always sat there in his long johns and
duty pants held up by suspenders. He always gazed
down at the desk, or scribbled, while people were talking. Millen was young. He'd turned down promotion.
He didn't have a girl friend. He had what Eames called
'ideals.' Now Millen looked straight into Charlie Rat's
face, he quit scribbling, and said: 'You say he slung the
trap over a branch. Whose trap was it?' Then, when
Charlie Rat didn't answer right away, 'Who owned the
trap?' Millen said.

"Charlie Rat spoke quickly over his shoulder to one
of the Loucheux. The Indian nodded. The Indian stood
and delivered himself of the single English word, 'Me.'

"'It was your trap?'" Millen asked him.

"The Indian nodded. Charlie Rat nodded. 'Peoples
needs ratses, we needs it!' he said.

"Millen shook his head and stood up. Charlie Rat
stood up. Millen walked over to the potbellied stove and
poured himself coffee. With his back turned, he said,
'Go harness the dogs, Lazarus, and tell King to come
in here.'"

"Whose statement did you say this was?" Eames
asked, without taking the pipe from his mouth.

"The driver's, sir."

"Who was the driver?"

"Lazarus, sir."

"The Eskimo Lazarus? Lazarus Sittichiulis?" Inspector Eames looked incredulous. His eyes were open
and he held his pipe in one hand.

"Yes, sir. He was out to school, sir, remember? Two
years."

The Inspector knocked the ashes out of his pipe, then
closed his eyes wearily and reinserted the pipe in his
mouth. "Go on."

Wild lifted the sheaf of papers up to eye level so that
he could see the Inspector, and behind the Inspector the
King, as he read. An extraordinary document, really;
he'd read it over beforehand. Not Shakespeare, but for

a duty report unusual to say the least. "'Go harness the dogs, Lazarus, and tell King to come in here,'" Wild read quickly and without any élan. Then, clearing his throat and composing himself, he began in the measured cadence that he felt the Eskimo's transcript demanded:

"It is dark outside and still snowing: minus thirty the thermometer reads. The hill overlooking the river is covered with five or six inches of snow, and more snow is falling. The river below is a grainy blackness. Trail will have to be broke. Not a single light on in the village, except the Christmas mass candles inside the church, and the hundred-watt bulb which lights up the window of the Arctic Red River detachment. All of the Indians are drunk, and Constable Millen and Constable King are hung over. The new snow crunches and packs underfoot, soggy and wet, the worst kind of snow to break trail in.

"In the valley the staked dogs are sleeping, curled up in round balls like stones, concealed by the skiff of new snow. There are real stones, too, drifted over with snow like the dogs, but the dogs are the stones near the stakes. When kicked the dogs spring to life, snapping and snarling. The lead dog sets up a howl. Still no lights in the village. The Christmas drunk will last into the new year, and King will be surly. The snow will continue to fall.

"Now the dogs stand harnessed, Eskimo-style, each dog on a lead of his own and flanged out like fingers in front of the Eskimo-style komatik. Not the best arrangement in new snow, but Indian-style, with the dogs in tandem, is too difficult, except when trail has to be broke through the woods. It will be river travel all the way to the Rat, and men can run if they have to. Better two men running than one breaking trail, and one riding. King will be riding.

"The door of the station opens, flooding the yard with light and blinding the dogs, warmth steams from the office and King comes out, hitching his suspenders up over his shoulders and pulling his parka down over his head. The snow crunches under his mukluks. Without

a word he sits down on the sled, ties the foxfur flap
across his chin, and, slipping his mitts on, sits huddled,
hung over, near the front of the sled, his back braced
against the pack containing the airtight. 'Well?' he
snapped, over his shoulder. Then scrunched himself
down on the komatik, and buried his face in his armpit.
In the window of the station the three Loucheux stood,
leering. The dogs whined and picked up and set down
their feet: their pads were beginning to freeze. Millen
was standing beside the potbellied stove, drinking coffee. King was curled up on the komatik, ready to go.
The dogs waited, whining and trampling tight little
piss-packed spots in the snow. No lights in the village
except at the station; no stars in the sky, not even the
Hunter. All human and animal life, what little there
is, has been crushed between the thumb and forefinger
of the earth and the sky. Ahead lies the river, frozen;
and the rivers it leads to, frozen; and the land those
rivers run through, and the people who live on the land:
all are dead, dead as Lazarus. And the Christmas candles, lit yesterday, make little difference this morning.
Only the dogs are alive, the dogs who have hopes of
breaking their traces, eating their drivers, returning
home to their vomit, the dogs who would rather be dead
than alive, but have no choice, no say. I, Lazarus, raise
myself to full height. The dogs await my command.
'Gemootik!' The lead dog springs in his traces, the other
dogs jump—all of them pulling and barking down the
slope to the frozen Mackenzie and over the drift on to
the hard riverbed. The light from the station at Arctic
Red River is the last light to be seen, and it too, like
the sound of my voice, any trace of my having existed,
disappears around the first bend."

"Why does he have to say that?"

"I don't know, sir."

"Why does he have to embroider? Cut everything
that follows his harnessing the dogs."

"It's out, sir. Shall I go on?"

Inspector Eames dipped his right forefinger in the
pot of dirty honey which sat on his desk, smeared the
inside of his pipe bowl, charged it with tobacco, and lit

the tobacco with a match. He signaled with the sooty
forefinger, and nodded with his eyes closed, wearily. A
layer of smoke wafted above Eames's head and over to
Corporal Wild as he read.

"Darkness along the riverbed, darkness and coldness; no light, no heat, no sound except the dogs' labored
breathing and the swish of the komatik's runners, no
movement except the snow falling, the sled slicing
through snow, the snow settling silent and shroudlike,
everywhere. The cold and the dark are forces, the wind
is a force, though there is no wind now; the frozen river
is a dark, windless channel through a desert of ice
stretching off into grainy blackness, blackness and
numbness that presses the land, squeezing the life out
of creatures. There is no time in this blackness. When
the sled with its sleeping Mountie and Eskimo driver
reaches Fort McPherson tonight, it will be the day after
Christmas in the year of Our Lord nineteen hundred
and thirty one. Until then, the sled is in space, surrounded by space, Arctic darkness and coldness pressing the life out of those who are racing through space
from mass light to mass light. Between Arctic Red River
and Fort McPherson, seventy miles by river, more than
twenty hours by dogsled, the men are no better than
dogs, and less well equipped...."

"Didn't they take the wind tent?" Eames said.

"I'm sure they did, sir. They always take the wind
tent. It's standard equipment."

"Why isn't it in the report?"

"The report hasn't been typed up yet, sir. We're just
getting the driver's statement, the transcript. Once we
have that, we'll know exactly what happened and we
can draw up the report however you like. We can mention the wind tent if you think it's important."

Inspector Eames took two puffs from his pipe, got up
from the chair behind his desk and walked over to the
window that looked out on Aklavik. Along the banks
of the frozen Mackenzie, winter tents with Eskimos in
them; between the tents and the RCMP station, dogs
staked in the snow, the four frame cabins with white
men in them—"G" Division, Western Arctic Sub-Dis-

trict. Eames was nineteenth in seniority in the Force.
There were three times as many inspectors below him
as above him, but most of them were young men. He
was fifty-two years old. Already this Johnson case had
consumed far more time than it should have, and each
year there were more cases like it, more white men
drifting north with a vague idea of trapping. Wild could
handle the paperwork, as he did on most of the cases,
collect the statements, draw up the report, submit it to
him, Eames, to sign. He took a long draw on the stem
of his pipe and let the smoke travel up through his
sinuses. Mrs. Urquhart, the surgeon's wife, walked
across the bleak townsite in her white foxfur parka,
giving the dogs a wide berth and not stepping on dog-
shit. Eames watched appreciatively while releasing the
smoke through his nose. Wild could handle the paperwork, but all the reports weren't in. Somewhere out
there in the frozen delta, beyond the town, a man named
Johnson was subverting the law and defying the RCMP.
Eames had sensed the presence of an adversary when
the man had first been brought to his attention: Corporal King and the special constable, Lazarus, arriving
by dogsled all the way from the Rat, King reporting
that contrary to the rules of the North, they had been
met with silence and refused entry to Johnson's cabin.
And while King told his tale, his face dark with frostbite, the special constable with him had stood skulking
in the corner, all six foot two or three of him, the tallest
Eskimo Eames had ever seen. Immediately Eames had
issued the warrant, sent McDowell and Bernard with
them, with orders to stick it to the man, rough him up
a bit.

The plantar's wart on the sole of Eames's left foot
burned. He kept the dead skin trimmed, but duty boots
and sweat from wool socks irritated the wart. Eames
felt no anger toward this man Johnson, just irritation.
He wondered now had he overreacted? Was this trapper
just another poacher like the Frenchman, what was his
name, that they arrested each year on the islands?
Caught this year with twenty-three white fox pelts and
a gangrenous foot. Pled guilty and was sentenced to a

fine of twenty-five dollars and thirty days, entire sentence suspended if he left the Territories. Eames remembered the last line of his report, a masterpiece, it seemed to him, as reports went: "Napoleon Le-Blanc"—that was his name—"in consideration of his freedom has left the Northwest Territories." Maybe Johnson was that type, a petty poacher. Still, he couldn't afford to make any mistakes. At fifty-two, he was replaceable by some bright, younger man, and Aklavik didn't really rate an inspector. Only thirteen years to retirement.

"I don't know," he said in reply to Wild's question, though he had forgotten what the question was. "Go on. We'll attend to details later. Just don't let any newspaper man get hold of that transcript."

"Newspaper man, sir?" Wild blinked. "What newspaper man? What newspaper? You think...?" he began, changing his tone. Eames recognized it as the student tone, in the presence of the Great Chief.

"On those few occasions when I do think, I like to think for myself, Wild. Just don't let that or any other transcript get outside this room."

"I wouldn't, sir," Wild said.

"And destroy it after the report's drawn up."

"I will, sir, I usually do."

Eames turned from the window to look at him: a good kid, bright, a year of college at Western, about the age his own son would be, would have been. "I know you do," he said. He flexed the fingers of his pipe-holding hand, then his other hand, while Wild watched. "Pull the file on this case, and let's close it," Eames said at last. He came back around to his desk, and sat down. "What do we have?"

"Not much, sir. I've got it all here." Wild opened a legal-sized manila folder, displaying two legal-sized sheets. He passed them to Eames. "The first one I drew up, sir, when Bishop Geddes informed you about this fellow Johnson, and we sent it to Melville; the other is Melville's report."

Eames studied the two documents; both seemed routine and straightforward.

Aklavik, N.W.T., July 12th. 1931.

The Constable in charge,
R.C. Mounted Police,
Arctic Red River, N.W.T.

It has been reported that a strange man going under the name of Johnson landed somewhere near Fort McPherson on the evening of Thursday, July 9th, 1931.

He apparently came down the river on a raft of two or three logs, tying up above the settlement and walking into the Post.

As far as can be learnt he had no outfit of any kind, neither rifle nor dogs, but appeared to be well supplied with money. He purchased some supplies from the trader there and is supposed to have made enquiries regarding the route to the Yukon.

Please make enquiries in your district and submit a report, but I do not want you to make a special patrol in this connection.

ANE/RSW

[Sgd] Richard S. Wild, Corpl. for Insp.,
Commanding Western Arctic
Sub-Dist.

Arctic Red River Detachment,
August 15th, 1931.

The Officer Commanding,
Western Arctic Sub-District,
R.C.M. Police,
Aklavik, N.W.T.

Sir: *Re: Albert Johnson*

Acting on instruction of the Constable in Charge at Arctic Red River while on the McPherson patrol, I made inquiries re the above mentioned.

At Mr. A. N. Blake's post at the mouth of the Husky River I interviewed Mr. Blake and he informed me that Johnson had left McPherson about July 16th and had passed his place on his way

down river to find the mouth of the Rat River.
Evidently he missed the Rat and returned to
Blake's post, and then proceeded up a creek at the
back of the house which leads to the Rat River by
a chain of lake portages. Mr. Blake informed him
that he did not think he could get over this route
with a large canoe, and would have to cache the
canoe and go overland. The man is fairly well
fixed for supplies as he purchased dry goods and
a full outfit from the Northern Traders Ltd. at
McPherson.

Johnson gave Mr. Blake to understand that he
was going over to the Yukon side and that he was
not returning. Since he has left Blake's he has not
been heard of.

I have the honor to be,
Sir,
Your obedient servant,
[Sgd] R. W. Melville, Const.

Eames looked up from the two documents, thoroughly dissatisfied. It wasn't that the documentation
was inadequate, but neither did it help him understand
the man; it was adequate, but it wasn't accurate, the
man hadn't gone to the Yukon. Eames absentmindedly
dipped his finger in the honey, which was grimy with
grains of carbon. He had meant to smear his pipe bowl,
but it was filled with ashes. He put his finger in his
mouth instead.

"Didn't Millen talk with this man?"

"I believe he did, sir, last summer."

"Don't we have a record of that?"

Wild shrugged. "He just talked with the guy, sir,
told him to get a trapper's license. The guy didn't say
anything. You didn't ask for a report, sir."

"I'm asking for one now," Eames said with decision.
Wild, rolling his eyes, pulled out pencil and paper. "And
I'm responding to Millen's report which has yet to come
in."

"Yes, sir," said Wild, prepared for dictation.

"Millen's report should state that Johnson wouldn't volunteer any information about himself, and that he was informed of the trapping license regulation."

"Yes, sir," Wild said, writing.

"Those are the two main points. Anything else that passed between them, Millen should note in detail. But those are the points to which I'll respond and when Millen gets that report in, and King's patrol gets back, I think we can wrap this case up."

"Yes, sir."

"Re: Albert Johnson," Eames said, and Wild began writing. Eames got up from his chair again, and paced back and forth from the desk to the window, from the window to the desk, puffing at his pipe which had gone out. There was no clear path between the desk and the window; an inverted twenty-five-gallon water stand blocked the way. He had to turn sideways and squeeze between the water stand and the metal file cabinet beneath the portrait of King George the Fifth each time he passed back and forth. Still, he continued to pace, and squeeze, and turn sideways, puffing his pipe which had gone out, while Wild, sitting cramped in the grade school desk that had been borrowed for dictation and statements, wrote down what he said as he said it.

"To Constable Millen, Arctic Red River Detachment. Re: Albert Johnson," Eames repeated. "I am surprised that you accepted Johnson's excuse for giving you no information. If Mr. Johnson's intentions are good, he can scarcely object to the police knowing all about him. I particularly desire that we have full information of the home address and relatives of men coming into our various detachment districts. In case of accidents or any of them becoming lost, the information would be of use to us and would assist the man himself. You are to keep track of Johnson, and if, when you next visit his place, your suspicions are aroused, you are to search his outfit (underline that, Wild) as you are authorized to do under the terms of Section 24 of the Game Regulations. On the other hand, if Johnson merely desires seclusion, you are to carefully explain my wishes regarding the information needed, and encourage him to communicate

with you, and state what his condition is and his whereabouts. (Add, after encourage him: 'and all others in
your district who may be remotely placed in winter
time.' We don't want this to seem too personal.)

"Where was I?"

Wild said in a monotone, "And his whereabouts."

"And his whereabouts. This practice was commonly
followed by all white men up the Mackenzie River after
the death of Nicol and Beaman on the Gravel River.
Got all that? New paragraph. Johnson may be going to
the Yukon. If that is his intention he should be asked
to drop you a line acquainting you of his safe arrival.
Long patrols can often be avoided by such co-operation.
Signed, etc. And I want this dated August 11th."

"August 11th, sir? That's four and a half months
ago."

"August 11th, 1931. And Millen's report should be
dated accordingly."

"Sir..."

"Yes, Wild?"

"Nothing, sir."

Eames stopped between the water stand and the file
cabinet, beneath the portrait of the King, and lit his
pipe.

"Now, about this patrol Millen sent, the one you have
the driver's transcript on, all you need to say," Eames
said, between puffs, "is on December 25th, 1931,
Constable E. Millen dispatched Constable King—get
King's initials—in company with Special Constable
Lazarus Sittichiulis, to investigate the complaint of residents of Fort McPherson. The complaint alleged—say
what the complaint was. The officers were also to ascertain if the man had a trapping license. Constable
King and Special Constable Sittichiulis arrived at
Johnson's cabin on the 28th in daylight. Constable King
spent some time knocking on the door, stating who he
was, and that he wished to speak to Johnson. Constable
King failed to get an answer. The door was never opened,
but Johnson was seen looking through a sort of window,
which he immediately covered when he saw Constable
King looking at him. Constable King decided to proceed

to Sub-District Headquarters, Aklavik, for instructions. Constable King and Special Constable Sittichiulis arrived at Aklavik on December 29, 1931. You got all that?"

Wild, writing furiously, nodded. "Should I mention a warrant, sir?"

"Was there a warrant?"

"No, sir."

"Well, don't mention one, then. Why would you mention one if there wasn't one? Sometimes you don't make sense, Wild."

Wild shrugged roundly. He stared at his pad, as though prepared for dictation, and doodled. Normally, Wild's doodling infuriated Eames, both at the time and later, when Eames would find intricate diamond- and heart-shaped designs on the draft copies of his dictation. Now, for some reason, Wild's act of defiance didn't bother him. On the contrary, standing beneath the King's portrait, Eames felt in control of the district, as if by means of words alone he was imposing order. He went on: "Now, for the second patrol, just make it part of the same report, another paragraph. Ready? In view of Johnson's suspicious conduct I issued a search warrant and, to prepare for all eventualities, had the patrol take rifles in their sleds as well as side arms. The patrol consisted of Constables King and McDowell, Special Constables Joseph Bernard and Lazarus Sittichiulis. They left Aklavik, Northwest Territories, on December 30, and reached Johnson's cabin... When King gets back, find out when they got there, the time of day as well as the date, tell what happened in detail, any exchange between the two parties, and the eventual disposition of the man named Johnson, or, it may be, the prisoner Johnson. Add Millen's letter when you get it, and prepare the report for me to sign, and send to Division Commander, Edmonton. All that clear?"

"Yes, sir," Wild said, still writing.

"And, Wild..."

"Sir."

"Shitcan that driver's transcript. I don't like things like that knocking about." Eames banged his pipe on the concave rock that served as an ashtray, beside the dirty honey, then he scraped out the bowl with a penknife. "But make sure it's shitcanned. Don't leave it around where some...somebody might find it."

There was a rustle of paper, while Eames searched his drawer for pipe cleaners.

"No newspaper man will find this, sir."

"Good. What did you do with it?" Eames said, suddenly suspicious.

"I ate it, sir."

"You what?"

"I ate it. I didn't have a match, so I ate it." Wild grinned, holding the transcript over his belly, and licking his lips.

Normally Wild's clowning infuriated Eames, but, strangely, this time it did not not. "Very good, Wild," Eames said without anger, but without a trace of humor. "See that you do."

2

"Two sleds this time, two dog teams. Bernard drives the other, Indian-style, while McDowell rides. King rides, Eskimo-style. Four dead men who don't know they are dead tracking a dead man who does. Along the frozen riverbed, mile after mile, the green of the spruce, dark wintergreen, against the white of the ice and the blue of the sky. The spruce, row upon row, crowd like soldiers along the far bank; on the near bank, willows. The spruce are straight and tall, but the front rank slant out over the river, like soldiers ready to fall. Where the Rat intersects the Husky, an Indian fish camp. Deserted. Through alder brush at the top of the bank a drying rack pole, covered with snow, a flatboat drawn up, also covered. A black dog sat on the bank. It did not bark."

Eames stood up at his desk and started to pace, between the water stand and the file cabinet, from his desk to the window and back. Wild, from his seat in the grammar school desk which faced Eames's larger desk, continued reading.

"The river the same as three days ago. New snow has fallen, but wind has blown, and there is the same depth of snow. The three-day-old tracks are visible near windblown patches of ice. The dogs sniff and follow the tracks, the drivers follow the dogs, the dogs and the drivers and the hung over Mounties follow the man who went in to stay. He has committed some crime, but no

one knows what. No one knows who he is, or where he
came from, or why he chose to come here. Only a desperate man would come here, Inspector Eames said to
King. Eames is right. So is the man. Both are right.
The last day of the year, no one is wrong. In Arctic Red
River, Aklavik, Fort McPherson, all over the world all
the mass candles but one have been snuffed, and when
darkness covers the world tonight it will be unrelieved
darkness. In darkness, no one is right.

"The spruce which line both banks lean out, ready
to topple. They will lean that way forever, sentinels,
forming a corridor through the Rat's delta through which
men and dogs may pass, staining the snow with piss
and tea to prove that they have been there. At mile
sixteen from the mouth of the Rat the corridor wide is
into a swale. Before, there was no horizon, now off to
the west there are mountains. Light blue, icy, and clear,
three humps stand higher than the high hills: a saddleback hump, twin mounds like large breasts, and a
long bowl-shaped range with a diagonal slash down the
middle, the Barrier Pass. The cabin is four miles below
this swale, out of sight of the mountains and hidden,
or nearly hidden, from the riverbed.

"The patrol drew up beneath a large S-shaped spruce
that leaned far out from the bank. Across the river and
in the trees smoke could be seen, a thin spiral rising
in the windless air. The cabin, which couldn't be seen,
was on a high bluff but set back thirty yards from the
river. Constable McDowell came over carrying his rifle,
and he and Constable King talked. The drivers were
busy staking the dogs, and unloading frozen dog food.
King pulled his rifle from the sled, and loaded it. Then
they walked across the riverbed and when they reached
the far bank, King waved. Some of the dogs were whining, but others had trampled spots in the snow and lain
down. The drivers left the dogs, and followed the Mounties. McDowell now checked the action of his rifle and
loaded it. Then King attempted to climb the hill directly
facing the cabin, while McDowell went around the far
side, to come up on the cabin's blind side. King on his
second attempt managed to reach the top of the bank,

but fell several times in the deep snow; also, he dropped his rifle in the drift and had to hunt for it. McDowell meanwhile had ascended the easier slope and had posted himself behind a tree, about twenty yards from the cabin. The two drivers, seeing King's difficulty, had scrambled up the hill on either side of him, but at an angle, without difficulty. So that when King, who had started first, reached the top, the other three were at their posts, one with, and two without, rifles, waiting for King to appear. His snow-covered rifle topped the hill first, and he, holding the rifle over his head, followed it. There was no sign of life from the cabin, except the thin spiral of smoke. There were, however, new loopholes bored through the log walls, just above the snow level. The loopholes had not been there three days earlier. King, red-faced and catching his breath from the climb, then yelling, 'JOHNSON!' rushed for the door with his rifle at the ready.

"Perhaps he expected Johnson to open the door, perhaps he expected to burst the door down. A shot through the door from the other side doubled King over and he fell to the ground. Immediately McDowell began firing rapidly into the cabin, while the man in the cabin returned his fire through the loopholes. Special Constable Bernard was nowhere to be seen. Constable King was crawling while holding his stomach and bleeding and vomiting across the open space in front of the cabin. McDowell was firing, Bernard was hiding, King was crawling in circles.

"I, Lazarus, who am a dog driver for the RCMP, and do not wish a promotion, on the last day of the year of Our Lord nineteen hundred and thirty one, reluctantly raised myself to full height and ran out to where King was thrashing about, picked him up as carefully as I could, and carried him back out of sight of the cabin, down the hill, across the river to where the dogs and Bernard were. I kept downwind of the dogs, and had Bernard bring the sled over, on which I laid King, making him as comfortable as possible. The sound of rifle fire across the river continued for some time, while King, who had passed out, continued to bleed. The dogs caught the scent, and had to be beaten. One dog died, and was eaten by the others, though we were beating them the whole time. Finally the rifle fire ceased and McDowell came running across the ice and yelling for us to 'Mount up, mount up!' The dogs had already been fed, the sleds were hitched. McDowell hopped on, and we left. A thin spiral of smoke continued to rise from the trees beyond the high bank. It was two in the afternoon, almost dark, but one could see from across the river the trampled snow where King had gone up, and the trail of blood where he had come down. I had frozen blood and vomit on my parka and windpants, and the dogs were hard to control. A diary of this patrol is appended."

Wild stopped reading and looked up, quizzical. "Do you want to hear the rest, sir? It's just a few lines."

Eames, who had been pacing, squeezing and turning sideways, between the water stand and the file cabinet, from his desk to the window and back, did not stop pacing. He nodded. Wild continued to read:

"December 30, 1931: Left Aklavik at 7:00 A.M., rested at noon, arrived Fort McPherson 10:00 P.M. Cold. 65 miles.

"December 31, 1931: Left Fort McPherson at 7:00 A.M., proceeded up the Rat River to Johnson's cabin, arriving 10:00 A.M. Twenty minutes unhitching dogs, feeding dogs, climbing bank, surrounding cabin. At 10:20 A.M. King shot through door. Forty minutes beating dogs, hitching sleds, waiting for McDowell. Departed Johnson's cabin 11:00 A.M. Cold. 26 miles.

"January 1, 1932: Drove all night, arriving Aklavik 7:00 A.M. Took King to All Saints Mission, notified surgeon. Half an hour unhitching, staking, feeding dogs. Cold. 80 miles.

"Total mileage for patrol: 171. L. Sittichiulis, Special Constable."

Throughout the entire recitation, Eames had paced. Now he stopped at the window and gazed out. It was almost dark outside, 2:00 P.M., but the Anglican Mission hospital was brightly outlined, and staked dogs could be seen in the dusk. "I don't like it," Eames said, "I don't like it at all."

"No, sir, I didn't think you would, sir."

"Then why did you take it?"

Wild shrugged. "Standard procedure, sir, to take two statements. Bernard didn't see anything, and King's not able..."

"What's the latest on King? I saw him this morning, a bloody mess. Urquhart said he didn't have the equipment..." He broke off what he was saying to stare out the window at the mission hospital. It was lit up like a Christmas tree. The rest of the village was plunged in darkness, not a light on, except in the RCMP station. It was he who had given the order for blackout, not wishing to overtax the old village generator. "But that's what they all say, at first, until they know whether...how is he?"

"Still critical, sir. The bullet entered here," Wild placed his hand a little below his heart, like a sloppy pledge of allegiance, "and came out here," he reached around to his back, beneath his arm. "Urquhart says he's lucky it went through. He says he'll probably live."

"Mmm." Eames continued to gaze at the Anglican Mission, until he realized he was looking for Mrs. Urquhart. He looked abruptly away. "Well, I don't like it," he said, "not at all."

"I have Corporal McDowell's statement, sir, all typed and signed. McDowell can type, sir."

"Let's hear it."

Wild shuffled through some papers in a folder, drew one out, placed several more in the space for books underneath his grade school desk. The papers fell through the slats of the bookrack, and he retrieved them from the floor. He read aloud:

"Re: Albert Johnson, Trapper. Rat River, N.W.T.

"Acting on instructions from the Officer Commanding Western Arctic Sub-District, I left Aklavik at 7 A.M. of December 30th, 1931, in company with Constable A. W. King and Special Constables L. Sittichiulis and J. Bernard. The patrol proceeded to the cabin of a man

known as Albert Johnson. The cabin is situated on the
Rat River, fifteen miles from its mouth, a few miles
from the junction of Driftwood Creek and the Rat River.
The latter place is also known as Destruction City, where
a number of miners are said to have perished in making
their way to the Yukon Gold Rush in 1898."

"A good touch," said Eames, listening attentively
while looking out the window. "The man can write. You
say he typed it himself?"

"Yes, sir," said Wild.

"Go on, go on."

"The patrol arrived at Johnson's cabin at about 10:30
A.M. of December 31st, 1931, and Constable King immediately went forward to the cabin, which is situated
about twenty yards from the creek where we had left
our dogs. I walked to the top of the creek bank, by which
time Constable King had reached the door of the cabin.
Constable King knocked on the cabin door, at the same
time saying, 'Are you there, Mr. Johnson?' Someone
inside the cabin fired as soon as Constable King had
finished speaking. The shot came through the closed
door. Constable King fell to the ground, but rose again
and staggered away into the bushes close by. I at once
secured my rifle and fired through the shack wall, drawing the fire of the man within, who shot at me twice,
narrowly missing each time. Retiring from my exposed
position, I worked round under the creek bank to where
Special Constable Sittichiulis had by this time gone to
the assistance of Constable King. With the help of Special Constable Sittichiulis, Constable King crawled, and
was carried, through the brush. It was easy to see that
Constable King's condition was serious. I decided to
abandon any idea of an attack on the shack, and to
return to Aklavik with all possible speed with Constable King in my cariole, accompanied by Special Constables Sittichiulis and Bernard.

"The patrol traveled all night and reached Aklavik
twenty hours later at about 7 A.M. I placed Constable
King in hospital, and had Special Constable Sittichiulis
stop and notify the duty surgeon as soon as we entered
the settlement. The surgeon, Dr. Urquhart, was in at-

tendance by the time we were able to get Constable
King out of the toboggan and into the ward. Signed,
R. G. McDowell, Constable."

"Now, there's a report," said Eames, brightening. "It
says pretty well what you expect to hear, and it says
it without any palaver."

"That's what I thought too, sir."

"File this as the official patrol report."

"What shall I do with the other one, sir?"

Eames thought a moment. "Destroy it," he said. "No,
wait." He pulled his pipe out of his tunic and, crossing
to his desk, dipped his finger in honey and smeared the
bowl and charged it. "Hold it until we can get a statement from King to corroborate this one, then destroy
it."

"Yes, sir."

Eames lit his pipe and took two or three tentative
puffs, then a long one. "But we'll have to cable headquarters. What's the date?"

"January 1st, sir."

"What a way to start the year," Eames muttered,
and thought, 'My plantar's wart.' He would have to lead
the next patrol, employ a posse if one were needed,
purchase all the equipment, and arrange for transpor-
tation, communication, administration, while in the
field. McDowell couldn't lead the patrol—only a constable—a good one, though. Millen? Why had Millen
turned down the promotion? Millen would have to be
in on it though, second in command. Maybe he could
leave it to Millen, once they got in the field. The special
constables he could do without, but they were needed,
as drivers. The dogs—how many? And dog food. At
least, thank God, they didn't use horses. And weapons—what should they take? They should go to blow
that shack down, total war. What about the surgeon,
in case of accident, and his wife? No, King would need
him here, and there would be no reason for her to go
without him. If she were a nurse...She wasn't. Nice to
have her here, something to look at, Aklavik further
afield than most women came. Only the Anglican missionaries' wives. He thought of the rector's fat wife at

Fort McPherson, and shook his head. "What a way to start the year," he muttered again.

"Telegram — to OFFICER COMMANDING, RCMP, EDMONTON."

Wild pulled out pencil and paper and commenced writing.

"REGRET TO REPORT CONSTABLE KING (King's an Edmonton boy, you know.)"

"I didn't know, sir."

SHOT AND SERIOUSLY WOUNDED BY TRAPPER KNOWN AS ALBERT JOHNSON STOP KING IN HOSPITAL AKLAVIK STOP ACTING ASSISTANT SURGEON URQUHART REPORTS KINGS CONDITION CRITICAL (no, change that to serious) STOP SHOOTING OCCURRED AT JOHNSONS CABIN FIFTEEN MILES FROM MOUTH OF RAT RIVER STOP MILLEN HAD INSTRUCTED KING INVESTIGATE COMPLAINT THAT JOHNSON TRAPPED WITHOUT LICENSE AND INTERFERED INDIAN TRAPLINES STOP KING REPORTED AKLAVIK TWENTY-NINTH THAT JOHNSON HAD REFUSED TO UNBAR CABIN DOOR NOTWITHSTANDING KING STATING HIS BUSINESS CONSEQUENTLY KING CAME TO AKLAVIK TO OBTAIN SEARCH WARRANT AND ASSISTANCE STOP

Eames stopped, too, cognizant that he had come to the critical part, and that for what he said here he would be held accountable. Cautiously, like a man putting weight on a hurt foot, he commenced slowly, editing mentally as he went and constructing from the two reports he had heard a third version which, when he had read it over, he would mark "Official," sign, send, and await the consequences. He hoped to phrase it in such a way that he would be seen as doing his duty, not grandstanding, and not flinching from danger, but merely following the *Constable's Manual* in apprehending a dangerous and vicious criminal.

PATROL CONSISTING CONSTABLES KING MCDOWELL AND TWO POLICE INTERPRETERS DISPATCHED THIRTIETH REACHING JOHNSONS CABIN ELEVEN AM

THIRTY-FIRST STOP MCDOWELL REPORTS [That was the best way to put it, that took the weight off his foot.] KING KNOCKED ON CABIN DOOR AND SPOKE TO JOHNSON WHEREUPON OCCUPANT FIRED THROUGH DOOR WOUNDING KING WHO WAS ABLE TO STAGGER TO SAFETY IN SURROUNDING TIMBER FOLLOWING WHICH SHOTS WERE FIRED THROUGH SPACE MADE BETWEEN LOGS NARROWLY MISSING MCDOWELL STOP MCDOWELL BROUGHT KING AKLAVIK TRAVELING EIGHTY MILES TWENTY HOURS [No one down south would appreciate that, unless they'd done Arctic duty; he would put it in anyway.] STOP SURGEON REPORTS BULLET ENTERED TWO INCHES BELOW LEFT NIPPLE [For a split subliminal second, he fantasized Mrs. Urquhart.] AND EMERGED SAME PLACE ON RIGHT SIDE STOP WILL LEAVE TO ARREST JOHNSON WHEN DOGS RESTED PROBABLY SUNDAY MORNING STOP DAILY BULLETINS TO FOLLOW KINGS CONDITION

"Send it collect, and rush," he said to Wild.
"How shall I sign it, sir?"
"Eames."

3

The next day, January 2, was filled with difficulties for the Inspector. He had known it would be, had foreseen some of the problems of dragooning and equipping a small posse of men in the midst of New Year's celebrations, of collecting and provisioning dogs and dogsleds, of procuring drivers and a guide. The overall strategy of a crushing offensive against Johnson's stronghold Eames had assumed in a moment of vision, as a field marshal might, dispassionately imagining the sudden mobilization of all the men and matériel at his disposal, their march to the Rat, the police warning to Johnson (this Eames would deliver, through a bullhorn), their apprehending him and demolishing his cabin. The logistics of such an operation would be enough to tax any inspector, but Eames was confident that his own men would respond, that the local trappers who were to comprise his posse would co-operate, that the supplies required for such an undertaking would materialize. Two factors, however, that he had failed to take into account, balked and frustrated him. The first was that New Year's Day fell on a Friday, which meant that January 2 and 3, being the weekend, were doubly lost days.

Eames himself was not a drinker. During his first eleven years of Arctic duty he had been—an alcoholic, he would say now, though never drunk or dysfunctional. But when he had begun to have memory lapses (of trifling details—a few minutes charging his pipe, then knocking it out fully charged; a half an hour out on patrol, then failing to make the entry in his report— never forgetting the things he would like to forget, the events which drove him to drink), he had quit cold. Within six months of his newfound sobriety, his wife had left him, and they had lived separately ever since, she "down south" in Calgary, he "up north," first at Hershel Island in the Arctic Ocean, then, following his promotion to inspector, at Aklavik. He suspected, in fact he knew, his sobriety had made her feel guilty about what she called her adaptation to his former self. Though he had never known what she did the four to six months of each year she was outside—visiting family and friends she'd always said—it had been her way of adapting to marriage with an RCMP officer, the spartan regime it afforded her, the oppressive constraint of living within the law.

Within a year of his turning sober and their permanent separation, she had moved in with a childhood sweetheart who had just been released after serving fifteen years of a twenty-year sentence at Kingston for manslaughter—he had killed a policeman—and who, as soon as he was out, so Eames had heard, turned alcoholic, petty larcenist, and common-law-wife beater. This regime seemed to suit Eames's ex-wife, misnamed Irene, at least according to the Christmas card he had received from her in yesterday's weekly mail run. On a field white with snow (or was it sand?), beneath a Maltese cross (or was it a star?), three men on camels were riding, one pointing ahead over the dunes or drifts; and she had captioned in under the pointing figure the single word "Alex," which was her name for Eames. The printed message and note inside read:

> Mercy and Truth are met together,
> Righteousness and Peace have kissed.
> Ps. 85:10
>
> Rene.

(P.S. Arnold too sends his greetings.)

Just as well, Eames mused as he glanced at the card on his desk, just as well that their son, who would now have been almost Wild's age, had died—mauled at age five on his way home from school by the dogs of an Eskimo dog team. That had been Eames's first time of remorse, and he had stayed sober a year; his wife's frantic behavior he had attributed then to her shock at the loss of their son. When after a year he'd begun to drink, she had calmed down, taken her normal trips out, and adjusted again to her lot as a Mounted Police-man's wife. Five drinking years later, when he'd turned sober for good, her renewal of frantic behavior per-plexed him at first, and occasioned his second time of remorse. It was then she had told him of fellow officers, subordinates, even native drivers she'd slept with; then reversed her story and said she hadn't slept with them. It left him numb. After six months of intolerable ar-gument he'd dismissed her finally, in his mind and in his petition for divorce, as a nymphomaniac, one who couldn't distinguish between the act and the urge, be-tween the fantasy and the fact of adultery. It was a distinction he himself had lately had difficulty making, regarding the acting surgeon's wife, Mildred Urquhart. But not really. He knew he had not lain with a woman or taken a drink since his wife left him ten years ago.

Now it was the weekend following New Year's and all of his men were drunk or hung over, except King, who was seriously wounded and in hospital.

Wild might, or might not, come in today, he knew how much work Eames had to do. Sergeants Hersey and Riddell, the two Signal Corps men, couldn't be called on, except to send radio messages; they were not Eames's men, after all, but regular army men, soldiers. He could, of course, deputize them as special constables to aid in pursuit of this outlaw, but that seemed extreme. Hersey wouldn't mind, he would welcome the outing, but Rid-dell, the old sergeant, would interpret such a move on Eames's part as panicky, and for Eames to panic was pagan. No, it shouldn't be necessary to swear in the two Signal Corps men. A few radio messages, a well-

organized posse, a lightning march to the Rat should
wrap the case up. Millen would need to be radioed, at
Arctic Red River, to meet the posse. The Indian who'd
filed the complaint, at Fort McPherson, would have to
be radioed to meet Millen and act as their guide. As
for the posse itself, whom would he call on? Eames
counted on his fingers. There was McDowell; but after
his exertions of yesterday, McDowell would need to rest
up, as would the two drivers, and, for that matter, the
dogs. They would need more dogs. Each of the trappers
who lived in Aklavik had his own dog team, and they
were all in town for New Year's, not out on their traplines. He would try all of them, but first he would try
Gardlund and Lang; maybe Verville, but Verville was
married. And Sutherland, that would make seven, eight
counting himself. The posse had to be more than patrol
force; a small posse might result in another defeat, for
from all reports Johnson was well entrenched and well
supplied with ammunition. But too large a force would
require too many provisions and more dogs than could
be mustered. The dogs would have to be fed, too, and
the distance between Aklavik and Johnson's cabin was
eighty miles, a full two days' trek. A base camp would
have to be established, perhaps at the mouth of the Rat,
and provisions cached there, perhaps from Mc-
Pherson.... Eames sighed, and limped to the window
to look out at the dogs and the bleak townsite in the
gray Arctic dawn.

It was 10:00 A.M., Saturday, January 2, 1932, not a
soul stirring in Aklavik, not a light on, except at the
mission hospital. It was blindingly lit, but shone fuzzy
and soft through snowfall. And gazing out the detachment HQ window Eames suddenly noticed the other
factor he hadn't taken into account, and the instant he
realized it, he resigned himself to it: the weather. The
temperature had dropped in the night—he knew without checking the outdoor thermo—and a blizzard was
blowing. The dogs lay hunched up, their heads buried,
as small and round as they could make themselves.
Around each dog a hummock of snow had drifted, like

a lopsided igloo, and some were already buried. Only the upright iron staking poles, here and there dotting the townsite, indicated which ridges of snow were chained dogs, and which were inanimate objects. He presumed all the others were inanimate, but they might not be. One might be a drunk Eskimo cooling off in the snow instead of fighting his wife—another reason why he couldn't take all of his men on the Johnson expedition. If there were a fire, or a murderous fight, and there was always one or the other or both around New Year's, there would need to be at least two men to quash it. There was no getting around it, he was shorthanded. 'Hersey and Riddell,' he thought resignedly, 'deputize them as the acting detachment, and they can transmit messages, too.' Riddell couldn't quibble with that, though Hersey would feel deprived of the action—too bad, he was a Signal Corps man. Having decided that, Eames limped to the front door of the detachment office, just as Wild, lightly clad in parka and duty pants, but without windpants or mukluks, burst in at the door, redfaced and blowing. "Sir!" he said, and let in a blast of cold air.

"Check the thermo, Wild," Eames said, "I was just going out too."

"Yes, sir!" And back he went. Eames closed the door after him.

Again Wild came in, with another blast of air. "Minus forty, sir. Down some." He stood in the doorway, removing his mitts, then struggling out of his parka, while Eames watched.

"Close the door, Wild," he said finally.

Wild closed the door and, having emerged from his parka, proceeded to his morning routine—three hours late, Eames reflected—drawing water in a pan from the inverted bottle, placing the pan on the potbellied stove, adding coffee. Wild stood by the stove, warming and chafing his hands, while Eames pulled on his mukluks, his parka, his mitts, and taking his toque from his parka pocket, said: "Wild, I'm going over to the infirmary. I want you to radio Millen and tell him to

meet us." Wild nodded. "Also that Loucheux at Fort
McPherson, Charlie Rat, I think his name is. He's to
meet Millen, and act as our guide." Wild nodded again.
Eames waited, but Wild just stood dumbly, his hands
behind him, like an automaton at parade rest. "Don't
you want to know when and where, Wild? You know
who, you don't need to know why, but don't you need
to know when and where? What's wrong with you, Corporal?" Without waiting for an answer, Eames stalked
from the room, leaving Wild by the stove, warming
himself.

As soon as he was out in the cold, bareheaded, he
remembered his toque, jammed it onto his head, and
stood still in the face of the blizzard. His temper cooled,
and his mind cleared instantly. 'Let every overwrought
fool,' he mused, 'and every hotheaded kid down south
come here and stand in a blizzard ten minutes.' He
pulled his parka hood over his head, and buttoned the
chin flap. He considered going back in to instruct Wild,
thought better of it, and started across the compound,
leaning into the wind which blew ice slivers at him,
avoiding snowdrifted dogs.

Acting surgeon James Urquhart was sitting on the
bench where Eskimo outpatients normally sat, in the
narrow hallway which served as a reception room of
the All Saints Mission hospital. An Eskimo woman in
a blue uniform—not the immaculate yellow nurse
McCabe wore when she was on duty—sat at the small
desk at the end of the hall, writing something. Eames
always looked first for nurse McCabe, whose first name
he loved to hear her pronounce, "Moira," but she was
not there. There were no patients, and the doctor was
leaning back against the wall, one leg crossed over the
other, which was braced against the bench by the opposite wall; a newspaper was in his hands. He was tall
and spare, with a ruddy beard, had run distance and
rowed for Oxford, and he often complained that the
chairs and beds which fit the Eskimos (with the excep-
tion of Lazarus, who was a giant) didn't fit him. A sign
he had devised and nailed above the doorframe announced:

PROCRUSTES' CHAMBER
ENTER.

Under this entry sign Inspector Eames passed.

"Have you seen this, Eames?" said Urquhart, un-crossing his legs, and crackling the newspaper as he folded it largely. Eames, in the act of unhooding himself and removing his mitts, felt a moment of faintness, envisioning headlines in the Edmonton *Journal* (he could see it was that) about a madman at large in the Arctic, a constable shot, and himself, the Inspector, dragging his heels. At the least he expected to see his yesterday's cable to HQ in Edmonton quoted. Urquhart folded the paper again and displayed the page, not the front page. It read: "Here Is the New Yardstick of 1932 Motor Car Values." Beneath the banner type, an auto was depicted with the caption: "ESSEX SUPER-SIX (70 HP) (Spd. 50 MPH)!"

"What do you think of that little honey, Eames? I'll bet you could tool down the ice from here to McPherson in less than two hours. Imagine!"

"Is that...?" Eames peered to see the date of the paper.

"Two days ago, came in with the supplies. Well," said the doctor, uncrossing his long legs and standing up slightly stooped, "I suppose you've come to see our patient. Sarah, fetch me the report, will you?" Then to Eames: "You've got your men trained, I must say. Your man was scarcely out of danger, what with the sled ride and blood loss, he had been comatose and was still trau-matized, yet he insisted as soon as he woke up this morning on making a statement. I've got it here—thank you, Sarah—signed by King himself, duly notarized by myself, and typed by my good wife; I trust it will suf-fice." He handed the sheet of paper to Eames, and went on: "He's resting comfortably now. You can look in on him. It took something out of him to make this state-ment, and he's still what I'd call critical."

Eames held the statement, typed by Mildred Ur-quhart, taken by the doctor, given by King, and it was as if he held in his hand a sparrow, warm and palpitating. The loyalty of his men, especially of King, but of all his men—McDowell, Millen, Wild, the regulars; the Signal Corps men, Hersey and Riddell; even the specials, Bernard and Sittichiulis—moved him as he had not been moved for a long time, not since the death of his son. He nodded mutely.

The doctor continued his chitchat: "I'd say it will be two weeks, maybe three, before he's up and about. He's lucky, you know. That bullet missed his heart by two inches, and if it hadn't gone through as it did he wouldn't be alive, what with the punishing sled ride. Your boys didn't get him here any too soon, I can tell you." The doctor patted Eames's shoulder fondly. "He'll do, though, he'll pull through all right." The doctor smiled patronizingly; he was Eames's junior by eighteen years.

"I don't need to see him," Eames said. He carefully folded the statement by King, and placed it in his parka pocket, next to his pipe. He started to pull out his mitts, and had his hand on his hood, but hesitated. "There was one other little matter," he said. "It's not urgent. If you're busy..."

"The day after New Year's." He shrugged. "Business will pick up, but now..." The doctor held out his long arms, indicating the empty office, his own idleness, his willingness to be at Eames's disposal. "What seems to be the problem?" he said, in mock solicitation.

"My plantar's wart," said Eames.

"Oh." The doctor was visibly disappointed, or so it seemed to Eames. But he motioned Eames to follow him past the desk and into the first little room off the hallway. There was a cot in it, and a stool. "Let's have a look," he said, and seated himself awkwardly on the short stool. Eames sat on the edge of the cot and pulled off his mukluk, then his two pairs of wool socks; the sock next to the left foot was slightly frozen, and pulled at the skin around the wart. "Lie down," said the doctor, and Eames lay back while the doctor examined the sole of his foot.

"Your feet sweat a lot," the doctor commented. It wasn't a question.

"No more than the rest of me," Eames said. From

his prone position he watched the doctor take some instrument in his hand, then he felt the cutting as the doctor carved into his foot. It wasn't too painful.

"It's alive and well," he said, "flourishing. How long have you had it?"

Eames thought. "Six months, a year maybe. It comes and goes. I keep it trimmed."

The doctor put away the sharp tool he had used, and leaned back against the wall, crossing his legs. "It's not a simple problem," he began, closing his eyes, "like a palmar's wart, or a digital wart—it's what we call in Britain a verruca or plantar's wart..."

"I know," said Eames, "I was hoping you'd cut it out for me, before I go on patrol."

The doctor, interrupted, opened his eyes. "Let me explain a few things about warts to you, Inspector. It's my duty to, as a doctor. First, there are over a hundred remedies for plantar's warts listed in the *Journal of Home Medicine*, which means, of course, that none work. On the other hand, a study conducted a few years ago, in which schoolchildren in a working-class district in London were allowed to keep their plantar's warts over a five-year period, during which time they were examined but not treated, indicated that seventy per cent of the warts went away on their own, poof!—just as they came. They came mysteriously, no one knows why, and they disappeared the same way, which leads us to conjecture that warts in general, and specifically plantar's warts, are not a physical ailment at all, but a symptom of something else—a state of mind, nervous tension, congenital deficiency, your guess is as good as mine."

"I have been under nervous strain recently," Eames said.

The doctor shrugged. "Who knows? We do know that warts are caused by a virus. The virus gets lodged in the skin and causes an abnormal growth, like a tumor, a benign tumor. What you've got is a tumor, but it's on the sole of your foot, you keep it alive by exercising your foot and keeping your foot warm and eating and resting—all those things you do for your foot, you do

for the the wart, too. As long as you're healthy, it will
be healthy—unless it decides to go away, which, as the
study indicated, there's a good chance of. As for cutting
it out..."

"Or burning it out," Eames intervened.

"Yes, I've seen that done too. Either way, you've got
a scarred foot, maybe for the rest of your life. And you're
on your feet a lot, aren't you, Eames? You go on patrols,
you walk around the compound?"

"Mmm," said Eames.

"The cutting or burning might not do the trick, you
might have to keep cutting or burning—that's painful,
and eventually you would be lame. The wart might
recur, in the same place or somewhere else. Pregnant
women have been known, immediately following childbirth, to have an eruption of hundreds of warts. And
sometimes the warts went away, and sometimes they
didn't. Are you prepared to do violence to your own foot,
and to keep on doing violence to it, if need be, when
the wart might just go away as it came, suddenly and
mysteriously? One morning you wake and it's gone, it
died in the night while you slept. Now, some people
claim to have charmed them away; others employ hyp-
nosis. Still others say you can think warts away—warts
in general, or a particular wart."

Eames looked at the doctor for the trace of a smile.
There was none.

"All things considered, thinking it away is the best
way, it's the method I'd recommend."

Eames sat up on the cot. He pulled his poor, naked
foot up over his knee and gazed at the gray crater of
dead skin, with the crusted core in the center; encircling
the area of the wart was a ridge of callus, to which tufts
of gray wool adhered. He reached down and picked up
his sock, and began pulling it on.

"That's my advice," said the doctor. "You do as you
want, it's your foot."

Eames nodded gravely, and tugged on his mukluk.
The foot felt to him like an alien being, propping him
up, prepared to walk for him, to perform all manner of

functions, but engaged in a life of its own, too, its own private war. He pulled his parka hood up.

"Nasty weather," the doctor commented.

"Mmm," said Eames, and pulled his mitts on.

"I suppose you'll let things ride for a while," the doctor said. "No pun intended." He smiled.

"I'll be in tomorrow to check on King," he said. "Thanks for your advice."

"It's free," said the doctor.

Eames wheeled about-face and passed through the hallway, under the Procrustean sign, and out the front door. The icy air buffeted him and clutched at his face. His foot, too, was sensitive to the cold; it sent up a signal, he winced. The idea of thinking the wart away crossed his mind like a cloud of unknowing. The very idea made him angry. He had deferred to his foot far too much already; he would heel it into submission. With resolute strides, he marched across the compound, the wind at his back now, veering left past the detachment station to the log shack in which the two trappers, Karl Gardlund and Knut Lang, lived when they were in town. No light was on, and he knocked loudly on the door. No answer. He kicked at the door with his foot, his lame foot, and heard groans from inside; he knocked again. The wind howled around him and in the brief time he'd stood there already a small skiff of snow had begun to form at his feet. He continued to beat on the door. At long last a shuffling noise inside, the latch clicked, and the log door opened inward to reveal in the darkness the prehistoric features, covered with hair and clothed in long underwear, of the trapper, Karl Gardlund.

"It's Eames," he said, "let me in." The door opened further, and Eames stepped inside the small, one-room cabin, its hide-covered floor littered with garbage and skins, its air foul with animal smells. The stench caused Eames's head to reel and gave him an instant headache. The long-john-clad figure shuffled in the twilight like a hairy gorilla, its powerful shoulders and too long arms groped over a huge pile of garbage to where a lamp sat;

its fingers fumbled with matches. Then the dim lamp went on: seal oil, black smoke, fishy smell. Eames stood in the dim light, the door open behind him, his arm up over his face, his nose in his armpit, breathing. The creature called Gardlund stood, stooping and blinking at him, across the room, and from the upper bunk in the corner he could hear the hoarse snoring of Lang.

"Happy New Year," Eames said in a muffled voice.

Gardlund blinked, and gazed stupidly about the cabin.

Eames partially closed the door behind him, but kept his arm up over his nose, except when he spoke. "Gardlund," he said.

Gardlund stood like a creature at bay. Lang continued to snore.

"King was shot, Constable King. Did you hear?"

Gardlund blinked.

"I want you and Lang to help form a posse." Eames emphasized the word "posse." "You know what a posse is?"

Gardlund nodded vaguely.

"To go after the man who shot King. We leave tomorrow morning. I want you to come with your rifles and snowshoes, and dogs, to the station"—he waved his hand toward the station, whose light from this vantage shone brilliant across the gray snow—"for a manhunt of several days, maybe a week."

Gardlund made no response, neither nodded nor spoke.

"You'll be paid," Eames said, "the regular wage."

"How much?" said Gardlund.

"Five dollars a day."

Gardlund seemed to be calculating the amount, seven times five, or formulating a question. Eames waited, breathing into his armpit.

At last Gardlund spoke on his own initiative. "Is there a bounty?" he said.

"A bounty?" Eames repeated.

"Like on a wolf. His nose, or his ear."

Gardlund's voice was flat, and his eyes bloodshot, but Eames realized at once what he meant and the idea both thrilled and repelled him. Contracts could be put out on men as they were yearly on wolves. When men were like wolves, why not destroy them, and bring in their noses as proof? It was the opposite of the doctor's advice about thinking diseased parts away. He wondered how Gardlund would deal with a wart. "No," he answered, "not yet."

Gardlund made no response, but Eames felt new respect for this creature. It was like hiring a gun. "Tomorrow morning at 0600 hours," the Inspector repeated, "with dogs."

Silence. The only sounds Lang's snoring and the wind's howling. Finally Gardlund said in a flat, inflectionless voice, "Tomorrow." Eames nodded, removing his arm from over his face, and went out through the door, closing it.

He had now only to notify the drivers and McDowell, but he stood outside the trappers' cabin, the wind blowing snow in his face, and reflected on what a difference there was between men: King, for example, summoning almost his last energies to make the statement Eames had in his pocket, and Gardlund, trapping and hunting brutes for so long that he no longer distinguished between men and beasts, but only between hunter and hunted. And Lang was even more mercenary than Gardlund. Yet these two were more or less civilized specimens compared with the one they would hunt, the half-man, the madman, the walker-alone, Johnson— in Eames's attempt to comprehend him, Gardlund and Lang were like two missing links.

He wondered, for example, whether Johnson took the trouble to cook his food. Some of the Eskimos didn't. Half stupified with cold, and themselves resembling the seal blubber they ate, they crammed the frozen meat into their maws. They used knives, flashing in front of their faces like an extra incisor, to slice the meat off at their lips; one old Eskimo he'd watched once, drunk, slice his nose off that way. Cut off his nose to spite his face, the joke went around. Eames remembered his foot; he was still debating carving the wart out, despite Urquhart's advice. What would Johnson do, he wondered? But Johnson was a wart, a wart on the body politic

whose guardian he, Eames, was. He was a tumor who
had to be cut or burnt out, unless he just went away,
suddenly and mysteriously, the way he came into the
district. The posse might arrive at the cabin and find
Johnson gone, find that he'd fled over the mountains
after the shooting of King. Then he would be the Yukon
inspector's headache, not Eames's. But it was unlikely.
He'd chosen Eames's district, just as the wart had
Eames's foot, and both seemed dug in for the duration;
wishful thinking wouldn't rout either Johnson or the
wart, but cutting or burning might, Gardlund and Lang
might if offered a bounty.

Eames started walking in the direction of the dogs,
between the detachment HQ and the hospital; all other
buildings had been blotted from sight by the blizzard.
The dogs worked in teams, though they ate one another
and were generally savage and surly; even Gardlund
and Lang lived together at times, vicious brutes though
they were...for a man to live like a dog, and alone—
to choose to live that way—like Johnson...Eames
steered toward his own bunkhouse, the cold sleeping
porch at the rear of the RCMP office. Then, feeling that
after the events of yesterday, and prior to those of tomorrow, he needed civilizing, he changed course for
Mildred Urquhart's. There was an enormous amount
to be done, but Wild could fret; as for McDowell and
the drivers, they would be asleep still, as King should
have been were he more of a natural man, and less of
an RCMP. Mildred Urquhart would appreciate that,
having taken, or at least typed, King's statement.

Abstracted, and unable to see anything but the snow
five feet before him, with here and there an iron stake
projecting, he stumbled. Immediately he knew, before
he felt the snap, heard the snarl—like being struck by
lightning, then hearing thunder—that he had lit on a
dog. He jumped back at the same moment as the snow
at his feet became a mad thrashing. The brute, luckily,
was at the end of his chain. Eames, angered, stared at
the animal's snout and into his tiny red eyes. He realized then that he had drawn his side arm, and was

holding it, foolishly, in one mittened hand. Shoving it back in its holster, he gave the brute a wide berth, and arrived at Mildred Urquhart's door shaken, but feeling more faith in himself and his instincts than he had felt for some time.

4

In Eames's opinion, Mildred Urquhart would be a beautiful woman in anyone's book. Tall, stately, full-bodied, and spirited, with a keen intelligence and a lively wit, there was about her a resonance that affected everyone who came in contact with her, especially Eames. Seated in his parka and mukluks at her kitchen table while she busied herself around him—she was never still, always active, yet her body and mind both seemed to plead for repose—there was something about her, he thought as he watched her, that made him feel both young and old at the same time. Old, because he was old—fifty-two to her thirty-five or thirty-six, he wasn't sure which—and old in spirit, too, as was everyone else in comparison with her, except children, who flocked to her door; but youthful, vitalized, more alert, because he had entered her ambit, which immediately placed him outside the restrictive compound of blizzards and dogs and trappers and policemen (both the well and the wounded), and doctors and nurses and patients. She was busy kneading bread dough, though she might just as easily have been playing backgammon, which she often did, or reading—she was an omnivorous reader. A copy of Malory's *Morte Darthur* sat on the table, with a red bookmark in it and a sprinkling of flour like fingerprint dust on its maroon cover. She was simply the Queen, that was all. When Eames thought of the Force as an abstract ideal, he didn't picture King George the Fifth, whose portrait hung on the wall of his office, he pictured

Mildred Urquhart as she was now, kneading bread dough, her arms bare and speckled with flour, her ample bosom, throat and neck flushed from the effort.

Her back had been to him, but now she stood at a three-quarter angle, so as to converse over her shoulder; and she was saying, as she kneaded the large lump of dough, working more and more flour into it: "Surely the men in this district, if there are any men in this district, will not return wrong for wrong. Bunce has suffered, I know that, but two wrongs don't make a right. If you men think so, we women don't, I can tell you." She seized the large lump of dough, tore it in two, and mashed the half lumps into two bread pans. "This one's for you, if you wait long enough," she said, smiling, and opening the door of the oil stove, placed both pans inside. Then she placed both hands on her apron, against her thighs, and pressed down, wiping them, untied the apron strings behind her back, and started to cross to the table, but stopped, remembering something. "I won't be a minute," she said, and disappeared into another part of the house. Eames was left, staring vacantly at *Morte Darthur,* while waiting for bread to bake. He wanted to smoke, but neither the doctor nor his wife smoked or approved of smoking, and when he visited here he never indulged. His hand was already in his pocket, rummaging for his pipe, but he pulled out King's statement instead.

King was "Bunce"—they all called him that, Eames didn't know why, since his real name was Alfred—and as he looked at the statement, signed in a scrawled hand "A. W. King, Const.," Eames thought warmly, 'Bunce.' The typing was flawless, he noticed. It read:

Western Arctic Sub-District Headquarters, Aklavik,
   N.W.T. January 2nd, 1932.
   Acting on instructions received from the Officer Commanding, Western Arctic Sub-District, Aklavik, I left Aklavik on the 30th December, 1931, in company with Constable R. G. McDowell and Special Constables Sittichiulis and Bernard.

We proceeded to the cabin of a man known as Albert Johnson, whom I had previously visited on the 28th December, 1931.

We arrived at the cabin about 10:30 A.M. of December 31st and I walked up towards the door, while Constable McDowell proceeded under cover of some brush to a position where he could cover me. Special Constable Sittichiulis went towards the rear of the cabin, and Special Constable Bernard stayed near the dog teams. I knocked on the door of the cabin, standing sideways to the building as I did so, and called "Are you there, Mr. Johnson?" I had just finished speaking when I felt a smash in my left side and heard the report of a gun. The shock knocked me to the ground, but I was able to regain my feet and reach the toboggans, where Special Constable Sittichiulis immediately came to my assistance. At the same time I saw Constable McDowell coming towards me through the brush and heard the report of a shot which was fired at him from the cabin.

Constable McDowell and Special Constable Sittichiulis fixed up the toboggan and put me in it, and immediately left for Aklavik, traveling steadily until the hospital was reached at about 7:00 A.M. of the 1st January, 1932.

A. W. King, Const.

What effort that must have cost him! Eames thought, gazing at King's scrawled signature. He could not have been more moved if the statement he held, typed by Mildred Urquhart, and given by Bunce King, had been written in blood. Mildred Urquhart came back in, the blouse she had been wearing changed for a sweater, the same woolen slacks on her legs and lower body. She wore slacks, she once told Eames, because the house was so drafty. In her hand was a jewel-studded cigarette case, from which the tip of a filter protruded. She sat down at the kitchen table and, pinching the cylinder between long fingernails, pulled it out and put the cigarette to her lips. Eames watched her with horror.

"I've been thinking," she said. "By the way, do you have a light, Alex?"

Eames nodded, and rummaged in his parka pocket desperately, and unsuccessfully, for a match. "I don't seem to..."

"It's all right," she said, and put the cigarette back in the case, and the case beside *Morte Darthur*.

"I didn't know you smoked."

"I don't, normally. Only when I think—it's not a habit. But I have been thinking about this Johnson fellow, you know, the one in Bunce's report?"

Eames nodded, and even while he braced himself to resist her opinions and to hold in abeyance his judgments, he was charmed by the sound of her voice. Always her voice struck a resonant chord in him, especially when she was "talking to win," so much so that were she reduced to a sound, a disembodied voice, he would travel for miles to wait in lineups to listen—as who would not?—to the Queen. "Mmm," he muttered.

"Well, all morning while I was waiting for the dough to rise I was reading this book"—she laid three fingers lightly on the cover of *Morte Darthur*, further imprinting the flour—"and while I was reading I asked myself, 'What would drive a man to such extremes, so that he would resist any effort to bring him back?' What do you think, Alex?"

Eames shrugged. "Some crime he'd committed. Fear of the police. Hatred," he almost said "of society," but cut himself short. "I'm sure I don't know," he said.

"I'm sure you don't, Alex." She smiled. "Well, the answer is love. The knowledge that he'd been hurt so badly that nothing, and no one, could make him well again. What does a dog do when it's been hurt?"

Eames pictured the huskies lying in wait between where he sat and his bunkhouse. "Die, I hope."

"But where does he go to die? He drags himself off to the bush to eat grass, or buries himself in the snow—to get away from the other dogs. I'm like that, if I'm sick I don't want James meddling around me, I want to be by myself."

"I see your point," he said.

"Listen to this."

He thought she was going to read from the book on the table, but she brought out a Bible instead. It was one of those tiny ones with the small print, and she had been clasping it under the table.

"Fingerprinting with one hand, holding the Bible in the other—you'd make a fine policewoman," Eames said.

She paid no attention. The type was so small she had to peer closely at it, and as she scanned and flipped pages in her search for some passage Eames concentrated on the way her lips parted and her tongue thrust partway out. He'd seen her that way when she was sewing, or engrossed in a book, or absorbed in a game of backgammon. It was fetching to watch her, but tiring, too. Never was she in repose.

"Here it is. Now, listen." And she commenced to read: "Set me as a seal upon thine heart, as a seal upon thine arm:/For love is strong as death; jealousy is cruel as the grave;/The coals thereof are coals of fire, which hath a most vehement flame./Many waters cannot quench love, neither can the floods drown it:/If a man would give all the substance of his house for love, it would be utterly contemned."

She looked over at Eames, who looked back at her, dubious, uncertain what to make of it. It was evident she had something in mind, some application of the Scripture, but what it was he could scarcely imagine.

"I'll just read on a ways," she said, "You just listen, and think—think about Johnson."

Eames nodded, ravished by the sound, perplexed by the sense of what she read. She read on.

"We have a little sister, and she hath no breasts: what shall we do for our sister in the day when she shall be spoken for?/If she be a wall, we will build upon her a palace of silver: and if she be a door, we will inclose her with boards of cedar./I am a wall, and my breasts like towers: then was I in his eyes as one that found favour."

She ended the recitation, and closed the book. Eames,

who was accustomed to thinking of Scripture as spoken by men in long bathrobes, with hair on their faces like Gardlund's, and a strange Mideast glitter in their eyes from eating too many figs, wasn't sure what to think. It was clear she had something in mind, and was giving him time to guess what it was. Normally he would have kept quiet, but since it was Millie, he tried. "You think Johnson has a sister?" he ventured.

She remained silent, her gaze fixed on him; it was an intense gaze, eliciting from him an answer, like those silences his teacher used to lapse into in the one-room school on the prairies. "You think Johnson's in love," he said, and even as he said it he laughed, but it was a scoffing laugh. "I give up," he said.

"I think," she said, emphasizing each word, "that you need me on this manhunt." Having said that, and having framed the statement in silence, she went on. "If there's to be no more bloodshed, you need a woman along. This man Johnson is hiding, right? And he's hiding from something, or someone. Now what, or who, is he hiding from? A woman, that's who. And who but a woman can bring him out? A woman drove him in there, and a woman can bring him out. A man, or a hundred men, he'll just fight. He's like Lancelot"—she waved to the book on the table—"he was the strongest knight in the land, and the one knight able to save King Arthur's Round Table—why? Because of his guilty love for the Queen, Guinevere."

At the mention of Guinevere, Eames remembered from somewhere the words 'Bad when she was little, worse when she was big,' then the image of her dancing naked on the Round Table for the assembled knights; he wondered vaguely if it was from the book she motioned to, which he had never read, or from his drinking days. At the mention of the word Queen, other images arose, among them Mildred Urquhart, fur-clad and armed with the Bible in one hand, a cross in the other, leading him and his detachment of men through the snow up the Rat to the trapper's cabin and a bloodless recitation. There would be no need for the doctor, he would be needed at home to tend King.

"Millie, that's just foolishness," he said, though secretly he admired her spunk. "This man is a killer. He'll be waiting along the way somewhere to ambush us. He's incapable of listening to reason, he's a tough and desperate character, a killer."

"Has he killed anyone?"

Eames had never allowed himself to think this far before, but now that he had said it he was sure it was so. "Yes," he said, and closed his eyes, tiredly.

"Who? Who has he killed?"

"I can't say. I really shouldn't be discussing it," he demurred. "All I can say is that your theory is interesting, but wrong. At first we thought we were dealing with a loner, one of those trappers—there's one every year—who gets depressed in isolation. Some of them wander into the post, others stay out and we have to go get them; mostly they do themselves harm. But that's not the case with this Johnson character. We now have fairly certain indications that we're dealing with a man whose hatred of the police is so intense that he would put himself in a position..." For a moment, as a result of her watching him, and his being forced to speak, Eames lost his train of thought. "...in the position he's put himself," he finished lamely.

"But isn't it a position of need?" she said. "Isn't he, in effect, crying out for help? And aren't we bound by the gospel to help any creature, however desperate he may be? The more desperate he is, the more we should help him."

Her logic flummoxed him. There was a relentlessness to it, not unlike Johnson's, as he imagined Johnson's to be. Perhaps Johnson should be confronted by the gospel, but he, Eames, was not the Christian to do it. Bishop Geddes, perhaps. No, Not Bishop Geddes. Mildred Urquhart, but that was unthinkable.

"No doubt," he said, getting up. "But Bunce went to help him, and look what happened. I don't understand you, Millie. You seem to be more concerned for this madman than you are for Bunce—or for me."

"Oh!" she said, and jumped up. He smelled it too, the bread. She opened the door and with an oven mitt pulled

out both loaves, burnt on the top. Still bending over the
bread, her sweatered breasts like two perfect loaves,
her calves and thighs trembling slightly due to the
stance she was in, she turned her head to look at him.
They both laughed. "Well," she said, standing up, her
arms akimbo, "come give me a hug, Alex, and make
me feel better." It was the first invitation she'd ever
extended, and innocent enough; her way of showing she
cared. She was fully dressed, and he had his parka on.
Still, when he more or less bear-hugged her, encasing
her whole upper body, shoulders and all, in his arms,
he felt the round globes of her breasts on his chest and
the warmth of her thighs on his thighs, and rather than
hold her overlong, he let her go prematurely.

"You're sweating, Alex. Take your parka off."

"I must go now, Millie. I've got to..." He couldn't
remember what, have a smoke for one thing. He was
affected by her as she was by the Scriptures. "Millen,
I've got to radio Millen, and Charlie Rat, and go wake
up McDowell, and..."

"You just think of what I read to you when you're
out there. And, remember, I'll be praying for you and
for him, too."

Eames clutched his pipe in his pocket. He wasn't sure
what it all meant, but he felt caught between Mildred
Urquhart and Albert Johnson, and both afflicted him—
differently, to be sure—but pain was pain. Both seemed
to embody some more or less pure ideal that he couldn't
understand, much less aspire to. And both seemed to
be pawns of implacable forces which urged him to fight,
to forgive, to feel strongly, to act in some way contrary
to reason. He didn't like the unstable feeling it gave
him, any more than he liked the parrot in the old sea-
man's shack on Herschel Island, which said to anyone
entering the shack, "Now, let us be men!" It disturbed
and upset him. He felt, now as then, he wasn't sure
why, both inadequate and, somehow, mocked. Too many
explanations, too few facts, not enough time, too much
snow, and thirteen years to retirement—eight, if he
took the option. "I will, Millie, and...thank you."

"Next time," she said, meaning, presumably, the loaf of bread.

Eames put his hood up and pulled out his pipe and charged it. The doctor was just coming in as he left; they met in the cold, enclosed front porch, amid footgear and snowshoes and dog harness leather.

"Hi!" he said. "You're out and about today." His nose was running, and his eyebrows bushy with frost.

"Right," said Eames, and plugged his pipe into his mouth, and lit it in front of the doctor.

"Vicious habit," the doctor remarked.

"Right," said Eames, and wanted to say, "Now, let us be men!" but said instead, "There's some bread in there for you," and opened the front door, pulling his mitts on and shielding his pipe—'My only pleasure,' he thought, 'my only Goddamn pleasure'—from the wind.

5

The temperature continued to drop and the wind to howl throughout Saturday and most of Sunday. Eames waited it out at the detachment office, getting the radio message off to Millen, and another to Charlie Rat. Millen and Charlie Rat were to meet the main group at Blake's trading post on the Husky sometime on January 4, his first message read, but he'd amended it to January 5. That should give him plenty of time to contact the men, requisition supplies, and move as one had to move in the Arctic, in the lulls between windstorms. No inspector in the south would understand the delay, but no inspector down south had to contend, as he did, with recalcitrant men and dogs, dirty weather, trappers like Gardlund and Lang, or Indian trackers like Charlie Rat. For that matter, none of them had a murderous trapper to contend with; and he wondered if he were Johnson's cat's-paw—doing just what Johnson wanted him to do. But he resigned himself to the day's delay on account of bad weather, and set about girding up his loins, as Mildred Urquhart might have put it, and to getting up his men, if they could be called his men, against the next day.

Gardlund and Lang came by, in the blinding midst of the blizzard, dogs hitched and ready to go. They shuffled and hunkered outside the door in the lee of the storm, kicking (the men) and pissing (the dogs), and when Eames communicated the change of plans to them

they seemed willing enough to "take the day off," as
Lang put it. That was the bone of contention, as Eames
knew it would be, and he granted them the day's wage,
told them to contact Sutherland for him, and be ready
to go the next day. Both men and dogs disappeared like
straws in the wind. He made a note of the extra day's
wage for Gardlund and Lang, and started a file marked
"Johnson." He decided not to attend church, though
Mildred Urquhart would be there, and spent the rest
of the morning trimming dead skin from a crater the
size of a quarter around his plantar's wart, and probing
its core with a needle.

Toward evening on January 3 the wind dropped, and
even though it was a Sunday, the Sunday following
New Year's, and though the temperatures remained
cold, $-40°$, Eames was able to get everything done. He
found McDowell in the men's barracks, in duty pants
and suspenders, playing poker and drinking rum with
Hersey and Riddell. McDowell hadn't shaved and still
looked haggard from the patrol of three days ago.
Straightway he asked Eames, "How's Bunce?"

"Coming along," said Eames, and pulled from his
pocket the statement taken by the doctor and typed by
his wife. "He gave this statement the minute he re-
gained consciousness. It corroborates your statement,
Mac." McDowell nodded gravely.

Mac was no crackerjack, Eames reflected, but he was
at least a good company man. You knew where you
stood with McDowell, and what you could ask of him.
He asked him to contact the drivers. He explicitly instructed McDowell to tell the drivers to equip the sleds
for a patrol mission of several days' duration, and to
meet him at the station next morning at 0700 hours.
Hersey and Riddell he told to stand by for messages,
and to act while he was out in the field as stand-in
policeman, should any local need arise. All three men
laid their cards face down on the table, following
McDowell's example, and listened as he spoke, and
grunted, each one, an acknowledgment—a knowing nod
from Riddell, the veteran sergeant, his cavernous mouth
clamped around a cigar; a quick "Sure, chief" from

McDowell; a tight-lipped "Check" from Hersey—no questions: they were eager for him to be gone, so they could resume drinking and gambling. It was all he asked, that each one understood where he stood, and what he expected of them; it was all he'd ever asked, even of Irene. Then he rousted Wild out of the sack and told him to be on hand in the morning to issue arms to the men, and to requisition in advance (Eames didn't care when he did it) dry food and dog food enough for the two extra teams. Having conveyed these instructions along with New Year's greetings to each of the men under him, Eames left the barracks and trudged back through the weirdly drifted snow to his own bunkhouse, the small, sloped-roof shed off the rear of detachment HQ.

He found the back door, which he had not used in days, drifted in. Behind him lights shone through the windows of the barracks and the Anglican Mission hospital, the church in the distance was brightly lit and, nearer him, in the tiny window of the two trappers' cabin, a single candle flickered. On an impulse Eames pulled up his parka, peeled down his windpants, out with his gear and pissed in the drift that sealed off his back door. As he wrote his name in the snow he gazed up and saw, dominating the northern night sky, the complete constellation of the Hunter: his shield, his belt, his sword, his outstretched arms; and off to the side—Eames searched, then found—the two dog stars, said to guard him. Eames shook himself, took a childish delight in having left his signature; then pulled up his windpants and trudged to the front of the station, went in and straight to his bunk, determined to get a good night's sleep before the ordeal of the manhunt.

The back room was cold, as he liked it, but he had trouble getting to sleep. First he lay on his back, then on his side, then on his other side, then on his stomach, until gradually, over a period of several hours, his mind became less alert, ceased to buzz with details—radio messages he should send; newspaper stories he should stifle; Mildred Urquhart pressing her warm globes against him, her thighs against his thighs, her bread

beneath his sword, while the Anglican rector read
Scripture—and finally he fell asleep. He dreamed he
was waiting in line at some customs or immigration
official's counter; there were people in line behind him,
and ahead of him was a young woman whose turn it
was to tell the official her troubles. She was about thirty,
tall, blond, and quite bright—very attractive, except
that her left leg was missing from the knee down. In
its place she wore a steel brace attached to a shoe, and
she was telling the customs official how she had come
to be maimed—describing in detail, and with great
intensity, why she was like she was. The customs official, a small, nondescript man (a little like Charlie
Chaplin, Eames thought, as he waited in line) held a
microphone for her to talk into, and had been listening
patiently to her story for a long time. Now she was
rising to the climax of her tale, pointing to her leg, or
to the steel brace where her leg should have been, de-
claiming non-stop and with suppressed rage into the
microphone held before her, when suddenly the little
man moved the microphone, then he moved it again,
then again; he came out from behind the counter moving the microphone—up to the air, down to the floor,
sideways, both ways—holding it a moment in each new
position as if listening intently, then jerking it to a new
position, and ran out of the office and off through a field
holding the microphone here, there, up, down, to the
air, to the ground, listening for a moment at each new
position, then spastically moving the microphone, or
being moved by it, until he listened himself out of sight.
All this while the girl with the brace for a leg watched
him, aghast, and Eames, who was next in line, woke
up...laughing—he was actually laughing out loud—
in the cold little room, with the toque on his head and
his holster slung over the chair, he laughed till tears
came to his eyes, cold tears; then he got hold of himself,
and quit laughing. Extricating his arm from beneath
the covers, he squinted at his watch. In the gray twilight of the Arctic night he could just make out the
time: 0430 hours. Another half hour he lay in bed, then
jumped up, grabbed his clothes and his side arm, and

went into the detachment office to dress beside the fire. . . .

The drivers arrived at 0630 and, shortly thereafter, the trappers. None of them came into the office. The hubbub outside of dogs snarling and scrapping kept the drivers and trappers busy, each with his own team—five teams in all, of seven dogs each—and Wild was in and out of the office, issuing rifles and ammo which he'd lugged across the compound from his quartermaster's stores, and checking each man off the list of equipment that Eames had drawn up. McDowell had not arrived yet. Eames downed a final cup of coffee and knocked out his pipe, then he donned parka and mitts and went out. It was his intention to assure Sutherland, who had come on Gardlund's say-so, that he was employed; and to encourage, with a pat on the back or a friendly word, each of the men of his posse.

It had been seven years since the Inspector had headed a posse—the last time had been to the Arctic coast, to bring in an Eskimo who had thought he was God—and while Eames didn't wish to inhibit the men, he did mean to run a tight ship. But in the gray predawn Arctic twilight, oppressive with intense cold, the hooded men were like phantoms: humpbacked and bent by some physical force, barely visible as here or there a driver raising his arm to strike, or two dogs at each other's throats, would emerge partway from the palpable cold, and then sink back into its swirl. The shadowy figures leaned on their sleds, holding their dogs by the reins, and Eames couldn't at first, with their parka hoods up and the oval of fur lining their faces, distinguish one from another. It was like gazing at five outhouse holes. Steam issued from each oval hole and Eames, exhaling steam puffs himself (his sinuses had plugged the minute he stepped out, and he was forced to gasp through his mouth), peered through the swirl of palpable air in an attempt to find Sutherland, but could only identify, of the five, Lazarus, because he was the biggest. With tears in his eyes from the cold and gasping for air, Eames limped toward the Eskimo's sled—his would be the lead sled—and assumed that McDowell, whom he saw trudging toward him, would ride with Bernard. He

tried to speak to McDowell, but couldn't make himself
heard above the din of howling and barking. He raised
his arm to point, an act which in itself tired him, and
McDowell, who looked hung over, nodded. McDowell
trudged over to Bernard's sled, though how he knew
Bernard from the three trappers, Eames couldn't tell.
Eames was headed for the big Eskimo's sled when he
felt something tug at his arm. It was Wild, with a rifle
and ammo cannisters for him; Eames took them, and
Wild disappeared in the swirl. One instant Wild was
there, handing Eames physical objects, and the next
instant he wasn't, neither there nor anywhere else; but
the objects were there, in Eames's hands, so he must
have been there before he vanished, and Wild wasn't
known for his quickness. Eames wondered if he was
experiencing memory lapses—a result of his drinking
days, or the intense cold, or both—then he forgot about
Wild.

He was stooping over, attempting to secure the rifle
and canisters beneath the laced-down tarpaulin, struggling, his mitts on, with the frozen ropes, when the big
Eskimo silently came up beside him and, handing the
dog reins to him, took off his mitts and untied the ropes,
shoved the rifle and canisters under the tarp, and with
a tug on the rope which rocked the sled, laced the tarp
down again. It was all Eames could do to restrain the
dogs. He had to dig in his heels, which hurt his wart,
and the rope chafed his hands through the mitts. 'I'm
fifty-two years old, and not fit,' he thought, but even
that thought was cloudy, as though it came from another mind than his own. Then the Eskimo pulled on
the mitts which he held in his teeth, took the reins from
him, and waited for him to get on. A shadowy figure
crouched on Bernard's sled—'McDowell,' thought
Eames—and the other three dog teams were ranged
around the two that had riders; first one, then another,
surging up suddenly out of the swirl, and subsiding
again, their drivers reining them in. Wild, when Eames
turned to look over his shoulder, stood in the door of
the station, which meant that the guns were all issued.
Eames longed suddenly for a cup of hot coffee; already

he felt dehydrated. But the sleds and supplies, the men
and the dogs were all ready, everything waiting on him.
Eames made ready to raise his hand, but before he could
actually do so, he felt the sled lurch; the others immediately started, as if in a race, the clamor of sled
dogs and drivers filling the air, and they were off: a
formidable force of seven armed men and thirty-five
huskies cutting keenly through the cold Arctic dawn.

As they bumped over the rafted shore ice that bor-
dered the river, then slid smoothly along the Mackenzie, Eames remembered the one thing he had forgot:
dynamite. He tried signaling Lazarus, but he had to
hold on, and the only way he could halt the pellmell
flight of men and dogs, though the dogs would slow
sooner or later, was by rolling himself off the sled onto
the ice. He considered it briefly. But the catchbreath
cold which plugged his sinuses clutched at his lungs,
he could scarcely breathe, and if the sled struck a bump
and bounced on him, he would be injured for sure, perhaps killed. The bonelike fretwork of the sled hurt his
ass, cramped his legs. It was all he could do to hold on,
and he held. Blake's might have dynamite; if not, they
could send to McPherson. Recalling momentarily the
maimed girl in his dream, Eames muttered aloud between short, gasping breaths, and amid the din of mad
dogs, "Blowthat...bastard...toKing...domCome!" Then
he nestled his face in his armpit and gripped the sled
with both hands.

He must have fallen asleep, or had a giant memory
lapse, for the next he knew they were reined up near
a frozen tree stump on the river; his arms and legs were
numb and his back ached. He climbed, or, rather, toppled, off the sled into the snow, then stood up and commenced beating both arms dully against his chest while
lifting his legs, like two dead logs, in a parody of running in place. The dogs were staked, he saw now, and
Lazarus had a fire going. Bernard was chopping a hole
in the ice for tea water. The three trappers were a short
distance away staking their dogs. A cold gray light
enveloped them: not quite light, for there would be no
dawn in the delta, only a lessening of night; and not

gray either, more like a blowup of a black-and-white
photo; but the mist of early morning had dissipated,
and it was cold. 'Must be minus forty,' Eames thought
with alarm, and wondered how he had held on. Mc-
Dowell approached him, and Eames quit beating his
arms, though he still moved his legs up and down, up
and down, heavily.

"You know..." Eames began. His voice cracked with
the cold; he tried again, "You know where we are?"

McDowell's unshaven cheeks were dark with frostbite, and circles enclosed bloodshot eyes. "No, sir," he
said, his voice like a raven's croak. "Down the Mackenzie somewhere." He shrugged.

"Get some tea," Eames said. He meant it as a sug-
gestion, but it sounded like a command. He was too cold
to worry about it. He resumed beating his arms and
strode on legs that felt waterlogged over to stand by
the bonfire. And now he saw Lazarus like a tree walking, a Christmas tree. He signaled Eames to step back,
and tossed the tree on the blaze, fulcruming its chopped
stump off his hip. He laid another pole across the massive tree stump, and jammed its end in the ice. Then
he took from Bernard the blackened tea pail, filled with
chopped ice, and suspended it by its bail from the pole
above the crackling inferno. All this he performed
quickly, smoothly, and silently, Inspector Eames noted;
while Bernard, having chopped and delivered the ice,
trudged off again to feed both their teams. The two of
them worked well together, routinely. The trappers had
their own tea pail.

Standing, his back to the bonfire, Eames began to
warm up, and as he warmed he felt more in command.
Within minutes, it seemed, Lazarus put in his hand a
tin cup filled with hot tea. The tea had an oil slick on
top, and some ashes, and when he took a sip the viscous
stuff was like syrup, thick and sweet. Then he spotted
the open lard tin on the ground, and the ore sample
sack filled with sugar. A second cup and he began to
feel human, except for his feet, which were numb. He
couldn't distinguish the foot with the wart from the
other; both were like stones, without feeling. After a

third cup, he had recovered feeling in all but the toes on his right foot, and the area of the wart in his left. The two drivers had returned to their teams, and the trappers were beating their dogs. McDowell stood dully beside Bernard's sled, as if reluctant to get on, and the sugar, the lard, the tea pail, and cups—all but his— had been packed. Eames slid the empty tin cup in his parka pocket and strode over to Lazarus' sled.

The big Eskimo had just finished checking each dog's harness and trace, and now stood impassively, waiting. Eames tried to think of something to say, a moment's delay, but nothing legitimate came. Slowly he got on the sled; McDowell had boarded Bernard's. Then they were off again; the tea break had been a sane moment in the otherwise mad rush upriver. They ran, the dogs flanged like hands, Eskimo-fashion, pulling sleds on which rode phantoms of men; they drove, the men, hands gripping the handles, one foot on, one foot off the sled crossbars. Eames watched the black and white crystals of night and day coalesce into gray at the end of the river, the river which seemed never ending. Then he let his mind sink into numbness: saw the spruce trees on either side slide into taiga, and taiga into a dark, hazy blur, and the Arctic sun, which never emerged from behind the leveelike banks, sink further behind the desert of ice they rode through, until the men seemed to Eames like six ignorant phantoms in pursuit of a wandering fire. Then they turned off the Mackenzie onto the Peel, and ten miles and two hours later, where the frozen tongue of another great river splayed off into dark grayness, the dogs turned westward and were reined in under cover of trees on the Husky, below Blake's trading post. . . .

January 5, 1932: Arrived at Blake's store on the Husky around 4:00 P.M. Dogs tired and men cross, especially the trappers. Inspector forgot to bring dog food enough, or underestimated the quantity needed for thirty-five dogs. Blake had some dried fish, but not enough. Teams put on short ration following the evening feeding. Bernard and I offered to set a net under

the ice, but Inspector said it would take too long, and
sent Gardlund to McPherson for dried fish and dynamite. About 7:00 P.M. Millen arrived from McPherson,
with Charlie Rat on his komatik, dead drunk, and Millen exhausted (he had driven non-stop, except to pick
up the Indian, from Arctic Red River last night). When
Gardlund gets back from McPherson there will be forty-
two dogs to feed, and nine men. Snow conditions good.
Weather cold.
Mileage: 81.

January 6: Gardlund arrived back this morning with
200 lbs. dried fish and 20 lbs. dynamite. Gardlund's
dogs tired, but Gardlund, who moves at all times like
a bear, able to keep moving, he says. Eames, after
breakfast at Blake's with Millen and McDowell, returned to the camp on the river and directed a late start,
around 10:00 A.M. Since the dogs consume the same
food, or nearly the same, whether working or resting,
he wants to travel each day, whatever the weather. Dog
food the main factor so far in his plan to assault Johnson's cabin. The weather no factor so long as it holds.
Before setting off, Eames held what he called a council,
with all the men present. The dogs, already hitched,
had to be staked. Half an hour to stake them. A fire
had to be built, and tea boiled, though nobody wanted
the tea. Everyone stood by the fire, while Eames spoke,
except Charlie Rat, who was too hung over to stand.
He sat in the snow at Eames's feet, bobbing his head.
Eames said Johnson's cabin was built like a fort, so he
had added dynamite to our supplies. He said he didn't
underestimate Johnson, and he didn't consider him
crazy. Johnson, he said, was "a shrewd and desperate
character." He expects an ambush, and Millen, the only
one except Charlie Rat to have actually seen Johnson,
agrees with him. Whenever Eames or Millen speaks,
Charlie Rat bobs his head.

McDowell now says he agrees. He thinks the trap
will be set in a canyon up the Rat. The canyon he de-
scribes as having two- to six-hundred-foot banks and
several spots from which a desperate killer could snipe
at the posse. This canyon, and Johnson's ability to am-

bush us in it, became the topic of a half hour's discussion. I, who have been up the Rat more often than McDowell, have never seen such a canyon; and the one patrol on which McDowell was on the Rat, with King, Bernard, and me, he was so hung over he saw nothing. In fact, there are no canyons in the delta, as everyone present should know, except Eames. But if a wolf runs out of a cave and tells you a bear is inside, you must believe him.

McDowell has given a name to his canyon, he calls it "Destruction Canyon," and in order to avoid Destruction Canyon and the chance of being ambushed in it, Eames instructed Charlie Rat to lead the posse a back way, which Charlie Rat said he knew, and to approach Johnson's cabin from the rear. As soon as we heard this, Bernard and I excused ourselves to go and unhitch our teams, which we had harnessed Eskimo-fashion, and to hitch them up Indian-fashion, for woods travel. Then we set off, around 11:30 A.M., with Millen's sled in the lead, and Charlie Rat giving directions, past the mouth of the Rat which led directly to Johnson's cabin, an easy day's travel, and on up the Husky for ten or twelve miles, where we turned off on a little creek and, after it ended, proceeded overland. After about four miles, the trappers and Millen being forced continually to disentangle their teams from tree branches, and all of us having to dig and lift our sleds out of drifts and over ravines, we made camp on a small pond and fed the dogs.
Mileage: 16.

January 7: The teams were fed, and all sleds hitched Indian-fashion. Off at 9:00 A.M. One mile out, Millen changed places with Charlie Rat, who was incapable of breaking trail, and who, due to drink or befuddlement of some other kind, had lost all sense of direction. It is certain that no dog team has ever been through here. Trail has to be broke, limbs have to be chopped, drifts have to be dug out, sleds have to be lifted over, and the men are in a constant sweat from chopping and digging and lifting. No one rides, all wear snowshoes. Charlie Rat is tied by a rope to Millen's sled, and the Inspector limps along, moving out of the way as team after team overtakes him, and gradually falling behind, until he calls a halt from the rear. He realizes that there is no trail, that the men would do better on foot, that the men are carrying the sleds and the dogs rather than the dogs carrying the men. But the idea of avoiding Destruction Canyon drives Eames overland, and he is convinced, as he said this morning, that "murderous fire would have caught us and killed us, at least some of us, had we proceeded the way Johnson expected us to, up the Rat with its canyons." Eames has never been up the Rat, though he thinks he remembers a patrol he led once in this region. His remembrance is vague. The Rat is as flat as the rest of the delta, as flat as this creek we are crossing. But no trees grow on it, and it is not drifted over as this is.

We proceed overland, the teams and their drivers taking turns breaking trail, at the rate of about a half mile per hour. Each half mile is hard won. I, Lazarus, who have never traveled overland in this country, and have never had a yen to, do not wish to ever again. The delta is Indian country, and I am content to leave it to them. The Indians do not like it either. They huddle in villages throughout the winter, living off welfare from white man and fish from the rivers, and who can blame them? Not I. Only a white man, like Johnson, would wish to live here, and only an Indian like Charlie Rat, or other white men, would begrudge him his cabin and his trapline, his lonely and dreary existence. But there is a law, I suppose, against living like Johnson, alone. Otherwise why would Eames lead us through here?

We came out on the Rat around 4:00 P.M., nowhere near Johnson's cabin, but six miles above it. The temperature around −45°, the dogs hungry and tired, the men exhausted, the footing through loose snow and willows difficult with snowshoes. We boiled up on the Rat, but the Inspector was afraid Johnson would find us and murder us if we camped on the river, or in the woods, so he directed that we return to base camp. We turned back and, retracing the trail we had broke, arrived back around midnight where we had started two days before,

all the way back at the mouth of the Husky. Dog food
was replenished from Blake's stores, and Eames spent
the night with the men on the river, being too lame to
walk up the hill.
Mileage: 24.

January 8: The weather holding cold and clear, we
got off around 9:00 A.M. and moved upriver to the mouth
of the Rat. The Inspector decided to blame Charlie Rat
for yesterday's blunder, and at the turn off the Peel,
where the Rat meets the Husky, Charlie Rat drifted off
toward McPherson. We proceeded directly up the Rat
River. No more was heard about canyons, and there
was no ambush. An easy day's travel by river put us a
few miles below Johnson's cabin. Here the Inspector
ordered camp to be made, dogs fed, and men rested.
Mileage: 16.

January 9: Broke camp at daybreak, 10:30 A.M., and
moved directly upriver to cabin. Halted within half a
mile, around noon. Across the river and through the
trees a thin plume of smoke could be seen. The dogs
were secured in the timber, the rifles were drawn, the
men spread out down the river and began climbing the
hill at several points so as to surround the cabin. The
sound of metal on metal, a cooking pot on a stove, could
be heard from the cabin. Then a curious sound, a man
singing:

"Beat the drums slowly, and play the pipes lowly,
Play the dead march as you carry me on..."

The Inspector held up his hand, and we listened as the
voice, a white man's voice, continued:

"Beat the drums slowly, and play the pipes lowly,
For I am a young cowboy, and I have done wrong..."

The sound carried through the closed door and across
the clearing. Then the Inspector picked up his bullhorn.
"We know you're in there, Johnson, and we've got you
surrounded. Come out!" The singing stopped, and there
was unnatural stillness. The spruce trees stood silent

and stock-still, unmoving, as the spiral of smoke curled
lazily through their tops. The snow in front of the cabin
was trampled and stained with boot marks and animal
blood, and a pile of frozen intestines lay off to one side.
A whiskey jack flew from the handle of an ax stuck in
a chopping block. Again the Inspector, crouching partway down behind the hill where King had climbed over
and rushed for the door, blared out through his bullhorn: "You're surrounded, Johnson, surrender!" The
men, the rifles, the silence—all seemed familiar to me.
I'd been there before.
Mileage: 4.

6

To Inspector Eames, hunkered down behind the crest of the snow-covered hill directly before Johnson's door, the silence which followed the two police warnings seemed ominous. The structure—an earth- and snow-covered dugout, about eight by twelve feet wide and long, and roughly four feet high—was only a stone's throw away, and between him and it was an open clearing of snow littered with animal entrails. To the right of the shack, where McDowell lay, stood a few trees, and to the left, where Millen was hid, were some stumps. Any advance would have to be made across that snow-covered clearing; any cover would have to be found behind those few skinny trees. The structure itself, as Eames scrutinized it, was squat and formidable, part earth and part log. It had been there long enough, and was built well enough, that it blended in with the site, which it commanded. It resembled, Eames thought as he peered over the hilltop at it, gun bunkers of which he'd seen pictures, with loopholes cut between the logs at ground level on three sides, and the muzzles of at least three guns sticking out through the loopholes, ready to fire.

Eames had joined the Force in September of 1913. He had joined partly to miss The War he'd seen coming, and he had missed The War. While buddies of his were being killed in the Ardennes, at Ypres, on the Somme, he had served as a peace officer in the Arctic. He had heard, from friends and from others, about going "over the top," and most of his friends who had gone over the top were now dead, or crippled, or had drunk themselves blind in the Legion. Eames had never, himself, been in a slit trench (though he had likened his marriage to one), nor had he ever gone up against a gun bunker, or against fire of any kind (though one old crazy Eskimo had shot arrows at him, from a distance of 300 yards). Now, at fifty-two years of age, his left foot nearly lame with a wart, all his nervous energy drained by the cold and by the circuitous route they had come (his first error in judgment: was he being overly cautious?), he knew it was his turn to do what millions of men had done in The War—go over the top.

As he crouched with his rifle and bullhorn behind the snowcovered hill, pulling off his mitts and putting on the canvas liners with finger- and thumb-holes, and flexing and working his fingers, he could see McDowell about twenty yards to his right and Millen a little further off to his left. Gardlund and Lang had been detailed to circle the cabin, to determine whether Johnson had left it. They had had a head start, and should be coming back now. They would signal to Millen when they were in place, and Millen would signal to Eames. Then the cabin, which reportedly had no back entrance, would be surrounded on three sides: with Sutherland, whom Eames couldn't see, at three o'clock, McDowell at four o'clock, Eames at six o'clock, Millen at eight, and Gardlund and Lang at nine and ten. The drivers, Bernard and Lazarus, were with the dogs in the riverbed, downstream and behind Eames. Now as he waited for Millen to signal that Gardlund and Lang were in place, Eames checked his watch and made a mental note of the time: 1300 hours. The siege had begun half an hour ago; the next tactical move was the raid.

The image of Rene and her "Righteousness and Peace have kissed" Christmas card came to Eames as he waited, their son and his death, their failure in marriage, his being passed over for promotion—all the hardships he had endured, never complaining, always consoling himself that he had been spared that long bloody halt in the mud that had destroyed a whole generation. And now, fourteen years after Armistice he was hunkered behind a hill crest, facing a shack dug in like a fort and outfitted like a gun bunker, with a madman inside. The madman had been there all along, it was Eames who had just arrived; it was Eames who had sent, and then led, his men here. If one or more of his men got killed, would the press make him out a butcher? The words of one of the German generals, oft quoted in the newspapers, returned to him now: "A good many men will be killed. But so long as no man can prove to me that a man can die more than once, I am not inclined to regard death for the individual as a misfortune." Eames gripped his Lee-Enfield and sincerely hoped it wouldn't, like the Canadian Ross rifles which were notorious for being deadly on the firing range but worthless in the trenches, jam or misfire. His magazine of cartridges, as he inserted it in the belly of the weapon, he prayed might contain no duds. Then, cautiously, he ventured a peek over the snowbank at the cabin, twenty-five yards distant.

Nothing stirred but the wisp of smoke ascending from the stovepipe; nothing sounded but the rasp of his own breathing, and the rustle of his mukluks and parka on the snow. In answer to his police warnings, there had been silence, menacing silence. Against his better judgment he picked up the bullhorn a third time. "Johnson!" he blared, and the name like a sonic boom reverberated through the clearing, the authority it conveyed surprising Eames. His voice, magnified, brooked no shilly-shallying: like writing a report—"This is Inspector Eames," it boomed—then signing it—"of the RCMP." It was the Force, and behind the Force was the Government, and behind the Government, the Dominion, and behind the Dominion, the Empire, and at the head of the Empire, the King...and the Royal Canadian Mounted Police always got their man. He didn't know what he would say next until he said it; after he had said it, he wondered why he had—was it Mildred Urquhart's influence? "There's no serious charge against you, Johnson. The man you shot isn't dead. Come out!"

He waited five, ten seconds. No response from the shack:
its log front stood like hide or plate, which Eames's
words could not penetrate, shielding some prehistoric
intelligence inside. Millen waved to let him know Gardlund and Lang were back. It was an affront to the
Force to wait longer. He raised his right hand above
his head, and looked at Millen, then McDowell; each of
them raised their right hands. Then, scrabbling for footing in the snow, and using his rifle for support, he
dropped his hand and went over the top....

Immediately, it seemed to Eames, there was rifle fire
all around him. McDowell and Millen were on either
side of him, firing into the shack, as he was, and from
three sides shots were being fired at the logs, dogs were
howling behind him, and bullets jumping and falling
beside and around him, both his own spent cartridges
and Johnson's shots making dull little thuds in the
snow. He found himself sheltering behind a tree, reloading with wet, shaky hands; one clip fell in the snow,
and he dipped his hand like a man with Parkinson's
disease into his pocket for another. His face was slick
with sweat and the tree dumped snow on him when a
bullet smashed into its trunk. Millen and McDowell
were nowhere to be seen, neither were the trappers.
Only he was exposed in the ring of fire, behind a thin
spruce tree, while little jetties of smoke and murderous
fire darted out of the cabin's loopholes as the madman
inside covered every approach and fired his guns in
every direction, not only rifle but shotgun blasts boom-
ing and raking the clearing. It seemed to Eames folly
to stand where he stood, but to break for the bank from
which he had come, or for the nearer bank behind which
McDowell was pinned, firing blindly into the logs,
seemed more than folly, seemed madness. Having reloaded, which meant he had fired a whole clip, ten shots
(when had he done it? he didn't remember having
squeezed off a shot), he pulled his rifle shakily up to
his shoulder, its barrel colliding with the tree trunk,
and accidentally triggered another shot into the snow
at his feet. Immediately the hail of a shotgun blast
riddled the snow next to him, and he hugged the spruce

tree for cover. The two shots that followed were directed elsewhere, then there was a lull—Johnson reloading—then another blast from the shotgun. Johnson had at least three guns, Eames had counted three muzzles, and was running from one to the other snapping off shots like billiard balls; the dugout was not much bigger than a pool table, and the barrels were stuck like pool cues through the loopholes in front and on both sides of his cabin. He could cover his flanks and the entrance, but not all at once; in response to the assault on three sides by six men he had developed a circuit.

Eames cowered quietly behind the spruce tree, awaiting the next shotgun blast and distinguishing between rifle sounds—all of his men had .303's—so as to calculate as nearly as possible Johnson's firing pattern. The series seemed to be shotgun, large rifle, small rifle; the only variant was shotgun, small rifle, large rifle. The shotgun fired every third time, though there was no reason for it to do so; Johnson could, if he wanted, fire twice in succession from the same loophole, though he would have to reload. But following the first shot, if one waited a moment, Johnson would be at another loophole.... Eames awaited, almost with eagerness, the deafening shotgun blast; when it came, he counted to three, then broke from behind the tree toward the cabin, about fifteen yards distant. As he ran, McDowell coming up over the top from his right, and Millen showing himself, yelling and firing, on the left, it suddenly occurred to Eames that if he could get in close to the cabin, inside the range of the guns which were sweeping the clearing, he could be—if not safe, at least less exposed—but he had to stay clear of the door... and the loopholes.

McDowell, in his run from the bank, came up with Eames now at the cabin's right corner; they ran side by side, both bent over (why, Eames did not know, the firing was all at ground level), along the front wall and, as they passed the door, McDowell with his rifle butt banged at it twice, trying to batter it in. There was a burnt spot in the pole door, a bullet hole, stomach level—and Eames felt his own stomach sink, and thought,

'Bunce'—then they were at the cabin's left corner. The
corners were safest; the notched log ends had no chinks
or loopholes. Eames laid his hand on the log ends to
brace himself—he was winded—and a black barrel
slithered out like a snake two feet away, and fired at
knee level. But he was inside its angle. The snake slithered back and he and McDowell ran back past the door,
both of them banging the door with their rifle butts as
they passed, and both of them running on to the cabin's
right corner again, where they stopped abruptly, align-
ing themselves with the log ends. It was from here that
Eames saw Gardlund and Lang, whom he had last seen
an hour ago, come over the top in a commando-like rush
on the cabin.

The two trappers had been detailed to circle the cabin,
to determine whether or not Johnson had left it. Struggling through deep snow and willows, they had climbed
the bank to the rear of the cabin and snowshoed across
the neck of the peninsula on which the cabin was built.
Spotting Johnson's cache, Gardlund had climbed the
tree to see what was in the drum and, finding nothing
worth plundering, had thrown the drum to the ground.
Then they slogged back across the isthmus of snow, and
took their places behind the bank about twenty yards
in from Millen. From this position they sniped at the
cabin's left flank, not expecting to hit anything, but to
divert Johnson's fire from Eames and McDowell, who
were rushing from the right side.

Gardlund, who felt they had earned their five dollars
that day, settled into a rhythm of firing. He was in no
hurry for the siege to break off: the longer Johnson held
them at bay and they stayed encamped on the Rat, the
more days' pay they would get. And shooting somebody
else's bullets at tiny holes in a wall (he liked target
practice) reminded him of the Army, which he had also
liked. Now he lay in the snow, next to Lang's lanky
body, his .303 nestled on top of the snowbank which
had melted and crusted around it, firing methodically
at each of the loopholes on the cabin's left side. There
were three, and he had ten rounds in his gun; he fired
three times at each loophole, once at the chinking be-

tween the logs, then rolled over onto his back and inserted a clip of ten more. As he lay on his back between rounds, gazing up at the trees around him, he counted board feet.

Gardlund had been a faller-and-bucker in B.C., before he came north to trap, and on the Queen Charlottes and Vancouver Island he had passed his days, from four-thirty in the morning until six at night, a saw in his hand, calculating the board feet in giant pines as he cut them. But there were no trees in Aklavik, or none worth the trouble of counting, so he counted white fox pelts instead, multiplying the number he hoped he would get by the price he hoped they would bring. Now he lay on his back between rounds, gazing up at the spruce trees around him, their stately butts and tapering trunks and not too branchy tops transporting him, amid rifle fire, to the rain forests of the Queen Charlottes. There was one tree, just to the left of him, a hundred board feet, if a foot—he guessed it 104; and, at twenty-one cents a board foot, and it wouldn't be less for such virgin timber, that would be . . . $21.84—for just the one tree! There was, of course, the problem of getting it out, but . . . *he* could cut that tree with a crosscut, fall it and buck it, in twenty, no—he eyed the butt, then the bucking joints, and thought how many saw strokes for each—in twenty-four minutes. In a twelve-hour day that would come to $(12 \times 60) \div 24 \times \$21.84 =$ . . .He was using as counters the bullets in his pouch—each clip held ten—as he loaded and shot them (in the trenches he had used his rosary, then an abacus), when he felt Lang's paw on his shoulder. Still on his back, Gardlund held his fingers on bullets and his figures in mind as he craned his neck to see Lang—the long, stupid Swede's face, the scraggly blond beard. "Yeah. What?" he said, interrupted.

Lang had the same look on his face that he'd had the time Gardlund had found him sitting inside the cabin, shooting Arctic cockroaches as they crawled up through a hole in the floor. The hole was between Lang's feet, Lang's elbows were on his knees, and he was holding the end of his rifle barrel three quarters of an inch

from the floor. "What the fuck are you doing?" he'd said.
"Shooting shoe-craps," Lang said. "You better watch th'
fuck out, or you'll shoot your foot," he said. "I'll shoot
my foot," Lang said, and swung the barrel an inch to
the left and blew his big toe off.

Lang had now that same look of focused vacancy,
and in gazing at him Gardlund lost track of his figures.
"What?" he said, disgruntled. "What do you want?"

"Them guys is havin' trouble," Lang said.

"So?" He could hear the firing of rifles and, now and
again, a shotgun. Millen yelling, dogs howling. "So,
what'd you expect—lunch break?"

"I think we oughta help 'em," Lang said.

Gardlund turned all the way over to face him, 'the
gentle giant' Lang was called in Aklavik, but Gardlund
knew better. He wasn't gentle, just morose. Gardlund
had kept him from suicide twice, once when an Eskimo
girl rejected him, and once when . . . he couldn't remember why. "Are you crazy?" he said. "Who gives a shit
what they do to each other?"

"I been in th' war," was Lang's response.

"So what?"

"I'm goin' over."

"Jesus!" muttered Gardlund, and turned to see Millen waving his arms like a lieutenant or an infantry
captain sending his men over the top. He had that look,
Millen did, of the officer (though he wasn't one, Gardlund reflected) getting his men out of the trench so
that he could come out himself. "What's keeping ya?"
he yelled at Millen, but Millen was too far away, and
too agitated, to hear. He, Gardlund, didn't see any advantage at all in leaving the spot where he was. He
finished reloading and turned, in a leisurely way, back
onto his stomach, when, all of a sudden, Lang's big paw
was thrust under his armpit and had lifted him up and
over the top and, to keep stride with the six-foot-four-
and-a-half Lang's lope, he was pumping his short stubby
legs pistonlike for all he was worth, just to propel himself forward without falling down: his rifle at the ready
and his bullethead braced, he was rushing the goddamned cabin and staring slit-eyed at the logs in the

wall with loopholes between them and purring like a
Comptometer as he ran: $8 \times 6 \times 4 + (2 \times 4) = \dots$ and
he was shouting, "JOHNSONYOUMOTHERFUCK-
INGSONOFABITCH!" with the suicidal Swede right
beside him.

Lang was loping and hauling Gardlund by the armpit and then Gardlund was running beside him and in
Lang's mind they were at Ypres (the second one) but
without barbwire and muck and the craters and shells
and thousands of men with a scared shitless shout running forward into machine gun fire raking the line and
men crumpling and falling and stumbling over the bodies and through the barbwire and then Jerry firing and
shouting scared shitless as they were and then Jerry's
mother—jump down her throat and bayonet her in the
oven and beat on her head—with his rifle butt he was
banging down Johnson's front door filling it with himself when it battered open and there in the well of the
dark earthwork like an animal crouched in a hole or a
man in a slit trench was Johnson but he was not scared
or surprised as Lang thought he would be...Lang stood
in the doorway, silhouetted by light from outside, a big,
an enormous target, with Gardlund beside and behind
him. And Lang continued to stand, stupidly, holding
his rifle, his eyes adjusting to darkness and searching
the deep pit before him in which, crouched motionless
in a corner, holding a sawed-off shotgun in one hand
and his Winchester with the stock blown off in the other,
Johnson waited until Lang could see him, then shot....

From his place by the log ends Eames watched the
two trappers reel back and run for the snowbank. Then,
while Johnson continued to fire through the doorway,
Eames and McDowell ran for the snowbank and dove,
Eames diving headfirst as he had when a boy, but forgetting to tuck and sprawling ungainly on top of the
bank, his legs stuck up in the air and snow in his face
and all over. He picked himself up and brushed the
snow from his rifle. Then he scrambled on down the
hillside, heedless of the hurt in his shoulder (had he
broken his collarbone?), to where the two trappers were
crawling around to meet him.

"I seen 'im!" yelled Lang. Eames could hear between shots— Sutherland and McDowell and Millen still firing into the logs—the sound of wood upon wood and some heavy instrument beating: Johnson securing his door.

"He was down like this in th' trench," Lang seated himself in the snowbank, "an' he had a automatic—pistols they was—in each hand, like this"—he grabbed Gardlund's rifle and held a gun in each paw, pointing across the river. "Then he seen us, an'...blooey!" Both rifles, the barrel of one about a foot from Eames's leg, blasted deafeningly in a direction not far from the dogs. Eames jumped back and, to catch himself, stuck his rifle barrel in snow.

"Are you crazy?" yelled Gardlund, and grabbed his rifle from Lang.

"I jus' wanted you to see what it was like." Lang sulked. "I jus' wanted you to 'preciate th' danger."

"I was there, asshole! I appreciate the fucking danger!"

While Eames backed away from the two wrangling trappers, and busied himself wiping the snow off his rifle, desultory gunfire continued above them. Across the river dogs howled dismally. Daylight, what little there had been, was rapidly fading. The riverbed and the opposite bank had receded since Eames had last looked, and resembled now a gray nocturne: the bank, the trees, the river between and the sky above were like lead, contracting visibly as a cold gray mist moved in to envelop them all. Eames shivered and realized that he was chilled to the bone. The sweat that fear and exertion had wrung from him, once the hazard was passed, had frozen on him; and, as he stood like a knight encased in ice countenancing the two trappers' antics, the winter light was failing and the world around him vorticing down to zero. "Bring up the dogs," he said through chattering teeth. "Build a fire, make camp." And having issued three separate orders, he himself trudged off to find firewood.

Shaking all over like a man with St. Vitus's dance, and without any feeling in either foot, Eames shambled along the ice until he spied broken willows and an up-ended spruce in the snow. It was about 250 yards downstream from Johnson's cabin, and a stone's throw from the wrecked cache; a seasonal feeder stream merged with the Rat, bringing deadwood and brush to its bank. As Eames struggled to haul from the snow the broken spruce top, he kept muttering to himself his father's adage, "Wood warms a man twice! Wood warms a man twice!" He was as cold as he ever had been, or ever wished to be, his concentration, if it could be called that, focused narrowly on the spruce top he was pulling, on the foot he braced with as he pulled, on his arms like two alien instruments, and on the frozen and dead wood he pulled. Johnson could come blasting down the hill and kill them all, Eames wouldn't care, he was too cold. He was too dehydrated by intense cold to think clearly, and his puny strength was no match for the half ton of snow in which the spruce top was buried. He seemed dazed, and wondered if he would pass out. The howl and whimper of dogs he could hear, and he smelled the faint scent of gunpowder. It hung in the air on the hill near the cabin, acrid and roily; but here it smelled more like snuff, just a pinch, unplugging his sinuses. If in his casement of ice he passed out, he would die like a knight in his armor—"of exposure," the inquisition would read, but he would know better.... He would know nothing. But "J. A. Urquhart, Coroner" would know less than nothing, for he would think he knew something.... Eames quit futilely pulling and simply held to the branch. He wished he had read *Morte Darthur,* he wished...he had not been, somewhere by someone (Mildred Urquhart, perhaps?), corrupted by sentiment, he wished...he had dynamited the fortresslike cabin. For what other purpose had he bought twenty pounds' worth, with caps and fuse, from the Scotch trader at Fort McPherson, who had got it to blast cellar space? ...The whimper of dogs had come closer, and the pounding sound of iron on iron, axheads on stakes. Then Lazarus was beside him and hauling with him at the deadwood, until it came: the spruce top popped free of the snow and, within minutes, it seemed to Eames,

Lazarus had a fire blazing, the dogs staked and fed, and camp made....

While Lazarus boiled tea and baked bannock, Eames stood with his back to the fire and issued orders—to McDowell to make flares from rags soaked in kerosene, to Sutherland and Gardlund and Lang to keep watch on the cabin, to Millen to unload the dynamite. While he gulped hot tea laced with sugar and lard, and wolfed down half a hot bannock, the men on his orders prepared for the siege and a full-scale assault on the cabin. "Pick a number, any number," he heard Gardlund saying, then saw Lang trudging off to keep watch on the man who was fortressed, and trapped, in the dugout. Eames noted the time—1800 hours—while continuing to warm himself....

Minutes later, it seemed, Lang returned and Gardlund trudged off. Eames gazed at his watch incredulously; he tapped it, wondering if the cold could have advanced it. But, no, two hours had passed, punctuated by the brief balelight of the flares thrown every fifteen minutes to light up the cabin and prevent Johnson's escape in the darkness. By 2100 hours Eames himself had recovered enough to clamber up the hillside and toss a few flares.

The dark hulk of the cabin in among the dark trees, like a giant dog among stakes, stood illuminated for a few minutes starkly distinct in the clearing; then the flares sputtered out in the snow and the squat structure sank into shadowy obscurity again. The shadows were not so thick, however, nor the night so dark—due to the presence of snow—that the men could not see any movement, if there were any, or shoot anyone attempting to escape, though no one was. There was only the one door, which opened onto the snow-covered clearing. If Johnson emerged, he would be at their mercy. The wonder, Eames mulled, was that he himself was not shot when crossing that clearing in daylight; that Gardlund and Lang were not shot in the doorway; that not one of the posse in a siege that had lasted for over ten hours had been killed, or even wounded. The psychological effect, perhaps, of their numbers, their firepower...perhaps Johnson's shots were random, or his sights knocked askew by the loopholes; perhaps he was deranged...in any event, concluded Eames, the man they called Johnson was doomed....Leaving Gardlund on watch, Eames came back down the hill and at 2300 hours ordered the dynamite thawed.

Thawing the dynamite was a delicate process; only small charges could be thawed at a time, and the fire had to be closely watched. As the caps and fuses got dried out, and the charges assembled, Eames and Millen took them to the top of the bank and hurled them at the cabin in the hope of dislodging the logs. But the small charges had no effect on the logs, and most did not even explode. Around midnight Lang volunteered to run with a football-sized charge up to the cabin and toss it onto the roof, and Eames ordered the rest of his rifle squad—Gardlund, Sutherland, Millen, McDowell—to position themselves in their earlier nests on the hill. On Eames's signal a volley of flares was thrown and they all opened fire on the brightly lit cabin. Johnson, surprised by the salvo, resumed his circuit fire pattern, firing from each gun in turn on three sides across the no-man's-land of the clearing. As the first set of flares sputtered out and the cabin sank back into darkness, the men on Eames's signal ceased firing and Lang went over the top, racing over like a fullback with the lit dynamite in his hands. Lang loped heedlessly toward the cabin, Eames expecting at any moment to see him crumple and fall, then he veered toward the cabin's left corner, where he tossed the charge on the roof and kept running on toward the snowbank. All of the men watched the charge. It fizzled for half a minute, then burst in a muffled explosion. The stovepipe went flying off through the woods in a shower of sparks and black soot. The cabin glowed like a jack-o'-lantern with tiny slits for teeth (the gun loopholes), a rectangular nose (the pole door), and a single patched eye (Johnson's window of animal skin) showing ghastly and pink its veins and membranes of dried blood and animal fat. Eames yelled, and the five men went over the top, firing as they ran at the teeth of the pumpkin in which John-

son, Eames thought, must lie stunned and defenseless.
Immediately their fire was returned, and all five men
ran for cover. No one was hit. The brief, dull pulse of
illumination had died, like a blown-out light bulb, and
the cabin sank back to a shadowy bulk like an unsleeping dog among stakes. Leaving Lang posted to watch
the cabin, the men descended the hill to have tea and
to rest before the next assault. It would be the last,
Lazarus informed the Inspector, because they had run
out of dog feed and would have to return to either
McPherson, or Blake's, by the next morning.

Not only the dogs, but the men too were feeling the
effects of the severe cold and lack of sleep, and Eames,
garnering his strength for a final offensive, ordered
Millen to thaw the last four pounds of dynamite. At
around 0200 hours the small squad of men—Eames,
Milen, McDowell, Gardlund, and Sutherland—trudged
back up the hill, relieving Lang, who trudged down,
and took their places around the cabin. Each of them
had his own route up the hill, and each his own nest
in the snowbank. The embankment was iced and packed
down from the pressure of weight and the men's body
heat at each of the five vantage points, and the glacis
was littered with shells. There was no talking, no exchange of any kind: the men were too exhausted, and
too dehydrated by the implacable cold, to expend any
energy other than the routine effort involved in trudging up the hill to their accustomed places, lighting and
throwing flares at the cabin, and firing at chinks in the
logs. Much of the moss and mud chinking between the
logs had been blown away, and flares, when tossed ac-
curately over the cabin, would illumine through a grill-
work of slits the cabin's insides. The cabin, above ground
level, was empty, as the brief brilliant light of flares
showed; the posse fired purposelessly and dispiritedly
into and through the empty window casement. It was
possible that a bullet might ricochet down, hitting the
man below ground, but unlikely; still the posse routinely threw flares and kept up their barrage on the
cabin.

After forty-five minutes or so of this pointless snip-

ing, Eames noticed that the fortress had become curiously silent. For some time Johnson had not returned
their fire, or exposed himself above the level of the
bottom log. Earlier the men had caught fugitive glimpses
of him. Now they saw nothing—no movement, no rifles—and heard no sound but the crack and the whine
of their own .303's. It was monotonous, and demoral-
izing. It was as though Johnson had left, though they
knew he had not. Eames moved laboriously behind the
snowbank to where Gardlund was routinely firing and
keeping up a conversation, apparently with himself, as
he fired.

"Gardlund!" Eames yelled. It came out a hoarse
whisper.

The trapper quit firing and muttering and looked
over at him. "Yeah?" he said finally.

"I think he's hit," Eames croaked, "or out of ammo.
He hasn't fired in half an hour."

Gardlund regarded him, Eames thought, stupidly,
as though he hadn't grasped what was said. The trapper
said nothing in response, but just stared, dull-eyed. 'He's
tired,' Eames thought, 'we're all tired.'

"I want you to go over the top," said Eames, "and
fire down in the pit—we'll cover you."

Gardlund regarded Eames, then the cabin. It wasn't,
Eames felt, hesitation on Gardlund's part, it was more
a lag in comprehension. At last Gardlund shrugged,
and turned over on his back to reload. He took a long
time reloading, long enough for Eames to crawl back
to where Millen was lying, and for Millen to crawl
around to where McDowell and Sutherland lay. The
four men set up a steady barrage, and at long last they
watched Gardlund run across the clearing until he was
at the cabin's left corner, where Eames had been standing when the thin black barrel had slithered out like
a snake at his knees. Then Gardlund went down on his
knees midway along the left wall, and, poking his rifle
barrel through a chink, fired randomly down in the pit.
Only then did the silence within erupt into gunfire, and
a hail of bullets and shotgun blasts drove Gardlund,
skittering along on his stomach, back behind the snow-

bank. When Eames got to him he was squatting, trapper-style, his back to the cabin, his arms hugging his legs which were drawn up under him, his head hunched forward, while a cloud of steam rose around him. Gardlund's ass-end emitted a sickening noise and an awful smell assailed Eames.

"You all right?" he asked the hunched-over figure. Automatically Eames's nose sought cover in the armpit of his own parka.

Gardlund without moving emitted another sick noise, and more steam rose around him, more smell. "Yeah," he said finally. Then, scooping a handful of snow, he wiped himself and duckwalked a few steps toward Eames, stood up quickly and pulled up his windpants, then squatted again, fully clothed. The men had quit firing, and so had Johnson; a vigilant silence pervaded the cabin and extended to its besiegers. "He could of killed me," said Gardlund, and, as he said it, looked directly into Eames's face as though this were a communiqué of importance, informed by intelligence. Eames tried to take it that way, though it seemed a truism. Gardlund was shaken, he guessed, and needed a rest.

"Okay. Why don't you go down and join Lang at the camp." Gardlund picked up his rifle and shuffled off. "And send up the dynamite, will you?" Gardlund halted and turned. "Send up the dynamite," Eames repeated. Gardlund shrugged, and ambled on down the hill.

Eames was left facing the left flank of Johnson's fortress, reflecting on something he had been vaguely aware of for some time, but had not consciously dwelt on. His left foot, the one with the wart, was fully thawed now, and had been for several hours. Both of his feet had been functional since Lazarus had made the fire and they had begun this last phase of the siege. He had had feeling since then, yet he had not limped. Standing as he was, aslant on the hillside, it was difficult for him to test the foot. He would try duck walking as he had seen Gardlund do—that would put pressure on both feet: balls, soles, arches, ankles. He executed a few awkward steps and confirmed his suspicion: both feet were burnt on the bottom, frostbit, and both were uniformly tender; but there was no difference between them. The wart, he was nearly certain, had been burnt out of its housing, and, whether or not it existed in some deeper recess, would no longer cripple and lame him. Eames exulted. Though not a man given to omens, he felt a resurgence of purpose, a recommitment to the mission they were bogged down in. He thought of Bunce: how must it have felt to have been shot here, in the unrelenting, undiminished cold? The cold like an unseen but ever felt enemy swirled round the men and swarmed through their weak spots, waging its war of attrition; it was constantly pricking and prying at one's toes, one's fingers, one's nose—whatever part was exposed for a moment—and draining the vital heat off. To have a gaping wound in one's stomach, through which the heat drained steaming away...and then the bloody sled ride...The mere thought of it gave Eames a chill, and he conjured in self-defense, while awaiting the dynamite, Mildred Urquhart. There was a woman who, if your feet were freezing (he had watched her do this for an Eskimo child), would pull up her parka and her sweater beneath it and press the cold soles of your feet up against her warm stomach, chafing your toes with her hands, and then, pulling her parka and her sweater up further, would thrust your cold toes right into the hollow between her warm-blooded breasts. He had seen her do that and had seen too the small mole on one of her nipples...not like your movie stars, Helen Hayes, all glitter and ice, or Greta Garbo, languid and lax, no...warm and full and soft and compassionate, a woman was Mildred Urquhart....Gardlund came trudging back up the hill, bearing the dynamite, and Eames strove to focus again on weapons and men, the stalemated siege in which they had been locked for over fourteen hours, the final and crushing offensive against Johnson, his discomfiture and defeat. Gardlund, shuffling up alongside him, handed him the packet, a hefty four pounds, with cap and fuse affixed and ready for use.

"Still warm," Gardlund grunted as he handed it over, and Eames received the warm packet gingerly, feeling the heat from it radiate up through his fingers and into

his hands, as though he held in his mitts a huge hot
potato.

"Go tell the men to throw flares," he ordered, "and
to get ready for the last try."

Gardlund stood staring at him as though uncompre-
hending; then, shrugging, he ambled off toward the
others.

At precisely 3:00 A.M., fifteen hours after the siege
had begun, Inspector Eames lit the fuse on the dynamite and, holding it in his hand like a shot, heaved it
across the clearing and against the front of the shack.
It fizzled for a moment up close to the door, then exploded. A shout went up from the posse as men in battle
shout when the enemy receives a direct hit, and Eames
watched incredulously as the entire front wall buckled,
causing the roof to collapse. A muffled roar followed as
several tons of gravel- and snow-covered logs caved in
on the man in the pit, while Eames yelled to Gardlund
to grab the flashlight and make a rush across no-man's-
land with him. Flares arced and sputtered and burned
on all sides of the cabin, ringing it with a phantas-
magoric light filled with shifting shadows and figures.
Together they rushed toward the gaping hole between
collapsed logs where the pole door had been, prepared
to find Johnson buried and dead, or at least stunned
and disabled. As they came within a few yards of the
shack, where King had been shot and Lang shot at,
Gardlund on the run switched on his light and flashed
its beam in the pit.

There, enclosed by debris and upended logs, Johnson
sat: his face a dark and farouche mask beneath a wide-
brimmed Stetson. His elbows rested on his knees, and
in his hands he held a sawed-off shotgun and a stockless
rifle. And he was...grinning (no: later Eames in seeking to describe that insolent face which stared at him
like a soot-blacked white man in a mistrel show, would
find a more precise word: leering), leering like a cat at
a mouse hole, like a gorged rat in a cellar, like a rabid
dog in a corner...leering like a madman, and he was
waiting for them....A single rifle shot shattered the
light in Gardlund's hand, and Eames in that moment

realized what Gardlund already knew: that Johnson from his stronghold could have killed them all many times over, and had for the past fifteen hours been playing some perverse game with them, whose rules, unguessed by Eames until now, they too had been forced to play by. While they had sought, in deadly earnest, to destroy his cabin and him, he had parried their blows one after another, and cunningly kept his distance. So long as they had not got too close, he had let them scurry away; but the instant they posed any real threat, he would kill them all without blinking. All this Eames understood instantly, and felt instantly thwarted. The realization that he was at Johnson's mercy, that his ordeal was Johnson's diversion, filled him with impotent fury—as though there were two different species of men, two distinct sets of rules, and no one had ever hinted that fact until now, past his fiftieth year. He had been let blunder on, and had led men (dull men like Gardlund, who was behind him now, laughing) to the position they were now in. Maybe there had been some warnings, but not since Rene introduced him to a mail pilot whom he guessed, later on, to be one of her lovers, had he felt so homicidal, so outmanned, outmaneuvered, and mocked. But it was too late: the pilot had flown; and Gardlund, the instant the flashlight was shot from his hand, had fled for the snowbank.

Eames stood alone at the brink of the pit, brilliantly silhouetted by flares which the men continued to throw, demeaned and belittled by an enemy he could not see clearly, whose guns he knew were trained on him and whose sneer he felt like a mad dog's fangs poised at his (and Mildred Urquhart's) bare throat. If he made a rash or foolish move, in they sank. He dropped his rifle and turned around slowly, defeat in every limb and angle of his body. Presenting his back to the enemy of all that he cared or stood for, ruefully he walked away. No rifle or shotgun blast followed the first shattering shot, and at 0400 hours the Inspector ordered a withdrawal from the ruined cabin, and a retreat from the Rat.

7

OFFICER COMMANDING
     R C M POLICE
          EDMONTON ALTA
RETURNED AKLAVIK FOUR PM TODAY STOP SURPRISE
WAS ATTEMPTED BY APPROACHING RAT RIVER OVER-
LAND AND ALSO TO OBVIATE RISK OF AMBUSH ON RAT
RIVER BUT DUE POOR INFORMATION INDIAN GUIDE
PATROL CONSISTING CONSTABLES MILLEN MCDOW-
ELL INTERPRETERS BERNARD SITTICHIULIS THREE CI-
VILIANS AND MYSELF DID NOT REACH JOHNSONS
CABIN UNTIL NOON NINTH STOP JOHNSONS CABIN ON
HIGH BANK OF LONG PROMONTORY COVERED DENSE
BRUSH AFFORDING POOR OBSERVATION AND NO
COVER FROM FIRE EXCEPT RIVER BANK STOP JOHN-
SON REFUSED TO LEAVE CABIN CONSEQUENTLY COM-
BINED RUSH WAS MÅDE WHICH WAS BEATEN OFF BY
HEAVY FIRE FROM TWO AUTOMATIC PISTOLS STOP
DURING ATTACK PARTY SUCCEEDED IN SMASHING
DOOR WITH RIFLE BUTTS WHICH SHOWED CABIN TO
BE DUGOUT FIVE FEET BELOW GROUND LEVEL WITH
LOOPHOLES IN LOGS FOR FIRING STOP DESULTORY
FIRE CONTINUED BOTH SIDES FOR FIFTEEN HOURS
STOP ABOUT MIDNIGHT COALOIL FLARES REVEALED
JOHNSON HAD REPLACED DOOR STOP AT THREE AM
PARTY BLEW IN DOOR AND BLASTED HOLE IN ROOF

WITH HIGH EXPLOSIVE AND AGAIN RUSHED CABIN
EXPECTING TO FIND JOHNSON STUNNED BUT WERE
MET WITH VIGOROUS FIRE WHICH INDICATED OCCU-
PANT PROBABLY HAS SHELTER EXTENDING BEYOND
LIMITS OF SPACE UNDER CABIN STOP PARTY WERE
FINALLY FORCED TO RETURN AKLAVIK THROUGH DOG
FEED AND OTHER SUPPLIES RUNNING OUT STOP NO
CASUALTIES SUSTAINED BY PATROL STOP AM RE-
TURNING TO CABIN AS SOON AS LARGER VOLUNTEER
PARTY CAN BE ORGANIZED WORKING FROM BASE AT
MOUTH OF RAT RIVER

                               A N EAMES

NIGHTLETTER
COLLECT

"Will that be all, sir?" Wild asked.

Eames stood heavily in the middle of the detachment
office. On his left was the inverted twenty-five-gallon
water bottle, to his right his desk with its dirty honey
and concave rock ashtray; in front of him Wild was
cramped in the little grade school desk brought into the
office for statements and dictation, and over his left
shoulder was the window looking out on Aklavik,
through which he could barely distinguish in the featureless gray blur the mission compound and, dotting
the snowdrifted clearing, a miniature forest of stakes
marking snowdrifted dogs. Familiar objects, but their
arrangement deceptive and nothing to orient by. Who
knew what aberrations they had undergone in his absence? Who could testify to him that this was the same
landscape, though it appeared to be? His own mental
furniture, too, seemed oddly disturbed, as though someone had rifled the files or ransacked the drawers of his
mind while he was away on patrol, though nothing
appeared to be missing. Nevertheless, he felt disoriented. He paced back and forth less than usual as he
dictated, and his pipe hung by his jowl between puffs.
Wild was staring at him.

"I'd like to see Lazarus' report on this patrol," Eames

replied. "I'd like to see what he says."

"He didn't make out a report, sir. He says he stayed with the dogs, sir."

"That's true." Eames nodded. "So he did." Eames continued to nod, standing in the center of the office, intermittently puffing his pipe. "Just as well."

Wild watched him warily. Any moment, he was sure, a great deal of work would fall on him, issued suddenly and without warning, like an avalanche, without any thought for his off-duty hours. There was a great deal of work to be done—reports on the last patrol, recruitment of a new posse, all the logistical arrangements and the paper work—and as soon as the old man came out of his stupor, he would undoubtedly tell Wild to do it. Wild had not entered the office during the week of Eames's absence, and was resolved not to stay late today. He was leery of starting the work avalanche, but Eames's odd silence was unsettling, and had the effect of opening up vistas of hours which Wild felt obliged to fill.

"Some newspapers came in, sir. I'm not sure where they got their information."

"Let's see them," snapped Eames, and eagerly snatched the first of several folded newspapers out of Wild's hand. Glancing rapidly at the front page, he read:

TRAPPER'S BULLET PASSES
INCH FROM OFFICER'S HEART
Injured man Recovering—Report from Aklavik Gives
Details of Strange Case—Patrol Determined to Capture Man Sought, "Dead or Alive"
(Special to Edmonton Journal)

AKLAVIK, Jan. 6—A shot fired at R.C.M.P. Constable A.W. King by a crazed trapper in a lonely cabin on the old Yukon trail last Thursday missed the constable's heart by a scant inch, a medical examination of King has revealed. The injured

man, cared for by Dr. J. A. Urquhart in hospital
here...

Meanwhile a patrol headed by Inspector Eames
is pressing forward steadily through the darkness
shrouding the Arctic. It must traverse...

It read as though Urquhart had been interviewed, but
Eames thought the word "shrouding" suspicious. Skip-
ping to the end of the article, he read:

Before leaving for the scene of the shooting Monday, Inspector Eames said he was prepared to bring
the man responsible back dead or alive.

Eames blinked. Was this one of his famous memory
lapses, or libel? He gazed dully at Wild, who was holding out to him a whole stack of newspapers. Setting
aside the one he had been reading, he took the whole
pile and, standing in the center of the detachment office,
quickly scanned the headlines of the paper on top. The
Edmonton *Journal* for January 7 announced: "Einstein
Agrees World in Motion: Famous Physicist Says Light
Can Bend." He was strangely tempted to read the article, but went on to the January 8 paper. Its headline
read, "Hitler Bargain with Bruening May Be Balked,"
followed by a longish article parallel with another
headed, "Unsuccessful Attempt Made to Kill Jap Em-
peror." Not noting on its front page the words, "Arctic,"
or "Trapper," or "RCMP," he quickly turned to the January 9 paper. "Germany Will Announce Inability to Pay
War Debts" dominated its front page. "Bruening to Tell
Powers Reparations Are at End. Quotes 'Iron Chancellor' Bismarck: 'All Politics Reduces Itself to This For-
mula: to Try to Be One of Three.'" ... Eames reread the
headline, though it made no sense to him. There was
no Sunday paper, and Monday's and Tuesday's were
missing. The next paper, the last in the pile, proclaimed
in banner headlines:

15-HOUR GUN BATTLE RAGES BETWEEN
TRAPPER AND POSSE
Bombs and Rifle Fire Fail to Dislodge
Man Sought for Wounding Const. King

Albert Johnson Blazes Back.at
Attacking Party with Automatics

FAR NORTH BATTLE

Inspector Eames Returns to Aklavik
for Reinforcements and Supplies

Eames read fearfully on. An eyewitness account had
been obtained, Eames wondered from whom, and the
newspaper report mentioned dog food, flares, three
rushing assaults, and the dynamite damage to the cabin.
There were no pictures, except of the new Bishop of
Edmonton on the occasion of his investiture, Rt. Rev.
Arthur F. Burgett, in robes, but the article spilled over
onto page 2, recapitulating the earlier account of the
wounding of King. Eames scanned the long column sub-
headed "Bombs, Rifle Fire in North Battle (cont. from
page 1)," and looked at two boxed ads for movies which
flanked it: "BEN HUR in Sound, with Francis X. Bushman," and "THE SIN OF MADELON CLAUDET, with
Helen Hayes in a performance that will touch your
heart with pity—her first talking picture." Handing
the pile of newspapers to Wild, Eames turned silently
to the window. His worst fears were not confirmed, but
the coverage was bad enough. There was a leak (not
the trappers—they were incapable of answering questions intelligently, even for money—and not his own
men: Millen, who had his ideals, or McDowell, a company man...of the specials, Bernard was as mute as
Little Orphan Annie's Punjab, but Lazarus...). Lazarus it must be—but why?

The leak left Eames feeling exposed, under pressure
from thousands of anonymous, misinformed readers.

Next he knew, there would be bleeding hearts sym-
pathizing with the creature the mere thought of whom
agitated Eames to the brink of nausea: the creature's
presence in the Arctic was a humiliation to Eames, and
his conjectured madness an outrage. Johnson, if that
was the man's name, was no more mad than...

Gazing darkly through the dingy window Eames
imagined the staked clearing before the mission compound as the no-man's-land in front of Johnson's cabin,
himself advancing on the enemy's gun bunker, a weapon
concealed in his hand. Star shells and flashbulbs burst
brilliantly around him. As Wild behind him said, "Did
you see this one, sir?" he was confronting again the
sullen creature whose gunsights he was lined up in,
when quite unexpectedly across the compound Mildred
Urquhart issued from the mission hospital in her foxfur
parka. Never had the sight of her so afflicted Eames.
Emerging blond and nimbused from the rubble of his
mind, she stopped and held her hands up—pulling on
her mitts, but Eames saw the gesture as forbidding him
to come closer—while at her back in his mind's eye the
gloating creature leered...Eames wheeled abruptly
away from the window, forcing his mind to be a furnitureless room filled with vague half-lights; the lights
in his mind were all bent, and armies of men bearing
forests of banners marched back and forth in the balelight.

"It's from the Toronto *Telegram,* an editorial."

"What?" he said vaguely.

"This one, sir." Wild handed Eames another newspaper, opened to the middle. Eames squinted at the
small, dark print which seemed to swim across the page
like sperm, or vermin. "A Pitiful Wilderness Tragedy,"
he made out finally. He skipped to the end, a blurred
word here and there stabilizing in the jellylike mess of
print he stared at:

> ...unfortunate...madman   must...slain...only
> solution...his problem...individual...surrender
> ...afflicted...

Then his sight went fuzzy and failed to focus. For a moment he stood suspended, deliciously experiencing a release of tension throughout his entire body, which broke into a sweat. It was then Eames realized, with a shudder of loathing, that he had shot his bolt in his duty pants...

He stared apprehensively at Wild, but Wild had seen or guessed nothing. He could have a stroke or a heart attack, and Wild would not notice the difference. With a limp hand he passed the newspaper back, and Wild took it. "Will that be all, sir?" Wild asked.

"Wild," he said quietly.

"Yes sir."

"You've had training in code, haven't you?"

"Some, sir. Not as much as Hersey and Riddell," he added quickly.

"I want you to devise a code," Eames said, and commenced pacing. His pipe still hung from his mouth, unlit. He stopped at his desk, and lit it. Wild, like a man in a valley staring up at a glacier, doodled around the written word "Code."

"All our messages from now on are to be sent out in code, unless I direct otherwise. You are to take full advantage of such civilian resources as the settlement of Aklavik affords. UZK, the local amateur experimental broadcasting station, is to be used—its equipment commandeered, if need be. Constable Millen and civilian Gardlund are to be outfitted and dispatched as soon as possible with orders to reconnoiter the area adjacent to Johnson's cabin, and to determine if the fugitive is still there. They are to report back, by runner or radio, prior to the departure of the next posse, which I personally will command, two days from now—what date will that be?"

"Friday," Wild said, scribbling furiously, "Friday, January 15th, sir."

"As soon as the code has been devised, let me know— and let no one else know except Riddell: he can signal it to Edmonton—so that the appropriate communiqués can be sent without interception. Have you got all that, Wild?"

Wild, scribbling desperately like a man buried in snow, nodded. Eames knocked out his pipe. "I don't want any more leaks," he said, "I want a strict code, and I want a small army. Riddell is quartermaster, and you're the liaison. Martial law will be strictly enforced. There will be a strict curfew, and the civilian population will be placed under protection until the fugitive has been brought to justice. You know what to do?"

"I think so, sir."

"Good. See that you do it." Eames struggled into his parka. "And don't waste any time," he fussed, his head hidden and his voice muffled. "This is an emergency situation, Wild"—Eames's head popped through the hole—"and these are dangerous times. Germany is rearming, Japan is expanding, the depression is still crippling the South. Where do you look for order, Wild? To the church? To the family?"

These last words were strident, derisive, and Wild knew better than to answer, unless he was forced to. The old man had been in this same mood before, around Christmas, when the mail came, but never to such a degree, or so bitterly. When Eames continued to glare at him with a contemptuous look, breathing all the while in short little gasps through his mouth, Wild shook then nodded his head in despairing agreement.

Eames marched to the door and opened it. He stood for a moment in the open door. "I'm going to Mildred Urquhart's to borrow a book." Then: "The world is in motion, Wild." .

Wild, saddened but not dismayed, closed the door after him.

Striding directly to the file cabinet, on top of which a half dozen books sat: *The Constable's Manual, Canadian Criminal Code, History of the Anglican Church in Canada, Royal Northwest Mounted Police—A History,* and *Crankshaw's Magistrate's Manual,* Wild took down *Codes and Semaphores: Canadian Signal Corps in The Great War.* Blowing the dust from its jacket, he sat down at Eames's desk and began crypting a message, using standard "A" code. Within half an hour he had the following:

PLEASE	INSTRUCT	IF	
214	214	214	
16740	12024	11138	
———	———	———	
16954	12238	11352	
PORTABILITY	INVADER	IMPORTUNATENESS	

PERMISSIBLE	TO	BURY	JOHNSON
214	214	214	
16338	22484	03250	
———	———	———	
16552	22698	03464	
PICNIC	TROTTING	CANNON	JOHNSON

WITHOUT	BURIAL	SERVICE	OR
214	214	214	214
23829	03227	20447	15570
———	———	———	———
24043	03441	20661	15784
DONALD	CANDENT	SHOW	OWED

DISCLOSURE	LOCATION	OF	GRAVE
214	214	214	214
07004	13470	15439	10218
———	———	———	———
07218	13684	15653	10432
DISSATISFIED	LUXURIATING	OSPREY	HAIR

Satisfied with the message, except for the word 'Disclosure," which he'd intended as "Disclosing"—but he could always add an "of" before "Location"—Wild closed the book and replaced it on the top of the file cabinet, next to *Crankshaw's Manual*. He read through his message again—it should cheer up the chief. He himself had found it more fun than doodling.

PART THREE

The Defile

1

The hill was deserted. The trees in the dark were pickets around a crush trap, the clearing an empty enclosure. He sat in the rubble amid smoking log ends, with gunpowder fumes in his nostrils, his eyes narrowed to slits which peered out at the dark, his ears humming. Slowly the humming died out. A wolf howled in the distance, long and forlorn; a second howl, more distant, faded away into silence. He lay back in the charred and warm debris and stared up steely-eyed at the Hunter. Cracks like rifle fire close at hand startled him, but he knew it was frost in the trees. Positioning near him his rifle and shotgun, he sank into much needed sleep...

When he awoke a gray, gunmetal mist had enveloped the ruins, and he was struggling to remember his body. He lay huddled up in a tight little ball against some barely warm log ends. Fingers of frost gripped his shoulders and the backs of his thighs; from the knees his legs had no feeling. He lay awhile longer not disturbing the air, while planning the things he would take: his ax, his rifles and shotgun and ammo, his eiderdown and other essential items—each pictured in its pre-dynamite state. He tried to move, but was hamstrung with stiffness. Then he leaped up, or tried to leap up, as he had often seen dead rabbits do when the scavenger's shadow appeared above them...but he could not do that either. The best he could do was to roll over on his stomach, then raise himself to his knees, then to his knees and his elbows, his hands and his knees, then push up with both hands until he knelt on one knee and one foot. His gaze like a lizard's swept the ashen-gray fog as, with the aid of a broken log end, he stood, if standing it could be called, on both feet. He was sweating profusely, yet there were parts of him frozen—both feet, one shoulder, his forearms and hands and parts of his face—frozen and numb and refusing to function. Tentatively, like a bear in a pit, he stamped one foot, then the other in the loose snow and gravel, packing the mound beneath him; then he stamped both alternately. With one foot he raked some splinters of charred wood together, clumsily fished from his pocket some matches and knelt down, falling over and burning his fingers... eventually he got a fire going.

Very deliberately, he began reassembling from the wreck of the cabin his outfit: hauling out from beneath timbers and snowburied ruins his soot-blackened packs and gunnysacks of equipment, weapons, supplies, blowing the soot off of them and laying them out along the larger wrecked logs, not haphazardly, but in a visual pattern which corresponded to his mental checklist. His rifles and the sawed-off shotgun, with ammunition for each: two boxes of fifty shells each for the .22 rifle; an ore sample bag of sixty shells for the .30-30; and a handful of 16-gauge shotgun shells—these he put loose in his pocket. The pocket compass he made sure he had on him, and a bundle of moosehide babiche for snowshoe lacing. One box Pony matches, and a bundle of sulfur matches wrapped in tinfoil, and another in waxed paper, along with a tin aspirin box containing fishhooks and one sailmaker's needle—these, along with a spool of thread, a loop of twine, four .22 shells, and a tinfoil wrapper containing two dozen liver pills he laid out symmetrically along two charred logs, then swept them all into an ore sample bag, which he placed in his parka pocket. His money—$2,410 in American and Canadian bills—his packet of pearls, his gold teeth, and bottle of gold dust, and the knife he had made from a spring trap, and the awl he had made from a file—both in moosehide covers—he put in his other pocket, along with the pocket compass. By now he was sweating and shivering. He scooped hurriedly into his packsack the lard tin and lid he used for a tea pail, with a tinfoil container of loose tea, a spoon, the eiderdown he used for a sleeping bag, the rifle and sawed-off shotgun and shells, and his ax with a caribou skin cover. Then, flinging the light pack on his back, and bending to lace on his snowshoes, he picked up his .30-30 and climbed out of the wreckage, not bothering to put out the fire he had built or to look over his shoulder. The dense, snow-covered bush at the rear of his cabin stood like a hand raised against him. He waded into its tangle of branches, then broke into a fast trot, maneuvering with the rifle aslant in his hands like a dog running through a thick woods with a long stick in its jaws....

He came out on a point overlooking the river, about four miles above his old site. The point concealed a low bluff on the river's north side, where the Rat opened into a mile-wide, flat swale which he remembered from the past summer: grassy and blue, surrounded by dark evergreen, in this first of a series of lakes leading up to the mountains he had spied knee-deep in the water a moose and her calf cropping horsetails. The Rat's swale was now frozen over, the whole scene unnaturally still, with coils of gray mist hanging over the ice field, obscuring the base of the mountains beyond so that only three peaks—a saddleback, twin mounds, and the slashed Barrier Pass—were distinguishable in the far distance against the gray, gunmetal sky. The peaks seemed not to rest on earth, nor to suspend from sky, but to float midway like a winter mirage without solid foundation, and between him and them lay a frozen expanse of flat swale and featureless taiga and countless ravines and foothills. On those bleak ridges nothing breathed, or could breathe, for long. He stood on the low point gazing across the ice field at the peaks which formed, like three broken teeth, the horizon, until the sweat he had worked up while running started to freeze. Then he built a small fire, and boiled up.

He continued abstractedly while gulping hot tea to scan the swale and high ridges for movement; for a full

half hour his gaze swept the ridges for signs of life, but
there were none. Only mile upon mile of nothing, nothing in sight but the frozen ice field, leading off into
other ice fields, with the iron-ribbed icebound hills rim-
ming the delta and cordoning off the high peaks. For
an instant, as though it were not he, but another, he
projected a man past the lakelands and foothills, toiling
up one of the peaks; the man had on snowshoes, windpants, parka...but the lack of trees, the lack of
trees....The figure toiled slowly up a vertical desert,
at – 75°, without fire, without food, without cover...how
much could the stick figure live without, and for how
long?...Then, as abruptly as he had placed him there,
he abandoned him. Pulling out his pocket compass, he
took a reading on the winter sun in relation to the
mountains, calculating quickly where due south was at
this time of day, midafternoon, and north at roughly
3:00 A.M., on an imagined watch-face, and east at roughly
9:00 A.M., and west at 9:00 P.M. Turning his back on the
mountains, he posted himself on the point to watch
down the narrow confines of the Rat and over its sullen
terrain to the curve four miles distant where his cabin
had been. This was the only point he knew of from
which he could maintain a watch, and still have a two
hours' lead. If, after a few days, he saw no sign of the
men, he would go back for his traps. If he did spy the
men...he knew every inch of the delta, and every turn
in the Rat: surprised or cornered, he would kill them;
left alone, he would let them live.

'Let him live'—the phrase which had hummed in his
ears at the cabin came back to him now, with the image:
the old man, the one who called himself "the Inspector,"
standing stupidly in his rifle sight line and throwing
his weapon down, blinking—was he waiting to be taken
prisoner? what would he do with a prisoner?—yet the
fool continued to stand there staring down into the
blasted pit directly in the sight line of the guns that
were trained on him. The old man could not see him,
but he could see the old man by the light of the flares
which the men continued to throw. And what he saw

was a man who, in the reverse situation, would kill him. He was not interested in what he saw, though he saw that the old man would come back. He would come back, if he 'let him live'; if he killed him, they would come back—it amounted to the same thing. Still the old man stood there, his stooped shadow in the dying flare light shrinking slowly—was he waiting to surrender honorably and have his sword returned to him? Was he waiting for them to drink claret together from the cellars of the dynamited shack? Then the old man squared his shoulders and wheeled about-face on his heel, and walked very slowly back to his lines. There had been no more firing after that, and no more flares thrown....

He continued to gaze down the frozen river, the three mountain peaks and an enormous expanse of frozen ice field at his back. He did not see how he could reduce himself further...a stick figure on the Arctic landscape, a speck.... If it was a matter of killing...he would rather not get into killing, he would rather keep it a game. If he saw the men first...that was too easy—that was just what they would be thinking, 'If we see him first,' and fearing, 'What if he sees us first?'—tiny antlike specks crawling across a vast white board, like spilled sugar or flour, each speck asking the other speck, 'Where is Johnson?' and none of the specks can tell. He grinned ruefully, and discovered a split lip. Was a strategy too much to ask, a plan which would put him in splendid isolation from the pack of ignorant specks?

Still squatting on his haunches and periodically gazing downriver he broke from a willow nearby a snow-covered branch. This he snapped into six segments and stuck them in the snow in the shape of a semicircle at his feet, representing the posse. Then, in front of the posse he stuck a larger twig in the snow, and around this single figure he laid four sticks—a box around himself. Reaching over the whole configuration, he ran one finger in a long, twisting rill through the snow—the river—and at right angles to the rill he tossed a charred piece of wood from the fire—the mountains. His play-

ing field and the initial disposition of his figures resembled this:

Glancing intermittently downriver, he began to deploy
his figures: the six twigs moved back to the rill, the
single stick moved out of the box toward the log representing the mountains. Two of the six advanced up
the rill in pursuit of the single figure, the other four
making flanking movements, two on each side of the
rill, until the six were again in a semicircle facing the
single stick figure.

Squatting on his haunches, the man studied the configuration and the playing field. The stick figure feinted
to the center, then outflanked the six twigs to the left;
the half dozen sticks shifted on their axis, and stood
facing him again. He outflanked them to the right; again
they shifted. Each time he outflanked the half dozen

sticks, they would shift on their center to stand facing him once again. Every flanking movement, due to the maneuverability of both sides, became a circling action: partial enclosure leading to flanking, which led to shifting and partial enclosure again.

He deployed his single stick back to home base, the box. But the twigs pursued him back down the rill and this time completed their encirclement because, when they reached his home base with him in it, they doubled their number—he broke off another willow branch and snapped it quickly into six pieces. Now twelve twigs were posted in a tight circle around the one stick inside the box. He continued to stare at the configuration before him—the same he had begun with, except that the enemy had doubled its number—then at the charred piece of wood and the playing field alongside it, which all of his twigs had abandoned. He tried to figure some way of getting his single stick through the tight circle of twelve, back up the rill, and over the boundary log. Now that his stick had returned to home base and got boxed in, he could see that the boundary log in the distance was his obvious goal.

For an instant, again, he projected a man past the lakelands and foothills, toiling up one of the peaks... the stick figure in his mind's eye had on snowshoes, windpants, a parka.... Then, as abruptly as he had begun his game, he left off. If it came to that, if worse came to worst, he would not be worsted. Once over the mountains he would be free... but he was not superhuman, he could not simply wish himself over. It was a matter of flanking movements and time, of laying down false trails and circling back on the wide playing field near the boundary, keeping the other side turning and guessing, cut off from its home base as he was cut off from his... that was essential: to avoid sheltering at any lean-to he'd built on his trapline or raiding any cache he'd constructed; above all, to avoid going back to his cabin where he would simply be trapped in the rubble.

At the thought of his cabin, blasted apart, he broke out in a sweat and his mouth grew unnaturally dry. An adrenaline surge convulsed him: squatting, his

breath came short as though he were running; staring,
his pupils dilated, then his eyes narrowed to slits. Suddenly he rose up and stomped on the stick figures,
grinding them into the snow in a fit of murderous rage.
Breathing in short, fitful gasps, he yelled: "Here is
Johnson!" In the answering silence he stood, listening,
then fell back on the ground, bathed in sweat and beginning to freeze. He lay on his back and glared up at
the indistinct sky. Arching his back and craning his
neck he gazed upside down at the mountains which
hung, sharp and enameled, like fangs from the roof of
the world; and continued to stare, his mouth gaping
wide, while the man he had placed there fell off, clutching and flailing and kicking, into a limitless
gray...Slowly he calmed, and as night settled over the
delta, unleashing a fistful of stars, he devised a round
of routines: dragging up wood for the fire, chopping ice
for tea, constructing a windbreak for sleeping....
Finally he slept, not deeply or soundly, but on the edge
of awaking and ready to leap up and run like the northern lights when flashed nervous above him, quicksilver
and wild, into the sword and shield of the Hunter. That
too passed at last, and he sunk into deep, dreamful sleep
as the fire beside him burned out....

He dreamed he was busy with something, or someone, but all the while off in the woods hung the carcass
of an animal he had killed and trussed up—a large
deer, or a moose. It was summer, and for the first few
days and warm nights the carcass was being bled, age-
ing, as in the South men said meat should age. But he
had made no incisions, there was no gash for the blood
to drain out; the stomach, too, was intact, though the
carcass was up off the ground and hung upside down
by its hooves, as it should hang. After several days he
became anxious: the meat would go bad. He wished
someone else would find it and butcher it, because he
was busy, but no one else knew about it. A week passed;
his worry and sense of waste grew acute. It was not too
late, still he could not free himself to go tend the carcass...it was not too late; then, with the passage of
more time—three weeks, two months: there was no

precise moment—it was. His sense of waste was intolerable. A terrible image of the great feed of meat dominated his mind: bloated with dark blood and gases, black with blowfiles and crawling with maggots it hung, trussed up and turning in the hot sun, while gobbets of rot-flesh and juices oozed to the ground which was crawling with beetles and scavenger crows, their blunt dropleted bodies loathsome and sleek, their shiny beaks tearing and rending....

He woke with a start to confront the northern lights' flashing play and the vast spectacle of an Arctic sky full of stars, yeasty and diamondlike in their brilliance, now one, now another, unfixed from its moorings and falling....He turned over onto his stomach. The dark line of mountains loomed against the night sky; the three peaks stood out icy blue, sharply etched like cut glass laid on velvet. The massive escarpment leading up to those peaks, by a series of deep ravines and dark foothills, was gray on its lower slopes with snow-covered taiga, but blue where the glacis began. The cover of snow beneath the night sky made the hills look foreshortened, but he was not deluded. *'If a crow were to fly, now, from that peak to me, it would fly at least twenty miles. But if I had to walk to that same peak...'* The thought trailed off, as it had begun, abruptly. The ordeal of the day before, and of the day before that, had drained him of all energy. He closed his eyes and went to sleep again....

He awoke to a sky filled with feathering snow like the down from torn pillows. He could not see fifty yards. Beyond fifty yards the gray and white stipples merged into whiteness and grayness, without up or down, east or west, backward or forward, and neither motion nor stasis. Everything was covered, everywhere. He smiled complacently to himself. Not even a moose could be tracked in this snowfall, not for days. The winter sun was absent, impossible to fix, and he remembered, oddly, his dream of the previous night. Fleeting impressions, fugitive imprints were all that remained, everything else was snow-covered...a moose in the shallows....a quarrelsome crow (or was it a raven?)...a river mumbling and whipping up whitecaps...the wave line where two rivers met, and their sandbar like a snowdrift...a tunnel-like passage through dense underbrush...and always, in every place, trees—he remembered the trees most of all, now that there were none, and the high, white mountains, and how the sun shone always on the mountains—for where there were trees, there was meat.

Pulling out his pocket compass, he calculated west: it was where he thought it would be, though there were no mountains before him, or trees behind him, only snow below and snow above and everywhere snow falling on snow. As yet there was no very great wind. He crawled out from under the blanket of snow that had fallen on him in the night, six inches at least, and stood up and shook himself like a dog and stretched his arms and his legs. Then, scooping up his few utensils and wiping the snow off of them, he strapped on his snowshoes and set out south-southwesterly across the frozen swale, his snowshoes packing the newfallen snow with a deep, pancake imprint which, as soon as he passed, filled again.

2

"Where do you want the dogs?" Gardlund had to shout to be heard; even so, only the odd word came through. Constable Edgar Millen, his six-foot frame squeezed into the komatik under the canvas, had twisted his head around to see Gardlund and cocked his hand near his ear. "The dogs!" Gardlund shouted again through wind-driven snow, and Millen nodded, leaving another decision to him. Gardlund didn't like it, any of it: the fucking blizzard, the fucking officer (he wasn't an officer, but he acted like one), the fucking mad trapper (no madder than him, only meaner), the whole fucking patrol. He didn't like driving the dog team right up to the wreck, though he didn't think Johnson would be there—*he* wouldn't be there—but neither did he fancy staking the dogs downriver and snowshoeing several miles, then having to snowshoe back, find the dogs, harness them, and—then where? These were Millen's decisions, Millen the man-in-charge; Gardlund was merely the driver and by Jeez he had driven—a day and a half through a fucking blizzard all the way from Aklavik up the Mackenzie, where the storm had first struck them, then up the Peel, following the dogs he could barely handle along a riverbed he could scarcely see; then at the drifts having to prize Millen out of his blankets while he ran ahead and broke trail, and always, always holding the dogs to the wind which, wherever they were on whichever river—the Mackenzie, the

171

Peel, or the Rat—shifted and twisted and turned itself
so that they were bucking the mother. There were cornering blasts, and blowovers near the deep drifts, and
even the odd little lull but, even then—he detested this
most of all—he had to pay strict attention. He would
just get settled into a rhythm of driving, the dogs running well, the komatik runners slicing through snow,
and him with both hands gripping the handles and one
foot on the komatik strut, the other foot pushing off
from the snow in a rhythm—the rhythm he'd learned
as a kid while riding a scooter—he would just be settling into the rhythm and treading the snow as if measuring it while making patterns with his heel and toes—
when the mothering sled would hit a deep drift, and
halt, and he'd be jarred forward, and the dogs would be
churning around in the drift, and he'd have to kick
Millen awake and wait for him to unwind himself from
the sled, then run to the front and pull the goddamn
dogs through, one by one, while Millen pushed from
behind, or, if it was a bad drift, he'd have to lace on his
snowshoes and break trail, or shovel a way through
with one snowshoe—whatever: what with the blizzard,
and dogs, and Millen, and drifts, he couldn't make patterns or measure. He had to navigate, break trail, and
drive, while Millen rode free.

They were coming out now around a big bend in the
river which Gardlund thought he remembered, though
he couldn't be sure in a blizzard, as being just below
Johnson's cabin: the bend where, the last time they had
come as a posse, Lazarus had staked the dogs. And
whether Johnson was there, or had gone, the last thing
Gardlund wanted was to take any chances—chances
on getting shot, getting lost, or on losing the dogs. To
have to walk out of this country, he mused as they
penetrated it further, would be like committing suicide
to avoid death; worse in summer than winter, but dead
was dead summer or winter. Johnson, if he were there,
could pick off the dogs one by one, as for that matter
he could snipe them off, Millen first.

Gardlund was bound and determined that Millen,
who lay half asleep in the sled, would lead this fucking

patrol. He'd like to see Millen tippy-toe through this
shit—Millen claimed he was a dancer. Some of the others claimed he was too, but if he was it was because
when he wasn't eating or sleeping, which was most of
the time, he was drinking but not enough to get drunk.
Gardlund had seen the type—boy-officers, ninety-day
wonders, cadet corps looeys—performing at parties and
on the parade ground but not in the field. Put them out
here and where were they?—snug as bugs in a rug;
chauffeured to the front to view "operations," then
chauffeured back again—to General Staff and wine
parties. Millen would have made a good adjutant—what
else were Mounties good for? Peace with the Indians
and parties for brass—Millen was made for the Mounties. The Mounties got ten bucks a day, every day; he
got five, for the days he was out here. He didn't get any
more than five for scrabbling blindly around in a blizzard or getting shot at while chauffeuring Millen.

He halted the sled and seemed to rush forward, as
rushing forward for the past eighteen hours he had
seemed to stand still. Slowly he lost his momentum.
The snow swirled around the sled and the men and the
dogs, all of whom, stupefied, stood like snow-sculpted
statues on the white ribbon of river. Then the dogs
started whining and pissing and digging holes in the
snow to lie down in, and Millen undraped himself from
the sled.

"Where's the cabin?" he shouted.

Gardlund pointed into an Arctic whiteout. Millen
peered.

"I can't see it," he shouted to Gardlund. "You sure?"

Gardlund shrugged, and groped under the canvas for
the dried whitefish which felt lumpy and long, like a
bundle of pine knots. As he hefted an armload, he wondered how many whitefish he carried (say, seventy-
five), how many to give each dog (there were six dogs
in all). Calculating $75 \div 6 = 12\frac{1}{2}$, he figured he would
give thirteen to three, and twelve to three, or twelve
to five, and fifteen to one—but that was only if there
were seventy-five to begin with....He couldn't see to
count the whitefish, though he could feel them like

sticks, he couldn't see the trees on the bank, or the bank itself, or the...

"Gardlund!" It was an officer's cry, the desperate cry (cloaked as command) of an officer in some kind of trouble. The fish were starting to fall, anyway. He threw the load as it fell from his arms in the direction of the dog team, half spinning so that some of the fish fell on all of the dogs, whether twelve or thirteen or fifteen he didn't know, care, or count. The dogs began snapping and wolfing, and again he heard Millen's voice: "Gardlund! Over here!" but couldn't for the life of him see anything beyond the blurred outline of the sled which stood five feet away. Fucking blizzard. Five minutes ago he had seen the bank on both sides, the outline of trees, and the curving shoreline of river for 300, maybe 400 yards; now he could see nothing. He peered slit-eyed in the direction the voice had come from, through a frenzy of blinding snowflakes—from now on he would think in six figures: 120487. 921745. A million was seven. "Gard-lund." The voice was weaker, more distant. As he felt for, and found, the long coil of rope and pulled it out from the sled, he thought: 'What if it's Johnson?' He knew it wasn't. Voices were distinctive; this voice was Millen's—something between a whine and an order—distinctly cadet-like, afraid of the dark (he tied the rope around his own waist), eager to lead but only when followed (he tied the other end to the sled handles), ready to die for his Country, his King (he tugged at the rope: it was secure), so long as somebody else did the shit-work (he felt for his rifle, loaded it, and with his rifle at the ready trudged off toward the voice). '999645.' '809343.' "Here!" he yelled. "Millen!"

Millen had blundered into a snowdrift at the edge of the river. In struggling to get free, he had lost all sense of direction. Hearing nothing but the cracking of the river ice below him, and the shrill whistling of wind and windblown snow around him, he had panicked and run a short distance downriver before stopping. Pulling himself together, he called out to Gardlund. But Gardlund might have gone on, the thought struck him, or be laughing to himself a short distance away. He had all the supplies, the sled, and the dogs, and no personal stake in the patrol. Why had the chief yoked them together, hip and shoulder like Siamese twins—a trapper who disliked the Mounties, a Mountie who mistrusted trappers—and now they were severed, a blizzard was blowing, and he was a pastry cook, really, whose martinet of a father had sent him to military school so he could be batman to men like his father so long as there was an England—"never send your kid to military school" he sang over and over every time he got drunk—but it was he who had crossed the Atlantic and worked as a farmhand and joined the Force to get shut of his officer-father. Gradually he quit calling and, watching the snow swirl around him, pictured the design on the cakes he had iced for the Governor General's trip to Aklavik. Using just sugar and butter and a drop of vanilla extract, he had created an armorial design as fragile as a snowflake.

The snow swirled around him unceasingly, but he stopped it again and again in mid-flight, focusing on a pattern and then letting it fade, then halting in mid-flight another pattern.... His body sat sprawled on the river ice, the snow corkscrewing around him, but he was not cold and his mind was dry, granular and distinct, like sugar or salt. On the cake for the Governor General he had inscribed, beneath the armorial design, "1931 Gov.-Gen. Akl." If he were a cake, he would inscribe himself thus: "9669 Rat R. 1"—he had to think what the day was—"15"—the year he knew—"32." In the snow beside him he drew his regimental number, 9669. Then he said it: "9669." Then he barked it: "9669!" When a few minutes later he heard a voice, not distant, yell, "Millen!" he struggled to his feet with the aid of his rifle and yelled into the void: "9669!" It was his batman, named Gardlund, come to see to his needs and lead him back to regimental headquarters....

The two men advanced cautiously on the burnt-out, snow-covered stronghold. The blizzard still blew, but there was a lull, and as they mounted the hill and crossed the clearing and entered the trees they could

see the blown-in front wall and collapsed sod roof and
the splintered log ends of broken-off timbers. The blizzard still blew, but here under the sheltering spruce
only a sifting of snow had settled over the debris-filled
crater. There was no sign of life, and they crept stealthily forward, removed from the windstorm which battered the delta by a ceiling of treetops and three thick
walls of forest—it was like walking inside an ice palace.
The only sounds were the cracking of river ice behind
them and the muffled roaring of wind overhead. Sift-
ings of snow dropped like sand constantly, obliterating
their bootprints as they crept toward the wreck. For
the first time in daylight they were able to assess the
dynamite damage, and, as they stared at the ruin from
twenty yards, they found it difficult to believe that
Johnson, or anyone, could have survived the main blast.
Scarcely a log was left standing, and all of the timbers
were charred by the terrific blast from close quarters.
Gardlund let out a low whistle. Except for the snow and
the trees, it looked to him like a section of Kraut trench
at Ypres—after the fifteen-inchers had finished.

"If he's not at least blinded, he's got horseshoes up
his ass," Gardlund said, and started forward with more
confidence.

Millen stood where he was, peering nervously all
around the clearing and scrutinizing every tree, as if
he faced an unseen firing squad.

"He's not here," said Gardlund contemptuously, and
spat yellow phlegm in the snow. He had taken to chewing tobacco again, after the stint with the posse, though
it gave him a queasy stomach and a light head. It was
being back here, in the place where the shoot-out had
been, under the same psychological pressure, that had
caused him to bite off a chaw as they mounted the hill.
Now, observing Millen's advance, or fear to advance,
he spit the brown cud in the snow: it steamed, then
sank, and he stepped on it and ground it once with his
boot as he trudged across to the wreck.

In the ruin itself they found nothing under the broken logs but chunks of old food—animal bones and
burnt bannock crusts—and a multitude of spent shells,

16-gauge and .22 long and .30-30, the corrosive hoarfrost already formed in them. Johnson was gone. There were neither tracks nor depressions in the new snow immediately around the cabin, and the two men, at Millen's insistence that they stay together, encircled the cabin several times in ever widening circles, but found only Johnson's canoe. This Gardlund staved in with the butt of his rifle, then they returned to the dogs and made camp.

Traveling the next day downriver, in a lull in the storm Gardlund spied smoke. It rose and dispersed among the trees he was counting off to the side and above them. He halted the dogs and nudged Millen, who was asleep on the sled. A dog on the bank started barking. His own dogs took up the challenge with a chorus of menacing howls. First one, then another, dark face appeared at the edge of the snowbank, flanked by the yapping black dog. Gardlund bit off a plug of tobacco and commenced chewing and staking his dogs, while Millen climbed out of the sled and clambered up the steep snowbank to meet with the Indians—eleven in all, lined up on the bank, outside a large winter tent with a stove.

While Gardlund stayed below with the dogs and built his own fire and boiled up, Millen disappeared into the tent and had tea with the Indians. When he came out, a half hour later, he brought an Indian with him. Gardlund, squatting at his campfire with his back to the bank, heard the two sets of footgear advancing toward him: the Mountie in boots crunching the snow and slipping every few steps; the Indian in mukluks slueing each step, almost silent. Gardlund didn't want to see either, the Mountie or the Indian—the only people he detested more were missionaries—but as the two advanced on him he cast a glance at crotch level and saw Millen scribble something and give it to the Indian. The Indian took the note in a hand without mitts and without fingers above the first knuckle. It resembled the mutilated paw of a beaver Gardlund had trapped once—just the paw, not the beaver; the beaver he had trapped later. The Indian had a thumb, though, and he

grasped Millen's note between his thumb and the palm
of his hand and thrust it into his skin pants, in the
region around his groin. The Indian continued to stand
where he was, a little way off, while Millen strode up
beside Gardlund.

"He's taking a message to Eames," Millen said.

Gardlund looked up at the boy-Mountie, then stared
into the fire.

"I've told him that Johnson has fled his cabin and
taken his outfit with him." Millen waited. "Anything
else I should tell him?"

"Eames will puke," Gardlund said, but he muttered
it more or less to himself and the wind was still making
a noise.

"Tell him what?" Millen said, and stooped down. "I
couldn't hear."

Gardlund glared at the Indian. The Indian looked
away. "Tell him the Indian is a Christian, and Johnson's no madder than we are."

"I don't think I need to say that." Millen frowned.
"Maybe he is, maybe he isn't—who knows?"

Gardlund shrugged, and returned to slurping his tea
and chewing his quid. Millen signaled the Indian, who
set out at a dogtrot downriver.

3

'Alas!' said queen Guenevere, 'now are we mischieved both!'

'Madam,' said sir Launcelot, 'is there here any armour within your chamber that might cover my poor body withal? And if there be any, give it me and I shall soon stint their malice, by the grace of God!'

'Now, truly,' said the queen, 'I have none armour nother helm, shield, sword, nother spear; wherefore I dread me sore our long love is come to a mischievous end. For I hear by their noise there be many noble knights, and well I wot they be surely armed, and against them ye may make no resistance. Wherefore ye are likely to be slain, and then shall I be burnt! For and ye might escape them,' said the queen, 'I would not doubt but that ye would rescue me in what danger that I ever stood in.'

'Alas!' said sir Lancelot, 'in all my life thus was I never bestead that I should be thus shamefully slain, for lack of mine armour.'

But ever in one sir Agravain and sir Mordred cried, 'Traitor knight, come out of the queen's chamber! For wit thou well thou art beset so that thou shalt not escape.'

'Ah! Jesu mercy!' said sir Lancelot, 'this shameful cry and noise I may not suffer, for better were death at once than thus to endure this pain.'

Then he took the queen in his arms and kissed her and said, 'Most noblest Christian queen, I beseech you, as ye have been ever my special good lady, and I at all times your poor knight and true unto my power, and as I never failed you in right nor in wrong sithen the first day king Arthur made me knight, that ye will pray for my soul if that I be slain.'

'Nay, sir Lancelot, nay!' said the queen. 'Wit thou well that I will never live long after thy days. But and ye be slain I will take my death as meekly as ever did martyr take his death for Jesu Christ's sake.'

'Well, madam,' said sir Lancelot, 'sith it is so that the day is come that our love must depart, wit you well I shall sell my life as dear as I may. And a thousandfold,' said sir Lancelot, 'I am more heavier for you than for myself! And now I had liefer than to be lord of all Christendom that I have sure armour upon me, that men might speak of my deeds or ever I were slain.'

'Truly,' said the queen, 'and it might please God, I would that they would take me and slay me and suffer you to escape.'

'That shall never be,' said sir Lancelot, 'God defend me from such a shame! But Jesu Christ, be Thou my shield and mine armour!'

And therewith sir Lancelot wrapped his mantle about his arm well and surely. And by then they had gotten a great form out of the hall, and therewith they all rushed at the door.

Then sir Lancelot unbarred the door, and with his left hand he held it open a little, that but one man might come in at once. And so there came striding a good knight, a much man and a large, and his name was called sir Collgrevaunce of Gore. And he with a sword struck at sir Lancelot mightily, and so he put aside the stroke, and gave him such a buffet upon the helmet that he fell grovelling dead within the chamber door. Then sir

Lancelot with great might drew that dead knight
within the chamber door, and then sir Lancelot,
with help of the queen and her ladies, he was
lightly armed in Collgrevaunce armour.

And ever stood sir Agravain and sir Mordred,
crying, 'Traitor knight! Come forth out of the
queen's chamber!'

And then sir Lancelot set all open the chamber
door, and mightily and knightly he strode in among
them. And anon at the first stoke he slew sir Agravain, and anon after twelve of his fellows. Within
a while he had laid them down cold to the earth,
for there was none of the twelve knights might
stand sir Lancelot one buffet. And also he wounded
sir Mordred. . . .

Eames blinked. He lay the book, face down and open,
over his knee which protruded up under the army-issue
blanket on his cot, and stared from his half-prone position at the book cover. *Morte Darthur.* Precious little
of Arthur had he encountered, and he was well on toward the end. He glanced at his wristwatch, 2100 hours,
and his gaze wandered off toward the shedlike toilet,
the door to which stood open and in which a twenty-
five-watt bulb burned. A cold draft issued from the toilet shed, keeping his sleeping porch, which was itself
a shed attached to the rear of the detachment office,
cool and frosted around the floorboards and in the corners, especially when there was a wind blowing. A wind
was blowing now, he could hear it outside, and as he
lay upright on his cot in his long johns, with two blankets drawn up to his chest, his breath frosted before
him. Through the vaporous air he could see on the shelf
in the bathroom a cylindrical can, black, with white
letters: "BRITISH ARMY FOOT POWDER." Placing the book
spine down on the straight chair which served as a
bedside table, alongside the kerosene lamp, he threw
back the covers and padded swiftly on bare feet into
the bathroom, picked up the can, and padded back swiftly
across the cold floorboards, shutting the toilet shed door
as he came. He sat down on the cot, pulled a blanket

up over his shoulders, and put his left foot up on his
right knee. Peering closely at the sole of his afflicted
foot, he picked some flakes of dead skin from around
the wart hole, then scraped the scar with a knife. The
skin around the wart seemed dead and encrusted with
layer on layer of callus. When he pricked at the core,
it was black—a thin black thread leading into his foot,
and easily cored with the knife. He dusted the sore spot
with British Army Foot Powder, sprinkled more powder
into his sock, and pulled his sock on. Then he stood up
and pulled on his pants and put on his tunic, his other
sock and his boots, his parka and mitts; checked his
watch again—2105 hours—and cast a last glance
around the room: at his clothes rack and basket of dirty
clothes, his stack of old issues of *The Force* on the floor
and *Morte Darthur* beside the cot (its bright maroon
cover lightly dusted with dandruff-looking foot powder),
and at the top of his chiffonier. In place of a backing
mirror, the rectangular frame contained a piece of plywood, with thumbtacks; thumbtacked to the plywood a
blue envelope hung. He strode over and released it and,
bringing it nearer the lamp, slit the envelope with the
knife, removed the letter, and read it. It was, he knew
from the handwriting, though he hadn't recognized the
return address, from Irene. It had arrived yesterday,
but he had put it aside, then had forgot it.

"Dear Alex," it read, "I know you will think it strange
after all this time for me to be writing you, but we have
never really lost touch and, anyway, we owe it to one
another to write. Really, you owe it to me, because I
did think of you at Christmas.

"The reason I am writing is to tell you I am on my
own now, Arnold having left finally. There was really
no way it could ever have worked, but I had to try it,
I guess. Anyway, I have taken a place at the above
address [Eames glanced at the envelope: Naramata,
B.C.—wasn't that a ski resort town?] as there was really
no other choice. It was the height of the ski season, and
all of the rooms were rented. Mine is a small bungalow,
just perfect for me, and I have a job on the local newspaper . . . [Eames blinked, and reread the last phrase, to

absorb it.]...on the local newspaper. I report local news and write a regular column called 'Here and There.' It is about odd happenings and strange people. Last week, for instance, a ski lodge owner thought he sighted a sasquatch!

"Now, Alex, it seems you are engaged in a search for some man that the papers in Vancouver and Edmonton call 'The Mad Trapper.'"

Eames stopped reading. He was aware of his frosted breath coming in short little puffs. So now they were calling the insolent brute the "Mad Trapper"—or Rene was; it was probably her name for him. She always was good at name-calling, blame-casting, summing up people by one characteristic—hadn't she called him "Alexander the Small"? Still, this new combination of Rene and Johnson was one he hadn't expected, and he felt suddenly beleaguered from both sides. He sat down on the cot, blinked, and steeled himself to read on.

"'...Mad Trapper.' Well, it seems a woman here in Naramata claims she was married to this man, Albert Johnson I think his name is. I've given her your address, and she will write you. She may be mistaken, of course. I know how these things go, having been married to you for twenty years. [Twenty years, he puzzled, and made a quick calculation. She spoke as though they were still married....] What I am asking is something else. Because of my connection with you, I've been assigned to write the story on this 'Mad Trapper' fellow. But nobody knows much about him, not even the big newspapers, I've checked. All they know is what they get from you. I don't want you to go to any extra trouble, as I know you are busy. Just send me what you send to the big papers, maybe a day or two earlier. If you can't do that, if your principles or whatever prevent you, then could you send me a little money, just enough to tide me over in my new life here until after the ski season? The press release will serve the same purpose, because I get paid extra for the article, or articles, about this Mad Trapper. It depends on how long it takes you to catch him, how many articles I can get from it. What I need, since you always said be precise, is about $200

a month between now and summer. I haven't asked you
for money before, at least not in a long time. I really
think you owe it to me now that I'm on my own.

Love, Rene."

Eames stared straight ahead at the pile of old issues of
The Force. Then he set down the letter and strapped
on his side arm, and opened the door to the office. No
lights were on in the office, but through the window he
could see, across the dog-studded clearing, lights blazing in both the men's barracks and the mission compound. Pulling his mitts on and his hood up, he crept
through the darkened detachment office like a phantom, like a phantom he felt. Thoughts he had none. He
had no desires, or purpose, or destination. Not of his
own. As various people pulled this or that string, he
jerked an arm or a leg, obeyed an order, initialed a
report, wrote a check—he responded. He stopped short
of the front door, as if caught like a thief from behind.
Standing up straight, he wheeled and strode over to his
desk, pulled off his mitts and took writing materials
out of the top drawer and wrote out a check, payable
to Irene Eames, for $1,000. On the bottom line which
read "For——," he wrote "ever," signed it, sealed it in
an envelope which he addressed and tossed in the box
marked "Outgoing." Then he opened the door and
breathed deep of the cold, and stood breathing deeply
a long time—ten minutes to be precise—before he shut
the door behind him and strode unswerving across the
clearing.

It was now by his watch 2120, and he should drop
in on Bunce in hospital; he needed to see the men in
the barracks, and check with Wild about tomorrow; and
he wanted to see Mildred Urquhart. He had done little
but read *Morte Darthur* all day, though he had told
himself that when he heard Wild stirring about the
office, he would get dressed and go in. Wild had never
reported for duty, consequently neither had he; and
here it was night; and tomorrow, depending on what
he heard from Millen (though it shouldn't depend on
that), he should be moving out with a posse. The cold

air in his face was bracing and stirred him to action.
One should never stay abed in the Arctic, as Rene used
to do: too easy to sleep a whole winter, one's whole life
away. Bunce would be asleep. Perhaps he would just
drop in on him, find him asleep, leave a note, then
depart.... He veered, in the midst of these delibera-
tions, away from the mission hospital on his left toward
Mildred Urquhart's to his right, then swerved again,
straightening his course, toward the barracks directly
ahead....

"Hey, Inspector! We thought maybe you'd died," Riddell hailed him, "but that didn't stop us. Look here!"

Riddell, a dead cigar clamped in his mouth, was surrounded by engine parts, piles of gunpowder, empty
beer bottles, and tools. One end of the barracks had
been turned into a workshop, all the bunks and foot-
lockers having been shoved together at the far end, and
Riddell and Hersey, the Signal Corps men, and John
Parsons, the retired ex-Mountie who had taken the option and lived on his pension, sat on the floor, while
the trappers Noel Verville and Ernest Sutherland looked
on. Wild, too, watched from a distance, glancing cov-
ertly at Eames as he walked in. Eames returned Wild's
glance with an I'll-deal-with-you-later frown, then
turned to the obvious center of attention, Riddell.

"I give up," he said. "What is it? A time clock for
Wild?"

Riddell set aside some engine parts, and stood up,
wiping his hands on his pants. "Him? You'd need a
bomb to wake him, an' that's what it is—it's goose eggs,
sir."

"Goose eggs?"

"I seen 'em in th' war," Sutherland said.

"You haven't seen none like these ones," Riddell said
around his cigar, which he rolled excitedly from one
side of his mouth to the other. "See, here's the cylinders
from a two-stroke motor, right?—you know that old
generator motor we had to rebuild?"

Eames, though he didn't know, nodded.

"Well, here's its cylinders." He held one in each hand.
"You fill them up with gunpowder"—he held them out

toward Eames, to show that they were full with the black powder—"then you plug in a half-minute fuse, see, with an extra length fed up through the intake port"—he indicated with one the fuse running into the other—"and then pass it out through a hole in the cylinder wall, which we haven't drilled yet. When we get those holes drilled—that's Parsons' job"—he nodded at Parsons, who silently nodded—"then we pack the powder with the piston and pass a half-inch bolt through the cylinder head to keep her packed down. There's your goose eggs, Inspector, guaranteed to give a good burst."

Eames nodded approvingly. "Very ingenious," he said.

"Only problem is, we only got two of 'em. An' what I hear, you boys was such bad shots the last time you might not even hit the right hill, much less lob 'em into the cabin. So, we got somethin' else. Show the Inspector, John."

Parsons, whom Eames had always liked—a man older than him and a sensible man who chose to live in the Arctic after retirement—got up from the floor where he had been sitting crosslegged. His well-oiled bass voice boomed loudly.

"Well, these are on the same principle, only we didn't have any more cylinder heads, so we used pipe instead." Parsons held up a length of pipe about a foot long, with small holes drilled throughout it. To Eames it looked like a bird feeder, lacking only the matchsticks for perches. "See, the holes are drilled on a bias, and the fuse is fitted snug, with a tin guard along the side"— Parsons picked up a strip of tin from the floor and held it alongside the pipe—"to protect the last half foot of fuse. The pipe, of course, is filled with gunpowder and, when that's done, we'll squeeze the ends together—"

"We'll get Land in to do that," Riddell interrupted, "he can bit 'em closed like he does his gun barrels—"

"—with a vise, of course, and then rivet the ends tight and, to make sure of a burst, we'll pour some hot lead in."

"What you'll have's a long-handled grenade," Riddell said, "a whole stock of 'em. I can't imagine any pit-cabin standing up to what these'll deliver."

"He may not be in the cabin," Eames said, 'he may be out in the open."

"You find 'im in the open and lob one of these—he'll be in the open, all right."

Riddell with a match lit his blackened cigar stub, amid guffaws from all of the men except Hersey. Hersey, who was always serious, had continued to sit on the floor and to tamper with some device, and now Riddell pointed to him. "You give ol' Herse here one a' these pipes to run with, like that torch he carried in Paris in '24—light the fuse first—an' he'll set a new Arctic record."

Hersey looked up from where he was sitting. He had been, as they all knew, an Olympic runner; he was still in good shape. "I don't carry grenades or shoot people," Hersey said simply.

"Son, you don't have to—you're in th' Signal Corps," Riddell said. There was a bantering edge to his voice, but it was good-humored. "Show th' Inspector the transmitter."

Hersey indicated without a word the portable transmitter between his legs: a field battery and a tube, with dry cells as filament supply. "It works," he said. "We're working on a receiver, too."

"Problem here," said Riddell, "is the rough sledding. We gotta figure out some sort a' box to keep it secure in, but we'll have it by—"

"Tomorrow," said Eames. "We're moving tomorrow. Wild?"

Wild, who had been sitting on a bunk at the far end of the barracks, moved reluctantly into the circle. "Yes, sir?"

"Has everybody been contacted, all the supplies requisitioned and the equipment issued?"

"More or less, sir."

"Well? More or less? What about"—Eames regarded the circle of men who were present: Riddell, Hersey, Verville, Sutherland, Parsons—"Carmichael? Has Frank been contacted?"

"No, sir."

"And Lazarus? Does he know he's going?"

"Not yet, sir."

"Not yet? Why, it's ten o'clock at night, man! We're leaving tomorrow morning. Tomorrow morning at 0800 hours," he said, turning to the men there assembled. "Has everybody drawn what he needs in the way of equipment, dog·feed, and weapons?"

The question, thus posed, had the desired effect. None of them had, and the trappers Verville and Sutherland hadn't even been told of the posse. They all, except Riddell, who knew what Eames was about and who often used the same tactics, turned on Wild and began demanding this or that item and accusing him of slackness. Riddell, rolling from one side of his mouth to the other the glowing cigar stub, resumed work on his goose eggs and winked at Eames as he left the barracks. Eames's last glimpse as he closed the door was of acting Quartermaster Wild in the midst of a badgering circle of men. It wouldn't hurt Wild to work all night, Eames reflected; he wouldn't work while they were gone.

Now as he stood outside the men's barracks, looking up at the night sky—the night was crisp and clear, though a stiff wind was rising, and he could see every star in the Hunter—Eames charged and lit his own pipe. Far above him the Hunter bestrode the winter night sky in splendid isolation: Eames liked the constellation for that. Also, for being the pattern into which the most stars could fit. As he stood outside the men's barracks puffing his pipe, he felt he should go visit Bunce but he disliked visiting hospitals and, mainly, he disliked . . . yes, the sick. Sickness was weakness, the sick were the weak; he had never been sick a day in his life and, while Bunce's was a special case and he genuinely felt for him, there was little he could say or do when he visited King, except talk about the so-called Mad Trapper, who undoubtedly was sick too. Bunce couldn't play cards yet, he couldn't read or be read to, he could scarcely sit up, and he seemed recently to have developed a sort of megalomaniac's interest in "the case" and the details of the siege, both of which subjects disturbed Eames. Really, he should visit Bunce, it would

be his last chance for several days...he turned toward
Mildred Urquhart's instead.

Mildred Urquhart was engrossed in a game of backgammon when he came in. Across from her, at the same
kitchen table and in the same place where Eames had
sat when he visited last, was her husband, reading a
newspaper but taking his turn when it came. James
was a quick and nonchalant player, while Mildred pon-
dered her moves; now she was intently studying the
board with the tip of her tongue thrust between her
teeth and her eyes shifting this or that man on the board
as she calculated her move. The dice had been thrown.
She glanced up at Eames as he entered, and gave a
peremptory wave of one hand, never breaking her concentration on the board. The doctor folded his newspaper largely, and held it like a shield between him
and the board and his wife, who was so intent on the
game. "Hallo, Inspector, it's been quite a while!" The
table was up against the wall on one side, with a chair
on each of its three exposed sides. Eames sat down quietly in the third chair, between the doctor and his wife.
"How's the reconstituted posse coming, Eames? Is this
second one bigger and better, and more determined, as
the newspaper says?"

"Is there..." Eames began in a normal voice, and
Mildred Urquhart glared fiercely at him, "is there
something in today's papers?" He whispered, and the
doctor nodded suavely.

"I'm afraid so," he said in a lowered voice, but not a
whisper. 'You won't like it, Eames, so why read it?" He
grinned urbanely at the Inspector, who was already
reaching for the newspaper.

"These things are my diversions," Eames answered
glumly. "Let's see."

"If neither of you wants to play with me," Mildred
Urquhart said sharply, "then don't. But the least you
could do is not interrupt when I'm already playing,
essentially, with myself." The doctor behind the newspaper which he passed to Eames raised his eyebrows
in mock fright. As he passed the newspaper he leaned

over behind it and whispered: "Interruption is more
than our first lady of Aklavik can endure. She has a
tiny little brow. Along with the tiny little brow, she
had hidden feelings. She is a lady, and a lady must be
deferred to. In a lady lurks an animal passion, but should
an act of passion be committed, nothing would remain
in her lady's soul but innocence." He wriggled his eyebrows again and leaned back while Eames, thoroughly
perplexed by this intelligence, held the paper and, forgetting himself, said aloud: "I was on my way to see
Bunce, I mean King..."

"That's *it!*" stormed Mildred Urquhart. "You two have
the manners of...hedgehogs!" She stood up in a flurry,
her face nearly livid, her "tiny little brow" agitated,
and her throat and neck above the sweater she wore,
Eames noticed, flushed and the vein in her throat palpitating.

"James has been baiting me all evening, Alex, I'm
not blaming you, you just gave him an occasion and,
believe me, he's always looking for an occasion to rile
me, it's his favorite pastime, it's his...perversion!" She
spit the last word like a bullet.

James, in response, stood up nonchalantly and said,
"I was, I admit, looking for an occasion to go make my
rounds, and now that you've provided that, Alex"—he
placed his left hand on Eames's shoulder—"I think I
shall, take my leave, that is. I'll leave you two lovebirds
to your game." He smiled mischievously, watching
Eames blush.

Mildred stared at Eames too, but compassionately.
It was clear to Eames that unfair advantage was being
taken by the doctor, and that she felt it directly. It was
at his, Eames's expense, but it might also be to his
advantage. While husband and wife stood and glared
at each other, Eames continued to sit stolidly in the
chair, clutching the newspaper. The doctor's hand left
his shoulder. "Here, take my place, Eames," he offered
congenially, and moved toward the front walk-in porch
where his parka hung. Mildred sat down and stared
straight ahead. Eames stayed where he was and stared

at the newspaper. "Really, Eames," said the doctor, returning, "why don't you take my spot? Mildred wants
to finish the game, and I don't. By the way, how's your
wart?" There was a lilt to his voice as he asked; Eames
knew it for banter.

"Fine," he said.

"Still holding its own?" Urquhart asked.

"Well, actually..." But he was cut off.

"If you're going, James, go—for God's sake!"

The doctor, unperturbed, wriggled his eyebrows at
Eames and, without a word, went. Mildred continued
to sit like a burning fuse, visibly seething, flaring up
now and again but not yet burnt down; slowly, as they
sat there (Eames was too distressed to read the newspaper at which he continued to stare) her pet subsided
and the fuse seemed to fizzle, then go out. Very deliberately, he got up and moved to the chair across from
her, vacated by Urquhart. He considered placing his
hand on her shoulder, but felt that too obvious, too
reminiscent of Urquhart's gesture. He studied the board.

Eames had never particularly liked backgammon,
but Mildred had taught him to play. Now he devoted
himself to the half-finished game as a diversion for her,
thinking it would be best if he let her win...but he
couldn't do that. A game was a game, rules were rules;
to play the game out was the least he could do—she
would probably win, anyway. He started to ask, Whose
move? but the cast dice showed it was hers. He looked
at her, she looked at the board, then she slowly reached
out her hand and with two of her men, blotted two of
his men. Eames cast his dice, doubles, and moved both
blotted men off the bar. Mildred threw, and was able,
except for her bar point, to bring all of her men into
her inner table. Eames, inheriting the doctor's nonchalant game, was far from bearing off. He cast his
dice, a five and a six, and studied the board.

"Alex," Mildred Urquhart said to him, and her voice
was soft and full-throated, "I'm sorry James said those
things to you. He shouldn't have"—here her voice hard-
ened slightly; Eames kept his eyes on the board—"he

shouldn't have, but...Alex, I want you to hold me"—
Eames kept his eyes on the board—"I want you to hold
me and touch me, Alex, and...and be gentle with me."

Eames swallowed and with sort of a blur before his
eyes passed an opportunity to blot one of her men. He
completed his move, and picked up his dice. Mildred
Urquhart gazed at him from across the table: her eyes
large, soft, limpid, her face beatific, her throat and neck
flushed with blood. Slowly and while still looking at
him, she reached out and touched his hand with her
fingertips. Eames, conscious only of the contact, swallowed noisily; it seemed noisily to him. There was an
extreme dryness in his mouth, and his lips seemed to
be pursing from lack of moisture. "Let's finish the game,"
she said in that fur-lined voice which Eames had heard
Urquhart describe so often as "a Mercedes-Benz, or a
Rolls-Royce hum—when everything's working just
right."

"Could I," he began in a voice exceedingly strange
to him, and very dry, "could I...have some water?"

"Of course," she said, and jumped up and brought
him a glassful. Standing at his shoulder, she handed
him the glass while her other hand brushed lightly his
neck and his shoulder and moved on down his arm,
withdrawing from him as soon as she touched him, but
in a lingering way. Eames had never been so discon-
certed. All his blood seemed to rush to the side she had
touched, and to certain other vital points of his anatomy.

"Let's finish the game," she said softly, and sat down.
Eames stared distractedly at the board, but saw only a
blur of points and circles, light and dark, within a rectangular box. He blinked his eyes and tried to concentrate, staring the more at the pieces.

"I can't," he said weakly.

"You can, but you don't want to, Alex," she scolded
him mildly. "It's because I'm winning, isn't it?" she
teased.

Eames looked at her helplessly.

"Never mind," she said, "come with me." And taking
him by his hand she led him through the living room,

which was lit with a lamp, into the bedroom, which was dark except for the light from the front room.

As soon as they passed through the doorway, she turned and pressed up against him, and holding his face with her hands kissed him again and again while rubbing her body against his. Eames, already overexcited, shot and she felt it and drew her hands slowly down the length of his body from his face to his groin, where she unbuckled and unzipped his duty pants, kissing him the whole while. Eames hardly knew what, if anything, to do. He was cognizant of the danger of the situation—should the doctor return and find them—but that didn't faze him; he was cognizant, too, of the fugitive nature of what they were about, and that Mildred might suddenly turn on him, as she had turned to him, in anger, but that didn't bother him either. Above all he was aware of an animal urgence detonating the sap of his body—as if he were an elephant who experienced rut only once every thirty-five years. And overborne by that dominant urgence his hands, which heretofore had moved checkers and initialed reports, groped their way as with a life of their own up under the closefitting sweater and full-laden bra till they rested at last on the globes of her warm and firm, full-bodied breasts. She meanwhile, ceasing to kiss him so vigorously, only brushing his neck or his cheek with her lips, pulled his duty pants together with his long underwear down over his hips—without help from him because his hands were employed—and proceeded quickly to unfasten and drop her own slacks. This done, she took hold of Eames's penis, which all this time had continued to drool, and with a combination of stroking and holding led him by it the few steps to the bed, and drew him down on top of her and, opening her legs to receive him, put his head at her lip and let him slide into her. Immediately Eames came again, and she tightened around him. Perceiving him shrinking, she moved fiercely around him, while Eames, not alarmed but physically tickled, shrunk more. While he withdrew further into himself, she wrapped her legs around him and grew more concentratedly agitated. But he continued to shrivel, while she continued to work, until there was nothing to work with. Finally she gave up. She released him and lay back, while he lay face down an appropriate few moments, sweaty from fear and exertion, extremely anxious to leave. "You can go," she said after a minute or so, without moving. "It's all right," she said, "go ahead."

Eames gingerly got off the bed and pulled up his long johns and zippered his pants, while she pulled a blanket onto her. Then he crept like a thief into the next room, pocketed the newspaper, and put his parka and boots on, and let himself out in the cold where the wind was still rising and the dogs were buried in snowdrifts. Eames's pants, which felt sticky and warm as he stood in the wind outside Mildred Urquhart's, began to stiffen and freeze. He groped in his pocket for his pipe, charged it and lit it, and strode across the clearing where, due to the air being filled with ice crystals, he could no longer make out the Hunter.

4

At the entrance to the hospital Eames nodded, passing beneath the Procrustean sign, to nurse McCabe, who was seated at the in-out desk in her nicely starched bright yellow nurse's uniform. It always reminded Eames of his favorite dessert, banana split. A brief little nurse's cap, also yellow, perched atop her coif of finely spun Irish red hair, like a tiara, and it was as a princess he had always regarded nurse McCabe, a princess in waiting on the crown prince (Urquhart), who was escort to the Queen (Mildred Urquhart), who seldom visited hospitals. But he did not regard her that way now, or, if he started to, did not complete the linkage. He was in a hurry, it was late—after 2300 hours—and he had much to do before the morning; this was merely one of many things which the Inspector of "G" Division, Western Arctic Sub-District, had to do tonight, as his brusque manner and brief nod (not to mention his stiff and frozen duty pants, the zipper of which he self-consciously checked) communicated, he hoped, to nurse McCabe. But there was time for courtesy, so long as the doctor wasn't around, and he seemed not to be; pressing affairs had not crowded the Inspector so utterly against the wall that he could not pause in his haste—on his errand of mercy, no less: a courtesy in itself—for a civil exchange with McCabe.

"How are you tonight, Moira?" he said fulsomely, and was aware as he said it of his male voice, his male

195

forthrightness, his male handling of the dipthong *oi* in
Moira—in short, of his voice and manner and approach
to the desk and the nurse as a voice and manner of
approach permeated with maleness. Nurse McCabe
seemed to appreciate this.

"Fine, Inspector," she said, tilting her tiaraed head
ever so slightly, "and yourself?"

"Busy, Moira: busy, busy—all this posse business...." His voice trailed off, suggestive of untold personal dangers and countless administrative details. "But
I wanted to see our patient before I left." (There was
room for compassion, even in wartime; there was chiv-
alry even here in the Arctic.) "How is he?"

"He's probably sleeping," nurse McCabe said, "but
you can wake him, Inspector."

This was a concession, Eames realized, and he was
grateful. "Thank you, Moira," he said, and moved toward the ward door.

"He's in room three now, Inspector. The doctor may
be in with him," she said. Eames panicked at this intelligence. "No, I don't think he is." This counterin-
telligence comforted him. "This way."

Eames followed nurse McCabe down a narrow hallway, past the room where he'd had his wart examined,
and another darkened room, to a door with a "3" painted
on it. As she opened the door into the room, dark but
for a night-light, Eames spied a single iron-posted cot
and on it a covered bulk, shroudlike and still.

"He's sleeping," she whispered.

Seeing the actual animal bulk of the sick man, and
feeling the muted atmosphere of the sickroom, Eames
hesitated. He had nothing whatever to say to the sick
man worth waking him for, and no news to report. He
was busy mounting his posse, King was asleep convalescing; he would have to break stride in his drive to
get Johnson, and King would have to wake up, all this
in the dark and middle of the night, when nothing good
could come of it. Why had he come? Was he so corrupted
with sentiment that he had to disturb a sick man? Or
was it atonement of sorts for his last misdeed—a good
deed canceling a bad? "It's all right," he whispered,

shrinking back at the door, and lying: "I'll come back tomorrow."

But nurse McCabe had already found and switched on the overhead light, and was calling, "Corporal King?" And now she was shaking him—a true daughter of Erin—and commanding him, "Wake up! The Inspector is here."

King, who was asleep on his side with his face to the wall, started awake and rolled over. "Huhh?"

"Easy now," nurse McCabe ordered, holding him down. "He has trouble getting to sleep," she said over her shoulder to the Inspector, who shrank further against the wall, "then he has trouble waking up. Don't you?" she said and, quickly checking his chest bandage and the one rubber tube leading into or out of King, Eames couldn't tell which, she brusquely left them alone in the room, closing the door behind her.

Eames ventured over to the bedside and looked down at King, whose wound, more than two weeks old, was still draining blood and pus. The bandage, a huge wad of gauze taped right around his ribs, was soaked at the bottom, and oozing an orange-colored fluid. King noticed Eames looking at it, looked at it himself, and reached for a tissue from a box on the bed table, wiped the orange-colored pus from his stomach, and tossed the tissue into the corner. Then he placed his hands on either side of his hips and pushed himself up in the bed to a half-sitting, half-prone position. Still holding his upper body free from the bed with his hands, he indicated with his head the pillow. "Push it up?" he said in a strained voice. Eames hurried to comply. "A little higher. That's it." The voice was strained and abrupt, and Eames let go of the pillow exactly where King said to. King rested his head and upper back against the pillow. The position, to Eames, looked uncomfortable, but King let go of the bed with his hands and closed his eyes. "That's fine," he said, "fine. What time is it?"

"It's"—Eames looked at his watch—"exactly 2317, nearly midnight."

"What day?"

"Friday, January 15th. Almost the 16th, Saturday."

Eames wasn't sure what to say next. Perhaps King had his eyes closed because of the light. "You want the light out?" he said.

King lay with his eyes closed, not answering. Finally he said, "I'm in a hospital, aren't I?" Eames nodded, though King's eyes were still closed. "I heard horses' hooves. They came nearer and nearer and got louder and louder—in the hallway, I think. When I asked, 'Who is it?' a voice said, 'None other than Zebulon Pike!'" King opened his eyes and looked at Eames. "Zebulon Pike," he repeated, and shrugged, but the shrug was with his shoulders only, there was animal pain in his eyes. "I see things a lot, chief. It's those bloody pain-killers they give me." Having given Eames a searching look, King closed his eyes again. "They keep me half drugged," he said, after an interval. "Doc says I'll be okay."

King lay with his eyes closed, breathing regularly. The tube to his wrist, which Eames decided was intravenous, brought clear liquid from a bottle on a stand beside the bed. The chest wound was dripping again, an orange pus. "You look fine," Eames lied.

King continued to lie quietly on the bed. After a minute or two, he started slightly and half opened his eyes. Seeing Eames, he said, "Zeb Pike again," and grinned horribly for a moment, then closed his eyes and his facial muscles relaxed.

Seeing King asleep, or nearly so, was like observing an animal closely. Eames felt as if a human being inside the animal form were making fun of him. But it didn't ire him. On the contrary, watching King sleep he thought: 'If you've seen a person sleeping, you can never hate him again. Even Johnson, caught sleeping and unaware, would not be hateful.' King's body jerked, and his eyes half opened again. "Not much company," he said dopily. "Good...see you." Eames took this as a signal to leave, and opening the door, turned out the light. He left King's sleeping form in the darkened room as he had found it, and walked as softly as he could down the hallway, trying not to sound like a horse. On his way past the desk, nurse McCabe said to him: "Did he tell you about Zebulon Pike?"

Eames nodded sadly.

"There's an Eskimo in room four from Old Crow, claims he's part of the 'Lost Patrol,' Sometimes he says that, other times he says he's Corporal W. J. D. Dempster."

"Maybe he is," said Eames, "maybe we all are."

Nurse McCabe glanced at Eames quizzically. "No, I'm Zebulon Pike," she said. "See?" And she hitched her skirt up slightly to show him her high heels and, Eames noticed, her ankles, her calves, and the line of her thighs beneath the skirt.

"So you are," he said. And, experiencing an erection against his duty pants still stiff with less than an hour's old semen, he stifled the impulse to say, "Very nice," though he thought it. What was happening to him? All of a sudden, after years of hard work and moral rectitude, was he being led around by his penis? In his very own district, of which he was Inspector, he had the impulse to fuck nurse McCabe—right there in the mission hospital!—where he would, no doubt, be discovered by the resident surgeon, whose wife he had just fucked! What was happening to him? Had he become a womanizer? Would he have to set himself against women as he had against alcohol? What had happened? What was happening? Who was Zebulon Pike? Eames hastily pulled on his mitts and drew up his hood and headed for the outer door, stooping unnecessarily under Procrustes. "Must run," he flung over his shoulder, and heaved open the door and breathed in a deep draft of ice crystals. The wind was blowing more now than it had even twenty minutes ago, and fumbling in his parka pocket for his pipe he discovered the unread newspaper. This he grasped at as at a straw as he hurried head down across the windy clearing toward the detachment office.

The office was dark, and as he switched on the light his glance was drawn to the box marked "Outgoing" with the letter to Rene on top of a stack of letters—

letters to the Commandant in Ottawa, to Area Superintendent Acland in Edmonton, to the Inspector of the
Yukon Division in Old Crow, and copies of cables to all
of the above as well as to the Hudson's Bay in Mc-
Pherson requesting supplies, to Northwest Airways in
Edmonton requesting an airplane (an oddball idea of
Riddell's), to the Director of Signals in Ottawa with a
description of Johnson—letters and cables and, now,
newspapers: the whole thing had got out of hand. Eames
sat down behind his desk and, taking his pipe from his
pocket, scraped its bowl with a knife. Black grains of
carbon fell out on the piece of white paper he'd laid out.
Then he dipped his index finger in the bowl of dirty
honey, turned his finger quickly, and brought the honey
to bear on his pipe bowl. He smeared it with honey,
charged it with tobacco, and lit it. Then, like a man
who has taken his last meal or made out his will, he
pulled the crumpled newspaper out of his pocket and
unfolded it before him. The story was on the front page:

POLICE PLAN NEW ATTEMPT TO TAKE MAN
Mounties Preparing for Third
Assault on Cabin of Albert Johnson
(Exclusive to Edmonton Bulletin)

AKLAVIK, Jan. 14—Electric lights in the
R.C.M.P. headquarters here blazed night and day
as Inspector A.N. Eames and his helpers prepared
for a third attempt to blast Albert Johnson from
his hide-out overlooking the frozen Rat River, following two repulses from the demented trapper's
smoking guns when he resisted arrest on a charge
of attempted murder of Constable A. W. King.

"This time we'll get him—get him dead or
alive," Inspector Eames grimly promised.

From a cache of dynamite left here by Dominion Explorers, home-made bombs are being fash-
ioned to toss into the cabin dugout of the crazed
trapper. Ammunition pouches are being reloaded.
Lee-Enfields and Colts are being overhauled to

make sure they function perfectly when the final test comes in the Arctic darkness around Johnson's battered stronghold.

"Three times and out," is the slogan of the bigger and better patrol leaving soon for a final test with the gunman who came out of the western hills, a man of mystery, origin unknown, who now is the most talked about man in the northland.

PLANS LAID

Plans for the attack have now been laid. Johnson will be given the customary chance to come out and give himself up. If this fails, then it will be a fight to the end.

Under cover of the Arctic darkness, lit only by the flickering dimness of the northern lights, muffled fur-clad figures—the volunteers for the forlorn hope—will inch forward on their stomachs through the snow with rifles at the ready and bombs in their hands. Like slinking shadows they will worm their way forward from tree to tree through the thick timber which encircles the low cabin.

A final word of command, and the rifles of the covering party will fire a volley.

Under cover of the sleet of lead smacking and smashing into Johnson's log defence, the bombers will dash forward and hurl their missiles into the cabin.

A grim relic of a narrow escape from death was brought back by Karl Gardlund, one of the Arctic trappers who accompanied the redcoat patrol. It is a shattered electric flashlight and was carried by Gardlund in the first stealthy advance on the silent cabin under the shadowing spruce. As the light flashed on, a gun flashed in answer from the cabin and a bullet clanked against the flashlight, shattering it. Gardlund was fortunately unharmed. This incident taught the posse a new respect for their defiant opponent.

DYNAMITE CACHE

F. M. Welton, Arctic trapper wintering in the city, stated that he had 1,100 pounds of dynamite cached at Aklavik, and this store will likely be used by the police in their final joust with the wanted man.

Two members of the posse which was routed by Johnson's blazing guns have been left in the hills to keep an eye on the future activities of Johnson while the posse prepares to invade his territory again.

It is believed that he will stand to his guns and grimly await the renewed onset of his attackers. As a bushman he must know that it would be hopeless under present weather conditions to take to the hills with a meagre pack. He would soon be run down, if he didn't perish of exposure first. And his chances in a gun-battle in the open would not be as good as they would be if he stayed entrenched in his dugout.

The base of the new patrol will be established at the mouth of the Rat River, 20 miles downstream from the cabin, and 60 miles from Aklavik, so that plenty of supplies and ammunition for the prolonged siege can be brought in by dog team from Aklavik and Arctic Red River.

Eames, although he had steeled himself for the worse, sat flummoxed and dumbfounded. It read like a report of what he ought to be doing, but wasn't, by someone familiar both with him and Aklavik. Definitely an "inside job"—no doubt about it. Eames puffed his pipe and dabbed his finger in the honey at the same time, removed his pipe and put his finger in his mouth, put his pipe back and with his licked finger turned the page of the newspaper. Articles about the moratorium on German reparations, and a corporal named Hitler making a bargain with Chancellor Bruening, about Japan's seizure of a Chinese-British rail line, about Gandhi being sentenced to prison—these and a large boxed ad for *The Sin of Madelon Claudet* had been relegated to the second and third pages; the Johnson manhunt and a City Council vote in favor of half-holidays on Wednesdays were front-page news, with Inspector Eames grimly promising to "get him—get him dead or alive." He could sue. First, though, he had to apprehend Johnson, wrap up the case, file the report, wash his hands of the dirty business. He turned back to the front page. "F. M. Welton." "Dominion Explorers." "1,100 pounds of dynamite cached at Aklavik, and this store will likely be used by the police." Maybe Wild knew about this, or Riddell. If there were such a cache—though where it was stored Eames couldn't imagine—he should know about it. The Inspector of all people shouldn't be sitting on top of a keg like that, and having to send to McPherson for piddling charges! It was outrageous, the whole situation. Eames felt like resigning.

His watch clicked and he glanced at it—2400 hours, plus a few seconds. This was the day he had scheduled for the showdown with Johnson. This was the fateful shoot-out date, after which he would deal with the carpers and critics who dogged and dictated his tracks. He was pondering what to do next, when Wild walked through the door. With him was Parsons, the old ex-Mountie, carrying two homemade goose eggs.

"I saw the lights blazing, chief, and we wanted to store these things here."

Eames glowered at him and stood slowly up, tapping with his sticky finger the newspaper which lay on his desk.

"Have you seen this...this rag?" he said threateningly, "the Edmonton *Bulletin,* yesterday's."

"Not yesterday's, chief. I saw the day before yesterday's. Put 'em right here, John." Parsons laid down the two bombs carefully, and covered them with a newspaper. "I didn't know yesterday's had come in. What'd it say?"

"The day before yesterday's," Eames corrected himself. "You saw it, then?"

"I saw it, chief."

"That's all I wanted to know," Eames said. He sat down.

"Well, if that's all, sir, we'll be off. Lots to do before tomorrow morning."

"*This* morning," Eames corrected him.

"This morning, sir, right. Have a good sleep, sir." Wild backed out through the door. Parsons' eyes twinkled, but he said nothing. Parsons, who had closely cropped steel gray hair and a salt-and-pepper beard, had been a Mountie when things were simpler, Eames reflected. They had never worked with each other, but got along well. Eames always felt in Parsons' company a resonant and supportive presence, like looking at old copies of *The Force*. Eames cast Parsons a disgruntled look. Parsons shook his head.

"Take it easy, Eames," he said in a voice that always sounded to Eames like an impersonation of God's. Parsons was the only person Eames knew who could make clichés sound profound. "We'll get the show mounted. All you need to do is give orders and make decisions, we'll do the rest. What do you care what those lunkheads down south say?"

"I suppose so," said Eames, "but..."

"Get some rest," Parsons said reassuringly in his deeply bass voice like God's. Then, like God, he went out, shutting the door behind him.

Eames stood up and paced lionlike between the desk and the window, between the file cabinet and the water cooler, beneath King George the Fifth's portrait. After six or seven turns he broke off abruptly, threw the newspaper into the wastebasket, turned off the light, and entered his small sleeping porch. Lighting and trimming the kerosene lantern, he undressed (all but his long johns, which were stiff around the codpiece) and crawled into bed. He sat for a moment so, staring at the chiffonier top, then picked up *Morte Darthur* and commenced reading where he had left off three hours ago:

Now sir Mordred when he was escaped from sir Lancelot he got his horse and mounted upon him and rode unto king Arthur sore wounded and all forbled, and there he told the king all how it was, and how they were all slain save himself alone.

'Ah! Jesu, mercy! How may this be?' said the king. 'Took ye him in the queen's chamber?'

'Yea, so God me help,' said sir Mordred, 'there we found him unarmed, and anon he slew sir Coll-grevaunce and armed him in his armour.' And so he told the king from the beginning to the ending.

'Jesu mercy!' said the king, 'he is a marvellous knight of prowess. And alas,' said the king, 'me sore repenteth that ever sir Lancelot should be against me, for now I am sure the noble fellowship of the Round Table is broken for ever, for with him will many a noble knight hold. And now it is fallen so,' said the king, 'that I may not with my worship but my queen must suffer death,' and was sore amoved...

Eames suddenly pulled his foot out from under the covers and started scratching the sole vigorously. After a minute or two of this he laid the book face down on the covers and padded into the bathroom, got his British Army Foot Powder, padded back and applied it, then picked up the book again. His eye scanned the page for where he had left off, and began reading at

'In the name of God,' said the king, 'then make you ready, for she shall have soon her judgement....'

There followed a long passage about the building of the fire to burn the queen, the shriving of the queen by her personal bishop, the weeping of her ladies-in-waiting, and the gathering of the knights of King Arthur's Round Table—each of them called by name: a long list—at the pyre where the queen was to be burned. All this Eames scanned cursorily, until sir Lancelot rode onto the field and fought his way to the fire.

...And so in this rushing and hurling, as sir Lancelot thrang here and there, it misfortuned him to slay sir Gaheris and sir Gareth, the noble knight, for they were unarmed and unwares. As the French book saith, sir Lancelot smote sir Gaheris and sir Gareth upon the brain-pans, wherethrough that they were slain in the field. Howbeit in very truth sir Lancelot saw them not. And so were they found dead among the thickest of the press.

Then sir Lancelot, when he had thus done, and slain and put to flight all that would withstand him, then he rode straight unto queen Guenevere and made cast a kirtle and a gown upon her, and then he made her to be set behind him and prayed her to be of good cheer. Now wit you well the queen was glad that she was at that time escaped from the death, and then she thanked God and sir Lancelot....

Eames yawned and set down the book and turned out the bed lamp. In the cool dark of his sleeping porch, snug and warm under his covers, he could hear the wind whistling outside and a dog howling. It would be windy and cold tomorrow, hard sledding against the wind as far as the Rat, and then drifts to contend with—the die was cast, though. What was his last cast? A five and a six—eleven—then she threw a double, snake eyes. To say the least. He felt, tentatively, his stiff codpiece; his prick like a blunderbuss recently primed rose miraculously under the covers. Nurse McCabe. He wondered what *she* would feel like—like dipping his finger in honey? The ladies-in-waiting...the queen...the king of the mountain...In his dream Eames was unhorsed by Zebulon Pike and orange pus dripped from his brainpan, but up the hill he kept charging, rushing and hurling, and as he thrang here and there on his way up the hill, he was flanked by both Bruening and Hitler and Japanese admirals, behind whom were ships, planes, and tanks. Eames kept on charging, bleeding and charging, urging his allies who walked behind him, behind as enemies walk, but the woman on top of the mountain was Mildred, despoiled and shriven for burning, or one of her ladies, a lady whose smock he could see up from his defilade down the hill. Up the steep hill he fought, waving with both hands his blunderbuss which weighed thirty-five pounds and squirted liquid fire and ammonia; like a wounded dragon he mounted the hill, dressed only in long underwear. All the rest were in uniform: tunics and striped pants and braid caps and gloves—the murderous uniforms. Only Zebulon Pike was less well dressed than Eames; he was naked—still Pike held the hill. Dreadnoughts and Mark IV tanks, biplanes and dirigibles were advancing against him, bunkers and batteries were trained on his position, armies of marching men carrying forests of banners were surrounding his stronghold—still Pike held the hill. And there were masses of reporters and photographers on neighboring mountains, writing stories and popping flashbulbs—the pressmen outnumbered the soldiers four to one. "We learned in 1848 that one against four was not a good ratio; two against three is better." It was Bismarck to Hitler, behind Eames's back. Still Eames fought on, onward and upward, oozing orange pus from his brainpan and drooling white fire from his thirty-five-pound blunderbuss, pushing Zeb Pike up, back, and over...Then he too saw what everyone else had been watching for a long time, what the reporters had been taking notes and the photographers flashing pictures of, what Hitler and Bruening and the Japanese admirals had all stopped to stare at and fallen into dispute about, and even King George the Fifth stood off to the side looking at it—a sign, which said simply "Pike's Peak." Eames saw it too. Zebulon Pike stood behind it. Then a voice like John Parsons' voice said: "This is Pike's Peak, and Pike's Peak it shall remain!" Some said it thundered; others said it was a voice. Eames was undecided, but inclined to agree with the side that said...Everyone forgot the queen....

5

POSSE PASSES SLEEPLESS NIGHT
PREPARING BOMBS, RADIO SINGLE
MEN'S BARRACKS BESIEGED BY WOMEN
An Eye-Witness Account by a
Roving Correspondent

AKLAVIK, Jan. 16—Electric lights blazed in
the single men's barracks in Aklavik as members
of the second "Mad Trapper" posse were rounded
up and brought in around midnight and told by
Corporal Richard Wild, acting quartermaster, to
"get some sleep." In addition to Corporal Wild and
Signal Corps sergeants R. F. Riddell and E. F.
Hersey, trappers Ernest Sutherland, Noel Verville, and Frank Carmichael, ex-Mountie John
Parsons, and Eskimo driver Lazarus Sittichiulis
were crowded into the barracks, where there are
bunks only for four. Three of these bunks are used
regularly by the mounted policemen. The fourth
bunk has been assigned to ex-Mountie Parsons.
Floor space, usually available, is taken up with
radio equipment and the litter left over from the
construction, earlier in the day, of what Sergeant
Riddell calls "goose eggs." These are dynamite
bombs intended to aid the posse in blasting the
"Mad Trapper" out of his stronghold on the Rat

River. It is felt by Sergeant Riddell that the posse,
armed with his goose eggs, will be able to "blow
the——to Kingdom Come!"

WHAT'S UP?

Quartermaster Sergeant Riddell and Staff Sergeant Hersey stayed up most of the night constructing a sheet metal box in which to carry a
field radio. The portable transmitter-receiver,
which operates on dry cells and weighs forty-five
pounds, is intended to keep the posse in two-way
contact with station UZK, Aklavik. Until 2:00 A.M.,
when amateur station UZK signed off, "the Voice
of the Arctic" Jimmy Ludlow could be heard in
the barracks broadcasting his nightly program,
"What's Up?" Albert Johnson, the Mad Trapper,
was loose in the delta, and Inspector Eames of the
Arctic was mounting his second big posse. The
posse was being quartered at the single men's barracks, and solitary trappers and wives of trappers
were asked to come into the compound. Albert
Johnson was described as follows:

Age	35 to 40 years
Weight	about 175 lbs.
Height	about 5 ft. 8 in.
Build	stocky; walks with habitual stoop
Hair	light colored
Eyes	light blue
Speech	believed to have a slight Scan- dinavian accent

Johnson is armed, and is a good sapper and a good
shot. Inspector Eames wants every available man
as soon as possible from all districts fully equipped.
Johnson is to be shot on sight. After 2:00 A.M. the
Voice of the Arctic signed off, and there was loud
and continuous static throughout the men's barracks.

WOMEN ARRIVE

At 2:30 A.M. trapper Noel Verville's wife arrived at the men's barracks. Felicia Verville has long been known as one of the most outspoken women in the Arctic, and it was she who organized the Trappers' Wives Against Fur Traders movement last year. Mrs. Verville complained about the quartering of the posse, and said she refused to sleep by herself. "I'll be——if I'm going to sleep in that shack without Noel," she stated to Sergeant Riddell. With Mrs. Verville were several other women, all of them the wives of trappers who were out on their traplines. They too were afraid to stay at home by themselves because of the madman. They had heard about Johnson over station UZK, Aklavik. Sergeant Riddell told them that the Mad Trapper only molested white women and Mounted Policemen, that he had never been known to harm trappers or natives. This quieted all of the women except Felicia Verville. She asked Sergeant Riddell was he scared?

"Yes, ma'am, I'm scared," Sergeant Riddell said, "as a Mountie, I'm scared."

"And you're only half a Mountie," Mrs. Verville responded. "I should be scared too, being a woman and half white."

She referred to the fact that Sergeant Riddell was attached to the Signal Corps, and not to the regular Force.

Sergeant Riddell replied that Mrs. Verville was right about his being "only half a Mountie," and that "goose eggs, or no goose eggs," he and Sergeant Hersey and the Signal Corps dog team were not budging another step toward the Rat until they had been properly sworn in and pay-rated. The newer members of the posse, trappers Ernest Sutherland, Noel Verville, and Frank Carmichael, expressed agreement with Sergeant Riddell, and Corporal Wild was dispatched to detachment HQ with this message for Inspector

Eames. Inspector Eames, who was already in bed, sent word back that there would be a swearing-in ceremony "first thing in the morning."

So there was a division, on the eve of the manhunt, between certain members of the posse. By 4:00 A.M. the ladies had been escorted home, the barracks were quiet, and the members of the posse slept until 7:00 A.M.

POSSE OUTFITTED

Buffeted by gale-force winds and numbed by −40° F temperature, the drivers fed and harnessed their dog teams. The dogs were so heavily drifted in snow that they had to be found by tracing their chains, then dug out. The dogs were coaxed out of their tunnels with fish, and by a combination of coaxing and kicking were finally put into harness. Sergeant Hersey, in charge of the Signal Corps team, had less trouble with dogs than the other drivers, due to his lead dog, Silver. Sergeant Hersey has developed a fond relationship with his lead dog, and when in the field sleeps with him. This is unusual among Mounties and trappers in the North, and unheard of among native drivers. By 8:00 A.M. all of the teams were harnessed, and the drivers took turns holding each other's teams while one by one they trooped in to eat breakfast and to draw their equipment. Sergeant Riddell served oatmeal and tea, while Corporal Wild issued Lee-Enfields and .303 shells. As each man picked up his ammunition and took his rifle down out of the rack, acting Quartermaster Wild checked his name off the list he carried around on a clipboard. Sergeant Hersey picked up a rifle and shells for Sergeant Riddell, who was busy packing and loading the portable radio.

INSPECTOR EAMES ARRIVES

By 8:45 A.M. all the dogs and men had been fed, the equipment issued, the transmitter-receiver loaded, the teams drawn up at the door, and ex-

Mountie Parsons and Corporal Wild had gone to
the detachment office to inform Inspector Eames
that all was ready. Promptly at 9:00 A.M. Inspector
A. N. Eames of the Arctic arrived. Due to the blizzard he was not able to speak to the members of
the posse, but he went from sled to sled, patting
the men on the shoulder and encouraging them.
After he had mingled with his men, Inspector
Eames, his back to the wind, faced the members
of the posse and held up his right hand. Some of
the men held up their right hands, some did not.
Inspector Eames then spoke some words, which
were lost in the blizzard, took his place on the
lead sled, and signaled the driver to start. Thus
were the members of the posse, including the Signal Corps men, sworn in under Arctic conditions.

Inspector Eames rode the sled driven by Special
Constable Sittichiulis, Sergeant Riddell was riding the Signal Corps sled driven by Sergeant
Hersey, ex-Mountie Parsons was on Mr. Sutherland's sled, and Messrs. Carmichael and Verville
drove the sleds with dog feed and extra equipment.

Present at the posse's departure from Aklavik
were Felicia Verville, wife of Noel Verville, acting
Quartermaster Richard Wild, and surgeon James
Urquhart. Mrs. Verville was dressed in a white
foxfur parka with wolverine trim, and blue
Hudson's Bay windpants. Representing the women
of Aklavik on this historic occasion, she was quite
striking in her farewells. Dr. Urquhart reported
that Corporal A. W. King, who was wounded by
the fugitive Johnson on December 31 of last year,
is past the critical stage and recovering nicely.
The posse of eight men and thirty-five dogs will
rendezvous with a special patrol already on the
Rat River where the notorious Mad Trapper,
Albert Johnson, is believed to be hiding.

January 16: An hour out from Aklavik the blizzard
struck with full force. The rider could not see his driver.

the driver could not see his dogs. Everywhere the same
gray frenzy of snow, confusing and covering everything.
The lead team proceeded by instinct, the lag teams by
smell. Steerage by sight was impossible. Each driver
followed the driver in front, the lead driver followed his
dogs. The posse proceeded blindly along the Mackenzie.
No bench marks to measure miles by. Nothing to measure time by except the slowing of one's own reflexes
and the dogs' pace. Frostbite and tiredness marked
time—four hours. Freezing and exhaustion—eight
hours. Where the Peel joined with the Mackenzie, the
lead team instinctively turned. No signal was given,
for no one knew where the turn was. Most of the drivers
were not aware that the river had forked, or that the
dogs had turned. Few of the drivers had any idea where
they were.

Where the Husky enters the Peel, the dogs halted.
It was now well after midnight, the blizzard still blowing, the men numb with cold, the dogs frantic with
hunger. The Inspector warmed himself and had tea,
then insisted on pushing on to the mouth of the Rat.
The river was drifting badly. The direction in which
the posse was headed had changed, from south to west.
The wind had been in the men's faces; now the drifts
were against them. The Inspector spoke to each of the
drivers. The drifts had to be broken through before they
got bigger. The dogs were rested and fed and again set
in motion.

The dogs tired quickly. The "Z" curve where the Peel
and Husky and Rat come together was choked with
drifts. Some drifts were fifty feet high. These mountains
of snow were impossible to go around, and had to be
scaled with tired dogs. Step by step the dogs balked.
Sled after sled was a tangle of strangling dogs and dog
harness bogged down in powdery snow pits drift after
drift. A few hundred yards and six hours later the posse
pulled up at the mouth of the Rat. The blizzard still
blew, but the dogs refused to go further and burrowed
holes in the snow. When beaten, they attacked one another. Each man lay down where he was, no one pitched
a tent.

Temperature: −40° (plus wind). Mileage: 60.

January 17: The snow has constructed a common grave covering men, equipment, and dogs. Soundless, painless, and warm, the posse lies under cover of snow while the blizzard howls fitfully. Strong gusts are followed by lulls, the lulls getting longer and the gusts getting shorter, but under the snow all is quiet. Under cover of snow I lie awake, remembering when I was dead. It was like this—soundless, painless, and warm. But it was above ground, in the air. The frozen sea stretched ahead endlessly, the frozen ground lay behind, and there were no trees. I was in an ice cave, surrounded by air. In the flat level distance were figures on an ice floe, but the figures were not men, but seals. The seals were the only creatures as far as the eye could see, and the eye could see everywhere, ocean and tundra, wherever the eye looked, there it went, and there was no water or land beyond it, and no trees at all, only ice. I was the eye. When I looked at the seals I was with them. When I looked away, I was there. Wherever I looked, there I was, and everywhere all was at rest and frozen, even the seals. The seals did not play, or fish, as seals do. They lay frozen on the ice floe, the ice floe lay frozen in the sea, only the eye could move, drift, or shut. Slowly it drifted away from the ice floe, it drifted away out of sight. Then there was nothing, no animals. Nothing to name, nothing to fear, nothing to know for all was the same, all was known. With nothing to look at and nowhere to go, the eye shut. It stayed shut until I felt heat and pain, first my hands, then my feet being rubbed with the oil, heat from the blessed candles, and saw shadows of men on the igloo walls, and in my mouth tasted the host and in my ears heard the words *Corpus Domini*...it was Candlemas Day. Then I was told I was frozen and had been dead for four days and that my name had been changed.

The posse lies covered with snow. Hummocks of snow mark the dogs, larger hummocks the men. I step around them like graves in a graveyard, but they will wake up when a fire is built for them. From the bank snow-covered trees slant out over the river. Masses of snow

supported by trees or suspended in air loom above me.
The alder brush at the top of the bank has drifted over
completely, and a piece of dry wood breaks beneath me:
a drying rack pole. An Indian dog starts to bark. No
one comes out of the tent. The Loucheux have always
been lazy, even for Indians.

An hour later one of the Indians wanders into our
camp. Immediately he is surrounded by armed men,
Eames asking questions, Parsons translating. The
Indian's hand dipped into his buckskins, and out with
a wad of paper. It had been peed on. Johnson has left
his cabin and taken his outfit, signed Millen. How it
got in the Indian's buckskins nobody knows. Another
round of questions from Eames, while Parsons translates. The Indian claims he was sent to Aklavik, but
circled back in the blizzard. He is on his way now, he
tells Parsons, who translates. This goes on for some
while, the Indian saying he wants to go, Eames telling
him he doesn't need to go, until finally Eames says he
is Aklavik. The Indian looked at Eames strangely, then
pointed up the hill. He said he was his camp, and pointed
a hand without fingers. This affected Eames strangely.
He asked Parsons to ask how it happened, and to translate exactly. The answer, a beaver trap four years ago,
persuaded Eames that this man would make a good
tracker. The fact that Millen had sent a message by
him vouched, he said, for the fellow's discretion. All of
the Indians here are discreet, silence is as natural to
them as mud to a pig.

At length all of his buddies were brought down, and
taking this veteran tracker and his ten cronies in tow
Eames insisted that we push on upriver. He wanted to
get past Johnson's old cabin, now that Johnson was no
longer there. The blizzard was fitfully blowing itself
out. The banks on both sides were visible, gray walls
above a gray floor. Eames rode turned around, his back
to the wind, his natives jogging alongside. None of them
ran close to me. The little black dog trotted ahead, just
out of range of the dogs. We passed Johnson's cabin
around 4:00 P.M.

Temperature holding. Wind SSE. Mileage: 24.

January 18: The mountains are there, so is Johnson.
The mountains stand, bare and enormous, they defy
anybody to cross them. A man who has got this far,
unless he is wounded, will try to go over. If he is wounded,
he will wait until he is fit, then try. The mountains
draw like a magnet and it is instinct—as a rabbit returns to his hold or a dog to his vomit—human instinct
to try to go over. I myself have tried, but in summer. I
remember the cut, McDougall Pass, the high steep walls,
and how the sun never stood high enough to reach down
into the crease. It was cold there, even in summer. But
there were no mosquitoes. All through breakfast and
the feeding of Eames and his Indians, and the tending
of the dogs, everyone watched the mountains and
thought, 'Johnson is there.'

After breakfast Eames called the posse together. He
had talked with his trackers and they had assured him
that Johnson would not try the mountains. The posse
would search the channels and blinds of the Rat to the
east and the south. Eames, with his back to the mountains, pointed in the direction we had come from and
toward the sun, which beamed on the mountains behind
him. Parsons translated. We stood at the edge of the
delta overlooking a swale, beyond it were foothills. The
swale was level and white, swept with a skiff of new
snow. If Johnson had walked here, no one would know
it. He could be holed up nearby, watching us, and we
would not know it. The snow covers everything. We
have food and dog feed enough for only four days, but
Eames says that experienced trackers can do the job in
a short time. Parsons translates. Eames and the Indians
will search to the east, everyone else will comb the
south Rat. Riddell will stay in camp to keep radio contact. Since Millen and Gardlund are out there somewhere, no one is to shoot on sight.

Hersey nods and strides over to Silver. About 125
pounds Silver weighs, and eats more than his share of
whitefish. While the rest of us looked at the mountains
and at one another, Silver jumped up on Hersey. Hersey
rubbed Silver's stomach and talked into his ear. If Johnson is found, it will be Hersey who finds him. Not that

Hersey is such a good tracker, but he is competitive.
He and Silver are the first to leave camp, then Suther-
land and Verville, Carmichael and Parsons, and finally
Eames in my sled with his Indians jogging behind.

The mountains, three peaks and two passes, moved
further away to the west. The mouth of the Rat opened
up at the edge of the delta and swallowed us: dogs, sleds,
and men. Now only the peaks could be seen getting
shorter and the trees getting taller, then only the trees
stoop-shouldered with snow, planted in snow, joined by
snow. There were no tracks. A few faint imprints left
by birds, a few holes around the skirts of trees where
snow had fallen from branches, a few shadows of
branches. All tracks, animal and human, had been
buried by the blizzard. Moose were yarded up for the
winter, bear and beaver and otter and muskrat were
in hibernation, lynx and fox and rabbits would only
now be venturing out of their holes. Johnson was holed
up too somewhere, but not where I drove Eames while
his Indians ran alongside, jogging off here and there
whenever Eames pointed to a hole or a shadow. And
the little black dog made so much racket that, had Johnson been there, he would have heard us two miles away.
But he wasn't there, no trapper would be. He was heading for the mountains behind us, his back to us, or holed
up in the foothills watching us as we searched the Rat.

We returned the way we had come. The sun sank in
the south and we came out of the gray cold delta into
the white cold swale, the mountains bare and enormous
beyond us, blue cold. Riddell was still working at getting his radio going, he could receive but couldn't transmit. Bannock and beans were served up. Jimmy
Ludlow's "What's Up?" came on. Felicia Verville was
organizing Wives of Trappers Against the Mad
Trapper. Constable King was improving. We heard Corporal Wild for ten minutes at seven, eight, nine, and
ten o'clock, then loud static for another ten minutes,
then Jimmy Ludlow. The radio was left on all night,
with loud music and crackling static. After the ten
o'clock sched everybody turned in: the Indians in their
skin tent, the Mounties in their silk tent, the trappers

in their canvas tent. I lay under the tent of the sky,
watching the same northern lights and constellation of
stars, both fixed and falling, that Johnson somewhere
in the Richardson Mountains was watching.
Temperature: −45°. Mileage: 8.

10:45 P.M., JANUARY 18, 1932.
STATION UZK, AKLAVIK

"...so this is Jimmy Ludlow, the Voice of the Arctic,
putting to bed another look at 'What's Up?' a little early
tonight. From now until midnight station UZK will
relay the ABC network programming, for your listening pleasure. G'night, Inspector. G'night, Sergeant Riddell. G'night, Albert Johnson, wherever you are. And,
remember, think nice thoughts." Static for twenty seconds, then a thin, quick voice. "The Heavenly Sounds
of Gus Arnheim's Big Band from the Coconut Grove of
the Ambassador Hotel in Los Angeles. First, Gus and
the boys in the band will play 'Stardust,' with Trummey
Young on tenor, then an extended version of their new-
est hit, 'Egyptian Shimmy.' Ready, Gus? Then dance,
America, dance!"

(In the Mounties' tent)

EAMES: Why doesn't Riddell stifle that thing? Awful stuff,
modern. The Germans and Japs serious. Is Johnson
a German? Can't picture him doing the polka or the
goose step. Millen could dance to that, amazing. Rene
always wanting to. The time I came in and she had
all her clothes off learning the Charleston she said.
I always believed her, less worry. Gone like a shot
when I gave up the drink. With her you had to be
drunk. Where's my pipe? *(Pulls out his pipe and
charges it.)* My pipe is the tent, tobacco my days, the
smoke is me going up. Johnson's no smoker. *(Lights
his pipe and sees the sleeping forms of Parsons, Riddell, Hersey.)* Birth the lighting, marriage the smoking, death the knocking out of the ashes. Wrap this
thing up tomorrow, next day at the latest. *(Knocks
his pipe out to the strains of "Egyptian Shimmy.")*
Awful stuff.

(In the trappers' tent)

VERVILLE: Felicia, Felicia. My head is big. You're my
big suck, Felicia. You never give me time to go down,
tonight I'll go down. Carmichael don't care. I miss
you, Felicia. Fifteen bucks already and we need it.
I always miss it when I'm out here, here...there.
Felicia....

(In the Indians' tent)

THE RUNNER: Keep animals away. Keep men awake.
Strange.

(Under the stars)

LAZARUS: No wonder Johnson came here. To get away
from the noise. Now we're here there's noise here
too. Johnson will have to keep going.

(In a tent a mile away)

GARDLUND: Weirdest sound I ever heard. Eleven beats,
there's no getting round it, not four and three, not
six and two, eleven. It's some weird animal, some
animal in rut in the middle of winter. One, two,
three, four, five, six, seven, eight, nine, ten, eleven!
One...

(Under the stars, in the foothills)

JOHNSON: They've got a radio with them.

6

Gardlund sprawled on the snowbank, elbows akimbo, bare hands pressing the cold metal case of the field glasses against his eye sockets. The lenses were frosting and he wiped with two fingers, not putting the field glasses down. Again the cache was distinguishable and he watched it for forty-five seconds. He pulled the binoculars away from his face, grimacing. Hairs from his eyebrows adhered to the casing. Blinking, he tossed the field glasses at Millen, then quickly put on his mitts. "Your turn," he said.

Millen sat in his usual stupor, upright against the spruce tree. The field glasses struck him, startling him. "You have to throw them?" he whined. He picked them up out of the snow. "Why do you always have to throw them? Can't you just lay them down? I'll get there," he said, getting up slowly. "He's not going to nip in and stock up in five minutes, it'll take him an hour."

"Eleven minutes," said Gardlund, "from the time he gets to the tree, gets up it, throws down a sack or two, and climbs down—eleven minutes: three, five, three, that's eleven. It takes you nine minutes to wake up and get set, that's if I throw them. Besides, if I hand them *I* have to get up." He watched as Millen fussed with the field glasses—getting himself in position, pulling his mitts off, first one, then the other, wiping the lenses, applying the cold metal parts to his eyes, focusing, wiping again. Eight and a half minutes, he reckoned, but now, finally, Millen was watching.

"Don't throw them next time," Millen's mouth said, his eyes glued to the field glasses.

Gardlund shrugged and rolled over onto his back and gazed up at the spruce trees. He had long since falled, bucked, and corded this particular stand; since nine this morning he had counted 1,780 board feet. The pastime had limits, especially when you were stuck all day in the same place. The alternative was to go slogging around on snowshoes as they had for four days. All they'd found were the two caches, untouched, with no trace of a track, and both well stocked with food. Johnson would have to visit one or the other sometime— while they watched this one, Riddell and Verville were watching the other—or give away his position by shooting game. No Jerry, this Johnson, but he had to eat. No hedgehog—a fucking fox. But the fox would return to the cache he'd made, and the food in the cache was the bait. They could plug him from here with their rifles; if they missed, there would be tracks. Good odds, four against one—Gardlund glanced over at Millen whose eyes were not quite to the glasses, he held the case about half an inch from his face—three against one, but Millen could cook, he could stay in camp and cook for them while they chased Johnson, then he could dance at the wake. There was something about him, about Millen...he reminded Gardlund of...who was it? He gazed vacantly up at the trees...it would come...

"Okay, it's your turn," Millen whapped the field glasses into his stomach like a football, then stumbled toward his tree. The tree had ice all around its base, where Millen's fat ass had been sitting all morning, no, half, no, more like three-fifths of the morning spent on his ass thawing and making ice.

...that was it—the Vilna offensive, the winter horror the Russkies suffered to relieve the French at Verdun. Mounting their drive when the thaw was expected—"*They expect us to cross that?*" Olaf said, "*without bridges?*"—the thaw came and the offensive was smothered in mud and in blood—"*We haf bridged it,"* Olaf's last words—the frost reappeared and whole armies were swallowed up in the stiffened swamps....Something about Millen, like Olaf and the whole Swedish regiment, but especially Olaf the Oaf...something about him let you know he knew he wouldn't make it. If there was to be a casualty, he would be it—Millen....

Gardlund took up the glasses and, rolling over, manned the observation post. The cache was still there, untouched by man or marauder, seven spruce poles which looked from a distance as though they'd been bit off by beavers, three poles joining three spruce trees, four poles laid across the triangle, supporting two gunnysacks. Twelve feet off the ground stood the platform, but it must have stood sixteen in summer. No dumb Swede, Johnson, no Swedish regular, and "believed to have a slight Scandinavian accent." No fucking Norwegian, a goddamn Finn maybe, or—who gives a shit?—a Latvian. Letts have to eat too....

Millen sat braced with his back to the tree, ears covered, eyes closed, mouth shut, his nose breathing into the fur of his hood, forming ice. It was cold, $-40°$, and all his sensors were drawn in warming themselves—hands, feet, arms, back, the top of his head—at a tiny fire which kept going inside him. The tiny fire was inside at the center, or slightly to left of center, of all his extensions. A small, raging furnace which he fueled periodically and constantly thought about stoking. Gardlund was different, Gardlund was animal, Gardlund moved and kept warm. Maybe he didn't get cold. Millen did. Maybe he didn't have to keep his fire stoked. Millen had to. Now it was his right foot: moving it didn't make it warm, he had to concentrate on it. He was thinking it warm, and thinking of moving it once it was warm, when Gardlund gave a sharp whistle. That was his signal that time would be up in one minute, get moving, get cracking, like a hawk on a rabbit. Gardlund was definitely animal, brutish, Johnson couldn't be worse, he would have to be better. He tried to remember Johnson and couldn't: Johnson kept blending with broad flowing waters, against the backdrop of riv-

ers he flowed like an animal—compact, powerful, vicious—a wolverine. Gardlund was a hawk. He feared
Gardlund, but if Gardlund ever smelled fear...he would
have to be cautious if he was to survive, he would have
to pay attention...but who could be interested in subhuman men who had stolen their chief traits from animals—cunning, fur-covered men? He would have to
become subhuman himself in order to survive, he was
becoming subhuman, brutalized—by Gardlund, by
Johnson, by the cold—that was why Eames had left
him in charge, because Eames was like him, Eames
didn't want to become brutalized and pulled rank so he
wouldn't be. "Millen's the only man here who's seen
Johnson, he's the only one who can give a positive identification, Millen's in charge." Who else were they likely
to meet out here, God? His father the major? That was
why he had turned down promotion, not for Eames's
principles. Eames was a dog, a house dog, a woman's
dog, Mildred Urquhart's lapdog. Eames was back in
Aklavik with Mildred Urquhart while he was out here
in the cold. The Indians were all right. They were animals too, but caribou, trappers were wolves. He should
have stayed a pastry cook, icing cakes for Governor
Generals. He should have known Eames would send
him here in his place—who else would he send? Not
Riddell, he was signals—who else, then? Why did anyone have to be sent? Why not just let Johnson go? They
wouldn't get him anyway, four to one wasn't enough.
Offer Gardlund a bounty, let Gardlund and Johnson set
traps for each other, shoot at each other, destroy each
other, let them fight each other for years, make friends,
share the bounty, send in reports—"Johnson is trapped
in an area the size of Great Britain. He has no means
of escape." Let it go on forever, who cares? Eames doesn't
care; Eames would prefer not to have to deal with it,
except for King's getting shot. King doesn't care, if he
does let him come out and hunt Johnson himself. Riddell doesn't care, except for his goose eggs. Verville only
cares about getting back so he can sniff Felicia and
smell where she's been. Verville is Felicia's husky, like
Hersey's Silver. Gardlund only cares about bugging me,

and his five dollars a day. I only want to keep warm.... The field glasses struck him square in his solar plexus, just to the right of his fire. Millen gasped for breath, then shouted, "Don't do that!" Slowly he unstuck himself from the ice, and hauled himself up with the aid of the tree. "Let's call it quits for today," he said, standing. The field glasses dangled from his right hand.

Gardlund stared at him. His stare became a leer, calculating, crafty. *"Macht nichts."* He shrugged, and began collecting equipment.

Millen watched him carefully, very carefully. Then he stooped down to strap on his snowshoes.

The two men trudged down the slope of the bank and across the end of the swale. There was no shadow, for the sun had not risen over the mountains. There was no wind, only snow-covered ice, and, fringing the frozen swale they walked on, gray snow-covered spruce. They carried their rifles and marched with their heads down. At the far side of the swale they mounted the bank and disappeared into spruce trees, then they came out on a frozen channel of the Rat. Along it they walked silently, closely bounded on either side by more spruce trees which stood frozen and still above them like lateral bars. Between the bars hung a gray sky. Heads down, they marched along the gray channel, stepping in their own snowshoe prints. Occasionally off to the side the taiga would part, the channel would branch, and they would pass a small swale, but their tracks led straight on and neither of them bothered to look up or to the side. Where the river widened with a high bluff to the left, and curved to the right, they both stopped.

"No need to take any chances," said Gardlund, and holding his rifle up with one hand he fired into the air. The crack of the rifle shot startled Millen—like an announcement of doomsday, cymbals clashing in utter silence, the start of an earthquake—and involuntarily he glared at Gardlund, who grinned. "You like that, sonny boy?" He leered, and fired again.

"Stop it!" yelled Millen.

Gardlund, grinning and holding his rifle out of reach

of Millen, fired a third time. He watched Millen, and
made as if to fire a fourth time, then lowered his rifle
and shrugged. "They'll know we're coming," he said,
and trudged on around the curve. Millen, after a full
minute, followed. He was sweating all over, and hot.

Across the river, at the end of the curve, a figure
stood in among spruce trees. A second figure appeared
beside him. The first figure waved, slowly, back and
forth with both arms, semaphore fashion. Gardlund,
stooped great apelike, brandished his rifle, then lowered it. They proceeded across the curve in the river
while the men in the trees picked up their gear and
came down the bank to meet them. The men moved
stiffly and slowly, at right angles to the river. Beneath
a gray sky bounded by trees, across a flat corridor of
ice between trees, Millen and Gardlund trudged toward
them. Behind them, on the bluff at the turn, the second
stage cache became visible. Two trees with poles lashed
between them, supporting a twenty-five-gallon red and
white oil drum. The oil drum was filled with flour and
sugar and tea in canvas sacks, and two five-pound tins
of lard. It had been a job to pry the lid off, and they
had considered stealing the stores, but had left them.
After four days of driving the dogs in a vain search for
Johnson, and three days of watching his caches while
the dogs rested, their limiting factor still remained dog
feed. Unless supplies arrived soon from Aklavik, they
would be forced to turn back. All of the men knew this,
and accepted it as a natural fact, like a blizzard or
Johnson's invisibility. Riddell had suggested that they
fish for dog feed, but Gardlund has said, "I ain't fishin'
for no goddamn dogs," and Verville had seconded Gardlund. Neither Millen nor Riddell knew how to ice-fish,
so the matter was not raised again.

Verville and Riddell fell in beside Gardlund and Millen, and the four men proceeded along the Rat's channel
toward their base camp. It was now dusk, though there
were no shadows since there was no sunset, only a darkening gray and a deepening cold and a coarsening of
the texture of the ice and snow they walked on between
the two banks of trees. Verville walked beside Gar-

dlund, Riddell beside Millen, but none of the men spoke,
there was no need to. After a week of camping together
each man had his task, and each was rehearsing what
he would do when he reached camp. Millen was rummaging in the food sacks, remembering what he might
find and where he might find it. He wished they had
stolen some sugar. He pictured himself producing a
three-layered cake, iced with sugar and butter, and
Gardlund's astonishment, Verville's glee..."for he's a
jolly good fellow" being sung around the campfire....Verville was chopping a hole in the ice where
he had chopped holes before, washing the pans in the
ice-slivered water while his hands froze and dogs whined
behind him, then he was carrying water to Millen and
beating the dogs that were howling, beating them
senseless, and wishing they'd stolen some flour...he
saw himself handing the water to Millen and Millen
handing him a tall stack of bannocks, he saw himself
watched by the dogs' greedy eyes and lunged at by their
snapping snouts as he threw them the bannocks and
the dogs leaping and straining and strangling themselves on their chains and gulping and slobbering and
scrabbling for morsels of bread in the snow...then
climbing into his tent and finding there waiting in a
warm sleeping bag—Felicia!...Verville cast a quick,
furtive glance at the others, then trudged on toward
the camp....Gardlund was building a fire, holding a
match to the dry willow sticks which flared brilliantly
into flame; then he was getting up firewood. He pictured
a deadfall not far from the camp and himself chopping
it: three strokes from the left, three from the right, a
strong blow on the middle—seven strokes for each cut,
three cuts, four logs, twenty-one strokes...except that
the log tapered, some cuts would require fewer
strokes...but there were limbs, too, and knots...now
the fire had gone out and he was down on his hands
and knees blowing, with Millen whining about no fire
to cook on and Verville badgering him about dog feed,
while Riddell...Riddell was hoping the batteries hadn't
frozen. He pictured himself turning on the receiver—
it worked! Then the transmitter—it worked too! Press-

ing the button and sending a message: "Patrol twenty-
five miles above Johnson's cabin, no sign of Johnson,
no second cabin, no dog feed, few supplies. Patrol withdrawing tomorrow to mouth of Rat. If no supply sled,
to McPherson. Riddell." Then turning on the receiver
and hearing, above the usual static and "no word received," Eames himself: "Message received. Hold present position. Supply sled en route. Continue search.
Eames." Dismay on the men's faces, especially Gardlund's and Verville's, resignation on Millen's, weariness and dismay...but they were congratulating him,
Riddell....

The four men emerged from the narrow corridor of
river into a large lakelike swale. It was now dark, as
dark as the delta would get under a gray, starless sky;
they could see as they rounded a dark line of trees and
entered the broad frozen swale several miles across to
another dark line, and darker lines beyond that, the
foothills, and stacked back beyond them, black mountains. The shallow swale was dotted with dark patches,
islands, and toward the nearest and largest of these the
men trudged across the lake ice, their snowshoes making slight squeaking noises and leaving little impression on the glare ice and hard wind-packed snow. They
were still a half mile away when the dogs started barking, and they could see squat dark forms and silhouettes
of two sleds drawn up near the shelter of an island. The
island was not near, nor was the far shore distant, nor
the horizon of mountains far distant; all was foreshortened in shades and textures of gray refracted from the
gray sky—from coarse-grained, to close-grained, to
crowded, to black: the lake ice, the far shore, the foothills, the mountains.

The men trudged on another quarter of a mile and
as abruptly as they had begun the dogs ceased to bark.
The four reached camp and, without exchanging a word,
each man set about his own task: Millen rummaging
in the food sacks, Verville chopping a hole in the ice,
Gardlund breaking off willow sticks and setting a fire,
while Riddell switched on the radio. Except for the rustle of canvas, the snapping of willows, the thuds of an

ax, the whining of dogs, there was silence. Riddell
switched off the radio, switched it on, switched it off,
then while Gardlund got a fire going, and Millen made
tea, and Verville fed the dogs, Riddell wandered off to
see what firewood, if any, he could find on the far side
of the island.

The overcast sky was not uniformly gray, a faint
moon lit a perimeter of cloud cover and from time to
time, with the passage of clouds, shone through onto
the snow. Riddell was circling the island in search of
deadfalls or brushfalls when the moon broke through,
lighting the glare ice. Directly athwart his path across
the lake lay a faint snowshoe imprint. He stopped and
looked off in the direction it pointed—away from the
island, toward the far shore. Neither he nor the others
had gone further than this, past the island; all of their
search had been southward. He stooped to inspect the
print, no more than a half inch deep in the packed snow:
the tail of the pancake impression was curved, not
straight like his own or the others' snowshoes. The next
print he looked at was straight, but the next one was
curved, the next straight, the next curved, and so on—
the frames of the snowshoes which had passed here
were homemade, leaving a footprint as distinguishable
as a fingerprint, peculiar to the walker-alone who had
made them. Riddell continued on across the glare ice
and small ridges of snow in the direction that the tracks
led, toward the far shore. Once he lost them but, ori-
enting by the island behind him—which was now a
dark patch a half mile away—and circling back on his
own tracks he found them again, and continued on with
the aid of the moon intermittently flashing and dim-
ming, like a signal light on a black ship at night, all
the way to the far shore.

There the trail mounted the shore and entered the
woods, where it was both easier and more difficult to
follow: the snow in the woods holding a deeper imprint,
but the absence of light under the trees becoming almost total. Riddell groped his way from tree trunk to
tree trunk, waiting for patches of moonlight. It was
impossible now to discern the telltale curve in the

frame's tail, and twice he confused his own with his
quarry's footprint. The trail was straightforward, however, and led with a few flanking movements at obvious
places—a deadfall, a dense thicket, a slight ravine—
up to the top of the ridge where, on the windswept bare
rock, he lost it and, afraid to venture out of sight of the
lake and lose his own way, he broke off the search and
turned back. Looking down the way he had come he
could see the faint glow of a fire near the dark patch
of island. Taking a fix on it, he retraced his steps down.

Reaching the woods' edge he saw a dark form trudging across the lake ice, rifle at the ready. The stooped
figure, when Riddell spotted him, was about fifty yards
from the shore. Riddell stifled an impulse to yell, and
stood hidden among tree trunks, waiting. There would
be time to yell if the figure were Gardlund, or Millen,
or Verville, or...but it was impossible to say with certainty from what direction the figure had come, or where
it was going, or who it was. It appeared to be following him from the direction of their own camp and was
probably Gardlund, but Riddell could not be certain.
Riddell had not brought his rifle, only an ax; he had been
outlined in moonlight across the glare ice and noisily
tracking through woods. The figure had appeared phan-
tomlike on the lake, sprung up fully armed from the lake
ice itself, with no apparent origin or destination, but barring his way back to camp. The camp was a full two miles
distant. He could spy the red hue of fire through the dark
patch of island. If only he had brought his rifle...he raised
his ax up to his shoulder, sighting along its curved haft,
steadying it on a tree trunk...it was an ax after all and
he lowered it, waiting.

The armed figure on the lake ice stopped about thirty
yards distant, stood several minutes staring into the
woods, then sat down on the ice. Riddell peered from
his hideout among the trees for details of clothing, but
it was too dark; for recognizable signs in the figure's
outline, but there were none. It was neither Millen nor
Verville, one was tall, both were cowards. But it could
be either Gardlund or Johnson—though he had never

seen Johnson, the police description fit Gardlund: five
feet eight inches, stocky, stooped. From thirty yards in
the dark there was nothing by which Riddell could distinguish one from the other, and both were nearby.
Gardlund he had last seen at camp, two miles distant.
Johnson had made the snowshoe track on which Riddell
and the figure were faced off. Johnson had crossed the
lake first, then Riddell. Now that Riddell was retracing
his own trail, what was to prevent Johnson from retracing his? Johnson may have seen the men coming
and crossed over the lake and climbed to the top of the
ridge to watch them. Riddell had followed Johnson's
tracks to the ridge, and was backtracking in a straight
line. But what was to prevent Johnson from circling
back to the lake and tracking his tracker, Riddell? There
was a good chance it was Johnson. Since the figure out
on the ice had decided to wait, Riddell had to wait it
out too....

Gardlund was flanked. To move laterally might put
him in cross fire, to move forward or backward might
force a shoot-out, and he was exposed on the lake. Who
knew who the man in the trees was, at the shoreline?
He didn't. He only knew it wasn't him. The man in the
trees wasn't moving, and neither was he. He had been
here before, in the Masurian Lakes region, between two
wings of a Finn ski patrol. Neither wing knew what
the other was doing, neither side knew who was who.
Nobody wants to be hit, but to be hit by your own...It
could happen, he'd seen it happen—a whole wretched
division of Portuguese shot by the British as they fled
from the Krauts at Messines...He wasn't moving one
way or the other, he was sitting right here, he was
waiting. He wasn't sure for what—morning...by
morning they'd be two frozen corpses, no doubt about
that. Mud and blood, only here it was ice and gangrene...the gangrene of the senses, he was beginning
to feel it, to not-feel it. He yearned for a cud of tobacco,
to calm him. What were the odds? The odds were...

"Asshole," Gardlund tried to shout, but his mouth

was so dry it came out a whisper. He put snow in his mouth and tried again. "Riddell!" he shouted hoarsely. "Get the fuck out of there!"

No answer. He crouched in the hard-packed snow which he had pissed on through his windpants, cheek snug against his rifle stock, peering at the formless dark shoreline until his eyes watered. There was no doubt in his mind now: it was Johnson. Johnson was drawn up inside the woods, behind a tree trunk, barricaded by a deadfall, defiladed, no frontal assault possible, no flanking, no retreat....He—Karl, Kerl, Dummkopf—was exposed. He could be picked off with a shot, a single shot, at any moment. He could be wounded, made to crawl, surrender, freeze...it was Johnson's whim that he live, that he continue to live, a whim that any moment...Slowly at first and then more and more quickly he began inching back on his belly across the lake ice, retiring as he retreated into a small dark room (was there a cellar off the slit trench?) while his gaze stayed riveted on the dark frontage of spruce with the sets of tracks leading into and swallowed up in blackness (straight ahead the muzzle black and formless of the *Sturmpanzerwagen* A7V drawn up at the end of the trench ready to rake it) wriggling his hips and snaking on his belly back (pinned, cross-haired, exposed beneath that enormous barrel) back across the lake two fucking miles...he would only have to belly-crawl a quarter of a mile, withdraw inside himself that far, no further...440 yards, 1,320 feet, 15,840 inches, he was crawling...and what if just as he crawled out of range, almost out of range, the sniper in the woods should chuckle to himself and, steadying his weapon's shank against a tree, and taking careful aim...

"Is that you, Gardlund?" a thin voice cried.

Gardlund stopped crawling backward, rolled over suddenly and fired five times at the sky, stood up slowly and with his back to Riddell—who was snowshoeing out of the woods and yelling for him to "Wait up, wait up, Gardlund!"—stalked three thousand four hundred and eighty seven yards back to camp.

7

TRAPPERS' WIVES FEARING
ATTACK OF DEMENTED MAN
SEEK SAFETY IN AKLAVIK

Albert Johnson Evades Police Posse

FAITH IN R.C.M.P.

Constant Vigil Kept by Force
One Woman Alone in Cabin

(Special to the Edmonton Journal)

AKLAVIK, Jan. 19—Terrorized because Albert Johnson, Arctic bush-crazy trapper, has escaped capture by the R.C.M.P. patrols, wives of trappers in this area are flocking into Aklavik with the avowed intention of staying until the wanted man is caught.

The trappers have gone back to their cabins to watch their traplines and to keep a constant vigil for the wanted man. They are heavily armed and ready for instant action.

While many of the women have come here, one, Mrs. Noel Verville, elected to stay at the Verville cabin, 40 miles from her nearest neighbor, while her husband went out to help in the search for

Johnson. Verville is one of the best trappers in the North and can make a longer and harder trip through the colds of the country than probably any other man in the region.

His wife is of the same pioneer stamp, and armed with a rifle she is holding a lonely vigil at their cabin while her husband assists the police.

RADIOGRAM

FOUND ON ARRIVAL RAT RIVER SEVENTEENTH IN-STANT JOHNSON HAD LEFT CABIN STOP SEARCHED RAT RIVER CANYON AND SURROUNDING HILLS FOR OVER TWENTY MILES WITH PARTY OF EIGHT WHITE-MEN AND TEN INDIANS FROM MONDAY TO THURSDAY STOP INDIANS IN PARTY SAY JOHNSON COULD NOT HAVE CROSSED HILLS UNDER PREVAILING WEATHER CONDITIONS AND THAT HE PROBABLY HAS ANOTHER CABIN STOP FOUR DAYS WIND STORM BLEW RIVER BARE OF SNOW AND PRACTICALLY NULLIFIED AT-TEMPTS TO TRACK FUGITIVE STOP CONSTABLE MIL-LEN AND THREE MEN ARE CONTINUING SEARCH AND HAVE SUPPLIES FOR NINE DAYS STOP MILLEN HAD CONVERSATION WITH JOHNSON LAST JULY AND DE-SCRIBES HIM FIVE FEET EIGHT INCHES FAIR HAIR LIGHT BLUE EYES SLIGHT SCANDINAVIAN ACCENT IN-CLINED TO STOOP EAMES

THINK MAD TRAPPER HIDING
IN ARCTIC WILDERNESS CABIN

Constable Millen and Three Men Start Intensive Search for Albert Johnson—Indians Assist— Word of R.C.M.P. Patrol's Activities Flashed Here

-----

(Exclusive to the Edmonton Journal)

AKLAVIK, Jan. 20—Albert Johnson, who three times has staved off Royal Canadian Mounted Po-lice patrols 80 miles from Aklavik, twice with withering gunfire and once by running away, probably is in hiding in another cabin. Johnson was gone from his cabin when the third patrol reached it on January 17.

Such is the official police information flashed out of the North Wednesday morning. Constable Millen of the Arctic Red River detachment and three other men are now trudging back and forth over the hills in an effort to find the second cabin in which Johnson is thought to be hiding.

The four men have supplies for nine days, and other members of the patrol are again outfitting at Aklavik and stockpiling extra supplies so that the search may continue.

For days the second posse beat the bush around Johnson's old cabin. They were assisted by ten Indians, the redskins giving valuable assistance to their white brothers. To the Indians, little marks left on trees or in the snow tell complete stories.

"The Indians in the party say that Johnson could not have crossed over the hills under the present weather conditions," a member of the party said. "They believe that he probably has another cabin."

Four days of high winds hindered the search by the Mounties and Indians, the gales blowing the Rat River ice and the hills clear of snow in which footprints might have been left. In their search, which lasted from Monday to Thursday, the posse checked every nook and cranny within a radius of 20 miles from the cabin, but found no trace of Johnson.

Following a thorough search of Johnson's cabin and his trapline camps, the Indians together with their families left for their caribou hunting grounds, where they will remain until April.

With rations to last them nine days, Constable Edgar Millen, Quartermaster Sergeant R. F. Riddell, and trappers Noel Verville and Karl Gardlund were chosen to remain and search as far as the Yukon Divide, if necessary.

The doggedness with which the Mounties are

continuing their efforts to "get their man" is typical of the police of the North. They are without modern equipment for laying siege to a hideout, and must make do with homemade bombs and grenades. There is no cover for the Mounties, and they offer ready targets for the sharpshooter Johnson.

Constable A. W. King, who bore the brunt of Johnson's first assault, is now considered to be out of danger and is convalescing at Aklavik.

RADIOGRAM

ALBERT JOHNSON WHO SHOT AND SERIOUSLY WOUNDED RCMP CONSTABLE KING ON DECEMBER THIRTY FIRST LAST STILL AT LARGE STOP JOHNSON IS BELIEVED TO BE MENTALLY DERANGED AND MAY BE HEADING FOR THE YUKON STOP INSPECTOR EAMES AND STRONG PARTY OUT TO ARREST JOHNSON STOP AS JOHNSON MAY ATTEMPT TO TRAVEL ALONG PORCUPINE RIVER ALL YUKON UNITS ARE ADVISED TO KEEP CLOSE WATCH FOR THIS MAN STOP ALERT RECEIVED AT FORT YUKON BY WIRELESS AND DELIVERED TO OLD CROW DETACHMENT TWO HUNDRED AND FIFTY MILES BY INDIAN RUNNER STOP NO UNNECESSARY CHANCES TO BE TAKEN IN EFFECTING JOHNSONS ARREST RCMP SUPERINTENDENT ACKLAND

POLICE HAMPERED IN ARCTIC MANHUNT BY INTENSE COLD

Fugitive May Make Good Escape Into Yukon Mountains

AKLAVIK, Jan. 21—Bitterly cold weather is hampering activities of the R.C.M.P. patrol searching for Albert Johnson, demented Rat Creek trapper, who wounded Constable King and later withstood a police posse in a 15-hour gun battle.

On Friday morning the official government thermometer at the radio station here sank to 48

below. In this paralyzing cold activities of policemen and dogs are naturally limited.

Johnson's bombed cabin is 80 miles from Aklavik on the banks of the Rat River, and it is
thought likely that the temperature may have
dropped lower there.

MOUNTAINS NEAR

Just a few miles to the west of Johnson's shack
lie the mountains of the Yukon, rough and full of
canyons and valleys where a man might conceal
himself for a lifetime without being found. The
fugitive would have to live off the land.

This would not prove difficult in the Rat River
area as it is an excellent caribou country. The
migrating caribou herds in their passage to the
west side of the Rockies follow the river valleys
and feed on the moss as they migrate.

It might prove tiresome, Northerners state, to
live entirely on caribou meat, but it can be done.

COULD AVOID SCURVY

A party of four prospectors in the summer of
1930 lived for 90 days on caribou meat and suffered no ill effects. Johnson, it is said, could avoid
scurvy by eating his meat on the raw side.

The greatest danger for a man traveling alone
in this country, according to V.H. Fisher, of Tynan,
Saskatchewan, who visited the district last year,
is from the large black and white timber wolves
which follow the caribou herds and slaughter them
by the dozens. The northern wolf has not yet been
taught to fear the rifle, and a lone man doesn't
look as capable of defending himself as a herd of
caribou.

AEROPLANE UNLIKELY

An aeroplane has been requested by Inspector
Eames for use in the manhunt for the Mad Trapper, R.C.M.P. Supt. Ackland reports. Inspector
Eames will probably handle the situation himself
until the aeroplane arrives. To this end, addi-
tional civilians may be deputized.

WILL MAKE HISTORY

The patrol in the field against Johnson will in all probability make history. It will go zigzagging back and forth across rugged country with the members urged forward by that "never give up" spirit which has made the Mounties famous.

It is not known here whether Inspector Eames stayed with the group which remained in the field, or went back with the others to Aklavik. Inspector Eames is quoted as saying he would be "surprised if Johnson surrenders."

8

A tree without snow on its branches. Skeletal sticks waving stiffly. Other trees sheltered beneath the ridge, tops pillowed with snow, trunks parallel, branches forming the uniform forest. The tree at the top was deformed. He made for the single wolf tree.

The snow on the ridge was hard packed. Wind funneling up from the lake below struck the prevailing north wind at the ridge. Precisely here, at the point of impact, the thrust from his snowshoes disturbed powdery snow and released sprays of ice crystals with every step which, settling, covered his prints. At the base of the wolf tree he stopped and looked back: no one had ever been there. The ridge as a vector of forces remembered no one. He was not there, he was here. How he came to be here was not known. The ridge did not remember him, nor did he remember the ridge. Lazy people walked ridges. He was not lazy, he had never walked there. There was the ridge, here he was. Next to him was a Y-shaped wolf tree. The tree did not move, except stiffly. Leaning his rifle against its crotch, and his snowshoes against its base, he climbed the tree.

This ridge and the ridges beyond it. The ridges coiled like frozen intestines with fingers of ice fields between. Gray then white, then gray then white, then gray then white, then purple: the mountains alone had blood in them. Their gorges rose massive but distant, not so distant now as the delta, the delta which lay flat and

gray to the east and the north. To the east and the
north directly below in the basin of a large frozen lake
the men and dogs were like grasshoppers, toiling across
an ice field. He stood in the crotch of a tree on the rim
of the world watching them, and they were to him like
grasshoppers: one man tracking, another man driving;
one man asking another man, "Where is Johnson?" and
neither man could tell. From the crotch of the wolf tree
on the top of the ridge he looked down on the men:
—How many of them were there?
—Four.
—How many directions were there?
—Four.
—How many of him were there?
—One.
—How many centers in a square were there?
—One.
—Was four against one too many?
—No.
—Was one against four enough?
—Yes.
—Were they likely to surround him?
—No.
—Did they bother him?
—Yes.
—Did he hate them?
—No.
—What were they to him?
—Grasshoppers.
From the crotch of the wolf tree on the top of the ridge,
the man looked down on the men in the ice field and
laughed. The laugh which began mirthlessly was not
loud. It was blown away by the wind. Then he heaved
himself down to the ground, strapped on his snowshoes,
picked up his rifle, and resumed his march along the
ridge, leaning forward into the wind which, as he passed,
covered his tracks. . . .

The creek at the bottom of the ravine was drifted
over with snow. He paused amid trees to examine his
tracks which from the top of the ridge downward had

become deeper. They would be child's play to follow. The hill opposite was deep in snow too, his track up it would be clearly marked. The ridges and the ravines were where the track must be broken. Lazy people walked ridges. They were lazy, they would stroll along the battlements and try to spot him from the high places. They could be picked off against the horizon. From any ravine he could mount an ambush, but he preferred to play hide-'n'-seek. The line of the creek, which followed the line of the ridge, he surveyed to where the ridge curved eastward, exposing the creek bed to the north wind. He followed the creek past the patch of glare ice for half a mile to a snow-covered shallows where stiff pussy willows and a stubble of reeds broke the surface, then he trampled a large area with his snowshoes, confusing his tracks. Reversing his snowshoes he backtracked the half mile to the patch of glare ice, where he crossed over the creek and proceeded up the far hill with his snowshoes on backwards until he attained the next ridge. Unstrapping and restrapping his snowshoes, he studied his tracks up the hill: deep and clear they led down. The diversion would work the first time; the two hours' effort would gain him two days. He gazed ahead at the mountains which stood stark and purple and seeming ice ages away. One ridge nearer the mountains. He proceeded along the windy ridge leaving such little impression that the wind, when it blew the snow he kicked up, made it no impression at all. . . .

The caribou were yarded up for protection and grazing the lee slope of a giant foothill between patches of scrub spruce and willow. They kept to the open, pawing the snow for caribou moss, bending their necks to nibble the moss, raising their heads to chew. Now and again one would start and the whole group would scatter, skittish. They were moving gradually along the flank of the foothill toward the defile up which he was traveling, the Barrier Creek. Wind funneled down out of the mountains along the line of the pass, doglegging, whistling, and howling, following the crease cleared for it by the spring torrents. He was in the crease, the caribou were not. But they were converging with him toward the pass. Provided men or wolves did not appear on their rear to stampede them, he could easily shoot one as they moved toward him. He counted twelve, all bulls. In two days he had eaten two rabbits, snared in their forms while he slept the four or five hours he had slept in two days. He felt his strength waning and his fat reserves burned off by cold. His joints, especially his knees, were stiff on awaking, and stiff and acutely painful whenever he stopped. The sight of the caribou had set his mouth salivating and his stomach pumping acids. To kill and eat was essential, but risking a shot...? All the trouble he had gone to, the false trails, the backtracking, circling, and flanking—all would be forfeit. His pursuers would gain an advantage in time, and time meant energy, and energy was critical, deteriorating as time decayed.... All this time he was moving, as the caribou were, toward what resembled a crush trap. A crush, not a trap, for there were no palings; he would not have time to construct them. He could get there first and set a foot trap with a noose where the animals would enter the crush, but in doing so he might spook them. He could not get there soon enough to set anything silent. He stalked up the creek bed another ten yards, then heaved himself against the bank at the same moment as he levered a cartridge into the chamber of his .30-30 Savage and sighted—all in one flurry of motion—and fired. For the first time since the siege at the cabin he fired, ejected the shell and reloaded, and fired again....

He lay, half lay, on his side in the rock-strewn ravine, propped up on one elbow, legs drawn up at the knees. There was no place to stretch out, and with no place to rest he was squeezed into cracks and crevices among angular boulders and rocks. In a crevice before him a fire burned. On a rock shelf nearby lay a bundle of sticks. The willow and poplar burned bluish, and gave off a thin haze of smoke. Strewn in the snow and on rocks near the fire were caribou leg and thigh bones, and forcibly lodged into the rock field a massive dead

log stood askew. Like a deadfall timber it leaned over
the fire, poised to break the back of the fire, but rigged
to provide a windbreak. A white canvas tarp was secured to the log and stretched apronlike over the fire,
dissipating the smoke. Fierce winds which swept in
great gusts down from the ridges, howling such threats
as "Strike!" "Kill!" and similar taunts, broke on the log-
secured tarp as on a mainmasted sail. But there was
always the fear that the sail might be split, the fire
scattered, and the man be again without cover. He half
lay, half crouched in the jumble of boulders gazing stupidly past the fire at the thick, awesome darkness which
rose vertically fifty feet, then inclined five hundred feet
higher to the lip of the ridge high above. There was
light at the lip, though it was night and immediately
below the lip black as night. The lip of the adjacent
ridge, pursed with the first, but not closing with it but
continuing like a mouth slit ear to ear, defined his narrow skyline. It was dark at the slit, but not so palpably
dark as the rock face descending five to six hundred
feet down to the rock-strewn ravine in which he had
fallen and where, except for a small bluish flame, he
lay, half lay, canyoned in darkness.

In the thick dark around him was both sound and
movement: movement of blundering beasts of prey
and of pursuing hordes, sounds of mountains crumbling
and of fierce winds springing up. In the thick dark enclosing him were void and brightness; in unbearable
intensity, void and brightness inseparable—the void
bright and the brightness void, and the brightness inseparable from the void. The power of both, unobstructed, assailed him; he listened and looked
distractedly.... Places remembered him, and he them:
a caribou head and guts on the snow; a narrow ridge
along a steep bank and the precipitous climb down the
bank. But there were few intervening traces, either in
memory or on the snow. Where he had come from, what
route he had taken, why he had come here was marked,
in the convolutions of brain tissue and on the intestinal
ridges of snow, only at critical junctures: a mass of dark
shadows in a deep ravine, the conjunction of ridges in

a wedge-shaped hollow, the cache of a caribou carcass
and the trek along Barrier Creek, the circling back, the
retrieval, the clambering up out of the creek to a high
narrow ridge, the gazing down into a mass of dark shadows, the plunge down...certain configurations in the
snow-covered terrain were retained in perfused brain
cells; intervening connections were lost...both on the
windblown snow on the rocks and in the mind of the
man who lay, half lay, by the fire breathing heavily,
having gorged two days on caribou meat, slept by the
fire between feedings, and consumed vast quantities of
hot tea. Now he lay with distended stomach and aching
jaw unable to rouse himself to any exertion other than
feeding the fire and, occasionally, belching. He had not
shit in five days, and felt nauseous. He belched and
poked listlessly at the fire, which sparked and popped
like a live thing. He leered at the fire, and poked it
again in the ribs, then tossed his poker stick on. With
drooping lids he watched the stick being consumed: first
beads of sap bursting out, then scales of bark black-
ening, then the wind-twisted stick untwisting, disintegrating into gray ash. A fierce gust of wind, obstructed
by precipices, howled fearfully through the ravine and
broke on the windbreak. He felt he must shit or vomit,
or both, so braced and bound up was he; he tried to
think himself empty, but could not.

—Was he striving for release from the first posse?
—No.
—Was he striving for release from a future posse?
—No.
—Was he striving for release from the present posse?
—No.
—What was he striving for, then?
—Release. He was striving for that.
—Was there a future threat now?
—No.
—Were there men who had risen against him?
—Yes.
—Was it on their account he had built a cabin, dug
a trench, constructed a cache, and reconnoitered a means
of escape?

—No. That had been attended to already.

—Was it on their account he had trained himself in sniping, in sapping, in trapping, in tracking, and in backtracking?

—No. That had been attended to already.

—For the sake of what?

—Just in case.

—In case of what?

—One never knows.

—So there was a future threat now?

—No.

—You are very cunning, to have prepared for future threats that do not exist.

—One cannot be too careful.

—You have not been.

He felt himself sinking and gaped stupidly up along the wall of thick dark to the slit far above him. With an effort of will he scanned the pursed lips. They were there still, the precipices: the bear with the hump on his shoulder, the hoodoolike snaggletooth, and the trappan—three salients of his fortification, five to six hundred feet high. The rest of the slit where the lips pursed, where an enemy walking the ridge and peering down into darkness would be instantly silhouetted, was smooth as skin, void and bright. The nauseous sensation of being constricted and squeezed into cracks among boulders and rocks rose like a gorge within him. With fumbling hands he pulled off his windpants and squatted over a crevice. The wind whipped his ass as he shit in the wind. His head cleared, his nostrils dilated.

—What more could a man ask?

—To not go through it again.

—What more could he do without?

—Food. He would do without food.

—For how long?

—For as long as it took.

He peered at the black, cloacal mass, steaming. With the ravine he felt a new bond: having eaten and slept here, and now shit. The sun would never penetrate the pursed lips. There could be no drenching fire in dull light, no plunging or reverse fire. Anyone lazy enough to walk ridges would not bother to search the ravines. Surprise was unlikely, encirclement impossible. The ravine was as entrenched as any natural defile could be. He built up the fire, and lay down. Before falling off, he scanned his horizon: the bear, the tooth, and the trap. They were there still, the shapes as familiar as cold sores on the lip of the canyon. He slept....

9

The men toiled up the long frozen sweep of the Barrier
Creek. On their right lay the windswept slopes of the
Bald Hills, with thin fringes of spruce and copses of
willow marking corridors through which caribou,
wolves, or a man might pass en route to the Divide. To
their left lay a maze of razorback hills and ravines,
rising and falling angularly like outworks of ancient
fortifications hedgehogging the Barrier Pass. By divid-
ing into two parties and traveling continually in half
circles—the two men in each party flanking out and
looping forward on a base line—they had by a series
of circling maneuvers tracked Johnson this far, and had
thoroughly familiarized themselves with his habits and
tricks, and his intended direction. He was slowly but
surely headed toward the Divide. He never crossed a
creek unless on glare ice. Invariably he followed the
ridges where the snow was hard packed and the slightest wind erased any sign of his tracks. He backtracked
on creek beds, reverse-snowshoed up ridges, and had
several times used his pursuers' trail. When ready to
camp he would strike a creek at its head, continue along
it until he reached timber, and, having selected his
campsite, would circle back for a mile or more to a
prominent point from which he could see anyone on his
trail without himself being seen. None of the men, tired
and cold as they were, underestimated their quarry.
Each half-circle advance was made warily, with one

man breaking trail and the other covering, and their
loops did not follow the lay of the land so much as
systematically scour the region within a half mile, and
no more than a half mile, of the Barrier Creek. In this
manner they had painstakingly tracked Johnson all the
way from the trail leading away from the lake, a trail
they had lost on the ridges but picked up again in the
ravines, ridge after ridge and ravine after ravine, all
the way west to the portage where the Bear Creek comes
down from the mountains to join the Rat. Thus they
had traced him through two old campsites before losing
his trail altogether. At the portage where the mountains began they had made a new base camp, brought
the dogs up, and determined to split up the next day—
one team up the Rat, and one up the Bear—for as long
as supplies lasted, or until one team found new tracks.

EAMES: Would Sergeant Riddell please explain to the
    Court why the patrol changed its tactics, why it went
    up the Barrier Creek instead of the Rat, or the Bear?
RIDDELL: Well, first of all, there's a difference there of
    maybe twenty miles, and it's twenty miles of some
    of the toughest terrain in Canada. You know that
    yourself. If we'd gone up the Rat, or the Bear, we'd
    never of located the fugitive's camp, and none of this
    would of happened. We'd be up there still, circling
    around. But we decided to search the region where
    there was the best chance of encountering the enemy
    and accomplishing our mission, which was to find
    Johnson and kill him. And we picked the Barrier
    Creek because the night before we started your
    Indian runner turned up.
EAMES: What night was this? The 28th?
RIDDELL: Right. We didn't know where he'd come from.
    All we knew was he was the same Indian you'd hired
    to track Johnson, and we figured he'd been out track-
    ing. Anyway, he told us he'd heard two shots the day
    before, and it sounded like they'd come from up the
    Barrier, or maybe from the Bald Hills. Then he took
    off, we didn't know where. But on the basis of his
    information it seemed best to stick together and go

up the Barrier, reconnoitering the Bald Hills as we went.

They toiled slowly up the Barrier Creek, Millen and Gardlund looping off to the left in search of fresh tracks on the ridges, Verville and Riddell circling to the right toward the Bald Hills. The wind off the slopes was fierce and their march up the creek had been strenuous, causing frost to form inside their fur clothing. Verville and Riddell kept close in the lee of patches of spruce and scrub willow, bending their circle to avoid gale-force winds. The stunted spruce fringing the slopes were four to five feet tall, blackened and burnt by windblast, and brittle and thick with dead branches. The two men followed the natural corridors between sheltered patches, walking abreast, or nearly abreast. There was no need to break trail: the snow had been tamped and trampled by caribou who had yarded and browsed and passed through some days earlier. The two men had reached the outer edge of their half mile, and were searching for a path back to the creek through the trees, when they came across a snowshoe trail cutting across the caribou tracks and leading up a small feeder creek in the direction of the Bald Hills.

EAMES: And what did you find up the Barrier, or on the Bald Hills?
RIDDELL: We found Johnson's tracks. I knew they were his because of the curve in the tail of the pancake—the tail of one print was curved and the other was straight, the frames were homemade. They were the same ones I'd seen back on the lake, four days before.
EAMES: Were you able to determine how fresh the tracks were, or where they led?
RIDDELL: No, we weren't. It was impossible to say how fresh the trail was, except that it was fresher than the caribou tracks. As to where he was heading, I was pretty sure they weren't reverse tracks, and my partner Noel Verville, who's a trapper, agreed. Where we disagreed was on whether Johnson had looped back to the Barrier Creek, or stayed hidden in the

spruce trees. It seemed likely to me that he might be hiding in the trees to ambush us, but my partner thought we should follow the track rather than lose time going back for the others. Finally we decided to follow the track as far as the edge of the woods, then go back. Which way to go and how far was a problem, and it slowed us down quite a bit.

With their rifles at the ready, and advancing abreast, the two men inched forward through the dense spruce thicket, peering anxiously ahead through the blackened branches, and nearly stumbling over the frozen caribou head and mound of guts. While Verville nonchalantly sliced off a piece of brisket and popped it in his mouth, Riddell frantically surveyed the spindly treetops in every direction—ahead, to the side, behind, to the far side, ahead—fully expecting Johnson suddenly to leap up from the brush and gun them down. But no wild man burst out of the bushes; the only sound was of wind in the spruce tops, wind through the branches, wind blowing the snow at their feet. They went on, Verville munching frozen brisket, Riddell peering anxiously in every direction and starting at each little sound, to the next turn in the trail about twenty yards further. Here they came upon two forequarters of caribou, carefully skinned and stacked in the middle of the trail. The men veered off to opposite sides and hid themselves in the spruce trees. The cache was not covered with snow and at any moment Johnson might come, striding back along his own path, for the meat he had left. After half an hour of hiding, the sweat in their parkas turning to ice and their stomachs gnawing with hunger, Riddell gave a low whistle and he and Verville emerged from their ambush and followed the trail a mile further—past the edge of the woods and out onto the slopes—where it became obvious to them that Johnson had made a huge circling movement which encircled their own, and was headed in the general direction from which he and they both had come.

EAMES: What did you and Mr. Verville do then?

RIDDELL: By that time we were too tired to be fully alert,
and too cold, and too hungry, so we cut straight across
the slope to the Barrier Creek. We crossed his tracks
again, but pushed on, 'cause we could see which way
he was headed. At the Barrier Creek we joined up
with the others and boiled up and ate supper.

CORONER: Johnson was known to be near, yet you built
a fire and had supper?

RIDDELL: We figured that he was the one being hunted,
not us. We weren't in hiding, he was. Besides, there
was four of us. One man kept watch the whole time.

EAMES: Would Sergeant Riddell please tell the Court
what happened then?

RIDDELL: We knew the big sweep he'd made on our side
of the creek was a circle to get caribou. He'd been
four days without food, or pretty nearly without—
we'd found a few rabbit bones at his campfires—and
we figured he'd be gorged and sluggish. Caribou meat
does that to you. So after supper all four of us set
out to search on Millen and Gardlund's side, that's
the left side. Now we're into wooded ravines and high
ridges, and it's late in the day, about four o'clock.
Millen and Gardlund hadn't found any tracks, but
we knew roughly where he'd crossed over, and we
knew any trail we picked up would be fresh. We
found his trail, then we lost it. We used the half-
circle method and found it again—a deep print, he
was packing meat—leading up a steep hill. The ridge
it led to overlooked a deep canyon, and for the first
time we saw smoke from his campfire. We wouldn't
of seen it, he was using just poplar and willow, except
that Gardlund smelled smoke and we searched the
ravine till we found it. He was down in this ravine,
he must of jumped down, a speck in a bunch of black
shadows. We could see his fire and his tarp from the
top of the canyon, otherwise we'd never of known he
was down there.

EAMES: Did you see Johnson?

RIDDELL: Not that day, no. We spread out along the

ridge and we watched for two hours, but none of us ever saw Johnson. The canyon was deep, and it was dark, and we were cold. All of us had frost in our parkas and we were so tired we could hardly stand up. With dusk coming on we were forced to return to our camp. We were pretty sure he'd still be there. He was trapped down there. We could prob'ly have starved him out.

CORONER: Why didn't you?

RIDDELL: I say he was trapped, and he seemed to be trapped, but it turned out he wasn't. Besides, he had more meat than we did.

JURY FOREMAN: Was the ravine completely enclosed?

RIDDELL: It was, except for a creek. The creek flowed out to another creek. It was T-squared, one ravine crossed another. Actually, it wasn't a bad hideout. But there wasn't any way out, once you were in, except the creek bed you come in on. Everywhere else was steep cliffs. So in that sense it wasn't a good hideout. It was blind, like a trap.

JURY FOREMAN: Are we to understand that Johnson had boxed himself in?

RIDDELL: Yep.

JURY FOREMAN: And yet Johnson escaped?

RIDDELL: Yep.

JURY FOREMAN: How? If there was no way out except the creek bed, and if you were guarding the creek bed, what escape route did he use?

RIDDELL *(shrugging)*: ?

CORONER: Well, surely he didn't fly out. When you searched his camp later, what did you find? Where did his tracks lead?

RIDDELL: We didn't go in so long as he might still be there. By the time we were sure he was gone, there'd been a snow storm. We combed them two creek beds and the ravine a full day—the ravine was nine miles long—and there wasn't any tracks. There wasn't any Johnson, neither. He was there—we know that— then he wasn't. How he got in and where he come out, we don't know.

EAMES: Does the Jury Foreman have any further questions to ask of Sergeant Riddell?

JURY FOREMAN: Just one. When you had Johnson trapped in the ravine, and surrounded, why didn't you use one of your bombs?

RIDDELL: They're designed to explode inside a structure. In the open they're pretty well useless. Besides, they were back at the base camp.

EAMES: Sergeant Riddell, would you describe to the Court the events of the next day, January 30th?

RIDDELL: Early Saturday morning we broke camp around seven. As luck would have it, a blizzard was on. We went straight across the hills the eight miles to Johnson's camp. In figuring out the best way to approach it, Gardlund and me overpassed it on the ridge, then we crawled down to the creek and took up our positions on the opposite side of the creek, about fifteen or twenty yards from Johnson's camp. Seeing us settled, Millen and Verville set off for their placements. We could hear Johnson in his camp coughing. We could also hear Millen and Verville snowshoeing down the hill. One of them slipped and it made quite a racket. We heard Johnson loading his rifle. It was a lever action, and he clicked a shell into the chamber. We could hear him all right, but no one could see where he was.

From where he lay across the creek from the camp Gardlund could see the side flap of the tarp, and he had a clear view of the fire. He had what his adjutant used to call "field of fire," except for a dead log which blocked the tarp's entrance. Thick snowflakes were drifting down from the ridge the five hundred feet he had crawled with Riddell. The snow fell relentlessly, filling depressions, mounding projections, leveling men, stones, and brush. Already the fire had been snuffed; now it smoldered and tried to breathe beneath the suffocating snow cover. Gardlund could still smell the smoke, see the campfire. Nothing stirred, no one was there. Johnson had rolled himself up in a ball and buried himself in

the snow. Even now he was burrowing out beneath
them. The camp was a trap, set by him, for them. It
was a Skokholm dunlin and they were birds to be walked
by a ringer into the trap, then removed for ringing by
means of a trapdoor. Johnson was invisible, like an
ermine. He had changed his colors and slipped away
past them, he was back at their camp eating their food.
A cough. It came from inside the tarp. Another cough,
like a caribou coughing. Maybe it was a caribou, maybe
there was a caribou under the tarp, it would come out
and meet them and moo. Then silence, the thick muted
silence of snowfall on snow, of snow on snowfall, of
snowflakes uncountable falling on snowflakes un-
counted. He wanted to rush the camp with guns blazing;
or pour enfilade fire down on it. They could do that,
Millen and Verville, from where they were on the hill.
Then Johnson, who didn't know Gardlund and Riddell
were watching, would be flushed out into a cross fire.
Why didn't they? Four against one to no purpose, they
always attacked one on one; they always spread out
and allowed him to hedgehog, he always burst out and
broke through. Why didn't the other two fire? In his
peripheral vision Gardlund saw lateral movement: two
large cranes swooping, two Finn ski patrollers, two
bull's-eyes, Verville and Millen. He saw them the instant that one of them fell: a clattering racket of metal
on wood and flesh padded by fat, fur, and snow—Millen,
of course. The sound, nearer, surer, of a cartridge clicked
into a chamber: metal on metal, metal in metal, metal
through metal. Johnson fired. Verville sixty yards up
on the hill vaulted an open spot. Millen after a three-
count hesitation followed and sprawled in the snow.
Again Johnson fired. Verville replied. Johnson moved—
suddenly rolling out and leaping up from inside his tarp
across the fire and across Gardlund's gunsights. Gardlund fired.

RIDDELL: For two hours we lay in position, with no sound
    or sign from Johnson's camp. Gardlund thought he
    had hit him, and the decision was made to approach.
    Gardlund and me drew straws. I lost. By the time I

had crawled around to the others, Verville was back
in his first position, about sixty yards above Johnson's camp. Millen was further down. He was holed
up under a cutbank about twenty-five yards from
the camp, just above it. I was easing my way down
the ridge—I'd circled around behind and up the back
side—when my eye caught something queer poking
up from the snow: thin and black, Johnson's rifle
barrel. I was making for cover behind a spruce tree
when a shot whistled by. Millen stood up. From where
he was he couldn't see Johnson's rifle. I yelled, "Look
out!" took a flying leap, landed on top of the cutbank,
and slid over in snow out of sight. Millen who was
right behind me stayed on the bank. I don't know if
he knew where the shot had come from or not. He
dropped down on one knee and fired twice. Johnson
fired three times.

From where he lay half buried in snow and hunkered
up under a cutbank Millen could see a dancing bear, a
clanging cymbal, and Death mowing snow with a scythe.
The wind-palsied branch was a scythe in a sword dance,
the dancer that held it was dead. The scythe sliced
through thousands of downfalling birds, assassinating
their feathers. The feathers were falling on Johnson.
Johnson the nameless, the faceless. Whenever he tried
to conjure up Johnson he saw broad rushing rivers, or
ice fields. Snow was not Johnsonian, snow was more
Millenesque. The snow from the lip of the canyon was
falling like butter, not animal fat, drifting down as
redundantly as icing on angel food cake. His own face
flecked by the buttery snow felt puckered and prunish,
deprived of sugar. The fire inside him burned low (he
rallied himself and peered over the cutbank), the fire
below him was out. Surely Johnson was dead, or at least
wounded. Surely Gardlund had at least winged him,
brought him to earth. Johnson was a large bird, he was
a small one; he was a sparrow and Johnson a hawk,
a sparrow hawk. The sparrow hawk had its eye on
the sparrow and the sparrow its eye on the ground.
The sparrow saw the shadow fall on him, but who saw

the sparrow fall? God? God was no help to the sparrow.
The sparrow fell, the hawk whistled off out of sight,
into the sun. The hawk had lice. Maybe the hawk was
God (God wasn't the sparrow), maybe the Goshawk had
lice...no, no. There had always been these two species,
the eaters and the eaten; he had been born among the
eaters but he was not of them, he was food. There was
food (that was him), and there were the eaters-over-
food (that was Johnson, Gardlund, his father, Eames):
four against one, but there were more of them, many
more, many many more, and there was still only one
of him. Not that he was unique, far from it. He was
afraid: weak and fat, and terrified—a pig in a pen full
of huskies. They were another species—Johnson, Johnson and Gardlund, Gardlund and Verville, Verville and
Riddell—a pack bloodthirsty and hungry...hungry for
whom? Not Johnson, Johnson was strong, they all feared
and respected Johnson, he was their leader (he happened to be on the other side, but he was their natural
leader). And not Gardlund, Gardlund they feared second only to Johnson; if Gardlund said quit, they would
quit; if Johnson killed Gardlund, they'd run. And not
Riddell either: Riddell had tenure, had been around,
was along for the ride. And Verville?—Verville they
laughed at (and pitied, because of Felicia; and envied,
because of Felicia)—Verville was one of the boys, one
of the pack. He had known all along...he was the one.
It was he who was surrounded, whom the pack hated
and held at bay, he who had withdrawn from the pack
and the pack pursued him, only him. (He had refused
to lead as his father had led. The pack asked only once.)
Did lightning strike twice? Did Death miss a stroke?
Was His scythe dull, His hawk hooded? Millen stood
up. He saw in motion ridiculously slow Quartermaster
Sergeant Riddell half dive, half fall through the air,
land on top of the bank just below, and scramble back
into deep snow. It was the clumsiest maneuver he had
ever witnessed. He heard Quartermaster Sergeant Riddell yell, "Look out!" before the sound collapsed and he
saw Johnson, or what he took to be Johnson—a black
Stetson hat on a mound of snow with a rifle barrel stuck

out—and dropping down flush on one knee and in the same movement loading his rifle he fired: once, twice. Then he executed the most perfect pirouette he had ever executed, followed by an almost perfect arabesque, except that when he spun the leg he stood on was not vertical but angled so that on the third shot he fell forward on his face.

JURY FOREMAN: Where was Millen in relation to where the shot came from?

RIDDELL: He'd turned right around, his rifle was at his feet and he'd turned right around so that his back was to Johnson. His rifle was empty.

CORONER: Did you see Millen fall?

RIDDELL: No, I saw him after.

EAMES: Would Quartermaster Sergeant Riddell please tell the Court what subsequently happened?

RIDDELL: I went up on the bank behind a large spruce tree from where I could see the mound Johnson was hiding behind. Gardlund by this time had also got behind a tree on top of the bank, and we both fired several shots at Johnson's rifle barrel, forcing him to withdraw it. I stayed behind the tree firing every time Johnson's rifle showed. This gave cover to Gardlund while he crawled through the deep snow until he came even with Millen's feet. He undid his shoelaces and tied them together to form a handle. While he was doing that I was firing to keep Johnson down. By this time Verville had come up. Millen was half dragged, half carried over the bank, where Verville and Gardlund examined the body to make sure he was dead.

CORONER: Was he dead, or just seriously wounded?

RIDDELL: We waited some three quarters of an hour to decide. When we left, Millen was getting stiff and cold and we were sure he was dead.

EAMES: Thank you, Sergeant, that will be all.

CORONER: Just one more question.

RIDDELL: Yes?

CORONER: How soon after death was the corpse retrieved?

EAMES: I can answer that, Doctor. Prior to receiving
     word of Constable Millen's death from Quartermas-
     ter Sergeant Riddell, I had sent Staff Sergeant Earl
     Hersey with a load of supplies for the patrol. En route
     to the Rat he met Sergeant Riddell, who was on his
     way to Aklavik, and being informed of Millen's death
     Hersey took it on himself, quite commendably I might
     add, to waste no time in waiting for a directive to
     retrieve the body, but to bring it on his return trip.
     It is due to Sergeant Hersey's efforts and his deci-
     siveness that the remains of Constable Millen are
     before us now, and soon to be flown to Edmonton for
     burial.

CORONER: Is Sergeant Hersey present?

EAMES: He is.

CORONER: Sergeant Hersey, you have heard the testi-
     mony of witnesses severally taken and acknowl-
     edged on behalf of our Sovereign the King, touching
     the death of Constable Edgar Millen, on the thirtieth
     day of January, nineteen hundred and thirty two,
     before me, J. A. Urquhart, one of His Majesty's Cor-
     oners for the Northwest Territories, on an inqui-
     sition being held in Aklavik, Northwest Territories,
     in full view of the body of the deceased, Edgar Millen,
     here and now lying dead: Do you swear that to the
     best of your knowledge this body before you is the
     same as that of the man you retrieved by sled from
     the scene of his death?

HERSEY: I do.

CORONER: The Court stenographer will record the tes-
     timony of Staff Sergeant Earl Hersey. Proceed.

HERSEY: I guess you want to hear how I found him, how
     I brought him back...

CORONER: In your own words, Sergeant Hersey, tell the
     Court in what condition you found the body, where
     you found it, how you transported it here, and any
     material difficulties you encountered on the way. A
     brief, factual account will be adequate.

HERSEY: Yes, sir. I set out from Aklavik at 0800 hours
     on the morning of the 31st. I did not know when I
     set out that Millen had been killed. It was a supply

run. Inspector Eames picked me because I used to be a runner; also, I have the fastest team. There had been a blizzard and the snow was deep. The dogs pulled the sled, while I ran along behind. As I said, I am a runner...

The frozen river is a cinder track. The banks are stands, the trees are people, the wind through the trees is the crowd's cheering. There and back again: 800 meters. At Paris I did it in under two minutes. The river I set out to do in under twenty hours. It was not a life-and-death struggle, it was more important than that. I will tell you how I ran the race....

The First 200. There are people all around the rails, thousands and ten thousands, but I don't hear them. When I spring from the blocks the cheering collapses, like air rushing from a balloon. There are other runners, but I don't let them dictate my race. The German—I glanced at him in the blocks, and never looked at him again until I passed him. He had the post position, but I knew I could move out and at the end of the first straightaway, a normal running stride out front, move over and edge him out. Until then it's just me, me and Silver. Silver is a good thing to run with, he always understands what you say. Watch your pace, I tell him, no faster (we could run a twenty-six, but I rein him in; a twenty-eight is what we're after in the first quarter). Think smooth, stride smooth, just below spring speed. Facial muscles relaxed, shoulders relaxed. If your face is taut, your shoulders stiffen, then your legs pump piston-style—like the German's; all right for 200, maybe even for 400, but not for an 800. There and back again, and we've got a load on; what we're aiming for is under twenty. That's right, easy does it, run smooth, we're moving up on him now.

(Already, before the race, I'd psyched out the German:

—What's your best, Jerry?

—I run 2:06 last week.

—I ran 2:06 last week too, but it was the first half of my 4:26 mile.

—*Aber*, I be ahead when you start.

—Then you better be seven seconds ahead, because today I'm going under two.)

There is no cheering, there is no crowd, there are no stands, there is only the wind in the frozen trees and the komatik runners slicing through snow and the scrunch of my boots on the river. Concentrate on not tensing up, think of yourself as floating in water— cheeks loose, head floating, not lolling, just floating— facial muscles relaxed, think ahead, even though you're cornering, constantly cornering, think straight ahead to the finish. And don't ride the sled, don't tire the dogs. The dogs are barking, but I don't hear them, I hear only the hum of internal machinery, the scrunch of the spikes on the cinder, the roar of the wind in the trees—a dull roar, nothing specific, no one in particular. I move out to pass the German, I meet up with Riddell... "Millen's been killed!" he yells...I don't break stride or hear him or see him except as a bench mark at the quarter, a phantom with a stopwatch. I'm listening for the split on my time...twenty-six, twenty-seven, "Twenty-eight!", twenty-nine—half a minute has passed...

The Second 200. Harder in some ways than the first, the second fifty miles is a matter of coasting, same pace, same time, same drive. If the split on your time was too fast, you don't consciously slow down, you glide; maintain the same pace and achieve the same time and if possible with the same effort. The German is running scared now, running scared and too fast. He kept his lead all the way to the center of the first turn, but I don't let it dictate my race. I move gradually up and alongside, glance at him, pass him, seemingly without effort...he comes with me, I keep up, he presses me to the outside on the turn, still I keep up: I keep up because nobody has that sudden burn after 300, and even if he had, even if he keeps it up, he will have paid more for it than I have...he begins to drop back. I move on and out and over to the post without the least hint of effort. He's already settled for second...I don't hear him, he's out of the race. I hear only the scrunch scrunch scrunch of my spikes on the cinder and the roar, the dull roar, of the wind. The wind yells, but I don't hear it. I'm sliding along on the snow's surface, two metal strip runners, one unit, the only sound breaking the slice of the snow is the scrunch of my wheel grips, the spikes, clicking off revolutions. Fast fluid motion, frictionless, effortless, touching and tagging the ground which here is rutted, drifted, and banked; I keep to the one narrow channel that corners, continues to corner, and then straightens out to the next corner or bend in the river or turn in the creek or uphill grade, around deadfalls, along cutbanks: there and back, eight corners, four straightaways, two complete circles, one race all the way to the finish is my only thought...now we're nearing halfway. The people alongside, and up to the rails, and around the stage cache where the body is stashed, they're gabbling and mumbling and clucking, but I don't hear them or see them, I hear only the click click click of the ratchets of the wheel turning, the windlass pulling, and the wind in the trees as the body is brought down—from the trees to the ground, from the ground to the sled, from the sled to the finish line—that, and my time at the half..."Twenty-nine"...Body and soul we glide out of the trees as the sled passes under the hillside; under the hills by a frozen stream we start back. I can see only snow-covered mounds and frozen hummocks, all white...

(—Well, but show me Millen. I shall never be able to make him out by myself.

—This mound is Millen.

—Millen, you mother, get your fat ass in gear. We have our third and fourth quarters to do....)

The Third 200. This is the hardest, halfway to three quarters, the spiritual low, the slump lap. Every race is won or lost in this quarter. We ran the third, Millen and me, as though it was the last: nose flared, eyes glazed, temples sunk, ears cold and contracted with their lobes turned outward, the skin over his skull taut and hard, the color of his face black beneath snow, he leered and glared and grinned at me. No, he said. The body said No, the legs said No, we can't do this again, we can't maintain this pace, we can't go faster. The

spirit says, You will. You don't have to go faster, just
keep up. There's no one else now, just us two. You will
go what seems faster to you, though by the clock it's
slower and slower...twenty-eight...twenty-nine...aim
for thirty this quarter, in your last quarter you can slip
back to thirty-two...We glide together from under the
hillside into the narrow lane of the river; there's no one
in sight, nothing, not even the finish, only a white expanse endlessly cornering back on itself, a mad dog in
a snarling fit rabidly chasing its tail, a ghostly lane
beneath a ghostly gray sky...

> When the head quakes
> and the lips pale
> and the nose flares
> and the eyes dim
> and the breast heaves
> and the breath gasps
> and the teeth ache
> and the jaws gape
> and the spittle dries
> and the veins bulge

and the legs fail, and the knees burst, and the feet
numb, and all strength fails and the senses darken and
freeze, then Death says: "This is my body, Constable
Edgar Millen, and with my body you must run." Then
Death winks, and says: "Do you like my body? Is it not
fine—fat, and white, and young—fine food for worms?
Ha Ha. Ha Ha Ha Ha. Ha ah ah..." Death gasps for
breath. "And so...shall you...be if you...run this
race...." Millen's body bumps and jerks, sits bolt upright in the sled, whines and wheedles and pleads:

BODY: Give it up, stop, why go on?
SPIRIT: Hold the rhythm, keep the pace, put a burst on,
   burn!
BODY: Too late, too late, when the bear is at the gate!
SPIRIT: He that is down needs fear no fall.
BODY: Worms shall eat my heart and my white side.
SPIRIT: I'll drive you to the finish line.

BODY: I'll drag you to the ditch.

SPIRIT: Don't waste your breath. Kick!

BODY: I have none, I want none, I am nothing. And as I am, you will be.

SPIRIT: I never was, and never will be, as you are.

BODY: As you are, I was.

SPIRIT: You're falling back. Pick up! Pull! Drive! Push! Burn!

BODY: The fire is out. I'm ashes.

SPIRIT: You're choking me, like a cat in a sack. Quit strangling me!

BODY: I've quit.

We moved out then, I made my move just where the body said quit. The race from then on was a triumph of mind over body, of breaking free and holding fast, of being released and in touch all at once. The aim is to fix the mind on the body, and not in the moment of death since death scarcely exists except in the mind or off to the side, when one stops to say there is Death, Death is there; but rather to fix the mind on some moment in the process of dying and running, of running and dying, somewhere toward the three-quarter mark. And even when the split is being called, as the clicks are being counted out, the runner cannot give way to terror, or tense up; he must tell himself no lies, and not fear Death... "Thirty"...

The Fourth 200. There is no break between the third and fourth, or between the second and third, or the first and second, no break in stride or mindedness as the splits are being called; yet there is a difference between the first and second, and between the second and third, and the third and fourth, a symptomatic shift that overtakes the many, then the two, then the one, then the no one who is running for all it's worth with what it has left to the finish. For whereas in the first there was a sensation of pressure, and the body felt as though it were sinking in water; and in the second phase a clammy coldness, as though the body were immersed in water; and throughout the third quarter a growing fever as though the body were plunged into fire; in the fourth

and last quarter...at first there is nothing, no bodily
sensation at all. The mind hears his split, he masters
his body, he enters his final phase. He has no kick, no
drive, no will, and the wind is against him. 'I am three
quarters through, I can't quit,' the mind thinks (the
body has already quit, the body is molten), 'I can't let
down. I can hold my breath from here to the finish, the
finish I've already finished but have to cross over, but
I can hear nothing, I can see nothing, I can feel nothing.'
The facial muscles are out of control, the head lolls, the
breath comes in gasps. All this is before the loss of
consciousness. And there is the eerie sensation of the
body being blown apart—fire bursting to air: the si-
news spring from the spondyl, and burst through the
bole of the hip, and descend to the brawns, and blast
the knee and the ham; and these descend to the ankle,
and splinter into smithereens the thirty-seven bones of
the foot, and the thirty bones of the toes. In like manner
the arms, and the bones of the hands, and the fingers
all boil and burst outward to atoms, like fire being
sucked into air. Then the finish, the second death of
the runner, the final death, death of the soul: I can
hear the scrunch scrunch scrunch again, far away
below, and the wind. It's strange that you should hear
wind, wind all around, wind over and under and
through. Far below the sled bursts to the finish: the
dogs burst, the corpse bursts, the man bursts—all
burst and lean forward out of themselves, almost out
of control. The runner's lean of fifteen degrees has
increased to twenty...to thirty; the arms which have
worked as a counterbalance are thrown backward now,
helter-skelter. You are not thinking smooth anymore,
or 'float' or 'glide' or 'drive'—you think, 'POWER
POWER LEAN LUNGE!'...the mind lunges almost
a whole running stride out in front of the body—the
nose sharp, the chin split, the eyes hollow—the body
which pants to keep up; the charged air makes contact
two full clicks ahead of the death's-head thrust through
the wire. Time...1:57...

CORONER: Touching the death on January 30th, of Constable Edgar Millen, whose body was retrieved from where it had fallen by Staff Sergeant Hersey, whose testimony you have just heard: Have the members of this jury, duly chosen and sworn, and charged to inquire for our Sovereign the King, when, where, how and by what means the deceased came to his death, reached any verdict?

JURY FOREMAN: We have.

CORONER: What is your finding?

JURY FOREMAN: We, the jury, find that the deceased, Constable Edgar Millen of the RCMP, came to his death by rifle fire from a man known as Albert Johnson, Constable Millen being in performance of his duty in attempting to arrest the man Johnson. And we are satisfied that no responsibility rests with any member of the party of which Millen was a member, or with the party as a whole, but entirely with the man known as Albert Johnson who was desperately resisting arrest.

EAMES: Is it the jury's will that I indict the man known as Albert Johnson with the charge of murder?

JURY FOREMAN: We are willing.

EAMES: I herewith issue the indictment.

CORONER: These proceedings are closed.

PART FOUR

The Compound

1

It had come back. The wart had a life of its own. Yesterday (or was it last week?) he had been walking so well, and today (or was it yesterday?) he was limping again. Actually, the limp as he considered it coolly had come back gradually; he could remember a tiny pinprick, then having to favor the foot on his way to the inquest, and even before that...

"Foot still troubling you, Eames?" the doctor said briskly as he walked past, crunching blue snow beneath him. "You'd better drop by," he tossed off *en passant,* "Cheerio!" and strode on toward his own house. Eames straightened up and quickened pace, veering off across the compound toward the darkened detachment office. The wart was the least of his worries he mused as he stared at a dog—the dog snarled—the least and the last of his worries. It was a minor irritant, really; a reminder to him of his own limitations and that he must not try anything rash, ill considered... "unseemly"— that was the word in his mind as he opened the door to the detachment office and let himself in the dark room.

Immediately, while he was pulling off his parka and before he switched on the light, he sensed someone else in the room. The sense was so strong that instead of turning on the light he called, "Wild?" but there was no answer. He groped for the light switch, found it, and flicked it, flooding the small room with light. No one was visible and the door to his sleeping porch was shut tight. Everything was as he'd left it—his desk, Wild's small desk, the water cooler, the file cabinet, the bookshelf, the portrait of King George the Fifth—except that there was some mail on his desk, a letter and some newspapers. The newspaper on top was folded, but in such a way—perhaps Wild had placed it so—that as soon as Eames spied it he saw the picture that dominated page one. Baleful and grim the face stared at him as troubled and tired he stared back. He knew before he unfolded and read it the name that would caption that face. He unfolded and read it:

"Albert Johnson, Mad Trapper of the Arctic, in Happier Days." The face was malignant and both older and saner than the soot-blacked and powder-burned face Eames remembered: that dark farouche mask Eames would never forget, insolent and grinning, leering out at him from beneath a wide-brimmed black hat...the picture caught nothing of this. But how much of the face had he seen, really, the flares dropping behind him, illuminating only the eyes of the killer, his teeth, and the gleam of his guns?...Eames scrutinized the photo more closely, then quickly unfolded the paper he held, whose bulk seemed small and its type unfamiliar. "THE OKANAGAN BANNER. All the News of the Valley, from the Rockies to the Pacific. Published weekly, Naramata, British Columbia."

There, filling the left half of the front page, as the picture dominated the right, was the column "Here and There"—by Irene Eames. Automatically he read: "Special to the Banner. The notorious Mad Trapper of the Arctic has been identified at last as a native of Princeton, B.C. Inspector A. N. Eames of the R.C.M.P. has disclosed..." He ceased reading and gazed into space. The serrated top of the lightweight newspaper and the contoured glass of the water cooler met and merged in his line of vision as a succession of dots, a gray line. He stared at this line for some minutes, then returned his gaze to the newspaper. "Velocity of Light Soon to be Known," a parallel column announced: "Experiments Expected to Give Definite Figures of Speed. Pasadena, Calif." Between "Velocity of Light" and the photo of Johnson was wedged a boxed column with fluted edges:

JOHNSON STORY DAY BY DAY

Here is the story of the Albert Johnson case, summarized for readers of the Banner:

Dec. 26, 1931—Constable A. W. King visits Johnson's cabin and is refused admittance. King was investigating complaints by Indians that Johnson had been stealing from their traplines.

Dec. 31—Constables King and McDowell return to Johnson's cabin with search warrant. King shot in chest by Johnson.

Jan. 10, 1932—First posse under Inspector A. N. Eames fails to dislodge Johnson from fortress after 15-hour gun battle. Fortress demolished by dynamite.

Jan. 14—Johnson gone when second patrol reaches cabin.

Jan. 16–21—Second posse under Inspector Eames searches delta around cabin but fails to find Johnson.

Jan. 22–29—Third patrol under Constable E. Millen searches foothills but fails to find Johnson.

Jan. 30—Third patrol corners Johnson. Constable Millen killed.

Jan. 31–?—Another posse? Another casualty? Will Johnson surrender? Can he escape?

The Banner, with its special hotline to the Arctic, will continue to keep readers posted on events in the Mad Trapper story as they happen.

Eames glanced once again at the picture of Johnson, refolded the paper along its original fold, and carefully laid it down. Ignoring the other newspapers, he picked up the letter with one hand, his pipe-scraping knife with the other, slit the envelope, and unfolded the letter. Grains of carbon from his knife blade adhered to

the letter; he brushed them aside, smudging the letter,
and read:

> Dear Alex,
>   We may have a lawsuit on our hands. Well, it
> won't be the first time, will it? And if you're as
> good this time as you were the last time, I'll have
> no complaints...

Eames glanced at his wristwatch—1950 hours—then
reread the first line. He read it first as a complete sentence; then as a main clause with a subordinate clause;
then, dismissing the clause "on our hands" as redundant, he reread again the main clause, isolating each
word: the subject "we," the verb "may have," the object
"a lawsuit." The noun he understood and the verb made
sense; it was the pronoun he could not relate to. He
read on:

> ...no complaints. Before you start getting upset,
> here's what happened. A man came into our office
> here, hopping mad. I recognized him, of course,
> who wouldn't, as Albert Johnson himself! He was
> Albert Johnson all right, from Princeton, B.C.,
> and he was the man in the picture our paper had
> run, and he had spent time in the Territories and
> had been a trapper, but he wasn't mad he said,
> and he hadn't killed anyone, and he wasn't wanted
> by you...

Once again the pronoun gave Eames trouble. He mentally substituted a noun, and read on:

> ...by [the RCMP]. This is the gist of what he said,
> I won't bore you with details. Why he marched
> into our office demanding retraction and threat-
> ening lawsuits, when every other newspaper from
> Vancouver to Montreal had run the same picture
> and story, I'll never know. Maybe it was my by-
> line. Did you notice it? Anyway, it was me he came

to, a small-time reporter on a small-town weekly, and he was as I say hopping mad.

I calmed him down (I could always calm people, remember? Remember Henry?) and the manager of the paper promised the man a printed apology. But he left muttering he might still sue, so I thought I should warn you. I personally don't think he will, but you...

Here Eames substituted an impersonal pronoun; it seemed to work, and he automatically substituted "one" for "you" throughout the rest of the letter:

...[one] never know[s]. It depends, probably, on how the case develops—[one's] case, up there, with the real Albert Johnson. If [one] should get a picture of him, dead or alive, I trust [one] will send it to me. It would help me get over this recent upset, which has hurt me professionally and emotionally. What with Arnold gone now, and my job here uncertain, I'm not really sure what to do. The manager Bob, he's a really sweet person, has said he might send me up there to cover the story first hand, that's if he can interest one of the big-city papers in going halves on expenses. So [one] may see me soon. Then again [one] may not. Who knows anymore? I thought it was a mistake to split up in the first place, it was Tommy's death I kept trying to run away from. Now I'm better, but I'm not 100% yet. I think of [one] up there, looking like Ramon Novarro in Ben Hur, [one] should see it, the most interesting and disturbing man I've ever in my life known. [One] I mean, not Ramon Novarro. Oh Alex, who knows anything anymore? Not I.

Love always,
Rene

Eames set down the letter and padded over to the
water cooler. Exceedingly dry and parched was his
mouth and his breath came in little short gasps. With
great deliberation he took one of the coned paper cups
from the dispenser, positioned it under the spigot, and
pressed the steel button. A bubble developed and burst
in the inverted bottle as the water drained into his cup.
his cup ran over. He drank, and drained himself another, then drank it. The night Tommy died he'd quaffed
whiskey like water, distended his stomach with the hot
amber liquid, while Rene in a fit of hysterical grief
babbled and sobbed and turned on the Gramophone and
tried to get him and then the Anglican rector to dance,
until the Anglican rector called her actions "unseemly"
and the doctor sedated her.... He downed a third cup,
and belched. Then he glanced at his watch: 1959.46,
47, 48, 49...broadcasts were to be every hour on the
hour.

He crushed his cup and tossed it in the trash can,
executed an about-face, squeezed sideways between the
water stand and file cabinet, and ignoring the pile of
newspapers and copies of cables sent, cables received,
switched on the radio he'd retrieved from the men's
barracks where Wild had hidden it. The dial stayed set
(Wild had his orders) on station UZK, and having turned
it on Eames moved away to take up his post at the
window, glancing at his wristwatch as he passed beneath King George the Fifth's portrait, 2000 hours precisely.... "Presenting your Treasury Air Show!" blared
forth from the speaker. "In collaboration with your
United States Treasury Department and the American
Federation of Musicians, James C. Petrillo, president,
ABC and affiliated airways proudly present Count Basie
and his orchestra, emanating from the Gardenia Room
of the Lincoln Hotel high above Forty-fourth Street in
New York. What do you have for the folks tonight,
Count?" "Well, Jack, I thought we'd start off with 'Aces
and Faces.'" "The Count will give out with 'Aces and
Faces,' featuring Frankie Foster on tenor. Let 'er rip,
Count!"...The jump tune began as Eames, fuming,
reached over the desk and fumbled for the tuner dial,

turned it...static...Wild deserved a reprimand for this...more static. "...the hundred-mile trip and reports that Constable Millen was shot and killed by Albert Johnson." The voice of Jimmy Ludlow, whiny and thin, soothed the reassured Eames. What disturbed him about radios, newspapers too, was their unpredictability—like women: turn them on and suddenly a man could be subjected to the entire German war debt, or Japanese aggression, or jazz from America...Wild deserved a warning at least.... "Constable Millen and party came on Johnson in dense brush. Inspector Eames requests that every available man, outfitted with rifle and ammunition, food and dog feed, proceed immediately to Blake's store on the Husky, where a posse will be formed on Wednesday. The Inspector wants every able-bodied man in the Territories fully equipped and sworn in on this posse." The boy had ad-libbed, but Eames didn't mind; he didn't mind small departures. What he did mind was... "This is a matter of the utmost importance. Johnson is to be shot on sight. This RCMP bulletin will be repeated...." Eames switched off the radio, stood staring a moment out the window at darkness, darkness grainy and gray, then at the pile of newspapers like the weathered leavings of a large dog on his desk. What he minded was...he wasn't sure what it was. He still had the sense of another person, whether in the room with him, or...he wasn't sure. He padded over and turned off the light, then steered for his dark sleeping porch.

It was cold in the sleeping porch as he fumbled for matches and lit the kerosene lantern. The chill of frost encroached from the corners, and a naphtha smell hung in the air. Eames quickly unbuttoned his tunic and unzipped his duty pants and undressed, slung his side arm over the back of the straight chair, and climbed shivering into his army cot. Huddled in his long johns beneath the covers until the chill had departed and some warmth had been trapped, he positioned his pillow and sat up in bed, the lamp on the chair beside him imparting a dull glow to *Morte Darthur's* maroon cover. He glanced at his watch—2012—then picked up the

book and opened it. A sprinkling of British Army Foot
Powder fell on his blanket like dandruff.

'Mercy Jesu!' said the king, 'why slew he sir
Gaheris and sir Gareth? For I dare say, as for sir
Gareth, he loved sir Lancelot of all men earthly.'
'That is truth,' said some knights, 'but they
were slain in the hurling, as sir Lancelot thrang
in the thickest of the press. As they were unarmed, he smote them and wist not whom that he
smote, and so unhappily they were slain.'
'Well,' said Arthur, 'the death of them will cause
the greatest mortal war that ever was, for I am
sure that when sir Gawain knoweth hereof that
sir Gareth is slain, I shall never have rest of him
till I have destroyed sir Lancelot's kin and himself
both, other else he to destroy me. And therefore,'
said the king, 'wit you well, my heart was never
so heavy as it is now. And much more I am sorrier
for my good knights' loss than for the loss of my
fair queen; for queens I might have enough, but
such a fellowship of good knights shall never be
togethers in no company. And now I dare say,'
said king Arthur, 'there was never Christian king
that ever held such a fellowship togethers. And
alas, that ever sir Lancelot and I should be at
debate! Ah! Agravain, Agravain!' said the king,
'Jesu forgive it thy soul, for thine evil will that
thou haddest and sir Murdred, thy brother, unto
sir Lancelot hath caused all this sorrow.'

Eames positioned himself a little more comfortably and
thought of his pipe. It was in the other room. The sense
of someone else in the room with him had abated now,
and he resolved to read on to the end of the chapter,
then go get his pipe, then do whatever it was he was
going to do, then...

Then came there one to sir Gawain and told
him how the queen was led away with sir Lancelot, and nigh a four-and-twenty knights slain.

'Ah! Jesu, save me my two brethren!' said sir Gawain, 'For full well wist I,' said sir Gawain, 'that sir Lancelot would rescue her, other else he would die in that field. And to say the truth he were not of worship but if he had rescued the queen, insomuch as she should 'have been burnt for his sake. And as in that,' said sir Gawain, 'he hath done but knightly, and as I would have done myself and I had stand in like case. But where are my brethren?' said sir Gawain, 'I marvel that I see not of them.'

Then said that man, 'Truly, sir Gaheris and sir Gareth be slain.'

'Jesu defend!' said sir Gawain. 'For all this world I would not that they were slain, and in especial my good brother sir Gareth.'

'Sir,' said the man, 'he is slain, and that is great pity.'

'Who slew him?' said sir Gawain.

'Sir Lancelot,' said the man, 'slew them both.'

'That may I not believe," said sir Gawain, 'that ever he slew my good brother sir Gareth, for I dare say, my brother loved him better than me and all his brethern and the king both. Also I dare say, and sir Lancelot had desired my brother sir Gareth with him, he would have been with him against the king and us all. And therefore I may never believe that sir Lancelot slew my brethren.'

'Verily, sir,' said the man, 'it is noised that he slew him.'

'Alas,' said sir Gawain, 'now is my joy gone!'

And then he fell down and swooned, and long he lay there as he had been dead. And when he arose out of his swough he cried out sorrowfully and said, 'Alas!'...

Marking his place with his finger, he thumbed quickly through page after page to the end of the chapter, then stiffly got up out of bed and padded directly to the door, opened it, and entered the office. By the light from the kerosene lantern he dimly perceived and picked up his

pipe, his open penknife, and some matches. He charged
his pipe from the tin of tobacco which always sat on his
desk, lit it and savored the first inhalation—the pun-
gent aroma stimulating his sinuses while the smoke
traveled out through his nose—and padded back
through the door to his porch. Climbing quickly back
in bed he picked up the book and scanned a half page
sprinkled with exclamation marks and asterisks (the
asterisks related to no notes he could find, either at the
bottom of the page or the back of the book; the exclamation marks all had to do with Gawain addressing
the king: 'Ah! mine uncle, king Arthur!' 'Alas! my lord!'
and so on) until he came to a passage underlined in
pencil (by Mildred Urquhart, he presumed), with a pen-
ciled-in asterisk in the margin. The marked passage
read:

'My king, my lord, and mine uncle,' said sir
Gawain, 'wit you well, now I shall make you a
promise which I shall hold by my knighthood, that
from this day forward I shall never fail sir Lancelot until that one of us have slain that other.
And therefore I require you, my lord and king,
dress you unto the war, for wit you well, I will be
revenged upon sir Lancelot. For I promise unto
God,' [this was doubly underlined] said sir Gawain, 'for the death of my brother, sir Gareth, I
shall seek sir Lancelot throughout seven kings
realms, but I shall slay him, other else he shall
slay me.'

'Sir, ye shall not need to seek him so far,' said
the king, 'for as I hear say, sir Lancelot will abide
me and us all within the castle of Joyous Gard.
And much people draweth unto him, as I hear say.'

'That may I right well believe,' said sir Gawain;
'but, my lord,' he said, 'assay your friends and I
will assay mine.'

"It shall be done,' said the king [here the un-
derlining ended], 'and I suppose I shall be big
enough to drive him out of the biggest tower of
his castle.'

So then the king sent letters and writs throughout all England, both the length and the breadth,
for to summon all his knights. And so...

Eames's eyes left the print and stared straight ahead
into space. He was vaguely aware of the chiffonier, its
dark bulk surmounted by the plywood mirror backing
within the scrolled frame with no mirror. It was directly
in his line of sight, but he did not focus on it. Instead,
he quickly itemized the things he must do, or make
sure had been done, before tomorrow morning. Had Wild
sent the cable requisitioning an airplane from Edmonton? Riddell's idea, but a good one. He'd had no confirmation from Wild that the cable had been received,
much less approved. No response either to the radio
broadcast asking for more volunteers: none, at least,
that he knew of. Should the search be postponed? No,
he should do what he said he would do, unless weather
prevented. Was there even one dog team ready to go?
He would like to have heard from Edmonton before
setting out; that was the main factor, really, the airplane. Even if it were approved, how long would it take?
Should he send a new cable requesting permission? He
knew he was putting off going to Mildred Urquhart's,
just as going there was a postponement of setting out
after Johnson, as that in turn was a distraction from
encountering Rene if she came.... What in all that he
did was something worth doing in and for itself? Where
did the series of distractions and diversions, weather
permitting and "I have the honor to request," post-
ponements and cancellations, all end? What did he do,
had he ever done, for himself? He could think of nothing.

As he thought about this, and drew a blank, his gaze
narrowed on a screwhead in the chiffonier frame, one
of the screws that attached the scrolled frame to the
plywood mirror backing. It was loose; it had been loose
for a long time. Without taking his eyes off the screwhead, Eames rose stiffly out of bed, sequestering in his
left hand the open penknife as he did so, shuffled over
to the chiffonier and tightened the loose screw. The

screw was countersunk, and he twisted it tightly: there was no chance it would ever work free again. Then he dressed—wincing as he pulled on his left boot—blew out the lantern and passed through the darkened office on his way to Mildred Urquhart's, taking care not to limp as he walked.

2

"Alex!" But Milred Urquhart did not fly from the table
to meet him and draw him into her charmed circle. She
sat, regal and flushed, in her place at the breakfast
table intent on the backgammon board and, across it,
on the large, florid man who sat stolid and huge in what
Eames like to think of as his place. A black cassock
enfolded the man.

"Hullo, Alex, old bean," said the doctor from over his
shoulder and behind his newspaper. The doctor was
sitting where he usually sat, at the side of the table
nearest the door. From the next room Eames could hear
music playing. Jazz.

"There!" Mildred Urquhart exulted. "Gammon me
now, if you dare! Alex," she said, quickly shifting attention (when she was playing backgammon, she could
not be disturbed; Eames, understanding this, had begun struggling out of his parka), "meet the Right Reverend Thomas Murray, Bishop of Athabasca. Thomas,
if I may call your worship that, Inspector Eames of the
RCMP." Eames was still in the midst of unpeeling his
parka when the large, florid man rose from his chair—
Eames could feel the floorboards give a little—and advanced to where Eames stood. The man, Eames could
sense, stood waiting to shake hands or buss him—did
they still do that in the Anglican Church?—when like
a worm he emerged.

"Inspector Eames?" said the divine, and held out a hand. It had a large ring upon it.

"Bishop," Eames muttered. He could not bring himself to say, "Your Worship," and surely the man didn't expect him to kiss his ring. They shook hands perfunctorily. The doctor watched from behind his newspaper.

"JUST AS GOOD—Ask Yourself Is It?" Eames read over the doctor's shoulder; a text of small print he couldn't decipher, then the conclusion: "NAME BRANDS—Ask For and Get Them!" From the next room a jazz tune blared mindlessly; it sounded familiar.

"The Bishop is here to say mass for those two sisters who had babies, Alex."

"Two sisters?"

"Lucy and Minnie Tatayanni," said the Bishop, "at midnight vespers, Candlemas Day."

"Then you're a Catholic Bishop," Eames said, surprised. For some obscure reason he felt relieved.

The Bishop nodded superciliously. "Is there any other kind?" he said, withdrawing his hand and sitting down heavily. The doctor threw Eames a large look from behind his newspaper and shoved a chair toward him.

"The Bishop writes books, too," said Mildred, impressed.

The prelate demurred: "Small books"—indicating with thumb and forefinger—"tiny little books of small significance and smaller readership. Catholic books. Are you a Catholic, Inspector?"

Eames sat down. He could hear from the next room the music stop and an announcer begin, "A little earlier in our program we asked the Count to stand by for something special. With Count Basie at the keyboards, Benny Goodman on clarinet will give out with that Basie breakaway, the 'One O'clock Jump'!" The music blared again.

"No," said Eames.

The Bishop continued to regard him attentively, as if waiting for him to explain, while Mildred regarded the Bishop. "He's lapsed something-or-other, he's nothing, and it's your move, Thomas." The Bishop acknowledged his Christian name briefly—a nod of the head, a wave of the hand—but kept his attention focused on Eames. The music attained a mellow climax in the next room. "May I ask what you are, sir? Religiously, that is. I am always curious to find out what motivates and sustains our law enforcement officers, especially here in our northern territories."

Immediately he said this Eames's foreboding sense of someone else in the room returned to haunt him, more oppressively now than ever. It returned, it regarded, it resided on the Bishop of Athabasca. "I'm a theosophist," Eames replied.

"Alex!" Mildred Urquhart gasped, and even the doctor peered out from behind his newspaper.

The Bishop of Athabasca nodded, as if he'd known all the time. "Madame Blavatsky," he said in measured tones, "was a great, an illuminated woman, filled with zeal for her work. But she was not, I think, very ...enlightened. When I was in London in 1922, I asked Annie Besant which aspect of Madame Blavatsky's teaching she and Rudy Steiner had fallen out over. For, as you doubtless know, Inspector, Steiner by that time had founded his own school, Anthroposophy, and he and Annie were on the outs. She told me they disagreed on the number of bodies a person was able to have, Steiner holding that the original seven (which in Madame Blavatsky's teaching were under the planets' influence) were reducible to only three—the physical, the etheric, and the astral, if memory serves. Annie stoutly denied this, and maintained her foundress's teaching. But she admitted to me over a bottle of wine—I hope I'm not betraying a confidence here—that had Madame Blavatsky been more informed in the new sciences, and less enamored of Swedenborg, she would have known there were nine planets, not seven."

The Bishop ended this recitation with a face more florid than ever. Mildred Urquhart stared devotedly at him. "May I have something to drink, please?" he asked, and Mildred jumped up, forgetting in her avid desire to please the Bishop both her pique at Eames and that he didn't drink. She set a tumbler of red wine at each of their places, and the decanter in front of the Bishop.

While the Bishop quaffed from and refilled his glass,
Eames stared morosely at his.

"Alex, I didn't know you were a theosophist, you
never told me," Mildred said, sitting down.

"It was my mother," Eames said, "she was ardently
religious and took me with her, and I...you might say
I had a happy childhood," he finished lamely, remembering as he stared into the murky liquid before him
the theosophical convention in Toronto—1901? 1902?
the Japanese were at war—and the medium in an au-
dience of at least a hundred pointing to his mother and
saying, "And you, I have a message for you from the
man who gave you the whiplash marks on your back."
Eames had been stunned, all the more so when his
mother beside him seemed to melt, as if to prepare
herself more fully for the ghastly tongue-lash that was
coming and could not be averted, beneath which she
winced visibly. When they got home that evening she
cautioned Eames, "Don't you dare breathe a word of
this to your father," then showed him the whip marks
across her back which she'd always told him were birth-
marks. Her father had whipped her when she was
Eames's age, she said, he'd driven into the barn in his
buggy and found her and..."I don't practice it much,"
Eames demurred, "but that's what I more or less am—
theosophist. And what about you, Bishop, what order?"

"Franciscan," answered the Bishop curtly. "It's my
move, is it?" he said, swiveling his head and attention
from Eames to Mildred Urquhart and the men on the
board. In the other room Jack Irish announced that
Jimmy Rushing would sing "Don't Cry, Baby" with Gene
Krupa on drums. Mildred Urquhart continued in wor-
shipful attendance on the Bishop, while Eames for his
part kept trying to dispel his strong sense of an alien
presence—not unlike the time thirty years ago at the
séance with his mother—but the message, if there was
one, eluded him while the presence of the Bishop op-
pressed him.

"Hi! Alex, did you see this?" the doctor was saying,
"Germany is throwing out the baby with the bathwater,

and—what's this?—your mad trapper has committed suicide!" He leaned over to include Eames behind his screen of newspaper.

"It's a damned shame," the Bishop was saying to Mildred, "in the literal sense of that word: a *damned* shame Germany has turned socialist. When I was there just ten years ago the students and workers sang in the pubs." The Bishop burst into song:

> "Wir versaufen unser Oma ihr klein Häuschen,
> ihr klein Häuschen,
> "Wir versaufen unser Oma ihr klein Häuschen,
> und die erste und die zweite Hypothek."

The doctor and Eames, startled by this display, hid behind the newspaper and giggled.

"It's bloody opera," the doctor whispered in Eames's ear.

"Is he Irish, or what?" whispered Eames.

"Next he'll shrive us."

"Now he'll translate."

The Bishop downed another glassful of red wine, holding one hand aloft to indicate he had not finished, then said with gusto: "Which rougly translated means,

> We are drinking up grandma's little house,
> her little house,
> We are drinking up grandma's little house,
> and the first and second mortgage!

Now you can't buy a drink over there after curfew, it's all private clubs, and the Catholic Center party is eroding, is eroding...Begorra!"

"I dared you to gammon me!" Mildred said fiercely, and there was that in her tone which like an ice pick pierced Eames so that, even as the doctor diverted him to the newspaper piece and began reading it aloud to him, Eames was drawn down to the seat of his unease: 'Sodom and Begorra!' he thought, 'I'm jealous!' and regarded with compassion for the first time in his life

someone other than himself, James Urquhart, who out
of his own need was reading to Eames something to
distract them both: "The airplane will be piloted by W. R.
'Wop' May, who achieved fame in World War One when
he and Captain Roy Brown shot down the Red Baron,
Manfred von Richthofen. With bombs and machine guns
May will attack Johnson from the air while ground
forces rush the demented trapper's stronghold. Supt.
A. E. Ackland—you know him?"—Eames nodded—"in
charge of 'G' division of the RCMP, is getting together
a store of ammunition and provisions for the beleaguered posse, and C. H. 'Punch' Dickens will take off
Wednesday morning..." The banner headline Eames
spied while the doctor read to him spanned the top of
the Edmonton *Journal's* front page:

AEROPLANE TO BOMB ARCTIC TRAPPER FROM STRONGHOLD
W. May, War Ace, Will Pilot Plane

"Where is there anything about suicide?"

"Right here," said the doctor. He pointed to a small
boxed column further down on the page. "Mad Trapper
Ends Life in Barren Lands," it announced. "Special to
the Journal. Report that Otto W. Lammer, solitary
trapper in the barren lands on the far side of the
Thelon..."

"Wrong trapper," said Eames.

"How many mad trappers do you have this year,
Eames? It's a bloody epidemic. Everywhere you turn"—
he turned the page—"I swear, look here! Here's another! 'RCMP Arrest Insane Trapper at Lac La Rouge;
Plane Aids Police'—good God, man, they're like warts
on a pregnant woman!"

Eames winced.

"I have heard of this trapper of yours," said the
Bishop, "and I must tell you I think it's a shame to go
after a man when he hasn't done any wrong."

Mildred Urquhart was fiercely nodding her head.
Eames regarded them both: the woman he loved (or
was it lust he felt for her? if lust, then it was mature

lust), and her new champion, the Bishop. The doctor
had folded his paper and put it to one side.

"He killed a man and wounded another," said Eames.
"Of course, they were members of the Force, not civilians. That's a hazard we run every day." He glanced
over at Mildred: no sympathy. "What would you do?"
he asked the Bishop. "You're a peace officer."

"I am indeed, I am indeed. In your situation, you
mean?"

"In my situation."

The Bishop fell silent. The Bishop appeared, like a
salted slug, to draw into himself. He could only proceed
by indirection, Eames noted, and here was a direct challenge.

"I've already told Alex what I would do."

"What's that, my dear?" said the Bishop.

"I would take me along, and let me disarm the man.
It was a woman who drove him into the bush, a woman
can draw him out." Mildred Urquhart's eyes glowed.

"Splendid!" roared the Bishop. "Well spoken! Well,
sir, you can't do much better than that!"

"It's a woman's scheme," Eames said brusquely, "and
you shouldn't encourage her in it."

"You have this nineteenth-century attitude toward
woman, Alex, which prevents you and others like you
from perceiving what you see with your eyes and from
understanding what's directly before you."

The Bishop grinned broadly, shifted his bulk in the
chair, and moved the backgammon board to make room.
The play had shifted. Eames had been sighted across
the table and was being called out by the Queen and
her Bishop. The King merely looked on bemused. Every-
Eames sallied forth.

"I don't flinch from what's before me. I don't always
meet things head on. I try to get around them, or leap
over them—this cursed thing, for example." He indicated the paper in the hands of his ally; but it was no
longer in the hands of the doctor, and he wondered if
the doctor were his ally. "I do my job," Eames finished
lamely, "I assume others are doing their jobs. If everyone did his job . . ." Here he glanced at the Bishop, who,

however, was busy bolstering the Queen to make her next foray. With the instinct of one alcoholic for another, Eames observed that the Bishop was high.

"What precisely do you think a woman's job is, and why do you outfit posses of men, subjecting them to great danger, when one woman might do the trick? One woman with love in her heart?"

"There's your answer," Eames began. But the Bishop with his loud baritone boomed him out.

"Well spoken, well spoken, like the Magdalene who loved her Lord! You, sir, respond!"

Eames colored, but continued: "As I started to say, you've answered yourself..."

"How have I answered myself?"

"A woman with love in her heart. There's no room for that out on the trail. Out there it's all backbreaking brute work, the men have other names for it..."

"Shit detail, right?" Mildred said, flushed.

Eames overlooked this. "But there is need of support for the men who are out there cursing and clawing so that you can be safe here. They need warmth, they need encouragement, they need hot food, and..."

"Prayers!" boomed the Bishop, so solemnly and with such emphasis that Eames, and the doctor too, wondered if the Bishop had just remembered the hour and was calling them all to compline. "They need prayers!" repeated His Worship, "which puts me in mind of a poem by Maria Janitschek. A woman challenges a man to a duel, and when he refuses on the grounds that woman exists only for prayers and long-suffering, she responds, much as Mildred here has:

'So wisse, dass das Weib
gewachsen ist im neunzehnten Jahrhundert!'
sprach sie mit grossen Aug, und schoss ihn nieder.

Which, roughly translated, means:

'Then know that woman
Has grown to maturity in the nineteenth century!'
She said with eye dilated, and shot him down."

Eames saw the folly of this move, even while he admired its boldness. The Bishop now dominated the table, he had advanced far beyond his own Queen, and was in a strong but exposed position. Eames could, he felt, pounce on him—either by attacking his position on prayer (whose value Mildred defended), or by taking him to task on the subject of woman (an issue sure to rouse Mildred). But the Queen might rush to her Bishop's defense, and no telling what arrows the Bishop might draw from his bottomless quiver of quotes. It seemed better to isolate him; the Queen would not aid him if she were under attack, and the Bishop might suffer memory lapses, or fall asleep, or pass out.

"I think," said Eames, adroitly sidestepping the Bishop, "that the point has been lost. We were talking about how to apprehend the so-called Mad Trapper..."

"Der sogenante Böse," muttered the Bishop.

Eames ignored this. "Not about woman's place in the posse"—a crazy idea, he almost said, but checked himself—"but about the effectiveness of resisting force with force, or with...something else."

"Love," Mildred Urquhart said.

"Love," echoed Eames, and felt panic. He wasn't sure where his next move would be. The Bishop was eyeing him like a mud turtle, ready to snap; the Queen like a hawk ready to swoop, was keeping the whole field in view.

Quite unexpectedly (for Eames) in this impasse the doctor began to read: "The rattle of machine guns and the roar of artillery was continuous as bluejackets advanced and the Chinese forces, centered in the Chapel, resisted attack. The Chinese used mortars for artillery. The Japanese continued their light artillery bombardment as well as their machine gun barrage. Japanese warships then swung into action, bombarding the village where the Chinese were still holding out, and machine gun nests on both sides of the river picked away at each other in a deadly cross fire. Japanese airplanes were also in action..."

"James..." the Queen interrupted. But the King ignored her and continued his own little end game, read-

ing as though to himself but more and more loudly:
"...a no-man's-land by day becomes a Chinese beehive
under cover of darkness when the eyes of the Japanese
airmen, alert to drop bombs, can no longer see their
targets. Scarcely a mud hut or tin dwelling has not been
blasted by aerial bombs or by Japanese naval guns, or
riddled by machine guns. The population of from eight
to twelve thousand is made up chiefly of Chinese fish-
ermen, river boatmen, and coolies. The Chinese vil-
lagers' morale, however..."

"James!" ordered the Queen, "stop it this instant!"

Doctor Urquhart stopped reading, looked with level
blue eyes at the Queen, at the Bishop, then shrugged.

"I do not immediately grasp the relevance," the
Bishop commented, pronouncing each syllable, "of this
lengthy and rather tedious reading. Is there some point
pertinent to our discussion," he asked, "which I, due to
befuddlement by drink, or our gracious hostess' dis-
tracting presence"—he bowed in the Queen's direction—"have failed to grasp? Kindly point it out, sir,
that we may respond."

"The news speaks for itself," said the doctor. "The
paper is the paper, I am I. One must do as the animals
do, who erase every footprint in front of their lair." The
doctor gazed coolly and directly at the Bishop.

The Bishop smiled. "If I understand you correctly,
sir, we are in perfect agreement. And it is of course true
that everything relates to everything else, while at the
same time nothing quite fits. I, for example, do not quite
fit this chair, or, shall we say, the chair does not quite
fit me. Yet here I am, sitting, and as the conversation
veers toward the heart of the matter I forget the ill fit
of the chair."

"We all risk missing the heart of the matter," said
the doctor.

"We do indeed," parried the Bishop, "risk it, that is,
and there are times I doubt not I have missed it. But
as such times I say to myself, 'Thomas,' I say..."

Eames was baffled by the turn the conversation had
taken. The chill tone of the two men, the lack of sub-

stance in what they were saying, perplexed and distressed Eames.

He glanced over at Mildred Urquhart. The bright, nearly feverish, gleam in her eyes, the suffusion of color in her cheeks extending up to the roots of her hair, and the warm gorge of blood her neck above her close-fitting sweater, made her seem more than ever desireable— incandescent almost. She was focused completely on the interplay between the two men, and Eames, of whom she was oblivious, felt his own gorge rise while his hand resting innocently on his groin was rudely nudged from beneath. He trained his gaze away from Mildred Urquhart.

"... goodness is where you find it, I say, as Our Lord's parable of the Good Samaritan teaches. You, sir, I do not for a moment forget, are our gracious hostess' husband, *ergo,* our gracious host." The Bishop closed his eyes and gave a little nod, a sort of bow, to the doctor.

The doctor acknowledged the Bishop's bow with a little nod of his own.

Eames watched them both. The nods and the bows were like ritual moves in some ancient martial art, whose rules Eames did not know, and whose stakes he could only guess at. The stakes in the present contest, he conjectured were . . .

The Queen: "No one has asked me what I think."

The King: "Your last word was 'love.'"

The Bishop: "Love it was. You and your word are the first and the last, the honored and the scorned one. Yours has been in incomprehensible silence, let your utterance now be of love."

With this flourish the Bishop deferred to the Queen. The King continued to gaze steadily at the Queen and the Bishop, and the knight at all three—King, Queen, and Bishop—as at some ancient formulation whose possible moves were well known and prescribed, except for his presence among them. And it occurred to Eames that the three of them, Murray and the two Urquharts, perhaps knew one another already; that this stylized game was a re-enactment of earlier, pre-Arctic pas-

times; and that he, Every-Eames, only muddied the
works by providing a point on which they could con-
verge. The simple triangle with which they were familiar became with his entrance a steep pyramid up
which they all struggled, and down which they all slid,
and through which they all tried to burrow, without
understanding or divine aid. The mere fact of his presence, though completely redundant, changed everything for everybody—could not the same be said of
every child born? And in the same reflex instant, against
a field black and white, he perceived with the searing
sting of a whiplash two of the many consequences of
his own blundering moves: the Queen gravid, whether
by King, knight, or Bishop, and spawning a pawn; the
knight on his horse seeking out a far castle, where
entrance must be denied him. Departure seemed to
Eames in that moment the most honorable of all moves.
If not departure, simple suicide.

"I have seen Albert Johnson," announced the Queen,
and at this intelligence all sound and thought waves,
even the radio in the next room, fell temporarily silent.
"I hesitated, Alex, to tell you before, but now I feel I
must." She glanced winsomely, yet defiantly like a little
girl who has peed her pants and kept it a secret, at each
of the three men in turn: first at Eames; then at her
husband; and finally, as though to solicit his sanction,
at the Bishop.

"Tell us what you remember, my dear," the Bishop
urged.

"It was earlier this evening, around dusk, shortly
after you arrived, Thomas. Both of you were at the
inquest. I had gone for a walk because I was feeling...disturbed. It was down by the river. No one was
near and the mists were beginning to come in, it must
have been around four o'clock because I could hear the
dogs rattling their chains for their food. I was standing
just at the edge of the reefed ice, he must have come
up from the river, or from behind, I don't know where
he came from, but all of a sudden there he was, not five
feet away, and I knew he had been there a long time,

longer than I had. I might have passed him by and not noticed him except for the energy coming from him."

"Energy?"

"It was like heat. But it was coming from him, not from me. It wasn't like when you startle a fox and both stand there frozen; it wasn't fear, it was heat. He was standing stock-still with two rifles, one in his hand and one slung over his shoulder, and he wore a skin parka, and he looked very lean, very gaunt, and I felt heat coming from him. I kept telling myself over and over, 'It's not you I fear, but I fear myself, and I fear for my friends, and I fear for the world, this crazy, crisscrossed world we live in...' then I started repeating my Jesus Prayer, over and over to the beats of my heart: 'Lord Jesus Christ, have mercy upon me, Lord Jesus Christ, have mercy upon me'... and then I began to cry. He hadn't moved, I hadn't moved, neither of us had spoken. He must have thought I was crazy..."

"Or afraid."

"Yes, afraid. For he said..." Mildred Urquhart swallowed two or three times, as though the words wouldn't come.

"What did he say, my dear?" the Bishop urged gently. The doctor and Eames glanced at each other, embarrassed.

"He said, he said... 'Don't be afraid,' he said. That was all. And when I looked up, he was gone."

"Which way did he go?" Eames asked. "Which way did his prints lead?"

"There were no prints," said Mildred. "There was nothing in the spot where he had stood."

Eames and the doctor exchanged glances again. "You're sure it was Johnson?" Eames asked.

"I'm sure," Mildred said, "as sure as I am that you're you."

Eames shrugged.

"Well," countered the doctor, "say what you will about hot encounters with men in the snow, I for one don't believe you saw Johnson. You may have seen someone, and been thinking of Johnson, but would Johnson have spoken the very words you were waiting to hear?"

"Did he have an accent?" asked Eames. "Johnson is supposed to have an accent."

"I doubt that you saw anyone."

"James," said the Bishop, "you have always been a skeptic. If she says she saw Johnson, who are we to doubt her?"

"I question the footprints," said Eames. "We might check tomorrow."

"I question what we might call her vision," the doctor continued, "not on the general grounds of skepticism, and not on the circumstantial grounds of no foot-prints—you know yourself, Eames, that the wind blows them away as fast as a man puts them down—but on the evidence that she herself has adduced. You say you were crying, and this stranger you call Albert Johnson said, 'Don't be afraid'? Is that what he said?"

"'Don't be afraid.'"

"Well, that's out of character for him, insofar as we know him. Here's a man who wouldn't speak to either King or McDowell after they'd traveled eighty miles to his cabin. The next time they went, he shot King. And how many words did he say to you, Eames, when you and the posse were within hailing distance for—what was it—fifteen hours?"

Eames shook his head. But he was intent on trying to analyze what was happening at the table. The play seemed to move laterally: between Mildred and him, between the doctor and Murray. If he moved this way, he got blocked by the Bishop; if he jumped that way, he confronted the Queen. The doctor, who was depicting Johnson as "a classic case of paranoia," seemed his ally, but even of him Eames was unsure. If he got up and left now, the three of them would be together; if he and the doctor departed, the Queen and Bishop would be alone. Either prospect disturbed him immensely. Like a bird tied by a string, who flutters in every direction but returns to where it is tied, Eames's mind returned to the square he was on, stalemated though he was. Here, after all, was where he belonged: seated at a table where he often sat, in Mildred Urquhart's kitchen, in

Doctor Urquhart's house. It was the Bishop who was the intruder, whose infallible presence set them at variance, King against Queen, Queen against knight. Eames glared murderously at His Worship, the Right Reverend Thomas Murray, Bishop of Athabasca, from whose mouth as from a slot machine new words were beginning to tumble.

"If I may say so, your so-called Mad Trapper is not a gangster, and he is not mad. It so happens I know him well. When I had the honor four years ago as suffragan Bishop to preside in Bishop Breynat's place at a confirmation in Dawson, I met your man Johnson. The name as you spoke it kept worrying me, and now at last it comes back. Have you ever noticed that; how a name will nag and tug like a thread until the whole cloth comes to mind? I remember him well. He was not so tall as you, Doctor, and not at all fat like me. He was younger than you, Inspector, by a good ten years, and in splendid physical condition. We took dinner together after the service—I think one of the girls confirmed that day was his niece, or related somehow—and my impression was of a man capable of marvelous endurance, and skillful in all that makes for effectiveness in the wilds. Would that description tally with your impression of him, Inspector?"

Eames felt balked and frustrated. "Did he have a thick accent?" he asked sulkily.

"As to that, I cannot say. The mass was, of course, entirely in Latin, and the conversation afterward was, as I recall, in German. I remember that detail because the food, too, was German, or rather Austrian: schnitzel, sauerkraut, schnapps. His German, I think, was flawless and, yes, I even recall something he said—what was it? something about war, a phrase he used stuck in my mind. He said, yes, we were sitting at table and dining, and he said something like—I'll try to translate as I go—'Since they started sitting on chairs and eating at tables, they have been waging longer wars.' I remember asking him who 'they' were and he said, and this is the phrase, *'die mörderischen Uniformen,'* the murderous uniforms. 'If you had to face the enemy na-

ked,' he said, 'you would have a hard time killing him.'
I asked him if he had ever killed a man and he replied
that he hadn't, but that his gun had. This intrigued me
and I, as I recall, asked him to amplify. He went on to
say something like 'Man is in love with his weapons.
What can we do against that? Weapons should be constructed so that they turn against the one using them.
Their terror is too one-sided.' Since we were speaking
of war, I asked him if it wasn't enough that the enemy
had the same weapons? 'No,' he said, 'the weapon should
have a will of its own. A man ought to be more afraid
of the gun in his hand than of the enemy.' Then he said
a curious thing, he said that war had become a religion,
only it wasn't like the old religions, which were religions of dying, the new religion was based on science
and was a religion of killing. When I asked him what
part God played in it, he said we must speak of a God
beyond the God the nations prayed to, that for him
belief in God was quite simply belief in something which
could not be killed, but—and he stressed this especially—it was not in God's power to save even one single person from death. He finished this long conversation
which, as you can tell, intrigued me sufficiently that I
have remembered it almost verbatim, with the strange
observation that it was impossible to imagine how dangerous the world would be without animals. How he
could move from God to the animals I was quite at a
loss to comprehend, until I asked him what he did for
a living and he told me he was a trapper. Then I understood. My impression of Johnson was of a man who
thought about what he was doing, and one who viewed
life in terms of himself and his trade. A trapper he was,
yes, but not like most trappers who have been shoved
to the fringe of society and forced to contend with the
brutes. Johnson struck me as having consciously chosen
his way of life—as you, Doctor, chose medicine, or I the
Church, or you, Inspector, law enforcement—as a vo-
cation, you might say."

The Bishop ceased speaking and an uneasy silence
ensued. Mildred's eyes were aglow and her skin flushed
at this new interpretation, while the doctor sat appar-

ently bored and impassive. Eames's response to the latest revelation was that everyone seemed to know Johnson; or was there a Johnson implanted by God in each man and woman's mind's eye which grew as faith grew till it brought forth its harvest: these dull recitations, with the imprimatur on them, concerning war and religion, weapons and schnitzel? For his part, he was secretly pleased that he had lost faith and that the doctor was a known skeptic. He was about to suggest that the two of them, atheist and agnostic, leave the true believers behind to swap sputum and sperm while they visited Bunce in hospital—Bunce, whom Goodman Johnson had blasted a hole through—when words from the doctor struck Eames like a truncheon and swept him and his horse from the board.

"Your impression of Johnson accords with my own. That sounds like the Johnson I know, though I knew him before the time you speak of, five, perhaps six, years ago."

Eames stared aghast at the doctor. He could scarcely hear the words for the high-voltage hum in his mind, yet the sense of the words came through clearly.

"I never mentioned it, Eames, not for any particular reason but just that it wasn't material, or didn't seem so, but when I was stationed in Mayo a man came in with severe lacerations on his shoulder and chest, not fresh ones, but they had grown septic. I think a lynx or a bear must have mauled him, though he never said. I treated him, the entire transaction lasted perhaps twenty minutes, he offered to pay, I told him the company paid me, he insisted on paying, I took it—American bills, this first time. The man was Johnson. He came in one other time, some months later, this time with an inguinal hernia; he also had an abscessed wisdom tooth, which he said he would pull himself. I explained to him about the hernia, which was so acute he could scarcely walk, how the inguinal type were common in males and as often as not healed themselves, like your malady, Eames, but more painful. I offered him drugs or surgery, but he said no, all he wanted was an explanation, and off he went—again, after having paid me, this time in Canadian money. I never saw him again, but he impressed me. There was something about him, a sense he gave off, that made him seem..." The doctor searched for a word.

"Self-sufficient," offered the Bishop.

"Yes, that of course, but so are most trappers. No, angular is the word I would use, angular and unapproachable. That's why I find it hard to credit your account of him, Mildred. That he should be here at all is highly unlikely, that he would speak is more so; but that he should say what you say he said is beyond credibility. I cannot imagine the Johnson I treated saying, 'Don't be afraid.'"

"You're not a woman," flared Mildred, "and you don't know how to speak to one. A real man speaks differently to a woman than he does to another man."

"I should think a 'real man,' as you put it, would be the same to all."

"Lord," the Bishop invoked, folding his hands in mock prayer, and raising his eyes heavenward, "may all men be good men, and may all good men be nice men."

"I like that," said Mildred.

"Lady Astor's prayer," said the Bishop.

"Alex," the doctor said, scraping his chair, "I'm heading to the hospital. Come, if you like. You could look in on Bunce, and we could take a look at that problem of yours."

Eames was already up and grappling with his parka, groping for his pipe and tobacco while struggling toward the head hole through which, when he emerged, he hoped to breathe.

3

What was happening to him? He had been drunk before and he had known grief, but the sense of escape he felt as he fled through the front porch and stumbled out the front door from Mildred Urquhart's kitchen into the vast freezer locker of Arctic night and the blow to the brain and shock to the system it dealt him, him or anyone else entering it, was out of proportion to anything he had seen, any word he had heard, any actual wound he had suffered in the circle of friends-turned-antagonists around the table of fire he had fled. The doctor, who without a word or look back was trudging off toward the hospital, did not seem to be so affected, and he was leaving the same round table, departing the same field of fire. So it must be he alone, Only-Eames, to whom whatever had happened was happening, he alone on whom the ends of the world and the eyes of the Hunter bore down. He shifted his gaze from the Hunter and sought out the Big Dipper, a constellation familiar from childhood. As a small boy he had sought the Big Dipper just outside the screen door of his parents' farmhouse, found it before going to bed each night, and felt comforted. Now, like a meathook dangling from the night sky, or a series of meathooks, the shiny stars their sharp points, he found it and felt even colder. Stability, maybe, but the stability only of undying threat, of a hand raised and poised against him

'or against anyone who soberly raised his eyes or his
hands to the dark god who hung it. No, something more
compelling than Mildred Urquhart, more alien than the
Bishop of Athabasca, more inscrutable than the resident surgeon was preying upon him and making him
want to get down on his knees and eat snow and howl
like a dog...The way things were going, had
gone....Everything since the advent of Johnson (though
things had gone ill before Johnson: drunkenness, death,
and divorce), but it was only since Johnson had come
into his life, only in life after Johnson—A. J.—that he
had been conscious of how ill things had gone, how
irreversibly badly, and only since then that the ends of
the world had been visited on him: the Bishop and
Mildred, Rene and the papers, even Germany and Japan—bullies and bishops and insatiable women—all
targeting on him, fixing him in their sights, training
their big guns on him or on Johnson, to obliterate one
or the other, or both...What had *he* done? What crime
had *he* committed? What enormity had he conceived
that he should be hounded and hunted, reduced to
searching out the Big Dipper and to regarding the unsleeping eyes of the Hunter as a personal threat? Why
should the tunic he wore, any more than the cassock,
be labeled "murderous"—especially when he felt naked
beneath the night sky, and skinless in front of people?
Where had Eames gone, and where could he be found?
What was happening to him?...

Standing in the snow outside Mildred Urquhart's,
his hand in his parka pocket, his pipe in his hand (he
knew in advance it would not comfort him: he might
reach for his pipe and pull out a snake), nothing familiar felt safe anymore. The familiar had not protected
him from the worst, for the worst was happening. But
the worst was not happening to him anymore, because
there was no "him" to whom it could happen. Eames
had died, and gone to theosophists' heaven. He felt himself expanding, his tunic stretching with him, till his
bulk filled the Arctic landscape and his uniform the
night sky. Over "G" Division, Western Arctic Sub-Dis-

trict, Eames in his duty pants stood, the embodiment
of law and order, at the head of a gigantic posse whose
number was as the stars of the Milky Way or the ice
crystals of the Mackenzie. Men, dogs, planes and supply
troops, trappers and trappers' wives, pressmen and
corpsmen, statesmen and churchmen—the galactic force
behind him filled the night sky and had no freedom but
to obey him: when he raised his right hand the force
swirled forward; when he put his hand down the force
rested. At the head of this force Eames felt himself
surging upward, higher and higher until he hung from
the Big Dipper. From the Big Dipper he looked down
to survey the whole Arctic—every nook and cranny,
every corner and crevice, of his entire jurisdiction: delta,
mountains, rivers, dwellings, all villages and solitary
sacks, every animal lair and dog run—no illicit activity, civil or criminal, could escape his scrutiny. With
astral sight Eames comprehended space, but not time
as certain seers did, and not time and space as the
founding few, such as Rudolph Steiner, had. Remote
above the Arctic and surveying as with insect's eyes
behind or stars above his head that frozen region, Eames
put his mortal shell in motion and limped between the
house and the hospital, even as his astral body hung
behind to spy upon the Bishop and the Queen inside
the house.... Every-Eames, having suffered the excru-
ciating worst of Only-Eames, emerged from the refiner's
fire of Mildred Urquhart's kitchen as One-and-Other-
Eames—and what pain, what harm, what suffering
could touch the man who underwent that distancing?
What sorrow or what sight could hurt him then? His
mortal shell might endure agony, or his astral body
behold anguish, but what the one endured the other
would not suffer, and what the other saw the one would
not endure. Released from pain that man would be released from pleasure also. Released from all such worries, one Eames now trod in the tracks of the surgeon
toward the hospital to visit King, while in the tradition
of Rudolph Steiner and Madame Blavatsky another
Eames hung from the meathook, the point of a star

piercing his cerebral cortex, as calmly he observed the Bishop of Athabasca and the Queen of Aklavik....

TRUST MEN LITTLE,
AND RELIGIOUS MEN LESS

(The Bishop is sitting at the kitchen table, the backgammon board at his elbow. Mildred gets up to shut the door to the porch, which has blown open behind the two men. She returns to the kitchen counter, between the sink and the oven, and begins preparing a platter of tinned meats, olives, and sardines, her back to the Bishop. The Bishop empties the decanter in front of him, drinking it all at one go, then commences tapping his foot and humming, then singing, a tune. The words he sings fit the tune he sings to, "When Irish Eyes Are Smiling.")

"Oh, they called me Hanseatic
  When at Freiberg I excelled,
  Jesus Mary and Heidegger why was I not expelled?

"Oh, they called me Maginot-minded
  When to Toulouse I went up,
  Mother o' God ha' mercy on my honors and my cup,

"Oh, they called me Little Papa
  When in Rome I climbed the stairs,
  Yegorrah man three Ph.D.'s are not for Peter's
    heirs.

"Oh, they'll call me Paddy Murphy
  When to home I turn again,
  And at home I'll be plain Paddy and nere traipse to
    Berlin."

(The Bishop stops singing and tapping his foot. He raises the empty decanter, peers at it, sets it down.)
—Oh dear, dear God, those were great times, great times. How did we wind up in this Godforsaken place, Millie? What's its name?

—Aklavik. It's part of your diocese, remember?

—The see, I should say. Considering the heresies rampant in some of the faithful. Your Inspector, for instance.

—You should meet his wife.

—Weeping God, why should I? I've troubles enough of my own. Any God's quantity of red wine down my gullet, another man's wife in my, ah, diocese, an inspector of the RCMP poking about—he's fond of you, Millie, watch out for that man—and this outlaw Johnson at large. Mother of God, defend us! And, Millie, I've a confession to make. Since we were last together, five, six years, I have not loved another woman, but—how shall I put it?—only separate parts of the female anatomy, and their wearing apparel: sweaters, for instance.

(Mildred, from the counter) I know.

—You know? How could you know?

—I know. I, too, have a confession to make. I love a man's foot. To be specific, Eames's foot.

—His foot?

—His left one.

—But why his left one? Does he have webbed toes, or turned toes, or no toes at all? I could make a song about that. It's not club, is it? Why his left one? Why his foot? And why, in the name of God, Eames's foot? Mildred, this is fetishism, and women are not fetishists.

—It has a wart.

—"A wart may be an adornment to an otherwise plain face."

—It is on his foot, his left one.

—"The Lord takes no pleasure in the feet of a man."

—That's why he limps. I have dreams of a limping man, his dead child and his dreadful ex-wife behind him.

—"Time and chance happen to all men."

—That's consoling.

—It's not meant to be. *Komm' näher.*

(Mildred comes over with the platter of food, and sits in his lap.) He's over fifty, you know.

—Who cares how old he is? (The Bishop begins kiss-

ing her neck, which she exposes for him while setting
down the platter of food beside the backgammon board.)
—I care. It's my birthday today.
(The Bishop continues kissing her neck.) Really?
—Really. James forgot, so did Alex. I'm, let me see
(she pretends to tally on the fingers of one hand, then
of the other, then of the first hand again) thirty-five!
Nobody writes me verses anymore, now that I'm thirty-
five. You used to send me verses from Marburg!
(The Bishop quits kissing her neck.) Thirty-five. (The
Bishop blinks and stares into space beyond Mildred
Urquhart's left ear.) Thirty-five, thirty-five ... you're sure
you're thirty-five, not thirty-six, or ... (A moment more
he stares into space, then recites into her left ear.)

> MILDRED is yet more alive
>   having come to thirty-five;
> If her heart she could contrive
>   life to stop at thirty-five,
> Love his chariot would drive
>   to the banks of thirty-five,
> Dismount his fiery steeds and dive
>   into the straits of thirty-five,
> Remorseful that he did not strive
>   to mate the Queen at thirty-five;
> Endgame for him who cannot thrive
>   beyond the bounds of thirty-five;
> Disaster for the rash who wive
>   before the age of thirty-five.

And now you see what it is to come for poetry to a
Bishop. The alternate lines form a true acrostic, and
the rhymes are alphabetical—an ancient Jewish and
Christian code, used, for example, in Proverbs 31 and
during the time of the Great Persecution.
(Mildred, elated, pulls up her sweater for the Bishop
to kiss her on the breast.) Ohh, Thomas, it's so lovely.
What a lovely, lovely verse. May I write it down?
—You may. (He releases her.)
(She jumps up and goes in search of writing mate-
rials. From the next room, she says) It's so ...

—Thirty-fivish. You're sure, quite sure, you're thirty-five?

(From the living room) I think I'm sure. Let's see now. Oh, listen, Al Bowlly's on the radio.

—Who's Al Bowlly?

—Who's Al Bowlly!!

The Bishop's question and Mildred's reply echo through space and over the Arctic, the genius of the tundra asking the genius of the tree line, "Who's Al Bowlly?", and neither genius can tell. The seven stars of the Big Dipper quiz one another regarding this eighth star, this wonder of the airways, but to no avail. Mildred Urquhart, age thirty-five, has left the kitchen, and walked through the living room where the radio blares, and entered the bedroom in search of paper and pencil...no immediate answer is forthcoming....

Eames limped toward the hospital, the words of a popular tune he had heard somewhere being sung in falsetto in his inner ear: "When my little Pomeranian met your little Pekinese..." Then it got garbled with another: "There's a ring around the moon..." But no moon shone over Aklavik, ringed or otherwise, only the tiny lights of the trappers' cabins and, off toward the river, the Eskimos' shacks, and ahead and behind him the mission compound cast fingers of light across the gray snow, shadowing the hummocks where chained dogs lay. If one did not walk in the darkness, would he be able to see the light...the lie...the lying down dog and the man standing...? A cold blast of wind struck at Eames as he walked, causing him to turn his head. A finger of light from a blown-open shack door raced across the gray snow and touched his face. In the open doorway were a man and a dog, profiled, the man's back to the door, the dog's rear to the man. The dog's tail plumed up in a panache on the side nearest Eames; the tail feathered and trembled like a flag of desire, then it drooped. The man in long johns hunched over and holding the dog reached behind him with one hand and pulled the door to. The pencil of light was erased. Eames blinked and came to a halt. Had the door really opened?

Had he seen what he thought he had seen? Was it Gardlund?—no, Gardlund was out hunting Johnson.
Lang?—but he was out trapping. Was it...he couldn't
bring himself to think it—Silver? Was that possible?
Or was it a vision, a glimpse into chaos? Had he seen
anything, really? One minute he was hearing a puppy-
love song from nowhere, the next minute visions
of...Sodom and Begorra! The Bishop of Athabasca's
naked penis suddenly leaped into Eames's mind's eye:
about the size of a husky's, but circumcised, with a blue
vein running the length of it, and a small white pimple
on the head. It stood blue and erect, quivering. Then
around it closed Mildred Urquhart's warm, moist mouth.
Eames shut his eyes and shook his head fiercely, stamped
his foot on the hard-packed snow, the left foot, until he
felt nauseous. One-Eames wanted to vomit, while Other-
Eames looked on disgustedly. Other-Eames communed
with One-Eames across space and time: 'This is not bad,
there's worse to come.' In pain Eames trod his solitary
path to the hospital....

—Mother of God, in the feathered glory of thy mouth,
o mother of God, o...mother...
—Mmm...

As soon as he entered the hospital he heard the radio
playing "There's a Ring Around the Moon." As he passed
beneath the Procrustean sign he decided to leave his
parka on—this would be a quick visit: no lectures on
warts, and no dawdling—just a quick, compassionate
visit with King. As he limped through the foyer and
past the nurses' station (nurse McCabe was not there,
no one was: it was after visiting hours—2210), he
reached out and turned off the radio. The voice died,
not abruptly, but gradually with a crackling, on the
words "around the..." and now Eames wasn't sure it
was the same song. He stopped and switched the radio
back on, but it took time to start up again, the next
word was lost, and he turned the radio down but not
off—as it had been when he'd come in—then limped
down the hallway to King's room.

In the darkened hallway he slackened his pace and wondered if he should be making this visit. It was long after visiting hours, it had been nearly two weeks since he had seen King; soon King would be flying to Edmonton, and he himself would be out after Johnson; they might miss one another altogether...he should have come sooner, he should not have gone to the doctor's house, he should, he should not have, he should...King's door was before him, on the left of the corridor, and it was open a crack, a pencil of light showing through into the hallway. Now that he was here, he would see him. Eames tapped timidly, and pushed the door open.

King was lying propped up in bed, a bedside lamp pooling light on his bandage and bathrobe. No tubes were attached to him and he looked in good shape, though subdued. He was holding in both hands some material which, as Eames entered the room, he let fall to his sides and proceeded to hide, under the covers, even as he looked up and said to Eames, "Chief, what a...what a surprise. I never in a thousand years expected to see you, not...not tonight anyways."

Eames left the door open behind him and moved toward the bed. The bed was not where it had been and it was awkward to know how to come at it; also, his left foot pained him. He cast about for a chair to sit on.

"Mind if I sit down?"

"Just toss those things on the floor, chief." But even as King said this, and as Eames removed the clothes, King seemed to be shoving whatever it was further under the covers.

"So how are you?"

"I'm fine. Fine. How you keepin', chief?"

Another tune by the same tenor voice wended its way up the hallway and in through the open doorway: "Brother, can you spare a dime? My luck is down and I'm..." The voice died out, then resounded: "Brother, can you spare a dime?"

"Posse leaves early tomorrow, so I thought I'd drop by. How's nurse McCabe treating you?"

King grinned. "Can you believe, I never even noticed her at first, I was that sick."

"You were in bad shape."

"Yeah."

King lay quietly in the pool of light, breathing regularly, his hands beneath the covers. The tenor voice in the hallway hit and held a high note—outside a dog howled.

"This is comin' off tomorrow, maybe next day." He indicated the bandage, yellow and pink with food stains and seepings, which covered his stomach and chest. King stared at the wall at the foot of the bed. "You know, chief, I been thinking. A guy has lots of time to think when he's in here. I been thinking off and on about that guy Johnson. I even had a dream about him." He glanced over at Eames, who nodded.

"You know, that guy, until he hammered me, we didn't really have anything on him. An' McDowell an' me didn't exactly come at him friendly-like, wagging our tails. We said 'Open up, Johnson, or we'll blast your ass'—somethin' like that." King turned his head and looked earnestly at Eames. "I've gone over it again and again, chief, exactly how it happened, an' it seems to me the guy was in the right, or, anyway, what he did was understandable, under the circumstances—I mean, put yourself in his place." He stopped speaking and continued to look searchingly at Eames, who met King's gaze but said nothing. "That's not to deny he's prob'ly a criminal, but just taking that one situation, the one that matters to me . . ." He broke off speaking and stared at the wall again.

"What was your dream?" said Eames. And his voice, even as he said it, seemed to him thin, almost falsetto.

King stared at the wall as if watching a silent film. "It was weird. There was a bunch of us, an' we all had numbers. We were lookin' for the one who had no number. But the one without a number had a name, an' none of us did, we just had numbers. We were making a lot of noise, tryin' to figure out the warrant, which was in code. When we finally figured it out it said, 'Seek him who is silent. His name is Johnson.'" King looked over at Eames and said, "I told you it was weird. An' it gets weirder." Again he stared at the wall. "We all drew straws and I was the one sent up to the cabin while the others covered. I was told to keep talking, it was only if I was talking that I'd know who the silent one was. I was supposed to ask the man inside if he was Johnson, an' if he said he was I'd know he wasn't, because the real Johnson was silent. But if he said nothing I was to shoot him, but I didn't know whether to wait for a count of ten, or five, or to shoot him right away...anyway, I went up, an' I said...tell me if this is boring you."

"No, no, go on."

"I went up an' there was this guy, it was Johnson, I was pretty sure it was Johnson, but I had my instructions, an' I'd decided to wait for a count of five...oh, yes, I almost forgot: he couldn't be seized, the warrant said, if we attempted to seize him he would outnumber us because he had no number...that's what the warrant said." King shrugged. "It's a dream, chief, remember that. Anyway, I went up, an' this guy named Johnson opened the door an' I said, 'Are you Johnson?' An' while I was counting to five before I shot him, I suddenly became him—you know how dreams are—but it was too late, I'd already shot, and as soon as I shot this Johnson guy said, 'I am he who was within you'—those were his exact words, 'I am he who was within you'—then he disappeared. Weird, huh?"

King continued to stare at the wall in silence, his eyes darting back and forth as if watching the flapping end of the film. Without looking at Eames, and in the same bemused voice he said: "I'm not sure I'm right for the Force, chief, anymore. Don't get me wrong, it was great, and I got more out of it than I put into it, I don't deny that. But I been thinkin'...well, Moira an' me 've been thinkin'..." He left off and shifted his upper body around. "It's different for you, chief, but I'm a young man..." The voice trailed off and merged, for Eames, with the final held note of the song, "diii-mmmme."

"Right," said Eames. "Well, you can't go wrong with Moira." Then, suddenly piqued: "What have you got there, anyway? Not old copies of *The Force?* Is it a girlie magazine you're hiding from Moira? It's none of my business, of course."

King blushed, and drew his hands out from under the covers. "Just a sort of a present, a going-away present...for you. It's not finished yet."

The fingers of one hand held a long needle attached to a large ball of yarn. The yarn was attached to the square canvas backing which was in King's other hand. The canvas material, covered with yarn, was about two feet square and covered with small squares, in a chessboard design. The bottom row of squares had not been finished, and letters and numbers were on it.

"Needlepoint," King said. "Moira showed me how, an' see, here's the inscription." He pointed to the bottom rank which read, "XII.31 '31 A.K.—A.J. II. .'32." "This here's the date I was shot," said King. "I'm waiting for you guys to get him," he said, "so's I can finish it off. It's for you, chief, for your office." He handed the needlework over to Eames, while he held the needle and yarn.

Eames held the cloth, which he supposed was a wall hanging, in both hands. The backing felt stiff and rough.

"You'd never believe how much work's involved, chief. I been working non-stop, almost. That's a buttonhole stitch, an' this is checker, those ones are cross-stitches, an' that's a basket-weave or tent stitch. There's others, too, even more complicated, but I figured these ones would do." King, holding the needle and yarn in his hand like an intravenous feeder tube, looked pleased with himself and beamed brightly.

"It's, uh, very complex," muttered Eames, "very...touching."

"I thought you'd like it, chief. Moira said you would too. She helped me with it. She got me the canvas and yarns an' she taught me the stitches. It's a joint gift, really. Soon's you finish off Johnson, I'll finish it. There's only a few stitches left."

Eames handed the piece back, and glanced at his

watch. The same tenor voice was singing, "Gotta date with an angel, Gonna meet her at seven. Gotta date with an angel..."

"Guess I'll go look in on the men," he announced, getting up. Standing at the bedside, looking down on King, Eames felt at an unfair advantage. He was up, King was down, but Moira could in a moment reverse that. Probably she and King were both waiting for him to leave. "Guess I'll go," he repeated, "before the men are asleep."

"They won't be asleep," King said, looking up at Eames, slightly impishly, Eames thought, but it may have been the light, the way it fell. "You might as well know it now, chief, you'll find out sooner or later." And once again King seemed to look impishly at him, as though he had secrets and yet more secrets to reveal.

"Know what?" said Eames, unable to guess.

"Your ol' lady's back," King announced flatly. "She was in here earlier, interviewing me for the papers. When she left here, she was headed for the barracks."

Eames received this intelligence standing up. He neither spoke nor made a move to go, he just stood there.

"She's still the same, chief. If anything, more so. Said she was here to cover 'the Johnson affair,' said she had your permission, and...anyway, I thought you should know."

"Right."

"Luck tomorrow, chief."

"Right."

Eames executed an about-face and walked from the room, closing the door behind him, and down the dark hallway into the music, which as he approached it grew louder and louder. But the music he walked into was not Al Bowlly's crooning, nor was it a radio broadcast. It emanated instead from his own sinciput, or from the spheres beyond, or from both: a sharp furioso in which triangles, xylophone, kettledrums, rattles, combed sticks, bells, blocks, whip, cymbals, bass drum, and gong percussed the brassy sounds of trumpet, trombone, and tuba. The further he walked and the closer he came to

the source of the noise—be it his own sinciput or the
spheres—the music merged in an appassionato of viols,
bass viols, and cellos all vying and veering off as he
stepped out into the cold and under the spheres' direct
influence into murmuring strettos and downward glis-
sandos and crackling pizzicatos. . . . The corridor, too, down
which he walked and from which he emerged was not
the same darkened hallway he had entered, but a path-
way from silence or a shelter from awareness which,
as he left it, stretched off into an immeasurable expanse. The corridor began from his head, was an endless
continuation of his head, the front lobe of which opened
it seemed into an Arctic expanse. As he faced the music
and walked down the hallway and past the nurses' station (at which nurse McCabe was now sitting, gaping
wide-eyed at him) he had the sensation of looking not
with his eyes but through a hole in the center of his
head, and of hearing not with his ears but through the
same hole, which was he. He was not Eames, but a hole
in Eames's head, gazing out along the hospital corridor
into an immeasurable Arctic expanse, hearing from
there the din of sound which issued from the vast void.
A bloodless, bright, ironspikelike hole, without benefit
of clergy—this was Eames; in whose headhole buzzed
and crackled the bass of the Bishop and the bell-like
tone of the Queen . . . as onward he marched, along the
men's barracks path, into the void itself. . . .

BAD WHEN SHE WAS LITTLE,
WORSE WHEN SHE WAS BIG

(Mildred Urquhart's bedroom. On the queen-sized
bed which dominates and nearly fills the room lie the
Bishop of Athabasca and Mildred Urquhart side by side.
A gold-colored spread covers them. From the next room,
muted by the closed door, the Ray Noble orchestra with
crooner Al Bowlly can be heard on the radio, but the
sound is tinny and thin. Mildred Urquhart lies staring
up at the ceiling like a Christian saint on her deathbed.
The Bishop, his Buddhalike bulk expelling and swell-
ing like a great air bellows, recites:)

—One fate comes to all, to the virtuous as to the wicked, to clean and unclean, to him who sacrifices and him who does not sacrifice...are you listening, Mildred?...this is the evil that inheres in all that is done under the sun: that one fate comes to all....Are you listening to God's representative, or to that Godawful music?

—Don't you think you should go before James comes back?

—Two things grieve my heart, a third arouses my anger: a warrior wasting away through poverty, a wise man treated with contempt, a holy man turning back from virtue to sin—the Lord marks this man out for violent death...violent death, Mildred....

—I don't want to hurt him, Thomas. He doesn't deserve to be hurt.

—Three things are beyond my comprehension, four, indeed, I do not understand: the way of an eagle through the skies, the way of a snake over a rock, the way of a ship in mid-ocean, and the way of a man with a maid.

—He was hurt last time, terribly hurt. I don't want to hurt him again.

—Three things my soul delights in, delightful to God and to men: concord between brothers, friendship between neighbors, and a wife and a husband who live happily together.

—Don't be sarcastic. You can spend the night at the men's barracks, or you can stay with Alex. Now, get up...

—Three things of stately tread, four, indeed, of stately bearing: the lion, the cock, the he-goat, the king...

—James will have finished his rounds by now. He can't make rounds all night. Here...

(She sits up in bed and pulls him up to a sitting position. He continues to quote.)

—Stolen waters are sweet, and bread tastes better in secret. But there are six things that Yahweh hates, seven that His soul abhors....

—Thomas, you're drunk. I've never seen you drunk before. No wonder you couldn't...

—A haughty look, a lying tongue, hands that shed

innocent blood, a heart that weaves wicked plots, feet
that hurry to evil...

—Hurry, Thomas, please hurry. (She helps him pull
on his long johns and drapes his cassock on him, then
pulls him up off the bed.) Now, are you going to the
men's barracks, or to Alex's?

—a false witness who lies with every breath, a man
who sows dissension among brothers, a...that's seven,
isn't it? Where are my robes? Where is my cassock? I
say Candlemas in—what time is it, Mildred?—where
is my Joseph's coat?

(She stands huddled and shivering, holding herself
with her arms, listening for the sound from the other
room.) It's—listen! that program comes on at eleven—
it's eleven-thirty almost. They're on you.

—Then is Aaron dressed. *Nunc dimittis servum tuum
Domine: secundum verbum tuum in pace. Quia viderunt
oculi mei salutare tuum: quod parasti*...do you remember it, Mildred, the holy mystery which in half an hour
I reveal here in—what is the name of this place?

(She slips into a loose-fitting silken housecoat.) Aklavik.

—*ante faciem omnium popularum. Lumen ad reve-
lationem gentium, et gloriam plebis tuae Israel.* God's
eyes, woman, where is my greatcoat? (He stands at the
door and recites, while she straightens the covers on
the bed.) *Domine sancte, Pater omnipotens, aeterne Deus,
qui omnia ex nihilo creasti*...do the words touch you,
Mildred? You studied to be a nun, didn't you? The Sisters of the Passionate Heart. Jesus Murphy, what a
sister you'd make! A rale thickeen, you are...

—A what?

—A pert hussy...*ut jussu tuo per opera apum, hunc
liquorem ad perfectionem cerei venire fecisti: et qui hodierna*...

(She opens the door and pushes him out, steering
him through the living room, where the radio blares
forth a jazz tune. The Bishop grasps her waist and hand
and turns her in a circle. Singing:)

—I wanna dance, can't fake it. I wanna dance, let's
make it...

—Quit! (She shakes herself free, picks up his great-coat and holds it for him. The Bishop twirls around, snorts playfully, runs at her and butts the coat like a bull.) Quit that, Thomas! Here, put your arm in here!

—Nine things I can think of which strike me as happy, and a tenth which is now on my tongue...

—The other arm. (She buttons his greatcoat. He hiccups.)

—A cup of cold water. You can't deny me that. *Et per intercessionem beatae Mariae semper Virginis, cujus hodie festa`devote celebrantur,* hear from the sink of thy kitchen the voices of this thy people who desire to praise thee with hymns and who have praised thee with a poem, and be propitious to them and to me, thy humble servant...

(She pulls him by his coat into the kitchen, sits him down at the table, goes over to the sink and turns on the tap.)

—The nine things I think of which strike me as happy, the tenth which is now on my tongue...

(She brings him water; he drinks. She stands him up and steers him toward the door. He recites:)

—a man whose joy is in his children, he who lives to see the downfall of his enemies, the happy man— mentioned earlier, remember him, Mildred?—who keeps house with a sensible wife, he who does not toil with ox and donkey, he who has never sinned with his tongue, he who does not serve a man less worthy than himself, the happy man who has acquired good sense *and can find* (The Bishop balks in the doorway.) *attentive ears for what he has to say...*

(She pushes him out and tries to close the door, but he wedges his foot in the doorway, reciting:)

—But hearken to me, Mildred my love, hearken and ponder my words. Three things which my heart dreads, and a fourth which terrifies me: slander by a whole town, the gathering of a mob, a false accusation—these are all worse than death. But, God between us and all harm, a woman's wrath...I am, as ever, in your power, my love....

(He removes his foot and she closes the door, bolts

it, and leans against it, trembling. Then she walks back
into the kitchen, through the living room, and into the
bedroom where, through the tiny snowdrifted window
she watches the Bishop shuffling along the path toward
the men's barracks, stopping every few steps to turn
toward the house and gesticulate. She watches him out
of sight, then falls back on the bed and, staring up at
the ceiling as the silken housecoat spills open around
her, draws the gold-colored spread over her, over her
legs, stomach, breasts, over her shoulders and arms, to
her neck. Beneath the cover she lays both hands on her
breasts, holding firmly the cups of her breasts, pressing
the nipples between her fingers; with her index fingers
she massages the nipples, touching and rubbing them
gently. Then she draws both hands down, slowly and
firmly, the length of her torso—across her stomach,
over her abdomen and along both hips and thighs and
into the groin, until both hands come to rest in the
warm, moist cleft of her thighs. Staring at the ceiling
and slowly pursing her mouth, the index finger of her
right hand explores the pursed lips of her vulva, then
slowly slides in....)

Eames was limping along the rutted ice path between the hospital and the men's barracks, the buzzing
and crackling of Bishop and Queen spinning giddily in
his headhole. The further he marched from the doctor's
house and the closer to the men's barracks, the faster
the dialogue spun through his head as it vorticed out
toward the void. He fast-marched a few steps: the words
spun dizzily. He limped slowly: the words spiraled lazily
down. All things were interrelated: Eames, Other-
Eames, the Bishop, the Queen, the doctor, King's wound,
and Johnson. All things were his: church, state, press,
home, hospital, Johnson. No one thing would disappear
without it all disappearing, no one sound would cease
until it all ceased, and it would not all cease until Johnson did—after Johnson the judgment—and maybe
(Eames dreaded to think this; he fought it; he thought
it), maybe not even then....Was there hope then for

Eames? Was there silence? He heard the grim hum of
the universe grinding inside his headhole, and hurried
on toward his next station of pain, the men's barracks,
to let one hostile sound oust another....

"Inspector!" The cry from Riddell was a cry not of
pain or of relief, but of puzzlement. He was standing
more or less in the center of the aisle between the two
rows of bunks. Carmichael and Parsons stood beside
him, one on either side, Carmichael focusing on the
floor at his feet while Parsons stared directly at Eames
in a silent appeal. Lang was lying down on a cot, while
Wild, three bunks removed from the central group,
peered down at them from a top bunk. Lazarus sat on
a chair by the stove, staring into the stove-hole. Ranged
against this array of embattled men, and holding all
six of them at bay on one side of the barracks, Rene
exalted stood: her mouth a slash of red lipstick, her face
chalk white with powder, her bobbed hair impossibly
blond. She wore a bright red suit coat over a black rib-
knit sweater above matching red (and tight) slack-
pants, which accentuated the curved coiled spring of
her body and its lean toward the men, as though ready
to strike, or strike again. A fistful of papers—Teletype
papers—she held clutched in one hand, and when she
opened her mouth (which even in the one or two minutes since Eames had arrived she had touched up anew
with lipstick: pursing her lips and smearing with a
quick hand, two clean sweeps), when she opened her
mouth words like bullets spewed forth, mowing down
men who stood, stared, listened, as her words like dum-
dums entered their ears, eyes, stomachs....

The barrage of words, which broke off at Eames's
entrance long enough for Riddell to cry out and for her
to apply new lipstick, was the most emphatic Eames
had ever heard (each word like a little explosion), and
when she stopped for a word she made a gurgling sound
so that no one else might cut her off or get a word in
edgewise (though Riddell had got one in, but only by
shouting). She was gurgling now, and taking Eames in

with a glance and a quick bob of the head, as though
pointing a gun at him and ordering him to join the rest.
Then she resumed her harangue, the red gash of her
mouth reopening and the barrage of words spewing forth
to catch him in chest, heart, and stomach....

"The cost, as I said, is negligible, and disproportion-
ate to the campaign. The third posse must succeed at
all cost, at any cost. Johnson has to be captured or
killed, and the Canadian public deserves to be told exactly how it was done. Are you using the eleven hundred
pounds of dynamite cached here in Aklavik? And if not,
why not? What use are you making of the Bellanca
aircraft which left Edmonton two days ago? Where is
it now? What instructions have you, Inspector, given
its pilot? And how many men are still out in the field,
and why hasn't the Yukon detachment linked up with
them yet? Have orders been issued for that? Is the Alaska
border patrol on alert? This madman Johnson can do
the impossible, or so the public imagine. Is he mad?
And who is he? Does he have a criminal record? These
are some of the questions the Canadian public wants
to know and deserves to be told, and all that these cables
which Corporal Wild furnished me indicate is that some
of these questions haven't even been asked, much less
answered."

With a gurgling noise she held up one of the cables
clutched in her hand to read, while ex-Mountie Parsons
continued to stare at Eames in silent appeal, and Eames
glared fiercely at Wild. "Just to give an example, this
one is a voucher, signed by the Inspector, drawn up no
doubt by his clerk. It reads in part, 'As regards the
necessity for purchasing the articles enumerated in the
voucher, I beg to report that we had sufficient camping
equipment in store at Aklavik for current needs, but
when extensive patrols were undertaken on the Rat
River in January, and as many as nineteen men had
to be accommodated in camp, I was forced to purchase
three stoves with elbows and pipes.' It goes on to detail,
with apologetic explanations, purchases of such things
as waste rags for flares, pilot bread to supply the camp
at Rat River, two enamel cooking pots, thirty-six flash-

light batteries, six-ounce duck canvas for a shroud for
Constable Millen, and two hundred and eighty-one dollars' worth of groceries, itemized. The whole is over the
signature of Inspector A. N. Eames, who has the honor
to submit, etcetera. And this is the food and equipment
voucher—excluding the posse's payroll: we'll get to
that—for the month of January! My point, gentlemen,
is this: if I were to wire this to the Edmonton or Vancouver or Toronto newspapers as a statement of the
expenses of the RCMP in their efforts to apprehend
Johnson—Johnson, who has already killed one man,
and wounded another—the papers, the radio, the government, why even the public would laugh! You're
treating this mission, the largest and most important
manhunt ever to take place in Canada, as just another
routine patrol! You're treating Johnson, and the manhunt for Johnson, in the same slack way that you'd
handle a pack of lost dogs!"

There was a slight gurgling sound as she selected
another paper from among those clutched in her fist,
and proceeded, before anyone broke in, to harangue the
men with it. "Or take this payroll voucher, again from
Inspector Eames but drawn up by Corporal Wild. It
reads, 'N. Verville, 28 days at $5 each, for a total of
$140. F. Carmichael, 18 days at the same, $90. John
Parsons, 10 days, $100'—why's that? Oh, I suppose
you're an ex-Mountie. 'Edgar Millen, 28 days, $280'—
well, he won't be collecting his! And so on. My point
here—wait, Inspector, before you interrupt—my point
is that this reflects a lack of imagination. A Mrs. Verville, whom I interviewed before I came in here (wife,
I presume, of the 'N. Verville' listed on this sheet), told
me that there were many persons willing to go out
against this outlaw, but that they had not been en-
couraged or permitted. Why not? Is it due to lack of
equipment? Is it from fear of over-spending your bud-
get? Or is it the fact that some of them are women,
some Eskimos, one, I understand, is a church divine—
is this the reason? What's the matter with you men up
here? Why is this madman still at large? Don't you have
enough troubles without him? Just you look at your-

selves!" She turned, for her peroration, point-blank on the Inspector. "Is this pitiful handful of pensioned-off Mounties and special constables and a trapper or two going to bring in a professional killer?—one who has already succeeded in repulsing you twice! What is your grand plan, your strategy, your overall approach? Surely you have one, Inspector!"

With that she formally turned the floor over to Eames. The men all shifted their gaze to him (except Lazarus, who sat staring into the stove-hole), and he faced a row of accusing eyes, as at a formal inquiry. It was the coroner's inquest all over, only this time the corpse was Johnson's, and Johnson was missing; or the scene in Rene's lawyer's office eight years ago, with himself on the carpet, and no correspondent. Eames, who stood just inside the door, wanted wildly to run out the door; he felt traumatized beyond the ability to make any coherent response. All he could think was, 'It's Rene'... using her torrent of words to drown him and browbeat his men, using her looks to gain attention and her trick of citing a text, turning her sense of deep hurt to blame casting and making everybody feel guilty.... It was Rene, all right; Eames was surrounded by Rene. Even now, having yielded the floor to him, she was waiting, pen and paper in hand, to take notes, to argue, to trap him. The Rene he had last seen eight years ago was a pet compared to the viper who glared at him now: her red and black chain mailed frame poised to spring, her face sharp and diamond-shaped, her eyes glittering, her tongue deadly.

"The men," he began, clearing his throat, "are not really responsible for the, uh, conduct of the manhunt. Insofar as anyone is, I suppose I am."

She nodded, and jotted down something.

"So I don't see the point in you, uh, airing these things, when I am the one responsible."

"You said that," she snapped.

He remembered that she always accused him of repeating himself, though this was the first time he had done so in years. He resolved not to do so again.

"If you want to talk about the conduct of the manhunt—its organization, the strategy behind it, the linking up with other units—it seems to me we could do so better in my office in private, or"—Eames focused his gaze and his frustration on Wild, who had supplied her with official papers—"perhaps with Corporal Wild in attendance, since as acting quartermaster he is essential to the success of the operation."

Wild, who was enjoying this confrontation from his upper bunk, comparing it with the quarrels his parents used to have, suddenly took on the expression of a ruined boy.

Riddell joined in: "That's a fine idea, Inspector. Wild knows things we don't, all right. He knew about them papers. Wild's the man to supply the info—tomorrow, after we're gone. And you got to get some sleep before we take off."

"I regret to inform you, Sergeant Riddell," said Rene, "that *I* won't be here tomorrow to confer with Corporal Wild."

"That's a shame, ma'am. You got to get back, though. We understand."

"I won't be here with Corporal Wild because I'll be with you in the field. I'm going with you," she announced, turning to Eames, "in the morning, with the posse."

The impact on Eames was the same as a firing squad's shots to a condemned man: he felt the shock but did not hear the sound. Something inside him collapsed, but there was no conscious awareness of outrage, no outward show of resistance.

Rene went on: "I have my own outfit. Special Constable Sittichiulis will be driving me. If anyone wishes to share my rig..."

The men all stared at Lazarus, who continued to stare at the stove-hole. The something within Eames which had collapsed began to encyst. His initial shock over, her design now took shape: from her mouth it took root in his stomach. The defection of Lazarus, the collaboration with Wild—these were strands in a web of

treachery and deceit which stretched from Rene's mouth
to the pit of Eames's stomach and, unchecked, would
enshroud the barracks, the compound, the Arctic—even
Johnson would not escape her; her design, Eames could
feel in his lower intestines, was total—the world. Someone had to stand up to her, soon, before she was fully
rearmed; a stand would have to be made on this or some
other issue, and who was there to make it? Riddell?
Both he and Parsons were from another era, couldn't
see the seriousness of the threat she posed, didn't appreciate the power of the press. Mildred Urquhart?
Maybe, but she was not threatened, and would be the
last to be challenged. Rene would move boldly, as she
had announced, straight for the jugular, for Johnson;
the Queen and her circle would be by-passed. Only
Eames sensed the danger, divined the design, saw the
need to dismantle her net before all were buried. But
Eames was down—or was he? who was he?—perhaps
his sole purpose in life was to neutralize Rene. The
world would owe him a medal for this, this act of extreme heroism in advance of the call, for no one perceived the danger yet, the design...

A cold wind struck Eames from behind.

"Gorra man! This is a gathering! Where the body is,
there the vultures will gather—eh, Inspector? I've come
for my bed, any bed. I don't believe I've had the pleasure, madame..." The Bishop advanced through the
door and past Eames with both hands outstretched to
where Rene stood. "I am himself, Thomas Murray,
Bishop of Athabasca. And you are...?"

"Irene Eames, Your Worship."

"Ah!"

They touched hands, the Bishop less fulsomely than
his approach had promised.

"So you are the worthy Inspector's wife! Welcome,
madame, welcome to—what is the name of this place?—
Aklavik! I have heard of you, madame, with the hearing
of my ears, now I see you with the seeing of my eyes.
And you, sir..." Flushed and florid, he turned so as to
face both Eames and her, like a priest pronouncing a
blessing:

"Happy the husband of a really good wife,
The number of his days will be doubled.
A perfect wife is the joy of her husband,
He will live out his years in peace."

Eames, thoroughly taken aback, tried to extricate
himself from this ludicrous farce, but the Bishop had
taken hold of them both—either to brace himself up,
or to draw them together—and his grip was surpris-
ingly strong. He held them each at arm's length while
he continued to intone in an unctuous voice, eyes closed:

"A good wife is the best of portions,
Reserved for those who fear the Lord;
Rich or poor, they will be glad of heart,
Cheerful of face, whatever the season."

The Bishop then opened his eyes and beamed brightly.
"Amen!" he proclaimed to the assembled group, all of
whom stared dumbfounded. Lang, who was a Catholic,
responded, "Amen."

"My ex-wife," said Eames. "We're divorced."

"Your ex-to-be, Alex," said Rene from the other side
of the Bishop. "The divorce is still *nisi*. Perhaps you
weren't aware of that, or had forgotten it. But thank
you, Your Worship, for your kind words. I couldn't agree
more."

"The words of Scripture, madame, they are truth,
and they are life. What brings you here, then? 'Who is
this coming up from the desert, leaning on her beloved?'
For a woman to come all this way . . . there must be some
purpose. Not many women . . . a reconciliation! Are we
witnesses to a reconciliation?" He closed his eyes and
recited:

"When two people come together, they fulfill
each other's desire;
So he who brings two people together becomes
a fulfiller of desire."

Rene glanced shrewdly past the Bishop at Eames, whose expression was one of anguished embarrassment. The men, also embarrassed, had broken ranks and begun to move about and whisper. Only Lazarus sat where he had sat, staring at the stove. Lang was snoring.

"Right now, Your Worship, I'm not even sure where I'll stay the night. I take it you're staying here."

"I have been invited," the Bishop said, "by Mrs. Urquhart, to spend the night here, or at our friend, the Inspector's." At this mention of him, the Bishop released Eames's arm, but continued to hold onto Rene's. "There are, it appears, those two bailiwicks, madame, available to such as we. We are transients and, by definition, require accommodation only briefly. Though I would remind the Inspector and his friends that 'some have entertained angels unawares.' Which prompts me to remind all Catholics here that Candlemas will be said in—what is the time, Inspector?"

Eames, surprised at the question, responded automatically. "It's 2342," he said, then resented having been asked.

"In precisely eighteen minutes, then, right over there, in that corner." The bishop pointed to the arms rack and the counter where the quartermaster's stores were kept. "Yes, that will do nicely. We'll draw this curtain, and...Candlemas, if I may remind you who are Catholics and prepare you who are not, is one of the oldest feasts of Our Lady, seventh century, if memory serves. It derives from a Greek rite of the fourth century, the Presentation of the Child, but had become by the seventh century in our own tradition a rite for the churching of women."

"The churching of women?" said Rene. "What's *that?*"

The Bishop, pleased for the question, and still propping himself on her arm, turned to her and purred unctuously: "The Church has instituted for Christian mothers the fine ceremony of churching. It is a rite whereby women, forty days after childbirth, may be purified..."

"To have sex?" asked Rene.

"...for the purpose of procreation, my dear, within the bonds of Christian matrimony. Which prompts me to tell a parable." The Bishop, still holding onto Rene's arm, turned to face the entire company and addressed it like a congregation. "On my recent tour of some of our Franciscan chapters in Central America, I encountered a bird called the booby. The booby stands about as high as a goose, has a wing span the width of a gannet's, and reminds one—in the way he looks, and the way he walks—of a penguin. There are red-footed boobies, and blue-footed boobies. The ones that I saw were blue-footed. The female booby is much larger than the male, and honks. The male booby whistles. Male and female, you can see them strolling in pairs down the beach, honking and whistling, the dominant female boxing the male with her wings, the diminutive male dodging her blows. Sometimes the male will strike back, but not often. When he does, his whistle becomes more guttural, almost a honk. In such cases, the female will either pommel him until he runs away, or she will cower and her honking subside into a cooing. On these rare occasions, for I am told they are rare, as rare as the birds have become, the bobbies are most likely to stumble into the numerous traps the natives set for them. These traps, one of which I caught my big toe in, are curiously constructed. They consist of a springe securely fastened to a stake, and they litter the beaches where the unwary boobies walk red-and blue-footed, honking and whistling. A menace to bird and bishop alike..." The Bishop seemed to lose the thread of his story while Rene and several of the men stood waiting its conclusion, ànd Eames, hearing in each of the Bishop's words a mockery of himself, agonized for release.

"Alex, I like this man!" Rene announced from the far side of the black-cassocked bulk between them. "Your Worship, why don't you come with us tomorrow? You can ride with me, on my sled."

The Bishop, still holding to Rene, blinked his eyes like a sleepy turtle. "I must prepare for mass now, but it is something I had thought on. We will take it under consideration, following vespers. As for sleeping arrangements—are you a Catholic, my dear?"

Rene shook her head—sadly, it seemed to Eames.

"Then why don't I stay here, and you go with the Inspector? I am sure the Inspector would rather have you than me—eh, Inspector?"

Riddell and Parsons were both watching him, while Rene from the distaff side of the Bishop was gazing at Eames with an expression on her face like the face in a painting Eames had once seen. The painting depicted Eve looking over God's shoulder—with a curious mixture of shyness and virginity, both inappropriate here— at the creation of Adam. Wild, too, was watching Eames gleefully from his top bunk, like some impish prankster in the clouds. And the Bishop had the effrontery to touch him again, this time on the finger, and say: "What about it, Inspector?"

Eames surveyed the faces assembled against him like some infernal jury, with a black-robed buffoon as judge, and Rene as accuser and witness. Blur-eyed with fury he turned on his heel and flung open the door just as a throng of Eskimo women, babies slung from their backs beneath their parkas, pressed through the small porch and into the doorway. Eames fell back, his gloved hand still on the doorknob, while they pushed past like a pod of humpback whales to a weir trap; then he strode out the door, slamming it hard behind him, and marched head down against the cold in the direction of his own quarters.

Behind him the men's barracks' door slammed a second time.

He wanted wildly to run, to sprout wings and flap up over the compound, above the bungled mess of his life—twenty years (if the divorce was still pending) married to calamity, and before that his mother with her weird meetings, and after that Mildred who had knighted and snubbed him—would he always be hounded and harpied by women?—Christian women who lived only for others... you could tell the others by their

hunted look.... Now Rene like a police dog was running
to catch him, to trap him in his hole, where, once caught,
she would tear him apart. He could feel her behind him
like an invisible tail dragging him down as he limped
across the compound...two hundred years to detachment HQ, and how many hours till morning? Could he
stand it? He could stand at attention all night in the
snow, or stop once for all and surrender...but what did
he have that she wanted? How could she be satisfied?...

In the dead waste and middle of the snow-covered
compound, hemmed in by stations of pain and chained
dogs, it seemed to Eames that his back opened up. Out
of his back, as from a hinged door, the body of an anguished giant—the experiences of the past twenty-four
hours—reared up and prepared to fling itself out of
him.

"Alex!" cried Rene.

The giant, poised to fling itself out of him, scrambled
hurriedly back inside him. Eames came to a halt. In
front of him, suddenly, two shadowy phantoms loomed
at him, then just as suddenly parted around him—a
man and his dog running past. Eames felt himself trembling, as though warts were erupting all over his feet,
up his legs, in his groin, his armpits, and along the
back of his neck. Was the universe coming completely
unhinged, or was it Only-Eames, One-and-Other-Eames,
After-Eames, World-Without-Eames? Emen. He stood,
shaken and waiting, on the ice-rutted path until Rene
came up alongside.

"I like that man!"

Eames trudged on. She joined him on the narrow ice
path, walking behind as an enemy walks. From behind,
she called: "You're limping, Alex. Anything wrong?"

Eames halted again, turned about-face, and surveyed the perimeter of the compound, the man and his
dog in the distance, the eyes of the Hunter overhead
and, lastly, Rene's vulpine face. A great heaving sigh
broke from him as he shook his head.

Together they marched along the rutted ice path
toward the fourth station in the mission compound, de-

tachment HQ of the RCMP, "G" Division, Western Arctic Sub-District.

Eames opened the door leading into the detachment office. To open the door seemed less churlish than not to open the door, and the door would have to be opened by one of them—they were both standing at it. He tried as he opened it, and held it open for Rene, to enter into a very small space in his mind: a clean, ironspikelike, perfect place, where nothing could affect him. Having located himself in this furnitureless space in his mind, he followed Rene into the office, and held her parka for her as she slipped out of it and, while she stood assessing the room, began to struggle from his own parka.

"What's there?" she said, indicating the door to his sleeping porch; and before he was out of his parka she crossed to the door and opened it, peeked in, and then went in.

Eames followed her in and brushed past her to light the kerosene lantern beside his cot. The wavering light illuminated the chest of drawers with the scrolled mirror backing, the pile of old copies of *The Force* in the corner, and the hinged plank door leading to the toilet. Eames stood on the side of the cot near the toilet and Rene on the other, nearer the door to the office. A gigantic shadow loomed behind her on the ceiling and the walls.

"What's that?" she said.

"The latrine," said Eames, and he took a step to the chest of drawers and began placing the contents of his pockets on the bureau top. His tobacco pouch he placed there, and his crookshanked pipe, a box of matches, and his penknife which he used to scrape his pipe. From a back trousers pocket his comb, a handkerchief, a crumpled-up cable with the words containing the radio announcement. From the other back pocket his wallet, and the piece of rabbit fur he always carried for his thumb, which sometimes froze. From his watch pocket the little compass he always carried.

"Do you always empty your pockets when you come into a room?"

Eames, who had scarcely been aware of what he was doing, stopped emptying his pockets and stared at the pile of objects on the bureau top. "Yes," he said, and fished from his tunic pocket a button which had come off his parka, two paper clips, and a backgammon checker which he studied and tried to remember how he had got it, before he put it down. "Don't women empty their pockets?"

"Women don't have pockets."

"Oh."

"Alex, why can't we be friends?"

The gigantic shadow moved upon the ceiling, and Eames winced. As a small animal, a mouse maybe, will wince before it sees or feels the hawk, and scurry at the casting of a shadow, so Eames prepared to scurry; then he saw that she was only applying lipstick—two clean sweeps—and back into her purse dropped the lipstick.

"Aren't we?" he said.

"If we could trust each other..."

"Can't we?" As he said this he scurried belatedly to his place behind the cot. With two quick yanks he unstrapped his holster and slung his side arm over the chair back.

"Your 'ex-wife!' Why can't you be honest about the situation? Why can't you face up to the fact that you're married, and quit talking as though you were single and a constable on Herschel Island!"

Eames shrugged. And now he had a shadow: it was round-shouldered and one half of it merged with Rene's massive outline. He moved a half step to the side to assert his own shadow. "I thought the divorce..."

"You thought! I'm sure it assuaged your conscience to think so! Then you could carry on with that doctor's wife who quotes Scripture and screws anything! Sending me a few hundred dollars...and even that I had to beg for."

"If it's money..."

"It's not." Then she began crying. Something white fluttered out of the purse which she clutched in her hand, and she daubed her eyes with it. "It's not...money.

Where is your mirror?" She stepped blindly toward the bureau.   —

"I . . . I haven't got one."

She glared at him and turned and stalked from the porch, tripping over the stoop, into the detachment office. The shadow, huge-backed and straight-shouldered, followed her out. Eames followed the shadow. In the office, Rene was stooped over, peering into the water cooler at a partial reflection, applying with a powder pad a chalklike substance to the skin around her eyes, her nose, her sucked-in cheeks. Eames stood at the far side of the desk, watching her. What to do or say he wasn't sure. His eyes lit on the *Constable's Manual*, and *Crankshaw's Magistrate's Manual* on the file cabinet beside the water cooler—they were no help, they had never been any help, and yet for years, the first ten years of his marriage, he had thought that every real situation in life could be covered by one or the other (augmented by the *Canadian Criminal Code* for extreme situations).

Her grievances—what were they? He had never heard any, not one. Perhaps she had some, he did not doubt that she did, but he had never heard them. Standing now in the well-lighted room, watching her powder her face, he tried to remember . . . She hadn't liked living in Aklavik, so what had she done?—bought a house in Edmonton, with a mortgage he still paid off monthly, but with ownership in her name only. She didn't like his not listening to her, so what did she do?—found an ear, in Arnold, who had other organs as well. She didn't like the long winters, so she spent four, then six, then nine months down south. All that was a long time ago, but he remembered it all with such vividness that it seemed seconds ago, or centuries—he had lost count, he had lost the ability to count or to organize thoughts, perceptions, sensations. . . . She didn't like his drinking, his lack of humor, his obvious enjoyment of Mildred Urquhart's company, his refusal to confide—there had been nothing to confide, on his part anyway; he had led no separate life, none whatsoever . . . he was dull, he was stingy, he was emotionless, he was Eames. And his grievances—what had they been? One only, only one....

"There," she said, smiling bravely and standing, her back to the water cooler and King George, facing him across the desk with the pile of newspapers and the picture of the imposter Albert Johnson between them. Eames felt a sudden craving for his pipe; it was in the other room on the bureau below the mirrorless back to which was pinned Rene's Christmas card: *"Arnold too sends his greetings."*

"That was silly of me. Forgive me. I know how you feel about weepy women and weakness of any sort. You needn't worry, it won't happen again."

Eames nodded coldly.

"But you simply must accept the fact, Alex...Alex, I'm back. And...I love you, I've always loved you."

"What about Arnold?"

"What about him?"

"Well, how is he?"

"How's who?"

"Arnold, the man you lived with, the man who sent me greetings at Christmas—Arnold."

"I've never lived with any man, no one but you—if you're a man, which I sometimes doubt. Oh, you make me so angry!" She wheeled around and her eye lit upon the picture of Johnson. "Here's a man! Well, not this one, he was like all the rest, scared. But the real one...I won't ask you what he's like, Alex, you wouldn't know, how could you?—you're too scared of him. But I'm going to find out for myself, I'm going with you tomorrow, I'm going to find that man and find out what he thinks— what he thinks about you, Alex, and this whole mad show!" Rene's arms opened up to include the King, the water cooler, the compound.

Eames, out of a mass of conflicting emotions and weighing his words carefully, said: "We started by saying we should be friends. I agree. There will be crises in our lives, there already have been. Perhaps you're going through one now. I know I am. But we're separate persons, and it's better that way. I don't question your situation, I don't know your situation..."

"If you don't know it, it's because you don't want to, because you don't care, you've never cared, you've never loved me, you've never loved anyone but yourself!"

Eames waited out this tirade in silence, before concluding his own. "I don't meddle in your situation, I support it, and I see no reason for you to meddle in mine. Johnson's part of my situation, he's at large in my district, and it's my job to bring him in. He's not at all how you picture him, and, anyway, you're not going!" The dispassionate statement was concluded with more passion than he had intended.

"Oh, yes I am. We're separate persons. You said so yourself. You can't have it both ways. Either I'm here as your wife, and you accept me as such, and drop the divorce proceedings, or you treat me as you would any other reporter from a big newspaper who had paid his way up here to cover this story, and hired his own sled and driver, and purchased his own provisions."

"You can't have Lazarus, he's part of the Force."

"He's a special constable, and you know what that means; and it's only here, in your district, that such exploitation takes place. You want that headlined in the newspapers?—'Inspector Eames of the Arctic Creates Special Constables, But Cannot Catch Killer.'"

Eames flinched, remembering his own qualms about the special constables "system." The Anglican Church was doing it, though, ordaining native priests with authority only in their own tribes, second-class priests. With a further qualm he remembered that the Catholic Church balked at the practice. He shrugged. "Suit yourself," he said, and in great weariness turned toward the sleeping porch, wherein lay his pipe, his book, his bed.

"Where do you think you're going?"

"I'm going to bed. I'm one of those half-men who requires sleep, not much, but a little. You're free to do what you want, with whom you want. Go to the men's barracks. Talk to the Bishop. He knows Albert Johnson. They chat together in German."

Hatred and hurt vied for Rene's face. Her lips curled

back in a sneer, her tiny teeth bared like a fox's. She spat: "You're so smug, so superior, you've never suffered, you've never loved...anyone. The closest you ever came to loving anyone but yourself was poor little Tommy the year he was killed." She started to cry again, and Eames, who thought this parting shot crude and vicious, nevertheless at the mention of Tommy felt strangely moved. This desperately insecure creature before him was also the mother of Tommy, whom he had loved. But Tommy was dead, his love for him buried, and any affection he may have felt for the hateful creature before him had long since turned, not without pain, to indifference. To probe these old wounds was madness, was maddening! A strangling sensation came over him, a fit of desire for tobacco, for drink, a breathless sense of claustrophobia—to be in the same room, the same town, the same world with this woman was more, almost, than he could bear. A choked cry escaped from his chest, his throat: "I am...going...mad!" he uttered, and lunged from the room...through the doorway into his sleeping porch, and on (as Rene pursued him through that door) through the second doorway into the stand-up latrine where, latching the frost-covered door behind him and holding it closed with both hands, he stood trembling and breathing in short little gasps in the dark as Rene on the other side pounded and pulled at the door, shrieking: "You can't get away! You'll never get away! Not after what you've done to me, you'll never lock me out! Open this door! I'll shoot through it, Alex, I'll shoot through this door, I swear it!" The pulling and pounding on the other side stopped. A stillness ensued in which, standing between the door and the toilet, holding the doorlatch with all his strength, he envisaged his side arm slung over the chair back. He heard floorboards creak and a metallic clicking. He knew this was not happening, not to him, not now. It was happening, but it was not happening to him, it was happening to...Johnson, it was happening to King, it was happening to the doctor, to Mildred Urquhart, to Hersey—to all of them, whether they knew it or not, whether or not they deserved it—it had already happened to Millen, it was happening to...Eames opened the door. And when he had opened the door, he was conscious of all the evils he had ever sustained, and of all that he and Rene had lost and of all the misery that had befallen them, as if all had happened in that very spot...and because of his perturbation Eames could not speak....

(Mildred Urquhart lies in her bed, her hands beneath the covers, massaging her breasts with one hand and with the other hand masturbating. A hurricane lamp burns on her bed stand, and from the radio in the next room the sound of a clarinet, reedy and thin, can be heard with a thirties' swing band. Her fingers move to the drummer's beat and she moves her bottom rhythmically, but her eyes are open and she stares as she mutters at the cone of bright light on the ceiling.)

...I never could get enough there was never enough to go round though they waste a million with their limp little sticks propped up by a pile of zeros it's the Elsie books I blame and the Christian religion and marriage investing yourself lock stock and barrel then the bottom drops out it's depressing I don't feel guilty Lord Jesus Christ have mercy on me James stalking and fuming and Thomas strutting and fretting and Alex limping around you'd think the world ending with Johnson out there in the cold could I call you Albert I'd like that or Al no that's too familiar Albert there's something I want to tell you what is it Millie I'm pregnant have mercy on me I saw you under the apple tree and I'm pregnant come away with me Millie I can't come away come away with me Millie I can't because I'm married I'm married and pregnant the two worst conditions for a woman to be in nothing fits if only I hadn't read the Elsie books as a girl I was one too more than most women and where did it get me O Albert have mercy this room and a poem at age thirty-five it was sweet of him always been good with words I suppose that's why he's a bishop not like that Anglican rector with his fat little wife blushing right down to her cellulitic legs and thick ankles while he leched at me over the pulpit I was watching his shoes little black patent leather mail order shoes he put on when he entered God's house and took off in the narthex typical workingclass Cockney but he never touched me except at the door leading out to his boots and his wife with her eyes on his boots Lord your kingdom is in a bad way kingdom come can I too I wonder...

(The Bishop stands at the counter where the quartermaster's stores are kept, facing the arms rack. He has spread a white linen handkerchief over the counter, and placed two candles, unlit, one on either side of the mass cloth. In a white alb, which he has put on over his floor-length black cassock, and trailing a long purple stole from his neck, he intones Candlemas with his back to the people. Lazarus, Lang, and the Eskimo women mumble the mass behind him.)...*Domine sancte, Pater omnipotens, aeterne Deus...*

qui omnia ex nihilo creaste, ut jussu tuo per opera apum, hunc liquorem ad perfectionem cerei venire fecisti: et qui hodierna die petitionem justi Simeonis implesti: te humiliter deprecamur; ut has candelas ad usus hominum, et sanitatem corporum et animarum, sive in terra, sive in aquis, per invocationem tui sanctissimi nominis, et per intercessionem beatae Mariae semper Virginis, cujus hodie festa devote celebrantur, et per preces omnium Sanctorum tuorum, bene dicere, et sancti ficare digneris: et hujus

who didst create all things out of nothing, and by Thy command didst cause this liquid to come by the labor of bees to the perfection of wax; and on this day didst fulfill the petition of the just man Simeon; we humbly beseech Thee, that by the invocation of Thy most holy name, and by the intercession of blessed Mary ever Virgin, whose festival is this day devoutly celebrated, and by the prayers of all Thy saints, Thou wouldst vouchsafe to bless and sanctify these candles for the use of men, and the health of bodies

plebis tuae, quae illas hon-
orifice in manibus desi-
derat portare, teque
cantando laudare, exau-
dias voces de caelo sancto
tuo, et de sede majestatis
tuae: et propitius sis om-
nibus clamantibus ad te,
quos redemisti pretioso
sanguine Filii tui: Qui
tecum vivit ...

and souls whether upon
the earth, or in the waters;
and wouldst hear from Thy
holy heaven, and from the
seat of Thy majesty, the
voices of this Thy people,
who desire to bear them
with honor in their hands,
and to praise Thee with
hymns; and wouldst be
propitious to all that call
upon Thee, whom Thou
has redeemed with the
precious blood of Thy Son;
who lives and reigns with
Thee ...

(She changes hands. Her left hand slides down to her
vulva, with her right hand she covers her heart. A vo-
calist has joined the band, and as the words of the song
float across the thick air and enter her murmurings,
she synchronizes her manipulations with the feel of her
heartbeat and the lyrics of the new tune.)...does he
ever get lonely out there with the wolves and the wolverines and the hum of his heart *sure do seem like magic*
when I met you by the river I was dreaming I was saying
I love you I love you over and over and the smell I smell
it now of sweat and woodsmoke in my heart *how you
happened by* Elsie always knew by the warm flush in
her heart before I saw him by the river and the dogs
howled twice I knew my true love by his smell *the beauty
in the sunset flame* James of antiseptic Alex of tobacco
Thomas *I never saw until you came* that sweetish sour
smell of sweat and wine that turns me off now it's gunmetal and the ice along his temples and the frost in his
wolfskin and the silence and the animals *and opened
up my eyes* gnawing its leg off as we came up did you
experience *walk into my dreams* palpitations or short-
ness of breath or blurring of sight no none of those
doctor *color all the scenes* only death judgment heaven

and hell all at once you've been reading too many romances they don't feel *open every door* except at the bone nothing to worry about any more than Eames's wart a simple psychomoter response *no one could before* at the bone smarten up Mildred it hurts in the marrow how would he know from his textbooks *yes it's just like magic* not by sight or by smell or by sound or by feel or by *I'm so glad it's true* flesh and blood numb and cold but my heart is awake and the prayer in my heart in the cave of my heart *a special kind of magic that is you* Thomas naked and prancing and demanding that I tie him to the bedstand and whip him it's disgusting it's *you baby you* decadent...

(The Bishop turns toward the people and raises his arms, his stole draping over his arms outstretched in blessing. All stand and repeat, as he turns back to the counter and the mass cloth and faces the arms rack, the prayer for enlightenment. As he prays, he lights the two candles.)...*Domine Jesu Christe, lux vera, quae illuminas omnem hominem venientem in hunc mundum*...

effunde bene dictionem tuam super hos cereos, et sancti fica eos lumine gratiae tuae, et concede propitius; ut, sicut haec luminaria igne visibili accensa nocturnas depellunt tenebras; ita corda nostra invisibili igne, id est, Sancti Spiritus splendore illustrata, omnium vitiorum caecitate careant: ut, purgato mentis oculo, ea cernere possimus, quae tibi sunt placita, et nostrae saluti utilia; quatenus post hujus saeculi caliginosa discrimina, ad lucem in-

pour forth thy blessing upon these candles, and sanctify them with the light of Thy grace; and mercifully grant, that as these lights enkindled with visible fire dispel nocturnal darkness, so our hearts illumined by invisible fire, that is, the brightness of the Holy Spirit, may be free from the blindness of every vice; that our mental eye being purified, we may perceive those things which are pleasing to Thee and profitable to our salvation; so

deficientem pervenire mer-   that after the dark perils
eamur. Per te, Christe   of this world, we may de-
Jesu, Salvator mundi, qui   serve to arrive at the never
in Trinitate perfecta vivis   failing light: through
et regnas Deus, per omnia   Thee, Christ Jesus, Savior
saecula saeculorum...   of the world, who in per-
                                         fect Trinity livest and
                                         reignest God, world with-
                                         out end...

(The song on the radio changes, and Mildred changes
rhythm with the new song. One hand still lies over her
heart, with the other she continues to masturbate. As
she synchronizes with the new jump tune and with her
galloping heartbeat, she closes her eyes against the
cone of bright light cast by the hurricane lamp on the
ceiling.)... a real Christian a real Christian girl always
saying the prayer every breath she took even when she
was sleeping *won't somebody love me got nobody near*
when I draw the air in I look into my heart and say
Lord Jesus Christ and when breathing out again I say
don't much care for lonely please somebody hear for an
hour two hours all day all night too *oh I'd treat you all
so sweet babe* a real Christian girl not for you Alex with
your mouth on my apples always craving but you
couldn't climb my tree Lord Jesus Christ *so won't somebody care* that terrible tobacco taste with stained teeth
comes limping *latch on latch on ev'rybody* beautiful thing
sticks it in *one* Lord *two* Jesus *three* Christ will they
never learn Wild you're a coward you could have if you'd
wanted to *oh make that thing sweat boy make it sweat*
beautiful thing the blue vein down the length I wonder
does the pimple *oh I'd treat you all so sweet babe* are
they all cocked to the left *and won't ask much for me*
Lord listen I renounce them all all poor men Elsie quit
saying the prayer with her mouth Lord listen listen
carefully to what my heart says *don't someone* have
mercy *out there* have mercy on me *listen* Lord
have mercy beautiful thing *I'm lonely* Albert his foot
have mercy I love it *I'm in need* I love you but I'm so
afraid *come on someone please* Albert O Lord it's alive

it's inside me it's bursting *love* I'm pregnant with apples and blue veins and membranes and rivers *me* corkscrews and woodsmoke I love you I love you I love you I love you…

(As Mildred writhes rapturously on her bed, the Bishop chants and the people repeat the recessional antiphon. Fats Waller sings over the radio in Mildred's house "Whose Baby Are You Now?" and the two Eskimo sisters during the recessional chant receive and take with them the candles.)

Adorna thalamum tuum, Sion, (O Sion, adorn thy bridal chamber) *et suscipe Regem Christum:* (and welcome Christ the King) *amplectere Mariam, quae est* (embrace Mary, for she who is) *caelestis porta: ipsa enim portat* (the very gate of heaven, bringeth) *Regem gloriae novi luminis:* (to Thee the glorious King of the new light) subsistit Virgo, adducens manibus (Remaining ever Virgin, in her arms) *Filium ante luciferum genitum:* (she bears her Son begotten before the day-star) *Dominum eum esse vitae et mortis* (Lord of life and of death) *et Salvatorem mundi. Amen.* (and Savior of the world. Amen.)

well whose baby are you now what mama's holdin' you tonight in whose cradle do you sleep who rocks you Albert I love you when you weep and makes it seem all right I feel you I smell you I'm drenched in your sweat and the stench of your woodsmoke I'm steaming whose baby are you now whose darlin' little boy I'm bursting inside and the river is rushing the ice is breaking the snow is steaming and glazing your smell is sex and the dogs have gone crazy who's tendin' to your needs an' givin' what you please whose baby whose big baby are you now Albert O Albert I love you I love you I love you…

PART FIVE

The Foothills

1

February 2 (Candlemas Day): The Eskimo women have taken away the mass candles and hidden them in a drawer. They will bring them out when a polar gale threatens, or one of their shacks catches fire, or when one of their children gets mauled by a dog, or one of their men is lost hunting. Or when one of the old ones lies dying, as I lay, or dead, then the priest will come and give the viaticum and say *De Profundis* and *Corpus Domine* while the candles are burnt on the ice ledge where the whale oil lamps used to be burnt.

This is the day, six years ago, when I came back to life. The lights of the world were all out then, except for the candles, even the fire inside had gone out. It was an eerie sensation, the gathering together of earth, air, and fire: the taste of the host, the struggle for breath, by the light of the blessed candles. Without the light, one would grope in the darkness and gasp for breath in the darkness. By the light of the candles he is able to see and to enter into thick darkness.

The Bishop gropes in thick darkness. He sits hunched over on my sled, and all of his movements are heavy and dull, but he is fearless. He understands what it is to die, though he has never died, and he understands what it is to live, though he has never lived either. The old ones would say he has never been born. He might say he has not been re-born. It is the same. When a man dies he is free. When he returns to life he remembers his freedom. Everything looks the same, but it is all changed and changing. He too is changed, and trusts nothing. He is free, the priests say, to enjoy all things, or, say the old ones, to wait out his time without passion.

Mrs. Eames is not with us. She was present at the men's barracks at noon, along with Mrs. Urquhart and Felicia Verville, but the posse has no women in it. When we were leaving Inspector Eames went over and kissed Mrs. Eames on the mouth and Mrs. Urquhart on the cheek and shook hands with Felicia Verville, then he came back and climbed on Bernard's sled. He and his wife seem to have reached an agreement that she would not go and the Bishop would go in her place. It does not matter to me who rides with me, but to the dogs it will matter. Perhaps the Inspector has heard from the old ones the saying addressed to the land:

"When we hunt, how should we hunt?"
"Hunt in the place where there is no woman."

Perhaps not. Wisdom does not always come from the wise. The Inspector, like the Bishop, gropes and gasps in the darkness, but he struggles against the thick darkness.

At noon the posse set off. The Bishop rides on my sled, and the Inspector on Special Constable Bernard's. Sergeant Riddell drives the RCMP team, and carries the field radio and the dog food. Staff Sergeant Hersey drives his own team, with Silver as lead dog, and ex-Mountie Parsons as passenger. The trappers Lang, Carmichael, and Sutherland each drive their own team, and the three new volunteers, also trappers, Constant Ethier, Peter Strandberg, and Ernest Maring, ride with them. August Tardiff and John Greenland are to be picked up at Blake's store on the Husky. If Blake also comes, when the main group meets up with the men in the field, the posse will number eighteen. Food for the dogs will again be a problem, and food for the men will be too, unless the plane comes. Inspector Eames is counting on a plane from the city, and on Riddell's ra-

dio, though the radio has never worked properly, and
no plane has been seen for a week. Of the eighteen men,
only Inspector Eames is a regular RCMP.

The posse drives on in thick snow and near darkness.
A wind from the north, thirty to forty-five miles per
hour, makes it impossible to see more than a hundred
feet forward or to the side. The Mackenzie River is
solidly frozen and drifted with rafted ice and snow dunes
all the way to the dogleg turn onto the Peel. The seven
sleds and dog teams and thirteen men zigzag upriver
around ice floes and snowbanks as high and as thick
as large buildings. My team leads the way, and in front
of me rides the Bishop, wearing around his neck the
gold cross, as in a funeral procession.

Temperature: −40° (plus wind). Mileage: 35.

February 3: The party pulled up below Blake's trading post on the Husky well after midnight. All of the
men were stumbling and the dogs falling down. The
Inspector and the Bishop, with Riddell and Parsons,
climbed the hill to Blake's post, leaving the drivers to
tend the dogs and make camp. Each dog had to be staked
and fed where it lay, while the men cursed and crashed
into each other—untying the frozen komatik ropes,
pitching tents in the darkness, building a fire, boiling
up. Around 2:00 A.M. I went to report to the Inspector
that camp was made.

As I climbed the hill to Blake's post the moon, past
the full, broke through low-lying cloud to light up the
river over which we'd just come, the other river where
we were camped, and the turn where the two rivers
joined a third. The long sweep of ice where the rivers
connected gleamed in a ghostly gray light, and I watched
a lone man on a sled make the turn, off the Mackenzie
onto the Peel and across the Peel toward the Husky,
following the tracks our dogs had made and steering
his sled toward our camp. As I watched from the hill,
the light from Blake's post glowing feebly before me
and the moon lighting up the glare ice, I could see that
the man was tall and hunched forward over a sled pulled
by only four dogs, but the dogs looked as big as horses.
The sled was bare and its bonework gleamed in the

moon's light. Then the moon disappeared behind clouds
again and the river below grew blurred, with shadows
of clouds merging with shadows of spruce and making
the bounds indistinct. I proceeded on up the hill to trader
Blake's cabin.

The Inspector, the Bishop, Parsons, and Riddell were
inside when I entered, but nobody looked up or said
anything. I stood inside the door just off the screened
porch, and it was as though I weren't there. They were
all seated around the potbellied stove, with Blake on
the far side, nearest the stove. A little table was beside
him, with a radio on it. Blake was hunched over the
radio, tuning it, but nothing but static came through.
The others sat listening to static. Millie, the Eskimo
woman from Coppermine, was standing behind the
stove. She looked at me, I looked at her, then she looked
at the floor. When she went around the circle of men
to pour tea, Blake looked up and I saw. Death was before
me. In the eyes, face, and neck of the man Millie lived
with. Death was before me in a flannel shirt and wool
pants. Blake was distracted and went back to tuning
the radio. Riddell, too, was fiddling with the radio; he
had the back panel off and was touching one wire to
another. The Bishop sat slumped in his chair in the
warm room, his gold cross rising and falling. The Inspector and Parsons were talking about a plane and gas
dumps. The Inspector broke off and looked over at me.
"Camp made?" he asked, and when I nodded, he said,
"Tell the men to bed down." I nodded again and glanced
briefly at Millie, who was looking at me, then left the
place where Death sat in flannel, fiddling with a radio.

On the way back to camp I searched for the rider,
but the river was clean: no sign of life, either human
or animal, and no sled tracks or prints. The wind had
erased all surface marks as quickly as they were laid
down. No one and nothing of substance had crossed
since last summer, and nothing of summer survived.
The ice covers thick swarms of bugs and the bodies of
small animals; its surface resists the larger, more du-
rable species. After several summers it buries them
also. In the end the ice covers all. By next winter Blake

will be below ice, the woman Millie will return to her people who live at the edge of the ocean. The ocean is ice and will cover her and her people. The man we seek will be covered with ice, as we who seek him will be. There will be a shoot-out on some icy river, and some will be covered now, and some later. Eventually all will be covered. The ocean of ice sends out fingers of ice to draw everything into its grip. The whole earth will become one closed fist of ice with everything frozen inside it. Then the rider will reappear. Now the rider has vanished.

The dogs did not bark and no guard has been posted. The camp was asleep on the ice. The Bishop is spending the night at Blake's post. My wind tent is empty and chill. I crawl into my eiderdown and fall asleep instantly. I sleep, but my heart is awake. My heart has been awake for six winters, though all around me sleep. Somewhere up this frozen river, Johnson is awake, and down the river toward the ocean, Mildred Urquhart lies watchful. Everyone else—in Aklavik, at Blake's post, and throughout the delta—sleeps through the long winter night. The rider who passed through our camp earlier, though the dogs did not bark and no tracks were left, never sleeps. He who feels it, knows it.
Temperature: −40°. Mileage: 0.

February 4: Off early, after a twenty-four-hour layover at Blake's. The layover spent between the post and the camp, fiddling with the radio and attending the details of living. From Edmonton Eames received word that a plane had been sent, and that a gas dump was set up at Fort Good Hope, further up the Mackenzie. The gas dump means that the plane will not need to have the oil drained from its engine while awaiting refueling. The plane means that the posse will have a supply line—bringing in dog food, men, and equipment—capable of outlasting Johnson; also that Eames will have eyes and a searching device capable of tracking down Johnson. This was the information Eames waited for. At 6:00 A.M. on Thursday the 4th, after the long layover at Blake's, the posse set out again, reinforced by August Tardiff, John Greenland, and Blake himself, Blake being the only man in the Arctic, other than Charlie Rat, who could identify Johnson.

The eight sleds proceeded up the Peel River to its branch with the Rat. There was no talk this time of taking the Husky, cutting through overland to the Rat, and surprising Johnson from the rear. There was no possibility of surprising Johnson, not with eight sleds, eighteen men, and forty-eight dogs—surprise would be Johnson's, if Johnson was still able-bodied. The plan, worked out in Blake's post by the Inspector and Blake and Riddell, was to overwhelm Johnson with men and materials. With the plane and a second posse from the Yukon and the radio maintaining contact, we are to search out Johnson and destroy him, or at least to surround and outlast him.

The posse drives on up the Rat. There are no canyons and no one is fearful of being ambushed. The sun in the South, which rose as we turned off the Peel, has not yet cleared the Rat's banks. But it will, then the stiff cold will feel less stiff, less cold, for an hour or two, until the sun sets in the North. We will push on. Even as I write this, while we boil up at Johnson's old cabin, I know we will push on past the Rat to the Barrier Creek, until we get to where Millen was killed. The Inspector is all business, all search-and-destroy, now that he knows the plane has been sent. At every tea break he orders Riddell to bring out the radio, but gives him no time to set it up properly, so that Riddell receives static, gulps down his tea, and then we are off, headed west again, knowing no more than we already knew—that Eames is in a hurry and the radio cannot be relied on. By the time we stop, if no blizzard comes up and we do not get lost, we will have driven:
Mileage: 24.

February 5: The linkup last night with the patrol proved unfortunate, and nearly fatal for Gardlund. All of the drivers were tired, and the dogs were exhausted. Riddell's team led the way, with Hersey's team close behind. Hersey's team was accustomed to leading, but he was unsure of the way and trying to keep them reined in. Once or twice on the river they broke out in the lead, but he brought them back in position just off Riddell's left shoulder. My team, with the Bishop as rider, was flanking Riddell's team further back to the right.

We resembled a wavering V of geese as we came off the river and moved out on the lake where the camp was. The moon was at full and lit the whole lake five or six miles across to the foothills. A frozen lake looks smaller in moonlight. As we rounded the bend in the river and spread out to enter the lake, Riddell pointed to an island two or three miles distant (in the moonlight it looked about a half mile away) where the patrol had last camped. As soon as he did this, Hersey quit reining in Silver, and Silver moved out in the lead. Hersey was worried, he later admitted, that Silver, reined in for so long, and especially at the finish, might hurt himself straining. He never considered that the other dogs might strain themselves trying to keep up with Silver.

So now we resembled a gaggle of geese taking off from the river and trying to fly on the lake. Gardlund and Verville from their camp saw us coming, or at least Gardlund did, and ran toward us. Running with his rifle at the ready, he veered slightly off to the side, my side of the advancing wedge, so as not to spook Silver— he knew Hersey's would be the lead team. At this point the Bishop, who had been quietly riding and nodding for about twenty hours, woke up, saw a man with a rifle running across the ice and, assuming it must be the Trapper and that only he, the Bishop, had seen him (for why else would the posse be traveling on, letting the man get away?), began frantically waving his arms and, when that didn't work (he said later he thought we were blinded, like the Aramaeans who followed Elisha), grabbed a rifle, jumped off the sled, and started running toward Gardlund and firing at him as he ran.

Gardlund, astonished, and not wanting to shoot back, which would mean firing into the tangle of men and dogs, threw himself down on the snow. He probably knew that a man in a panic will pull the trigger too fast and fire high, so he threw himself down head-on toward the Bishop, who all the while ran and fired at

him. I was trying to turn the dogs into the Bishop, but
they would not turn. Then, when they did, they turned
in between the two men, into the line of fire. Yanking
them back, I let them go on toward the camp and Verville, who by this time, with all the hullabaloo and
thinking their camp under attack, had doused the fire
and run off in the other direction. It was Lang, finally,
who got his dogs turned to come up behind and then
alongside the Bishop, and Lang who jumped off his sled
and tackled the Bishop. The Bishop said later that when
he heard the dogs coming and then got knocked down
by Lang, he thought seven devils were on him. Hersey
said it reminded him of football, and Lang thought he
should get the V.C., but the thing was so clumsily done
it was like a fat man being trampled by geese. Gardlund, meanwhile, as the Bishop and Lang rolled in the
snow, jumped up and caught Lang's spooked team as
it ran by, and all was eventually calmed except that
Gardlund would not accept the Bishop's apology or sleep
in the same camp with him. So then there were two
camps: Gardlund and Lang sharing a tent on the other
side of the island along with the other trappers, while
Verville stayed where he was, and let the Bishop share
his tent. This he did to spite Gardlund because, as Gardlund said, Verville masturbated all night, and, as Verville said, Gardlund counted his strokes. But all of the
trappers, except Verville, camped on the other side of
the island. Riddell, who had been with Lang, moved
into my tent.

It makes no difference to me who I sleep with, or if
I sleep with anyone, or if I sleep. The last time I slept
with a woman was nine years ago; since then I have
slept alone, in training, as Hersey says, for eternity.
Maybe. Hersey, of course, sleeps with Silver, Eames
with his pipe and Parsons, Blake with his cancer and
Tardiff, Riddell in my tent with his field radio.

At intervals throughout the night Riddell would wake
up, switch on his field radio, get static, tune the machine, get more static, then switch the dial off. Several
times in the night he did this, like a monk at his prayers. Perhaps Riddell and his god have nothing to say

to each other. I who was in the tent the whole night can attest to the fact that no message was sent and none received. Yet next morning Riddell had a bulletin for the Inspector, not an important report, but a report. It was supposedly from MacBrian, at RCMP HQ in Edmonton, and was dated 5:30 A.M. It said: "I have been given to understand that a large number of persons in the Northwest Territories have learned the telegraphic code and tune in with their radios and listen to the messages sent over your wireless system, and because of this there is alleged to be no secrecy in connection with wireless messages throughout the North. Perhaps Johnson himself is listening in? MacBrian."

Eames received the message in silence. He did not doubt its truth, or question its source. Riddell, I am sure, does not doubt his radio either. I, who have spent the night with them both—Riddell and his field radio— have this to say: either the radio or its receiver is not to be trusted.

February 5 (second entry): Got moving around 10:00 A.M. and covered the twelve miles to where Millen was killed by 2:00 P.M. The last mile or two very steep and tough sledding and the dogs had to be staked in a ravine off Barrier Creek. The trappers, all except Gardlund and Verville, stayed with the dogs. The advance party, consisting of Parsons, Gardlund, Verville, Riddell, and myself, was instructed by the Inspector to approach Johnson's last camp as if Johnson were still hiding out there. The shoot-out occurred six days ago. Johnson, if he were foolish enough to be waiting for us, would have frozen or starved by this time, or died of boredom. A statue or corpse we would find, which is what the Inspector expects, just as he expected Johnson to be in his cabin a week after it was destroyed. In his pep talk to us at the base of the hill which leads up to the ridge overlooking the hideout, the Inspector said there were rules. Johnson, he said, would be waiting for us because Johnson was learning the rules. Also, Johnson was tired. When Riddell said he doubted that Johnson was tireder than we were, and when Gardlund offered the Inspector ten-to-one odds against Johnson's still being there, the

Inspector said he never wagered on life-and-death matters but that he would accompany us. Gardlund said this was no life-or-death matter, it was more important than that. Then the six of us set out to find Johnson.

When we reached the top of the ridge and looked down, it was obvious no one was there. No fire, no camp, no sign or trace of anyone having been there, ever. The Inspector instructed the four of us to approach the hideout exactly as it had been approached, while he and Parsons looked on. Johnson would be confused and surprised by the re-enactment, he said. Riddell and Gardlund were to circle the ridge and crawl down the ravine and come at the camp from behind. Verville was to descend the slope directly ahead, and take up the position he had held when Millen was shot. I was to take Millen's place, Verville would instruct me. We waited, Verville and I, for Gardlund and Riddell to reach their positions. Riddell could be seen in the scrub brush and willows, but Gardlund was quickly lost sight of...

...no tracks to be seen, no movement, nothing. Gardlund lay in the stiff pussy willows computing, devising...for days he had been devising the game which would last the duration, while computing his chances of winning. All were involved, each sled a team and each driver a captain...the number kept shifting, but so did the game, in complexity, in difficulty...there were now seven stations, the same as the number of letters in the name JOHNSON...but JOHNSON was not the name, he knew that already, JOHNSON was a red herring, a will-o'-th'-wisp, a wandering fire leading Eames on, throwing the other teams off. Behind JOHNSON lurked the true name, the identity of what they were after, which Johnson was busy ferreting out and ahead of them all in pursuit of...perhaps Johnson would win. Johnson was, without doubt, his chief, at this point his only, competitor...even without knowing the rules of the game or the number of stations. But Johnson had rules of his own, not their rules, and Johnson determined the stations...Johnson had the whole landscape to play with and he was playing for keeps...

Here was a station. The third one for Gardlund,

*though it might be the fourth, or the seventh, or any
number between one and seven. The stations were ordered, but Gardlund did not know their order, only
Johnson knew that, but Johnson did not know their
number, he, Gardlund, knew that . . . so they were evenly
handicapped or disadvantaged. Johnson was running
ahead at this point, but not far ahead . . . no more than
one station, one letter . . .*

*As Gardlund figured it, a station was wherever John-
son displayed himself, whenever he showed himself he
left a clue (though they might not know he was showing
himself, he might be hiding and watching and laughing
at them, but whenever he laughed at them he left a clue)
in the form of a letter. And the letters were parts of a
name. That was the only way it made sense. The posse
didn't know who they were chasing, Johnson didn't know
why they chased him . . . but the chase must make
sense . . . Gardlund would make it make sense. Johnson
was playing a game with them, laying down parts of an
alphabet code as he went. It was up to Gardlund to break
the code, crypt the name . . .*

*The Name . . . He lay in the stiff pussy willows gazing
out on a snowscape of letters: angular, rounded, and
broken . . . A's and S's and Y's . . . the entire landscape
was marked out and mapped and involved, the delta
and foothills and mountains beyond, all groaned to give
birth to the name, to yield up their letters toward the
true name of the figure all were pursuing . . . two letters
he had divined. Now he lay on his back in the stiff pussy
willows straining hard at the third . . . he prayed it would
be a vowel. Perhaps the remaining four could be guessed
from the third? Then he would know what no one yet
knew, then he could laugh at the others and stage an
ambush for Johnson and pilot the posse home safely . . . or
let Johnson go, but let him know that he had got there
first, Gardlund . . .*

*He reviewed, as he had done hundreds of times, the
two letters he had deciphered.*

*First, there was the pit-cabin letter. He was pretty
sure it was the first. There had been little difficulty finding the station, but finding the letter, and divining that
there was a letter to find, that there was a game being*

*played, had been difficult. It had taken a trapper, but
more than a trapper, it had taken a wizard, which he
was. He smiled to himself, ruefully...Even he had not
realized until later, when he came to the second station—
the single wolf tree—then it had dawned on him that
Johnson was laying down clues with his tracks, and of
all the posse, of all the men pursuing Johnson, only he
was picking them up...if the posse wasn't to be completely skunked, it was up to him alone, Gardlund...*

*The letter at the pit-cabin was T. He had not at the
time noticed it—who would?—but once he got onto the
game, looking back, the letter leaped out at him...even
at first sight it had struck him as curious, the canoe in
the tree, not leaning, not standing, but wedged perpen-
dicularly at right angles so that from any angle, almost,
you approached it you were confronted straight off by a
T...a strange way to cache a canoe, he had never seen
anything like it, a canoe wedged like that would not see
another season (he'd made doubly sure, staving it in)...it
must be a sign, but for whom? and to what...a sign, or
the prank of a madman?...*

*And the second letter? No difficulty, once he was look-
ing for signs...but he wasn't yet, then...the two struck
him at the same time, at the wolf tree—the Y and, rea-
soning back, the T—the combination of the two con-
vincing him that the letters weren't being laid down in
order, but as the landscape permitted. So it must, Gardlund figured, be an anagram-code. And from then on,
while the others poor-mouthed about Johnson's backtracking, his traveling ridges and crossing at leads, and
about how his tracks disappeared, from the moment of
his discovery of the letters (and with them, of the ana-
gram game), he was off...in the hunt with and for the
Mad Trapper...*

*...Gardlund sighted along slender stalks with fur
nodules, some snow-covered, some not, of stiff pussy willows...trying, as he had tried for six days, to decipher
the letter, the letter...the letter was before him, this was
the third station, it must have a letter (his third, though
it might be any from two to six, he knew that), an X to
go with T and Y...it wasn't X though. He might run*

*through the alphabet, as he had many times... but that
was so random... no, the letter should strike him—O!
or A! or M! or Q!—between the eyes, like a sledgehammer
stunning a steer... he had to be that sure, as he was of
the other two letters...*

*With a sudden lurch he rolled over onto his stomach
and took in the scene once again: the tarp and the fire
and Johnson were missing, but he could picture them,
how they had looked... no letters there, all had vanished
like smoke... his gaze traveled slowly up the sides of the
canyon, past the slope where Verville and Millen (now
Verville and Lazarus) were hiding, to the bare ridge
where Parsons and Eames stood... gazing up, as Johnson must have, he spied them: three structures, snow-
covered and squat, rocks or stumps—were there three
letters here? or just one? one at least... his heart beat
like a trip-hammer... he must put himself in Johnson's
position, he must view the ridge from Johnson's... with
his rifle at the ready and hunched forward he ran, drawing fire, panicky fire, overhead... good thing Riddell
wasn't firing, or Lazarus... it was Verville, no danger... into the abandoned hideout, where, plunging full-
length on the snow, he squirmed on his stomach under
the upended tree. A bullet zinged in the tree trunk above
him and he heard Riddell shout at Verville. Cockpitted
in what had been Johnson's position, he raised his gaze
slowly, fervently up the five-hundred-foot canyon to the
mouth high above... the shapes were still there, starkly
outlined against the gray sky like cold sores on the lip
of the canyon... not one, but three letters (as there had
been three men after Millen was killed, or three shots
fired in killing him, or three hours spent... who cared
why?)—there were three!... Gardlund studied the canyon formations... quickly he shuffled himself around,
still on his back, still gazing up, to scrutinize them from
another perspective... they still spelled the same, and in
order: H, E, L... Gardlund concentrated as he had never
before concentrated....*

...this exercise took two or three hours. When it was
too dark to see one another, the Inspector sent Parsons

to call us all back. He himself had already left. The
dogs were hitched up and the posse mushed back under
cover of darkness the twelve miles to base camp.

No sign of Johnson, but Gardlund mistaken for Johnson and fired on. In the past twenty-four hours Gardlund has been fired on twice, first by the Bishop, now
by Verville. To draw fire the first time is considered
mere chance, the second time is considered bad luck,
but to draw fire a third time is held to be fatal—so say
the old ones who have taught us this. Does Death, who
rides the radio, and is at work in Blake, have Gardlund's name also?

When we converged on Johnson's hideout there were
no tracks to be found and neither packed nor pissed-on
snow where he had lain, but there was Gardlund. And
Gardlund was grinning as Johnson grinned in the pit-
cabin.

Temperature: −40°. Mileage: 24.

February 6: The entire party, except Riddell, rode
out of camp at 9:00 A.M. to circle and search the ravine
in which Johnson last camped. If you cannot catch
Raven, you catch his feather. Seventeen men, seven
sleds, fanned out through the foothills, the main party
along Barrier Creek. Small parties explored the ravines
and streambeds which feed into the main watershed.
Between feeder streams is the frozen tundra, kept hard
and packed by the wind which blows day and night
without ceasing, always drifting, always erasing tracks
and prints from the ridges.

Even a blind pig picks up an acorn now and again.
It was Hersey and Silver who picked up Johnson's tracks.

Hersey was driving Silver up a feeder stream when
he discovered fresh snowshoe tracks. The tracks were
certainly Johnson's, one curved, the other one straight.
Hersey followed the tracks along the bed of a stream
half a mile, then they suddenly vanished. There was a
bed of mashed and broken reeds not far from where the
tracks ended. These might have covered Johnson's exit
from the streambed up the hillside, but a thorough
search of the whole ravine failed to show any prints
leading into or out of the streambed.

Hersey believed that Johnson, having walked along the streambed, reversed his snowshoes and backtracked along the same route. But there were no prints at the other end of the trail either. A fallen tree trunk covered the creek at that point, but the snow on it was undisturbed. I myself saw the tracks, and can verify Hersey's report.

At the same time, fresh tracks laid down by the same homemade snowshoes, the left one with a bent tailframe, the right one straight, were found by three different parties on three different creek beds, four to six miles apart. This showed that Johnson had been crossing over the tundra from streambed to streambed, probably during the night when less impression is made on the snow, then circling back eight to ten miles to his own track. The old ones say, greedy choke puppy. Johnson, who earlier on had gained time with these tricks, is now wearing himself down to no purpose. Has he, like the dog, let go the bone for the shadow? Has he grown so fond of the chase that he has given up hope of escape? Or perhaps the rider who passed by our camp has caught up with Johnson, and is directing his movements?

The Inspector decided to divide the posse into day and night patrols. The day patrol might stumble on Johnson sleeping, the night patrol might run into him on the trail. My team was assigned night patrol duty. As soon as the posse returned to base camp, at approximately 8:00 P.M., I went to my tent to rest up.

The tent was busy. Most of the night men came and went while I lay in my bag trying to sleep between the day patrol just ended and the night patrol soon to begin. Hersey and Blake came to consult with Riddell, who had been alone in the tent all day with the radio. They came to get the broadcast bulletins, and to listen to static, and drink. Riddell always packed a liter of rum with his camp gear, and Blake produced three forty-ouncers wrapped in old army socks. Hersey wasn't a boozer, but he didn't like to miss out. He sat nervous and tense with the two of them while they drank and fiddled with the radio. When the Inspector arrived they just fiddled, while Riddell explained to the Inspector how he had fixed the radio.

"It's mainly the aerial," he said. "We're down in this valley, see, chief, an' the signal's weak and fading because of all the jouncin' around on the trip here an' the cold weather—cold runs a battery down faster 'n use does—so the signal has trouble getting outa the hole we're in down here."

I lay in my bag with my face to the tent wall, but I knew the Inspector was nodding, nodding and wishing Riddell would quit talking as I was.

"Once it's out, it goes a long ways, though it fades quick. The signal, that is, our *old* signal." A long pause while Riddell drank. Blake drank. The Inspector and Hersey refused the bottle, and waited. I waited, wanting to sleep. None of them were on night patrol duty.

"So I took this old Zepp I had here and altered it to a Horizon—that's shortwave band names. What it means is, there's more punch at the beginning, when it needs it to get out, but the signal fades quicker. It's like makin' a sprinter," he said to Hersey, "out of a long-distance runner."

"No." Hersey's reply was quick, clipped, and instant. "You've rigged a hurdler instead of a sprinter, with one giant hurdle at the beginning—a steeplechase."

"A wild-goose chase," mumbled Blake.

"Picture," Riddell began again in a loud voice, lighting up a cigar in the tent, "instead of a long, low curve—that's your Zepp—a parabola—that's your Horizon. Anyway, on my first call out with this little honey Aklavik picked up and acknowledged a steady R-6. Now, it didn't last long, I'll grant that, but long enough to let them know we were picking up their scheds."

"Does this mean we're able to transmit as well as receive?"

"Short messages, chief, a few words. But if we transmit the same few words over and over, they'll get the message. An' we can pick up what they send. See? Listen to that, chief! There's a bulletin coming through now."

The dull static coming out of the radio crackled and hummed, like a dwarf clearing its throat. Riddell turned the dull humming up. A thin little voice from far away said, "AJP, do you read me, this is XYZ Aklavik no code, do you read?"

Riddell tuned frantically until he got less crackle, then pressed the transmitter button and talked into the felt-covered spot on the box. "We read you, XYZ, this is AJP, go ahead." He let go the button, and listened. All of us listened: Blake, the Inspector, and Hersey listened; I listened too, in my bag.

Loud static, then out of the static a crackling, and out of the crackling a thin, small voice: "XYZ Aklavik to AJP advanced. Canadian Airways ski-plane arrived today via Mackenzie River, pilot Wop May. Plane to depart Aklavik tomorrow, carrying eight hundred pounds dog food and supplies. Landing strip at junction Barrier Creek and Rat River. Pilot requests posse move camp twelve miles west to airstrip. Plane will attempt landing tomorrow. Repeat: Plane will attempt landing tomorrow. This bulletin will be repeated every hour until 0100 or until acknowledged. Request acknowledgment. Over." Then a loud crack as though the speaker had been shot, and the static crackled again.

I closed my eyes and tried to sleep amid static and cigar smoke, knowing that whether or not the night patrol went out, there would be harnessing and feeding to do in the dark, and whether or not camp was moved before dawn there would be little enough sleep that night. I listened for the dogs, and not to the men who, once the Inspector and Hersey went away, set about drinking and fiddling with the radio again. Only once in the middle of the night I woke up, it must have been 3:00 A.M., or maybe later. I remember thinking, 'The night patrol hasn't been sent out and the camp hasn't been moved,' and hearing Blake and Riddell snoring and the radio going full blast, loud electrical static, the kind of sound the northern lights might make if they were in the same tent with you. And then—I wasn't dreaming it, because I never dream—a voice came over the radio, clear and smooth like the American announcers, a voice like the priest's intoning mass when he administers the *viaticum,* rich and oily and inside your inner ear. The voice, in a soft and silky whisper, said: "I have heard your urgent requests for men and dog food and I, Death, have dispatched Peter Moses and Stephen Moses, with ammunition and five hundred pounds of dog food, with instructions to proceed to La Pierre House and place themselves under the command of Constable May. These two men are Indians, expert trackers, and both of them owe me favors. I have also sent instructions to Constable May to join with Frank Johnson of La Pierre House, who is a crack shot, and to pick up James Hogg who is trapping near Loon Lake, another marksman. These five men are on their way from the Yukon. Another six, all of them trappers, have gathered in Aklavik, where they await my orders. Captain Wop May, who lured the Red Baron to his death and shot down thirteen other German pilots for me, will be landing his aircraft today, weather permitting, with eight hundred pounds of dog food and a replacement for my friend Constable Millen. No efforts should be stinted and no man spared in the manhunt you are now engaged in. It has reached the pitch and frenzy of a small war, a police action being waged between your group, which I will add to, and the man who flaunts you and defies me and must be destroyed. He is described as follows..." (The standard police description followed, in a different voice, as though Death who rode the airways had dismounted, stood aside, and let some little man in some remote broadcasting station—Old Crow, Yukon, it turned out to be—with his pitifully small voice and puny equipment, speak for Him. The description ended, as it always did, "Johnson is to be shot on sight." Then Death came back on.) "...I, Death, will continue to track and to accompany Johnson, dogging his tracks and weakening his will to resist. Be assured: When he backtracks and squanders his strength doubling back, I, Death, am behind him. When he builds a small fire and tries to rest for an hour, I, Death, am beside him. When he faces the mountains and considers trying to cross them in winter, I, Death, am before him. Wherever he goes and in all he thinks and dreams, both by day and by night, I am with him. He is strong, but his strength diminishes daily, while the strength of our posse increases. He is skilled, but so is Riddell, so is Parsons. He is competitive, but so is Hersey, playful, but so is Gardlund. Religious, but so is ... Ha-Ha-Ha-ha-ha ... *le fou*, the Bishop, is with you. Be of good cheer, I have overcome Johnson ... Ha-Ha Ha-Ha Ha-Ha Ha-Ha-ah-ah ..." The broadcast broke off in a consumptive cough, but it was Blake, not the radio, coughing. I sat bolt upright in my sleeping bag and switched off the loud crackling noise, then slept until the drone of a plane woke the camp, and Eames ordered everyone out. Temperature: −35°. Mileage: 40.

February 7: Gardlund was already gone, and with him the trappers, to set up camp at the new site. They had departed at dawn, and left the rest of us sleeping and Eames hopping mad, not that they had gone to do what all of us should have been doing, but that half the camp could depart while the other half slept. It struck a blow at what Eames called his "unified command."

The Bishop too was unhappy. It being Sunday, he had intended to say mass for the men before breakfast. In the haste and confusion, and with half the camp gone, the Bishop wandered about while the rest of us packed, and had to content himself with what he called "quick prayers" over each team and driver. Whether he used the same quick prayer for all, or varied it from team to team I do not know, but the prayer he uttered over me and my dogs was:

"Let GOD arise,
and let his enemies be scattered.
Depart from me, ye wicked,
I will keep the commandments
of my GOD!"

This he bellowed, both eyes shut, one hand gripping
the sledwood, the other hand on the driver. Whatever
one may think of him, the Bishop is the Bishop.

Then the ropes were tied, the dogs were fed, breakfast was wolfed down, and we were off, Riddell's radio
like an ark of the covenant riding secured to my sled.
Death rode the sled that I drove. At one place on the
trail the box toppled, the dogs churned in a slushhole,
and Riddell and I trying to right the top-heavy sled
must have switched the receiver button on. The radio
squawked, spooking the dogs. Riddell groped in the snow
and turned the switch off, but the harness lines had got
all tangled. One of the dogs choked to death, and I had
to cut some of the lines to prevent others from choking.
Then the cut harness had to be repaired, the other dogs
quieted, and Riddell had to check his precious machine
to make sure no harm had come to it. His fiddling disturbed the dogs further. Even though I am on the side
I am on—the side with radio contact throughout the
Arctic, an airplane piloted by a war ace, a chaplain to
bless the men in the morning, under an Inspector who
has unified command—I could not help but think, as I
repaired my harness and heaped snow on my dog, what
one man with high courage can do. He can outwit a
posse, and pin down a patrol, and hold Death at bay
for a season. He can move with freedom from delta to
foothills, along rivers and over mountains. He can think,
act, and dream, show mercy or punish, reveal or conceal
himself, resist or surrender—in short, he can act like
a man. If, while he does this, he can make a game of
it, or set a goal for himself and achieve it, he pipes the
tune Death dances to. If he fails, he pays the piper, but
the failure is his. Either way, he is on the right side,
though it is not the side that wins. The winning side
will be ours, with our radio, our airplane, our dogs and
our men, our equipment. But his defeat will be *his* defeat, while Death rides the sled my dogs pull.

The posse linked up at the new campsite, near where
the ski-plane had landed. The rest of the day was spent
hauling and stacking supplies the plane had brought
in. Only Hersey went out on patrol, found a fresh set

of tracks, followed them through a creek bed, then lost them when they led up to the tundra. Riddell was ordered to go up with the pilot and make an air search of the foothills, to see which way Johnson was moving. And a patrol of five men from the Yukon was sighted, coming over the McDougall Pass.

Temperature: −35°. Mileage: 12.

2

Captain Wilfrid "Wop" May wiped the frost from his pilot's door window and peered through the pane at the air-speed indicator which hung from the wing, out where the strut veered away from the slipstream. The spring-loaded needle registered 70–80, not bad with the load he had on. When the son of a bitch froze up, which it would, he could fly by the seat of his pants—the center of gravity on these high-wing monoplanes was right under the seat of your pants—that's if his long johns weren't frozen by then. It was cold in the cab.

A dollar watch in a rubber pad hung on the dash of the two-seat Bellanca, and a magnetic compass. Flying low into Aklavik yesterday along the Mackenzie River, he'd had a 500-foot cloud base and an open space up to 5,000 or 6,000 feet, the compass needle spinning like a clock hand—which way was up? which way was down? He'd half expected Wiley Post to come zooming out of the clouds and pass him upside down, waving. But Wiley didn't like ski-planes. Who did? He'd have to remember the two thirds more runway and the little ski on the tail-skid, no brake, also the friction and the heating up of the big skis—let her sit twenty minutes and she'd be iced in till breakup. The minute he stopped, the men on the ground had to move her.

If there *were* any men on the ground. If there weren't, would he bother to land? Would he unload? He'd have to be quick. He couldn't budge the big plane by himself.

He could spin the prop and climb in in time, he could take off by himself. But why bother to land if the men weren't there? Why bother to fly if you were going to worry about loading and unloading cargo? Next, he'd be worrying about a Blighty one, or about his bad eye, or this Boche they called the Mad Trapper...

Below him was a wilderness of worries. But they were all below him, out of sight. Out of sight, all right. Conditions weren't exactly *Clear-And-Visibility-Unlimited*. From 1,200 feet the delta below looked white on white, dark white with light white obscuring the dark white—like flying inside a milk bottle, the milk bottle turning and sloshing its contents up one side and down the other—like dawn patrols over the trenches, fog rising from one side, chlorine gas over the other. Everything looked like everything else—this was like that, that was like something else; now there was war, now peace, now mercy mission, now police action. All it amounted to was that men liked machines, they liked speed and freedom inside the milk bottle, the sensation of not being trapped in a trench, of being up in the air above it all and feeling the plane roll, buck like a horse, nearly spin *(O, spinning Jenny, where will you land? Will you land on a Jerry in upside-down-land?)* while the wind whipped the snow a thousand feet in the air, giant plumes of snow rising, subsiding, never quite touching the skis *(It's a dangerous mission, we don't deny that. Not many men know how to duel, but Captain Brown thinks you can be taught.)*, never quite touching the plane and the little man in it, the little man with his gigantic payload strapped in his puny cockpit.

That was the worry: the single shot in your payload—a fluke shot and you were fried. It had happened to Richthofen; it could happen to him. All those legends about the Aussie AA guns' accuracy and the Baron's death wish—they weren't true. He knew they weren't true, and Brown knew they weren't true, even though he and Brown had got credit for the Red Baron, official credit, half a kill each (in the end he had given his half to Brown)...He had trimmed her out pretty well, set his horizontal stabilizers so she'd fly tail-high to offset the ton of gear he had on, and his verticals to offset the prop torque. In ninety miles in this whiteout he could fly two perfect circles, while the magnetic compass turned as the world turned, as the top of the world turned, as the monoplane turned—dizzily. A blast of wind made him tighten his grip on the four-way stick, and adjust the left aileron slightly. His hand on the throttle and his foot on the rudder were steady. The Bellanca had broken out of the clouds and into a clearing between cloud bank and snow plume, casting a 1,200-foot shadow. May stole a quick glance at the map which lay spread out beside him. At the next break in the whiteout he should be able to spot the juncture. The Barrier and Rat, traced on the map in red ink, he had marked "Ancre" and "Somme." Aklavik was rechristened "Wipers"... It wasn't strafe from Brown's Camel, either. Everyone knew that, though for the sake of the D. S. C. Brown concealed it, and he concealed it for Brown's sake. But it wasn't Brown's obsolete Camel that had brought down the Baron's triplane. Brown was too jumpy and nervous, had the shits and was scheduled for sick leave. He shouldn't have gone up that day. *(Just a quick pass over the front, May, between Albert and Hangard. You'll be on the outside-left. If we spot any tripes, stay away from the dogfight. If a Boche singles you out, piss off home.)* It had seemed safe enough, the young pup with the dog team, tagging along at 12,000 feet and watching the white puffs of friendly AA, while the others dove down to inspect... A break in the clouds. His cargo, nearly a ton of it—tear gas bombs, dynamite, ammunition, dog food (Dog food! Didn't these people take anything with them?)—stuffed into his fuselage and seriously impairing his loft, he felt dragging at him like a huge heavy tail. The single wing of the Bellanca cut the air at an angle, casting a curious shadow—like the "Lady of the Limp" atop Albert cathedral, trying to fly or... Clouds again. The dogfight raging below, between Brown's seven Camels and what must have been fifty Albatrosses and Fokkers. Vickers and Spandau fire darkened the air at 6,000 feet. Mackenzie's Camel struck in the back and nose-diving, taking a

Fokker with him. A flame-colored tripe banking to gain altitude—presenting a perfect target—then diving back into the battle. May at 12,000 feet, under orders, circling, hanging back, watching...Another clear patch. The spruce tops of the Mackenzie delta stood dark and distinct against the monochrome snow. A long, deep depression of white, without trees, cut the taiga in two, snaking its way like the railway-cutting between Ypres and Comines. That must be the Peel, or the Husky. From 1,200 feet he could see below better. But the higher he went, the farther ahead he could see. From 6,000 feet he could see all the rivers, and alter his course. From 12,000 he should be able to see the whole delta, from the Arctic Sea coast all the way to the Richardson Mountains...Cloud bank. A second tripe rose like a bright butterfly, its petrol tank fully exposed. Bugger the orders! He dove and fired, missed, and shot after the tripe into the dogfight. Again the tripe was lined up in his gunsights, again he triggered a burst. The triplane staggered and swooped. His first kill?—request confirmation. Straightway he was in the beehiving middle of the Red Baron's dread Flying Circus, flame-colored tripes spurting at him from all sides, Spandau bullets spraying and missing by inches, so many of them he knew not to bank but go into a tight vertical turn, hold his guns open and spray as many red tripes as he could. One gun he held open to long—it jammed. Then the other. Frightening, really...Looking down through the break in the whiteout, he could see the trees thinning, the tundra beginning, foothills beneath the clouds and the tops of mountains above. If you went high enough you could see the whole system, as once on recon he had climbed to 18,000, hoping to see the whole S-shaped front, 400 bloody miles long, from the North Sea coast all the way to the Swiss Alps. He had seen only nineteen large craters from mines, but millions of pockmarks from shells, and the squiggly lines of the Central and Allied trenches laid out like dead nervous systems—some with square, some with zigzag traverses—with saps like nerve endings branching out everywhere. The whole landscape below him was gray. But

once you went over 12,000 feet, you could not spot the
men on the ground...Ass-tightening, when eight flame-
colored Fokkers of Richthofen's Circus, the dreaded *Jasta
11*—their colors a warcry, their guns rattling—came
banking and diving and spitting at you, and both of
your guns jammed, while 20,000 of the enemy below
and another 20,000 in your own lines stood up in their
graves watching the show—the wolf pack pursuing a
pup—and firing shots into the dogfight...The Mac-
Kenzie delta was suddenly visible with its frozen rivers,
snow-covered lakes, and thousands of Christmas trees—
no men visible—not like the Ypres Salient with its
wounded trees and wounded men and the sky reflected
in thousands of watery shell-holes. The air-speed indicator on the wing strut registered 80. With his stick
he depressed his back elevators slightly, forcing the
nose down and leveling out the tail-heavy Bellanca...Then spinning out of the mess and heading
west into the sun. Leveling out and looking around,
nobody following. Setting himself to hedgehop home,
west on the Somme and then south along Morlancourt
Ridge. Feeling good at having spun out, then hearing
the rattle and seeing the tracers of Spandau fire from
behind. A red tripe on his tail. Cursing his Camel and
useless guns, cursing his luck. Had he known then that
it was Richthofen, with eighty kills to his credit, closing
in on eighty-one (it flashed in his mind: Richthofen after
his head wound had grown cautious, went after the
stragglers and greenhorns; but surely this wasn't
Richthofen himself—maybe Voss, or Goering, or Udet,
or Wolff), had he known...Nobody knew who this Mad
Trapper was—was he scatty, or shirty, or gone stone
piache? He might be a squarehead—no one seemed to
know. Only that he was down there—behind that ridge,
maybe, or sheltering up that ravine, or dug in in some
glory hole. If he was going to have to do more than haul
cargo, and he probably was—air recon, bombing, strafing, the whole bit—he liked to know who he was bombing and strafing and blowing to Sweet Fanny Adams.
Or maybe he didn't. Maybe it was better not to...Diving
and twisting and turning and every other evasive ma-

neuver he knew, but nothing he did seemed to shake
off the German who was riding right on his tail. Closing
the gap now—fifty yards, forty. Brown managed with
his old Camel to bank and come down to assist, firing
a good burst at the Fokker before he overshot and pulled
out. Then it was just the German and him, him and
the German—Richthofen (though he didn't know it was
him) after his century mark; May on his puppy-dog
mission, not knowing what he was going to do and his
pursuer not able to figure him out (did poor flying save
him?)—flying wildly up the Somme River valley below
the level of bordering hills, hills grim and gunmetal
gray like mountains of corpses, mass graves (The Devonshires held this hill. The Devonshires hold it still.),
wanting wildly to turn back, or bank up, or spin out of
the deathtrap—but where is there to go but ahead?—
while the German behind him fired burst after burst...A
roll of the Bellanca spun the playing card that hung in
his cockpit from the sun visor, bringing "IF ONLY..."
then "EVEN THOUGH" then "IF ONLY" then "EVEN
THOUGH" to face May with his one good, his one injured eye—it was his right eye had caught the steel
shaving ten years ago on his on-the-job-training tour
through the factory of the National Cash Register Company in Dayton, the year he'd got married and given
up flying—so that even if "EVEN THOUGH" was facing him, "IF ONLY" fronted the world, and vice versa.
The card ("Mfd. by E. Erdman's, Mich., dist. by The
United Church of Canada") had been a gift from his
mother. The card spun again, bringing "IF ONLY" to
face May's good eye...He was vaguely aware as he
careened at a hundred miles an hour, 500 feet above
the Somme River, with the Germans on one side, the
Allies on the other, of Aussie AA machine gun crews
firing wildly at both of them, and of the threat of rifle
fire, the single infantryman firing the single shot from
his mud-coated, rusty Lee-Enfield or Mauser, which
would end the war six months early for the one it hit;
and then, vividly, of taking the curve in the river near
Corbie...Nearing the junction of the two creeks, the
low flat white depression ahead he could see. The Rat

looked cushy for a short distance, but soft and depressed
like a short trench with zigzag traverses. They would
have to trample the snow for takeoff. His good eye
scanned the treetops, while his game eye stayed cocked
straight ahead on the river—a trick he had learned.
Knowing your limits, and calculating your chances. The
Red Baron, killed by a single shot, wasn't twenty-seven
years old yet... Taking the curve in the river, but
Richthofen had beat him to it by cutting over a hill,
and when he banked out of the curve he was duck soup,
too low down between the Somme's banks to turn away.
He had to keep himself from pushing the stick and
plunging into the river. The German at fifteen yards
had him broadside, and then for some unaccountable
reason the red triplane banked away—as though its
pilot, disdainful, were sneering at him and shrugging
him off (he even imagined he saw a sneer; he did see
the German rip off his goggles). The flame-colored tripe
(so close that now he could read its nameplate—"Mil-
itär" Flugzeug Fokker DR.-1"—and its number—
"425/17"—Richthofen!) climbed a little and hovered and,
as he glanced behind in stunned disbelief, did a spin
and a half into a field... Overshooting the river at 500
feet, he banked the plane, turned, and nosed down. There
were men down there, a ground crew... The Baron is
dead. Long live the Baron!... Now the slow part: landing, getting the plane moved, getting the cargo un-
loaded. Men always wanted to talk, and to fly—all men
wanted to fly and to shoot from a plane. He throttled
back to minimum glide speed, with his good eye watching the needle swing toward the red mark out the left
window. She'd stall out at 40. He set his four-way stick
ahead and glided in around 50... Each of his thirteen
kills in the six months left of the war had been dog-
fights, none of them duels—dueling had died with
Richthofen... His good eye shifted between the air-speed
indicator and watching for possible leads in the ice,
snow-covered deadheads, or buried rocks in the river.
His game eye stayed cocked on the foothills and treetops
as suddenly he dropped below them. Twenty feet from
the ground he closed throttle, pulled back on the stick

and started his round-out. As his tail-skid, then the two
skis touched down, he was still scanning the blur of
branches and trunks for he wasn't sure what—a rifle
barrel? A sniper's lookout?...At thirty-six, May had
grown cautious....

3

May turned on the fuel tap above his head, strapped himself in, and waited.

"Switch off!" he heard from outside.

"Switch off!" he yelled from the cockpit.

"Suck in!" he heard, and responded, "Suck in!" He watched his oil pressure gauge as the prop was turned over three times.

He waited, checking briefly his trim tabs and throttle, then leaned out the door to see where the guy by the tail of the plane with the ax in his hand was standing, and where Riddell, who was turning the prop, was positioned. Riddell seemed to be an Old Soldier. The tail-man was a Sky Pilot: he didn't even have his parka hood up and was standing facing the slipstream.

"Contact!" Riddell yelled.

"Contact!" he yelled, and turned the switch on. Riddell gave the prop a good turn, jumping back as he did so. She caught, and he eased the stick forward and let off the throttle. He could feel the tail lift off the ground but hold fast, as Riddell clambered into the cockpit and strapped himself in, puffing. They sat until the oil pressure settled in green, then slowly he advanced the stick—to around forty, to fifty. The rope on the tail-skid was holding. May opened his door to signal the tail-man: the Sky Pilot's hood was up now and his back to the slipstream. The ax went up; the ax came down. A sudden lurch. They were released and up off the river

and into the air on less than a forty-foot runway, like
a lark; like a bat out of hell, the Bellanca was clear of
the riverbank and ski-lifting upward and over the tree
line, then banking, then turning, all the while gaining
loft. Riddell with a grin pointed down at the Sky Pilot
standing, an ax in his hand and a rope at his feet, in
the river; he gave a Gone Phutt signal. They were up
off the ground and just under the clouds, cruising the
foothills at 500 feet, two Old Soldiers, laughing...

"Captain W. R. 'Wop' May took Quartermaster Sergeant B. F. Riddell up and showed him all the foothills
and canyons branching off from the Barrier Creek. The
Barrier Creek runs parallel with the mountains which
divide the Northwest Territories from the Yukon. The
head of the river is twelve miles west of the base camp
established by the RCMP posse. In that twelve miles
of no-man's-land were dogsled and snowshoe tracks,
single and double, circling or straight, reversing or ending abruptly, as thick in places as the human and animal tracks at the annual police games in Dawson. The
entire area, from the juncture of the Barrier with the
Rat River to the Barrier's source in the mountains, was
pitted and pocked with dogsled and snowshoe tracks—
so many, in fact, that Sergeant Riddell in a special radio
bulletin said, 'It looked like an army had marched there.'

"Sergeant Riddell was wearing a faded blue army-
issue parka with wolf trim, reminiscent of the togas
donned by Other Ranks in Roman times...

"Isn't that a nice touch?" Irene Eames asked, standing where Corporal Wild usually stood and reading to
him from the typescript she held in her hands. Wild
was seated where Inspector Eames usually sat, behind
a desk littered with papers, listening attentively to her.
He nodded enthusiastically, encouraging her to go on.

"...Roman times. Captain May, well-known Canadian war ace, who among many other exploits helped
to bring down the Red Baron and flew diphtheria serum
to the stricken community of Fort Vermilion, gives a
Gorblimey effect with his soft cap and suave manner.
It was that unassuming manner that lured Baron von

Richthofen to his death in April of 1918, and that same
calm professionalism, perfected by numerous mercy
missions, barn-storming junkets, and bush pilot flights
throughout Canada, that will assure May's fearless
pursuit and swift capture of the Mad Trapper of Rat
River....

"I had to work May in somehow," Rene stopped to
remark.

Wild nodded approvingly.

She studied Wild for a moment, assessing the sin-
cerity of his approval, then read on:

"Meanwhile, Inspector A. N. Eames and his posse
are advancing on the ground to support Captain May's
assault from the air. The Mad Trapper, between the
posse's advance from the east and a party of men closing
in from the Yukon, will be caught in a pincer movement
on the ground, while being kept under constant sur-
veillance from the air. He will be called on to surrender,
or to be killed. This is the first time in history that a
manhunt has been conducted by airplane. Captain May,
who was the first to carry airmail to the Arctic, and
one of the first to perform mercy missions by airplane,
will soon have another first to his credit: the capture,
dead or alive, by airplane of the man whose identity
has baffled the world and whose presence has terrorized
the Arctic."

Irene Eames quit reading aloud and, with a mock
curtsy, laid the typescript in front of Wild, who was
sitting at Eames's desk. "How's that?" she asked.

"Amazing," said Wild. "Especially since the whole
thing is based on a radio bulletin of two sentences, one
of them garbled because Riddell was drunk. We know
that Riddell went up with May, and we know it was
May he went up with, but how do you know, well, for
example, how do you know what they were wearing?"

"I just know," said Rene. "They always wear the
same thing, and it's something my readers are interested in. Anyway, you didn't write it, so don't criticize.
Just say it's 'fine,' or 'amazing,' or..." She moved quickly
around to Wild's side of the desk, between the file cabinet and the chair he sat on, under King George the

Fifth's portrait. Laying one arm around Wild's shoulder
and with her cheek next to his, she began to read over
his shoulder. "There!" She pointed. "Parallelism. And
here, alliteration. And here again..."

Wild shrugged, Eameslike. "I'm no writer," he said,
"but I'm good at headlines. Here...." He picked up a
pen and doodled a bit, then scribbled out on a clean
sheet of paper:

A Limited Engagement,
ENTITLED:
BOMBED
A Most Depressing Performance.

Rene took the pen from his hand, and wrote:

A Piercing Play,
ENTITLED:
STRAFED
A Most Illuminating Drama.

Wild took the pen from her, and scribbled:

A Chilling Scene,
ENTITLED:
FROZEN
A Play Without Words or Acts.

Rene took the pen from him, and wrote:

A Stirring Drama,
ENTITLED:
MINED
A Most Uplifting Performance.

They both laughed. Wild turned himself in Eames's seat
and put his arms around Rene. They kissed.

"Desk duty isn't so bad, now, is it?" she said in his
ear.

"As long as they're out there, and we're in here, it
isn't. It's cushy. I don't know how long it will last..."

She kissed him again, several times very slowly on the face and on the neck above his stiff collar, whispering between kisses: "Don't worry...baby...don't worry...just pray...for bad weather...and Johnson...what else..." She quit kissing Wild and stood up just below the King's portrait. "What else do you have to do, before...?"

"This," he said. He moved her typescript to the side of the desk and laid out six letters, two in blue envelopes, three in white, one in off-white and legal-sized, with a printed return address: "Jesse A. Timms, Attorney at Law, York Mills, Minnesota." All six were addressed, five by hand, the one legal-sized by typewriter, to "The Inspector," or "Inspector Eames," "R.C.M.P. Post, Aklavik, Northwest Territories," or "The Arctic." Most included "Canada" in the address, and were postmarked "U. S. A." All of the envelopes had been slit, the contents read, and the letters stuck back in the envelopes for answering. "They're all 'missing persons' inquiries," said Wild, "and they all assume that Johnson's their long lost. Here, for example." He opened a white letter, postmarked "Joplin, Mo.," spread it out on the table and read:

Feb. 2, 1932.

Dear Sir,

I will rite you a letter in regards to my father Albert Johnson who your men will have killed by now. I want you send me all details and also his picture would also like to hear from the aviator Wop Maye. My father has been in that part of the country for several years trapping and mining I never thought he would loose his mind. I never saw the picture that came out in the paper or would of got it. My mother and dady has been supprated for 20 years so she has lost track of him but I never did so that will explane why he was there alone. I am 29 years old and have 3 more brothers and no sisters so as a boy I sure do want to no all about father, if you dout him being my father I can send all the profe you ask fore. I am trusting to you to send me what I ask for just as I always said only one father I love him as ever altho I no he did rong he is still the only father I ever will have he was a stern father with us boys and it is hard to think he turned out like that.

Yours very truly
Marvin Johnson
RR 3 Joplin, Mo.

Rene and Wild stared at each other for a moment, then burst out laughing. "This one," said Rene, pointing. Wild opened the legal-sized envelope, spread out the typed letter, and read:

Jesse A. Timms
Attorney at Law
York Mills, Minnesota

Gentlemen:

A client of our, Mrs. Sadie Johnson, has reason to believe that the Albert Johnson, referred to in news dispatches as a trapper and fugitive eighty miles from Aklavik, is her husband.

When this man is brought in, please ascertain if he formerly resided at, or near, York Mills, Minnesota, and if his wife's Christian name is Sadie, and if her name was Fuller before his marriage to her.

Yrs. truly,
Jesse A. Timms
Attorney at Law

Rene, becoming enthusiastic, pointed to the letter postmarked "Md." Wild opened it next. It read:

Berwyn Md.
R. F. D. Box 11
Jan. 17, 1932

Dear Sir

Please send me all info re the mad trapper, A. Johnson who resides near Aklavik, NWT.

This is bec. I have an uncle by the name of A. Johnson who left the States for Canada before the World War. We have not heard from him since.

Sincerely,
Mr. Johnson

"More?" said Wild.

"More, more!" said Rene, clapping her hands. "This one." Wild opened the letter, and read:

Sandy, Oregon
Feb., '32

Sir,

I have been following the news about one Albert Johnson, who is my brother....

"This should be good," Rene said, putting her finger on the word "brother."

"It is," Wild said.

...He was trapping and prospecting in Alaska for years now, Arlie was no crook, them teeth was for me as he in his last letter to me in Seattle, Wash. 18 years ago was to bring me a Gold Set.

I can prove everything, if Joe Murdock of the Burrard Hotel, Vancouver was alive or we could get Bill Low his bartender, they would tell of our parting 25 years ago. I came in from the Okanagan, he come from Alaska, we stayed there to match money. He was broke to $200, I had $600 and give Albert half, so he had $500 starting back

to Alaska to buy traps and an outfit. Around 1906
I went to Seattle, I have been backward and forward in B. C. and have tried to locate him.

I had a letter in Tacoma telling me he would
soon come down or I was to meet him in Alta.,
where a nephew of ours was. He died in Alta. 2
years ago. His name was Lonnie Johnson, he was
in the world war, he never got better, his wife
went back to Liverpool and when he could not find
me he may have gone a bit queer.

Albert is not as old as you may think. He was
always older looking than he was. There is a man,
warden of the State Pen at New Westminster, Pat
Devine is his name, he knows me well. Let me
know how old you figure Albert is, about his height,
and how many teeth in his top plate. I was in
Tacoma one Saturday night in Ned and Curly's
saloon, took a little too much, Sunday morning on
the street car got sick and leaned over the back
end and spit a $35 set of teeth out of my mouth,
the highest price spit I ever done. When I told
Arlie about it he said not to worry, he would bring
me a pure gold set...

The letter continued, but Wild pushed it aside. "Look,"
he said, and opened three more, laid them out in a row
for Rene's inspection, and pointed to a canvas mail pouch
in the corner, beside the file cabinet. "There's more. I
started drafting answers to this batch, but those...it's
like letters to the North Pole, a real blizzard, and the
mail hasn't come today yet." Wild shrugged.

"Poor baby," Rene crooned in his ear, "poor little
boy." She glanced at the three he'd laid out, and Wild's
answering efforts:

"I am writing on behalf of a Mrs. Emma Oddson,
who resides in this city, and who feels Albert Johnson
is probably her son."

"I BEG TO ACKNOWLEDGE RECEIPT OF YOUR INQUIRY
THE 7TH INSTANT..."

"I am writing to you for the purpose of find out whether Albert Johnson, the Mad Trapper of Rat River, is the same Ernest Johnson who disappeared from Buffalo about ten years ago and for whose arrest different warrents charging grand larceny were at that time issued."

"I BEG TO ACKNOWLEDGE RECEIPT OF YOUR INQUIRY THE 7TH INSTANT REGARDING THE ABOVE NAMED AND IN REPLY TO REQUEST THAT YOU FORWARD A FULL DESCRIPTION OF..."

"When this man is captured please notify: Daisy Lou Gillman, Kennebunk, Maine.

"P. S. Try and give age."

"I BEG TO ACKNOWLEDGE RECEIPT OF YOUR INQUIRY THE 7TH INSTANT REGARDING THE ABOVE NAMED AND IN REPLY TO REQUEST THAT YOU FORWARD A FULL DESCRIPTION OF YOUR_____AS ABOVE, ALSO GIVE FULL DETAILS AS TO THE DATE HE LEFT_____AND FROM WHAT PART HE CAME AND USUAL OCCUPATION, ETC. YRS. TRULY,"

Rene, who was leaning one arm on Wild's shoulder and had one buttock perched on the desk, swiveled his chair around toward her and buried his face in her breasts. "Poor overworked baby," she said, stroking the back of his head and tousling his hair, "you need help."

"I have to draft a letter of condolence to Millen's parents, too," Wild mumbled.

"Alex will have to sign, won't he?"

"I s'pose," came Wild's muffled voice.

"I can sign for him," she said pensively. "I always did. I always opened and answered his mail."

Wild quit nuzzling long enough to say, "Did the chief know?"

"I did it whether he knew it or not. The trouble it saved him outweighed his rage when he found out, and he didn't often find out. He'd lecture me. I'd do it again. Finally, he gave up. I did it because the woman he'd

gone with before we were married continued to write
him love letters. He never saw them. I intercepted them
all, and answered them all. It was fun. It got so I looked
forward to the weekly love letter."

"Didn't she notice the different handwriting?"

"Alex types. Only his signature had to be written, and
it got to where I could sign 'Alex' better than he could.
She got better love letters from me than she would have
from him! After two years of letters back and forth—a
love letter a week, and this after we're married!—I arranged a meeting between them in Chicago, a week-long
lovers' tryst at the Palmer House Hotel. Only Alex, not
knowing about it, failed to show up. Ann, that was her
name, was furious. I enclosed in his last letter to her an
earwig: 'From the heart of the Arctic and Eamesy'—she
actually called him that: Eamesy—'an earwig for Ann.'
Served the slut right. I'll sign the letter to Millen's parents, why not? I've had lots of practice. Here, how's this?"
She thrust Wild's head aside and grabbed a pen. "What
was his first name?"

"Edgar," said Wild.

"Really?"

Wild nodded.

Rene grinned and attacked the paper, stabbing with
periods, slashing with dashes, stippling with ellipses:

Dear Mr. or Mrs. or Mr. and Mrs. Millen—

Your boy fell in the front line of duty, he was
the first to charge and the first, and only, to fall.
Hardly a mark could be found on his body, and it
is being returned to you for burial. His spirit, however, of gentleness and courage, of dedication to
the Force and to Christian ideals, will remain forever a legacy to the three lads who fought by his
side. As one of his buddies remarked at the Coroner's Inquest, "Edgar was always a good pal to
fight by, you always felt safe beside Edgar."

Please be consoled in the knowledge that Edgar
died leading a gallant attack on the hideout of a

man who remains unidentified, but who is generally considered insane. His comrades, inspired by his sacrifice, press on to avenge you, and society, for the loss of your son. Since Edgar's death, their battle cry has become: "Greater love hath no man than this, that he should lay down his life for two trappers and a Signal Corps sergeant."

> Yrs. in Symp.,
> Inspector, "G" Division,
> Western Arctic Sub-Dist., R. C. M. P.

"How's that?" said Rene, her nostrils flared and her pupils dilated. A blue vein pulsed in her neck.

"Fine," said Wild, making himself small in the chair, "that's just fine. I'll...I'll type it later."

"No. You'll type it right now, and I'll sign it. You'll send it."

"Right." Wild nodded.

"I really shouldn't be here," King said. He was sitting up in the hospital bed, in new yellow pajamas with a blanket over his legs, a writing pad braced on one knee and a pen in his hand. Moira, in matching yellow uniform and a little starched cap, was busy sorting and piling King's clothes on the chair and the floor, those washed and those to be washed.

"You'll be off soon enough," Moira said, without stopping what she was doing. "You're better off here where I can keep an eye on you and not in that filthy men's barracks. Why, anyway?" She stood up abruptly, hands hanging stiffly down at her sides, and turned to face King. "Don't you like us?" With her eyes she indicated the room, which was changed. A desk lamp had been brought in to provide the indirect lighting by which King was now writing his letter; the needlepoint chessboard had been hung on the wall over his bed, its bottom rank still unfinished; and a potted geranium sat on the sill of the window from which new yellow curtains now hung. The entire room looked brighter, smelled cleaner.

"I do, I do," King said, and nodded and continued to nod. "Of course I do."

"Then why would you say you shouldn't be here?" Moira asked, still standing, her fingers fidgeting with a button and buttonhole on her starched uniform, facing King.

"Because this is a hospital room, after all, and I'm not sick. I was sick, but..." King's voice trailed off.

"You'll be leaving soon enough," she said, "both here and Aklavik. You'll be flying out to Edmonton and I'll be left here." She bent again to her task of sorting King's clothes.

"You'll go with me," King said, moving cautiously in an effort to get out of bed and go to her.

"No, it wouldn't be right. Your folks want to see you, not me."

"I won't go without you," King said. "I'm quitting the Force, anyway."

"You've said that, but..." She stood in the middle of the room, bent over slightly and with her back to King, no longer sorting or folding his clothes, but generating tension in her own healthy stomach and communicating it to King's wounded one.

"Moira!" King said, and made movements to get out of bed.

"Have you got the letter done yet?" she said. She went over to him, sat down on the bedside, and leaned over and kissed him lightly on the lips. "Let's hear it."

King lay back on his pillow, relieved. Bringing the letter up into the light, he started to read: "Dear Mum and Dad... I started a couple of others, but I was afraid they might upset Mum. This is the one I thought I'd send." He started again:

Dear Mum and Dad,

Thank you for the handknit toque. It looks fuzzy and warm, though I haven't had a chance to wear it yet. In answer to your question, Dad, there are no birds here, just ravens. You're lucky to have heard the first cuckoo. As for me, I'm quite well, and have taken up needlepoint. As you know, I was admitted into hospital for a slight wound, but will soon be discharged.

One of our fellows wasn't so lucky, maybe you read about it. He got in the way of the fugitive's guns and was killed. It's a good thing I was here in my neat little room with the flower and cards you sent, Mum. I have curtains, too. As to plans, I'll be coming down for a visit as soon as a plane has room for me. It would be great to go grouse shooting, Dad, like we used to.

Your loving son,
Alfred

King stopped reading and brought his eyes to meet Moira's, which, far from glaring at him, were staring off into space.

"There's no mention," she said listlessly, "none at all." She adjusted absentmindedly the little starched cap which had got tipped in her kissing of King, as slowly she rose from the bedside.

"Wait!" said King. "Moira, listen," and he read as he wrote: "P. S. A nurse may be coming with me." But Moira was still in the act of rising, and of gliding out of King's room. "Moira, I can't upset them," he called from the bed, "I just can't! They've read about Millen, and the Mad Trapper, and..." Moira continued to glide from the room, filling her own and King's stomach as she moved away from him with tension and ulcerous turmoil. "Wait, Moira!" King called from his bed, "wait..." She disappeared into the hallway, leaving the door open behind her. King glared at the letter still in his hand, crumpled it up and tossed it into the corner where two other crumpled balls lay. Then he began composing another, muttering as he wrote: "Dear Mum and Dad, Thank you ever so much for the toque...."

Dear Sir or Madam:

Your brother, uncle, son, father, or husband
ALBERT JOHNSON, otherwise known as THE
MAD TRAPPER OF RAT RIVER, was bombed,
strafed, mined, shot, or found frozen, starved,
dead of exposure, partially eaten,

his nose hands entire corpse collected and pho-
    ears feet
tographed for positive identification.

The R. C. M. P. requests confirmation of the
identity of the deceased, and burial instructions
from next of kin. You are also required to fill out
and return the Personal Possessions Claims Form
enclosed, for immediate release of any belongings
found on the deceased, except currency or stolen
or illegal goods, which are subject to seizure for
defrayment of costs.

Please accept my own personal condolences, and
deepest sympathy from the entire Force.

Sincerely,
Inspector, R. C. M. P.

"There!" said Rene, who had been leaning over Wild's
shoulder at Eames's desk. "That ought to do it. Type it
and I'll sign it."

"He's not dead yet," said Wild.

"He will be. And when he is, you just strike out the
words that aren't applicable. What's the matter?"

Wild looked worried.

"I won't release it to the newspapers until he is dead,"
Rene assured him. "And these people don't matter. Not
one of them will reply—you'll see. Really, you should
send it telegram form, and ask them to cross out the
words."

"Why?"

"People believe a telegram. Nothing is more upsetting than to learn that a telegram lied."

"I'll do it this way," Wild said sheepishly.

He positioned himself at the typewriter, inserted paper and carbon, and began to type, "Dear Sir or ..." "Do I have to do it now?" he asked.

Rene flashed a glance at him, first of anger, then a warm flush suffused her face, throat, and neck. The blue vein in her neck began pulsing. "Mama's little boy wants to go to Daddy's bed? Come on, little boy, with Rene."

Loosening his tie and unbuttoning his khakis, Wild followed her into Eames's sleeping porch.

4

"Wash me in the water
That you washed your dirty daughter
And I shall be whiter
Than the whitewash on the wall.
Whiter
Than the whitewash on the wall.
Oh, wash me in the water
That you washed your dirty daughter
And I shall be whiter
Than the whitewash on the wall."

Riddell broke off singing and downed another swig
of the Demerara rum he had produced from his parka
pocket. With the back of his mitt he wiped his mouth
and handed the bottle, swathed in an old sock, to Māy.

They were cruising at 900 feet over the foothills and
canyons that led up to the Richardson Mountains. Above
lay a soft, fluffy ceiling of cloud, merging before them
with the white sides of mountains. Below lay the steeply
treed foothills, the deeply trenched cuts of ravines, the
ridges of ice and flat tops of tundra, the branched system of streams, creeks, and cuts that flowed into the
Barrier Creek. Like a grooved pan with grease hard-
ened in it, the tilted floor of the ground met the sides
of the mountains where the ceiling of cloud cut their
tops, forming a visible wedge within which they were
flying. The pan had a top, sides, and bottom, and in the

grease on the bottom were small marks and signs as
though an army of ants had marched there.

"It's a bloody circus down there," yelled Riddell.
"Lookit that duckboard-track, an' there's another, outa
nowhere to Sweet Fanny Adams—a regular jig-a-jig!
Where's th' bloody Kelly's Eye going? Eh?"

"Trumpet-cleaning, I hope," May yelled back.

"Eh?"

"Trumpet-cleaning! Gone West!"

"Righto! How's about the old River Ouse?"

May nodded, but a quartering wind had come up
from starboard which he had to counter by crabbing.
He had already figured out the head wind by doing a
180°. Now he was crabbing into a quartering wind of
about 10 mph, trying to keep his A/S indicator down to
around 45, just short of stalling—creeping, in fact. The
plane crept over the broken terrain of the foothills, casting a shadow, not drifting. It was surprising how much
light filtered down through the cloud bank, and how
tracks in the snow would leap up at you from a mile or
more away. Situation stable. Riddell was watching from
his copilot's window, and May peered out the pilot's
window at the picayune tracks on the ground. Aston-
ishing how distinct they were, and how many of them!
Like peering down at a rat's maze or a trench system—
not a single rat or man visible, but the tracks and signs
of packs and armies of them. Where was this Butt-
Notcher? Was he in that funk-hole? Behind that revetment? May didn't care *who* he was, *where* he was
would suffice. But searching the snow in the wedge-
shaped core of light surrounded by whiteness, May felt
like someone entering a temple and looking for a men's
room. It was, somehow, obscene.

Riddell yelled, "Pass th' River Ouse, mate!" and surprised to find that he still had the bottle tucked between
his legs, May handed it over and feeling an updraft
went into a bank and rudder in the same movement,
putting the stick back a half inch to bring the nose up
and turning before the white sides of mountains, which
so much resembled cloud banks, smacked them both
senseless. He should have been paying attention—the

updraft had warned him. Now he had a quartering wind off his tail and a little, not much, but some, wing ice. He could feel his lift falling off, then his air speed. Irrationally he blamed it on Riddell: a copilot shouldn't drink, and he shouldn't tempt the pilot...If he hadn't felt that updraft...He decided to bring her down to 300, cure the ice and track the bugger both. He pushed the stick ahead and dropped the nose. "Here we go!" he yelled to Riddell. "Dirty Work at the Cross Roads Tonight!"

"Roll on, Duration!" Riddell roared back, gripping his bottle and grinning. Like a regimental sergeant-major, Riddell started singing:

> "It's down in the deep dugouts,
> I've seen 'im, I've seen 'im,
> Down in the deep dugouts,
> I've seen 'im,
> Down in the deep dugouts."

Riddell sang lustily as the plane swooped down, over the ravines, over the ridges, close to the treetops.

> "It's hanging on the old barbed wire,
> I've seen 'im, I've seen 'im,
> Hanging on the old barbed wire,
> I've seen 'im,
> Hanging on the old barbed wire.

"What!" he roared. "D'ja see that?" And May looked back just in time to spot, away from the main concentration of trails, a faint single trail at the head of the Barrier Creek circling off to the west toward some timber. May nodded and did a quick bank and rudder, keeping the timber in sight and letting the nose drop to 200 feet, then leveling out and searching the ground as it sped beneath them. Riddell had his nose pressed to his copilot's window and was wiping his breath from the pane. They passed over the trees and May swung back around, pulling the nose up this time. In the turn, and banked for the turn, they both could see clearly out

Riddell's side the faint snowshoe track at the head of
the Barrier circling off to the west and ending in timber
alongside the river; then, what they had not seen before,
the more distinct track joining the faint track and both
as the two became one proceeding on toward the mountains. Riddell winked at May, and May nodded, did a
right bank and rudder keeping the nose up and followed
the single fresh track.

"He's there all right, chief! We couldn't 'a' been more'n
a half mile away when the updraft off the mountains
forced us around. Look, here's the river an' this here's
the Divide." Riddell knelt down and traced with a stick
in the snow two parallel lines. Eames and Parsons stood
watching. Ten feet away at the open fire, Gardlund,
Lang, and Ethier looked over at the three men, but
remained seated on logs by the fire. The hum of a plane
could be heard in the distance, and the crunch of boots
coming up from the river. A light snow was falling.

"An' we're here, only about twelve miles away." Riddell, still kneeling, touched the line he had drawn in
the snow representing the river.

"So the Barrier Creek ends about twelve miles from
here, toward the mountains?" Parsons waved vaguely
in that direction.

"Righto. An' here's that canyon where Millen stopped
one, an' this here's the pass you can see." Riddell pointed.
"Well, you can see it when it's not snowin'. Now, Johnson worked hisself clear of this canyon an' this here
stand of timber—that's where we went through the
motions, chief, remember, with Lazarus playin' Millen?"

Eames nodded.

"He worked hisself clear o' there and traveled on the
bald tundra awhile." Riddell drew a line from the river.
"His tracks is clear as day across there, then they stop."
He jammed his stick in the snow. "So where do you
s'pose he went to?" Riddell squinted up at the faces of
the two men, then, grinning broadly, he drew another
line which joined the line representing the Barrier
Creek. "Well, he hit the next crick an' come down it till

he got on the Barrier again, circled back and headed straight up. Reaches the head o' the river an' again he takes to the tundra, where the snow's packed. Where next? Your guess is good as mine, 'cept I seen 'is tracks from the air." Riddell held his stick like a swagger stick, poised, then swept the snow at his feet in a wide angle arc. "Circles back on his trail till he comes to this draw where there's a sparse bit o' timber." He stabbed the snow several times to represent trees. "It was right in there that he camped—three, four days ago." Riddell stopped and looked up at the face of Eames, and then Parsons, gloating. But the two Mounties remained impassive, staring down at the lines in the snow.

"Then he heads back on his old trail an' doubles it up for a while—there was so many tracks there it looked like an army'd been through—gives up on that an' travels up *this* creek"—Riddell drew yet another branch line—"which leads toward th' Divide an' alongside th' Barrier head, well, watch closely now, here again he hits th' bald tundra, travels back parallel with th' mountains an' his old trail, heads down *this* creek"— he drew a fifth line—"to strike his old trail again on th' Barrier Creek just about four miles from here— that's where we seen th' faint track leadin' into th' timber." Riddell looked at Eames, then at Parsons. Putting his hands on his knees, he stood up.

"Before doing all this he must have climbed a high ridge and looked things over," said Parsons.

"This ridge," drawled Riddell, drawing in yet another line with his foot. The snow at their feet was pitted and pocked as though small animals had battled there. The Bishop came up.

"Well, boys, he's up and off again—a beautiful lad! What's this little conference about?"

"Anyway, the last we seen before the updraft forced us back, he was workin' his way up th' Barrier toward the Barrier Pass."

"Impossible!" boomed the Bishop, wading into the conversation. "Through those mountains?"

Riddell dragged his foot back and forth through the lines he had drawn. "I'm just tellin' you what I seen,

and the story writ on the snow." He placed his boot on
the Barrier Pass, and obliterated all the small creeks
and tree lines. "That's all I'm sayin'."

"Sounds to me," said Parsons, "like he was trying to
get back to the delta, and possibly to his cache. Trying
to find a way around us, and couldn't."

"No doubt the plane scared him off," declared the
Bishop.

"Or the dogs, or the smoke from the fire," Parsons
said.

"In any event, he was fainthearted. But that doesn't
much sound like our man, does it, Inspector?"

Eames, who had been gazing down at the ground
and at Riddell's boot, lifted his gaze as high as the
Bishop's groin, where in other circumstances a chasuble
would have hung. A stillness like the stillness before
madness had come over Eames, though he was not mad
and he was far from still. His lips were twitching, his
eyes blinking, and all his facial muscles—the six employed in smiling, the eight in frowning, as well as all
the others—were performing at cross-purposes: giving
off signals where none were intended, responding where
no response was called for. He could not be sure what
his face looked like, only that it felt in parts convulsive,
in other places frozen—which was why he was keeping
his head down. His internal system, too, was in turmoil
and all his soft muscles—not to mention his arms, legs,
and skeletal muscles, all six hundred of which seemed
in seizure—felt knotted and traumatized. Slowly Eames
shook his head, and again he shook his head slowly,
though the shaking felt more like the jerking or twitching of spasm. Then abruptly he turned, wincing because
of the wart as he executed a stiff about-face; and leaving
the circle of three, and avoiding the other three who
sat by the fire—coal-biters all—Eames steered stiffly
toward his blue miner's tent which sat empty and dark
in the circle of tents between the fire and the ring of
staked dogs.

Stopping down and entering the tent, the first thing
he did was to fall on his knees and attempt to light the
kerosene lantern which hung from the tent pole. His

fingers were trembling and he had trouble grasping, and then lighting, and then holding a match—his fingertips were without feeling and his hands powerless, and he was fumbling about in the dark—but finally he managed. Then, still in a kneeling position, he struggled out of his parka, taking care in his gropings not to upset the lantern, though he nearly knocked down the tent pole. Then he sat and with great care unlaced his boots and removed both them and his windpants. By now he was puffing. He sat, clad in his woolen one-piece long johns with the flap at the rear, and three pairs of wool army socks, until he got back his breath, then he crawled feet first—solicitous of the left foot, which went last—into his brown eiderdown, which was damp on top where he had been sitting, and frost-rimed inside where he had lain sweating for five nights. These blundering, elephantine rituals marked the start of the sixth night of Eames's ordeal, the third phase: for before this phrase, as he reckoned them, had been the one of Rene's return and the Bishop's arrival and Mildred Urquhart's defection; and before that had occurred the first phase, of the nightmare siege at Johnson's cabin and his first encounter with Johnson, bracketed in Eames's mind by the wounding of King and the killing of Millen; and before that . . . Eames could not remember back further. Events before that, even Tommy's death and the breakup with Rene, seemed horrific exceptions to a more or less stable existence, one in which rules, limits, and natural law still pertained. Since the irruption of Johnson into Eames's life and the chaos his coming unleashed, no rules comprehended and no limits prescribed the agony Eames had lived through. Thoughts could not lessen nor rituals stay the terror knotting Eames's bowels: his dread of the unpredictable (Johnson and Rene); his fear of the unreliable (Mildred Urquhart and Wild); his suspicion of the bizarre (the Bishop, Wop May); and his general loss of faith in the ability of normal human beings (Parsons, Riddell) to maintain clearheadedness and fair-mindedness when constantly outfaced, outflanked, and surrounded by the unpredictable, the unreliable, and the bizarre. In this

last category—of more or less decent, rational beings—
he included himself. Recalling his murderous rage in
the face-off with Johnson, his insane jealousy of the
Bishop, his fitful lust for Moira, his niggardliness and
then his fearfulness in the face of Rene, and in spite of
all, or perhaps because of all, his ridiculous theosophical pride, when he inventoried his conduct of the past
month—just a month!—he was appalled to admit that
he had indulged in every deadly sin but two, gluttony
and sloth, and for gluttony his now nearly constant pipe
smoking might qualify him, whereas for sloth his mind
and body yearned for sleep as he imagined Johnson's
must. No amount of sleep seemed to satisfy, and no rest
to relax him; besides, he was troubled by nightmares.
Just last night (he remembered now as he lay down
again) he dreamed he had got up from bed and padded
in slippers and bathrobe to the toilet, and on returning—not to his bag in the tent, or his cot in the sleeping
porch, but to the queen-sized bed in Mildred Urquhart's
bedroom—he returned to bed down with Rene. But
Mildred and Rene were in the bed together, naked and
flushed and laughing together, not actually doing anything, but looking as though they had done . . . everything:
the vein in Rene's neck was pulsing and her lipstickless
lips were swollen and wet, wet the whole area around
her mouth and her eyes looked glazed and lusterless.
And as Mildred Urquhart got up out of bed to make
room for him beside Rene, he noticed the flush of
Mildred's face, neck, and throat, and how ruddy and
chafed her thighs were. Eames ignored her and climbed
into bed, but still Mildred stood by the bed, naked and
huddled in the chill air, *her* mouth and *her* chin moist
and pink and her eyes watching them wistfully. Then,
with Mildred still standing there, her arms folded awkwardly over her warm, pendulous breasts against the
cold, he mounted (dutifully, it seemed to Eames in his
dream) Rene's small-breasted, long-waisted, boyish
form, which lay unresponsive beneath him. And dutifully as he worked his will, and as Mildred Urquhart
looked on, Rene continued to lie nonchalantly and to
read the newspaper she had stuck up between them . . .

Remembering this dream now, and dreading its sequel, as his numbed right foot and burning left one—the wart felt like dry ice—probed the recesses of the sleeping bag, unsticking the top from the bottom where the two layers had frosted together, Eames's mind sought a diversion, any diversion, and his hand produced from under the bag a weirdly mauve-colored, frost-covered *Morte Darthur*. Taking care not to upset the tent pole, he turned himself over onto his side and, wiping his cheek with the sleeve of his long johns (his left eye had begun twitching and watering, and the rheum started to freeze on his cheek), he opened the book to the page he had dog-eared. In the tent's eerie blue light he read:

> So upon Trinity Sunday at night king Arthur dreamed a wonderful dream. And in his dream him seemed that he saw upon a chafflet a chair, and the chair was fast to a wheel, and thereupon sat king Arthur in the richest cloth of gold that might be made. And the king thought there was under him, far from him, an hideous deep black water, and therein was all manner of serpents and worms and wild beasts foul and horrible. And suddenly the king thought that the wheel turned up-so-down, and he fell among the serpents, and every beast took him by a limb. And then the king cried as he lay in his bed, 'Help! help!' and then knights, squires and yeomen awaked the king, and then he was so amazed that he wist not where he was.

Eames blinked (his right eye—his left had continued to twitch). From outside he could hear the whining of dogs and the murmur of men: men huddled in darkness around a campfire, dogs burrowed in snow against the cold. Far in the distance a wolf howled. The dogs set up a chorus of deep-throated bays, reassuring themselves. Gradually the noise subsided. The wolf howled again, dolefully. A few answering yelps tapered off into whines. The murmur of men went on unbroken, their shadows on the tent wall unmoved.

Eames felt himself nodding off. The arm which was

propping the book had gone numb, and the pain from the wart had subsided. His feet mercifully, both his feet, had no feeling. He shifted around to free the pinched arm, and tried to wiggle his toes. Blinking both eyes, he read on:

And then so he awaked until it was nigh day, and then he fell on slumbering again, not sleeping nor thoroughly waking. So the king seemed verily that there came sir Gawain unto him with a number of fair ladies with him. So when king Arthur saw him he said, 'Welcome, my sister's son, I weened ye had been dead! And now I see thee on live, much am I beholden unto Almighty Jesu. Ah fair nephew, what been these ladies that hither be come with you?'

"Sir,' said sir Gawain, 'all these be ladies for whom I have faughten for, when I was man living. And all these are tho that I did battle for in righteous quarrels, and God hath sent me to you of his special grace to give you warning that in no wise ye do battle as to-morn, but that ye take a treatise for a month day. And proffer you largely, so that to-morn ye put in a delay. For…'

Eames could scarcely read the print as it swam before his eyes, black letter old style on a field azure. "'…an ye fight to-morn…doubt not ye shall be slain, and…many mo other good…God…'"

The book fell from his hand and his eyes closed, his breathing relaxed; he fell into Arthurian slumber, not sleeping nor thoroughly waking. As he breathed through his mouth and muttered, Eames dreamed he was leading a charge up a hill, his regimental sword still in its scabbard. Behind him an army of men, hedgehogged in tanks and drawn up in horse ranks, and flown over by planes, thronged the slopes. These, and the innumerable horse- and dog-supply trains and motorized support vans which clogged the valley, were stalled and the charge up the hill halted because a vicious rumor had been circulated by newsmen that a personal hate was consuming the commander-in-chief. This was Eames, and he was just at that moment consulting his Field Marshals Riddell and Parsons and Air Marshal May, when the enemy showed itself.

The lines were drawn up and the troops deployed like those at Thiepval ridge, with a come-hither center and detachable flanks designed to enfold the opponent, but the opponent was Rene, and Eames when he spied her waxed wrathful. Her vulpine face was sharp and quick, and quick her feline stealth as she descended. When she glanced at Eames and his lieutenants through her slits of eyes, the men felt themselves sighted and watched from machine gun emplacements. Her gash of mouth had not opened yet, but the men could see it was air-cooled and capable, once triggered, of continuous firing. She stalked down the hill and halted at point-blank range and stood, brassy and bold. "I am still Mrs. Eames," she said, then screamed: "I am still the wife of this man!"

Eames, breaking off his staff meeting and drunken with rage, drew from his scabbard his sword and raised it to strike her when Tommy, aged three or four, came scurrying out of a nearby bush to stand by his mother. Eames glared at them both, and there was about Tommy something so like his mother that Eames turned on him his full wrath. In a towering rage and brandishing his sword, he roared: "Come out from under your mother!" And to Rene: "Get him out of there, or I'll kill the little son of a bitch!"

Eames's wrath shook both him and the hillside. Before him the two were like animals in a windstorm, Rene small and cowering and Tommy (who now looked like Wild) smaller, burrowing up between Rene's legs in terror. Then both Rene and Tommy were burrowing up underneath the legs of a giant, the Pike of this peak who had stalked down the hill in one stride. And as Eames and his forces fell back in terror, the giant with great drunken guffaws roared and sang drunkenly in Eames's face:

"Oh, do not drive those sparrows away,
    You may be a sparrow yourself someday.
    Who is the man with the big red nose?
    Who? ah? Who—ah—ah!"

And sneezed. At that sneeze was a terrific upheaval,
the foundations of the world being shaken as the hill
turned upside down, and the giant plunged as they all
did—down, down past the planets and stars, through
a half-million galaxies of planets and stars with known
names, and another half-million unnamed, the men in
their plummeting downward, and outward, spreading
out from each other as they scattered free-falling through
metagalactic space, until they were bunched or clus-
tered—each one of them: Eames, Millen, King, Lazarus, the Bishop, Parsons, Gardlund, Lang, Wop May,
Riddell—in small clusters, but the bunches were separated by great expanses, the expanses between them
uniformly empty and filled with nothing, nothing at
all.... They were star clusters, each one fixed in relation to all the others. When one of them moved, the
entire cluster moved; when one was at rest, they all
rested. As one by one the stars within their formation
died, or decayed, and fell out of place—first King, then
Millen, then Blake, then ...—the fixed circle tightened
and the same rule applied to the fewer as to the
more.... But Johnson (for he was the giant, Eames could
now clearly see that) was on a vast hydrogen cloud,
surrounded by ionic fields, as inaccessible now as before. The death of stars did not affect him, nor the con-
version of matter to energy, or energy to matter ... as
their circle was, so was his cloud, a fixed form. Stones,
planets, interstellar gases, other large structures explored past them—there was only the one direction of
motion: outward—dissolving into atoms, electrons,
quarks, each of these smaller structures as fabulously
intricate as a snowflake ... but their star formation remained fixed and their cluster intact. This went on for
light-years, time, times and a half. Gradually, almost
imperceptibly it happened so slowly, their star formation shrunk. Now it included only Eames and his three

lieutenants, Riddell, Parsons, and May. But the original form stayed the same, the lower structures remaining intact in the higher, only the lights one by one had gone out. Then, out of the star cloud of nebulous gases, plasmic and formless with seething, inextinguishable life, the Voice of Johnson spoke: "KILL THE LITTLE SON OF A BITCH!"...

Eames woke with a start, trembling and sweating. Frost had formed around his nostrils where he had quit breathing when he'd begun panting and the lantern, a nebulous light, was smoking and needed its wick trimmed. He reached up and extinguished it, then he made himself small in his bag. His blue miner's tent, cold and dark though it was, was less cold, less dark, than his dream. The men outside were gone now, the fire damped. How did Johnson sleep, he wondered—without fire, without food, without shelter—or did he? Did he just carry on, mad for sleep? Eames's body craved sleep, cried out for it, but his mind dreaded more dreams. He needed withdrawal from the tensions of coping, not a magnification of problems. He would rather keep watch with the naked eye than gaze through a telescope all night long. But there was no need to keep watch—Gardlund, rhythmically spitting tobacco, was on lookout; the trappers took turns. A truce, if not peace, Eames required: a six hours' truce during which he could rest and renew his powers and gather his forces for the next day's assault on the mountain. Johnson could have a sleep too, build a fire, do whatever he liked except break the truce, spoil Eames's sleep. Contracting in his own mind a truce until daybreak, Eames rolled over onto his stomach and positioned himself for deep, dreamless sleep. Sleep without night-sweat, nightmares, the wart, and the great thirst he always woke up with. He lay still a moment, sensing something undone. He opened his eyes and stared at the tent side. A luminous patch cast by the moon compelled his attention. His body, and especially his head, was loath to move. Drawing his arms up slowly from within the warm covers, then wearily lifting his head and bracing himself on his elbows, he closed his eyes and muttered aloud: "God grant I may not lose my mind." He remained braced in a prostrate position, his eyes closed, not unmindful of the warm air escaping from the depths of his bag and the cold air on his shoulders and arms, the sweat in his long johns beginning to freeze. Time was always a factor. If he didn't act fast, he might chill or catch cold. Eames sneezed. He sneezed again. "And may Rene get over her anger and be content, whether with me or another"—he shrugged—"with me, then..." He shrugged again. "As for me, I solemnly vow as I did with drink ten and a half years ago, never to touch a woman again, so help me God." He stayed braced upright on his elbows for another few minutes, hearing from time to time a dog whine, the crackle of tobacco hitting the fire, and his own sudden sneezes. He continued to hold his body alert and his mind in abeyance, then as abruptly as he had braced himself for the effort, he gave up and lay down for the truce and the sleep it would bring. He could not bring himself to make peace with Johnson; he had tried, but it couldn't be done...not by him, not by pledges or vows, not tonight...he was too old, too tired....

PART SIX

The Mountain

THE FIRST DAY

Rock. Around and above the rock, space. The space was not empty. Wind shattered shale and hurled it at him with needles of ice, blinders of snow, taunts, threats, cries: "Kill!" "Climb!" "Hide!" No place on the rock, no break from the wind, no tree, shrub, no crevice, no cover. Windswept rock, in every direction, from every direction the wind.

He was in a bowl formed by mountains, hundreds of mountains thrown up, folded over, hammered and shattered and shaped by the forces beneath and above, mountains resisting as he was. Where he was those forces were strongest, and he could not resist long. To stop was to stay in a trap that would spring the instant he set his weight down, a steel trap he had to get out of. The Barrier was the way out. He was on the trappan, exposed. Weak from starvation, numbed with cold, mad for sleep, dehydrated from so much exertion in such cold for so long, but alive. Bait, but live bait. A target, but moving. Still able to slither across the trappan and, by placing numbed legs one in front of the other and using his rifle for support, to crawl up and out and climb over the trap jaws, then to stand at the top of the world!

Squinting, he lifted his gaze, lizardlike, to the top of the world. The teeth of the trap loomed above him, massif after massif, tooth after tooth, snow-swathed and sunlit they gleamed in the sun, the mountains. He was in shadow. He was in the very mouth of the mountains, a morsel. He wanted to hide in a cleft of a rock, very small. He was exposed in the bare waste and middle of a hundred amphitheaters ruined and empty, with fierce howls sweeping across them: "Kill Johnson!" "Hide Johnson!" Gigantic, majestic, impassive, and cold, the mountains had a soft, silken look like the fur of some animal, silken at a distance but fierce on approach, like an ermine, or a white fox.

Would it be possible at the world's top to stretch out his hand? Supposing he lifted his gun up, and fired. Would the bullet advance beyond the world's top, or would something compel it to stop? Were there limits, and what was beyond space—the void?

While he gazed stupidly up at the sky, the clouds' undersides became lavender-tinted, lavender and mauve and outlandishly colored by the cold sinking sun, but he did not find this remarkable. Nor did he think it an event worth his notice when the sun, withdrawing its light for the next twenty hours, silhouetted the mountains while it sank to the world's underside.

At sunset the mountains were pink like an animal's underbelly, or the teeth of an ermine. . . .

Things making for offenses should be known; things not making for offenses should be known. What was an offense should be known; what was not an offense should be known. A slight offense should be known; a serious offense should be known. An offense that could be canceled should be known; an offense that could not be canceled should be known. An offense originated by action should be known; an offense originated by inaction should be known. The original offense should be known; all subsequent offenses should be known. A series of offenses leading to defeat should be known and acknowledged.

"Was there an offense involving defeat, and where was it committed?" On the trapline.

"Against whom?" The Indian.

"What was it?" His pulling up the Indian's traps and slinging them, when they had already been set and did not belong to him.

"And did he feel ashamed, was there doubt in his mind, was his energy stirred up and did he give way to anger or violence on that occasion?" Not on that occasion, no.

"Then where was the offense? Where was it committed?" At the cabin.

"Against whom?" Against King, the Mountie.

"What was it?" His refusal to open the door to King and the man with him, after they had traveled eighty miles by dog team.

"And did he feel ashamed, was there doubt in his mind, was his energy stirred up and did he shove his bowl aside and squat inside his cabin, hunched against the door, silent, angry, shoulders bent, head lowered, brooding, speechless? Did he argue with them?" No, he did not argue.

"Then where was the offense? Where was it committed?" At the cabin.

"Against whom?" King again.

"What was it?" His refusal to be called out by King and the man with him, or to let them in when they threatened to break down his door, after they had traveled another 160 miles by dog team and returned with a search warrant. His shooting King through the door when King threatened to shoot him.

"And did he feel ashamed, was there doubt in his mind, was his energy stirred up and did he feel taunted, bullied, trapped in his own cabin and harassed beyond reason? And did he try to kill King?" No, he did not try to kill King.

"Then where was the offense? Where was it committed?" At the cabin.

"Against whom?" Against the leader of the posse, Eames.

"What was it?" His refusal to come out and give himself up, after they had surrounded his cabin and called him out with a bullhorn and fired on him for six hours.

"And did he feel ashamed, was there doubt in his mind, was his energy stirred up and did he feel besieged, hunted without cause, trapped in his own den,

and while their hate was on harassed to the point of
madness? And did he try to kill them?" No, he did not
try to kill them.

"Then were was the offense? Where was it committed?" At the cabin.

"Against whom?" Eames again.

"What was it?" His refusal to kill Eames or any of
the others after thay had surrounded and tossed bombs
at his cabin and had attempted to kill him for fifteen
hours. His refusal to kill Eames or to take him prisoner
or use him as a hostage, and his ridiculing him instead.

"And did he feel ashamed, was there doubt in his
mind, was his energy stirred up and did he lapse into
a battle trance as one by one they lumbered up over
the top of the snowbank, throwing flares like Verey
Lights and dynamite like Mills bombs, in a poorly executed, suicidal raid, just like the British? And did he
aim to kill them, any of them?" No, he did not aim to
kill them.

"Then where was the offense? Where was it committed?" In the ravine.

"Against whom?" Against Millen, the patrol leader.

"What was it?" His shooting and killing Millen when
Millen stood up, and all four were advancing on him.

"And did he feel ashamed, was there doubt in his
mind, was his energy stirred up and did he feel trapped
like a mad dog in the ravine, did he see no other way
out, and did he say to himself, I will draw the line here,
and did he shoot to kill Millen, both shots?" Yes, all
that and more.

"What more?" That was the offense leading to defeat,
the last but not the first offense. The first offense was
cutting himself off in the first place, but not altogether,
for he had glanced at the Indian girl in the store, asked
the priest where to find a canoe, purchased goods from
the Hudson's Bay trader, answered the Mountie's questions, ignored the Indian, asked directions from the second trader, and then cut himself off from human contact,
but not altogether, for he had brought with him weapons and traps, an ax and a compass, matches, and money,

and he rode in a canoe not of his own making, wearing clothes which he had bought, so he had not cut himself off altogether, but had simply taken the most useful things and left the rest. He had built a cabin, set a trapline, made stage caches, and thought himself outside the law and laughing, he was laughing as he built the cabin, laughing while he set the traps and made the caches, laughing when he shot the first and ridiculed the second and when he shot and killed the third policeman, laughing all the way to his defeat.

"Then these were the offenses leading to defeat: seeking to cut himself off but not altogether, taking things not his own, speaking and refusing to speak, killing and refusing to kill, having one's little joke, and onslaught to others—to the point of killing, to the point of refusing to kill: these were the offenses leading to defeat without doubt for the man who must be destroyed. And was he now prepared to be destroyed?" No, he was not prepared.

—Then what was your reason for entering the delta, if not to be destroyed?

—Release. I was striving for release.

—Was there a previous anguish you were striving for release from?

—Yes.

—And was it linked with a previous endeavor?

—No. It was merely sudden.

—And was that anguish present now?

—No. A new anguish had arisen.

—And this new anguish, was it linked with fresh endeavor: the attempt to cut yourself off but not altogether, speaking and refusing to speak, killing and refusing to kill, having your little joke, and so on?

—No. It was merely sudden.

—Then what prevents you from present endeavor, since you do not link it with future anguish?

—Endeavor now is useless, only previous endeavor is useful.

—Explain.

—They have dynamited my cabin, robbed my cache,

wrecked my trapline. I am starving, weak, and cold, in need of food and sleep and fire. My needs cannot be met by striving now.

—Your needs are few.

—They are urgent.

—A man who is of small possessions, few desires, and has learned what is and is not an offense, having subdued all passion in himself, and extinguished all remembrance of himself, if such a one has right perspective and high courage, he is not confined to any district or excluded from the mountain, but climbs with ease and can move up and down at will. Such a one may live alone without offense.

(Johnson chafes his hands, as if before a fire. He counts on his stiff fingers up to seven. He slaps his face and stamps his feet, rallying his senses. He cocks an ear and listens to the howling of the wind and the hum of his own heart. He counts again on his numbed fingers, calculates. His split lips, dry and stuck together, part in a hideous grin.)

"Of these seven, is it possible to leave one out, and allow the man who has the other six to climb the mountain?"

"Yes, that could be done. We could leave out possessions. For what do possessions matter? You need your gun and ax and eiderdown, your parka and windpants, your mitts and toque, your moccasins and snowshoes—without them, you would surely die. And your compass, the gold teeth and pearls, and your money—what do these matter? You may need them. Yes, we can leave possessions out, if you have few desires, no passions, no remembrance of yourself, right perspective, and having learned what is and is not an offense have high courage."

"But of these six, is it not possible to leave out one, and to permit the man who has the other five to climb the mountain?"

"Yes, that could be done. We could leave out passion. For what do passions matter, if you are alone? Your anger and your hatred and your arrogance and greed will harm no one if you see no one, signal no one, and shun all human contact. Passions can be left out, provided you have few desires, no remembrance of yourself, right perspective, and having learned what is and is not an offense have high courage. If you have these five, you may climb the mountain."

"But how can I have right perspective when I have not yet climbed the mountain? I have been stumbling through the delta, hunted like a dog, where one cannot tell his own track from the animals'. Right perspective is what I search for. Could it not be left until after I have climbed the mountain?"

"Yes, Johnson, that could be done. We could leave out right perspective. For what does right perspective matter when a man is desperate? If you have the other four— few desires, no remembrance of yourself, knowledge of what constitutes offenses, and high courage— you might then attain right perspective. That could be done."

(Johnson grins. The flesh of his cheeks is drawn back in a grimace like a rodent's snout poking up from the snow when the snow melts down around it. From a perch in the mountains a sparrow hawk shrieks: "Eich! Eich!")

"There is the little matter of Constable Millen, of course, but what does Millen matter? If you have only the one skill, courage, and have harnessed yourself to endeavor as to a dead body, and avoid any action involving destruction, you may still climb the mountain, though like a man crippled by past deeds, blinded by passions, and burdened by possessions and desires, you will find it hard going.

"Hard going means: burdened by possessions and desires, blinded by passions, crippled by past deeds.

"Involving destruction means: if it is the dwelling of ants or if it is the dwelling of earwigs or if it is the dwelling of mice or if it is the tunnel of rats or if it is the eyrie of eagles or if it is the nest of ravens or if it is the perch of sparrow hawks or if it is the yard of caribou or if it is the den of foxes or if it is the hut of ermine or if it is the lodge of beaver or if it is the cave of bear or if it is the dwelling of any other animal or

any living creature, or if it is connected with shrubs or if it is connected with trees or if it is connected with dog runs or if it is connected with houses or if it is connected with Indians or if it is connected with whites: this means *involving destruction.*

"Harnessed to endeavor as to a dead body means: bearing defeat, for just as a flat stone which has been broken in half cannot be put together again, so he who has deprived another human being of life is one who must bear defeat.

"It might still be done, though, and you might do it, if you renounce all thoughts of revenge, and seek only freedom."

—I renounce all thoughts of revenge. I seek only freedom.

—You may go over.

(Johnson stumbles across the low slope, fodder-footed, his five-foot-long snowshoes slapping the rock where it has been swept clean of snow. Two ravens hunched on a bluff to his left croak obscenely.)

THE SECOND DAY

The PHILOSOPHER, *the* PHYSICIST, *and the* BIOCHEMIST
*come out and occupy the gallery of one of the high
peaks looking down on the bowl-shaped arena. Johnson is seen far below, a black speck, toiling across the
Divide. The* BIOCHEMIST *has with him field glasses,
a thermometer, and a small slate blackboard with
chalk. The* PHYSICIST *has a spectrometer to measure
heat loss, a bolometer to measure heat differentials
at a great distance, and a tele-entrometer to measure
entropy. The* PHILOSOPHER *carries a tellurium sele-
nide infrared intensifier, which he attaches to the infrared telescope he has brought and proceeds to set
up.*

PHIL. *(apologetically, as he sets up his instruments)* These
    must be kept cold.

(The PHYSICIST *and* BIOCHEMIST *wait for him.)*

PHYS. Are we prepared to begin?

PHIL. *(Fastens snap-lens in place.)* There!

BIOC. As I understand it, we are to keep ourselves as
    much as possible out of the calculations, but we are
    to make a statement describing the subject's prob-
    ability of survival as a life-support system. Is that
    correct?

PHYS. We are to keep ourselves entirely out. What you
    call the subject is no different from an atom in a
    black box, or a vapor trail in a cloud chamber. There

413

may be an uncertainty quotient in the equation, but
the statistical probability factor will take care of that.

PHIL. There will be a subjective element in our description, since the measuring device has been contrived
by an observer. Bear in mind that what we observe
is not Johnson himself, but Johnson exposed to our
method of questioning.

PHYS. Of course, if you take the entire actual world of
matter and energy for your subject matter, it is ir-
reducible to logic and resists formulation because it
is not altogether answerable to law. There is always
a surd element at the basis of substance. Here we
are dealing, however, with a measurable mass moving a finite distance at a calculable velocity—those
are my variants—and the internal components, such
as organ specific needs, our biochemical colleague
can compute. I think we expose ourselves to unnecessary error by introducing a subjective element.

BIOC. From the biochemical point of view, in order to
consider an ecological situation in which the adap-
tive individual is confronted with an altered environment in such a way that both are changed by the
encounter, it is necessary to have an observer who
stands outside the whole complex. The complex in
this case consists of two simpler parts: Johnson and
the mountains.

PHIL. Such standpointlessness is factually impossible.

PHYS. But imaginable. Take the equation of state and
the energy equation, for example, in thermodynamics. Together they completely determine all the
thermodynamic properties of a substance. While it
is not to be supposed that the principle of entropy
applies to living as it does to non-living systems, the
important thing is that such an equation exists.
Physics would be unimaginable without ideal experiments leading to mathematically precise and ob-
jective results.

(*The* PHILOSOPHER *shakes his head.*)

PHYS. In any case, what we are after here is the probability quotient of the completion of an event, taking
into account all the factors—physical, biochemical,

and others if others exist—involved in that process.

BIOC. What do you mean by "event"?

PHIL. What do we mean by "Johnson"?

PHYS. Johnson? For the purpose of this experiment I take Johnson to be a thermodynamic system with boundaries. A system because he represents a definite quantity of matter bounded by a closed surface...

BIOC. Skin, I presume.

PHYS....which is impervious to the flow of matter, or energy. In this case, the boundary or control surface is further insulated by clothing which retards heat flow from the one heat reservoir, which I call Johnson, to the other heat reservoir, which I call the surroundings. Heat is always associated with a process, and Johnson is a system in process of being degraded. Let us call him J. $J_1 - J_2$ = the flow of energy across the boundary in the form of heat loss and work done. The energy flow in the case of J is irreversible.

BIOC. But heat is not something J *has*, it is something being generated in him by chemical breakdowns and enzyme outlays that require replenishment. As he starves, experiences stress, and struggles against the cold, his basal metabolic rate will increase, food stores will be depleted more rapidly, and essential vitamin deficiencies will occur. C deficiency will cause delayed wound healing, his blood vessel walls will become very fragile, small hemorrhages will begin to occur throughout J's body, and we should be able to see purpuric blotches over his entire skin. *(The* BIOCHEMIST *takes up the field glasses and peers through them at the distant speck, J.)*

PHYS. He is also losing heat through work. Heat is a function of J's total energy, E, which is in process of diminishing to thermal equivalence with his surroundings. We could calculate this in at least three ways: his kinetic energy, KE, is diminishing as he pushes ahead; his external potential energy, PE, is augmenting as he climbs uphill; his internal energy, U...

BIOC. *(putting down the field glasses)* I can't make them

out from this distance, but I know they're there.

PHYS.... his internal energy, U, is diminishing...

BIOC. Yes, as he uses his vital fat and protein reserves. Glycogen, his carbohydrate store in the liver, was used up in the first twenty-four to forty-eight hours. That's another reason for the purpuric blotches. I'm sure they're there...

PHYS. We could denote this change thus (the PHYSICIST scratches in chalk on the BIOCHEMIST's slate black-board):
$$(E_2 - E_1) = (KE_2 - Ke_1) + (PE_2 - PE_1) + (U_2 - U_1)$$ in J's process of diminishment toward a state of thermal equivalence with his surroundings.

PHIL. But Johnson's surroundings are losing heat too. The entire universe, as work is done in it, is losing energy as Johnson is, slowly converting itself into heat and vanishing into space until nothing is left except a dead ocean of energy at the lowest possible level, say $-272°$ Centigrade below the freezing point of water—incapable of doing any work.

PHYS. I do not think that is relevant to J.

PHIL. But it is true.

PHYS. It isn't useful. The availability, A, of a given system is the maximum useful work that can be obtained in a process in which the system comes, or is coming, to equilibrium with its surroundings. J's surroundings happen to be the earth's atmosphere, so the end state of his process will take place at atmospheric temperature, T_0, and atmospheric pressure, P_0. Remember, J is starving. His food stores will be depleted very quickly, more quickly, for example, than the seasons will change. I think we can take the surrounding environment as a fixed constant in J's case.

BIOC. I think the cold will get him first. His skin and subcutaneous tissue, especially fat, act as heat insulators. As he loses fat, due to increased basal metabolic rate, he has a lowered resistance to cold. Due to his lowered resistance, the cold stimulates the sympathetic centers of his posterior hypothalamus, causing piloerection, abolition of sweating and constriction of the blood vessels in his skin. His heat production will be increased up to 50 per cent through shivering, with a commensurate heat loss. Increased activity of the thyroid gland will cause an increase in thyrozine output, which in turn will increase J's cellular metabolism. This is also being increased by the adrenaline and noradrenaline released by his sympathetic nervous system in response to stress: cold, exertion, and fear. I presume that J is anxious. All these factors affect, to J's detriment, his consumption of energy and food requirement. Then, too, there is frostbite to think of, drowsiness, coma. Even if he has, as he might have, a basal metabolic rate 16–20 per cent above normal, once his body temperature goes below 85° the hypothalamus is no longer able to regulate temperature.

PHIL. Gentlemen, gentlemen! All this is very informative, but it is positing an end state without having clearly defined a beginning. The empirical datum with which it is necessary to begin is that the subject cannot maintain himself by concentrating upon himself. The materials which he needs for maintenance are to be obtained not from himself but from the external world. While it is true that there is nothing in the mind that was not first in the external world, except error, it is also true that mind is nature made self-aware. And just as a limited portion of nature is involved here, which we term "Johnson," so the degree of awareness, too, is limited. Limited, and, what is worse, fallible. Should Johnson's goal be the survival of the self, as it probably is, this would in no way alter the nature of his quest, which is to find the elements necessary for his survival, and these range all the way from water and food to the approbation of his fellows.

BIOC. Water, yes. Without water he would last only a few days. Death due to dehydration occurs with a 10–20 per cent loss of body weight. I assumed all along that he was picking up handfuls of snow, though snow will not give him the trace minerals that he needs, but he can do without them in the short run.

In the long run, of course, six to eight weeks, let us say, he will begin vomiting blood and will experience lesions of gums, loosening of teeth, bloody stools, and cerebral hemorrhaging. B deficiency will add stomach, heart, and nerve problems. But that is the long-range forecast. He probably won't last that long. Probably he will produce very little urine in an attempt to conserve fluid. But he does have an obligatory urine output of four hundred milliliters per day to flush his system of toxins. Otherwise . . .

PHYS. Uremic poisoning.

BIOC. Curtains.

PHIL. The needs are animal, granted. The best interests of the individual are served by the reduction of organ specific needs, and the drives function to reduce basic tissue needs. But once a drive is fired it acts on its own and cannot be recalled. Drives acting thus are powerful and often blind. They do not necessarily stop when the needs are reduced, but continue on, dragging the individual with them. The drive for survival may become so obsessive that it inhibits all other drives and draws on energy resources unknown to science. Thus those exaggerations of action which the Greeks recognized as "outrageous behavior." Incredible feats may be performed, boggling the imagination.

PHYS. J is not likely to provide any surprises. Look at him. (*All watch for a moment the black speck toiling across the bare white horizon.*)

BIOC. He is beginning to stagger. Arterial oxygen saturation is probably down below 90 per cent. It's the cold. Plus the altitude, though an increase in respiratory rate doesn't usually occur until eight thousand feet.

PHIL. That name-and-shape we call Johnson is still capable of incredible feats.

PHYS. Since energy can neither be created nor destroyed, I fail to see where these energy resources would come from. Energy may be transferred from one system to another, but the total amount remains constant. Even if we disregard for a moment the thermodynamics of J's situation and regard him as a free body, he is still not isolated, but boundaried by other free mechanical bodies. He has extensive and intensive properties, and these are all calculable. Classically speaking, the ratio of any force component to the area on which it acts is called a stress, and in general there will exist nine such ratios.

PHIL. But it is true, is it not, that in addition to this gross material calculation, other forces must be taken into account, electromagnetic for example, and nuclear.

PHYS. They are not relevant to J.

PHIL. Doesn't the weight of a body vary with movement, and doesn't a moving body undergo a contraction?

PHYS. Only at very high speeds. That is hardly relevant to J.

PHIL. But what is relevant and of importance to J is that matter itself can be transformed into energy. Matter and energy are two conditions of the same substance—in the present case, J.

PHYS. But the energy is not without form, and it must be approximately equal in amount to the matter transformed.

PHIL. Precisely! If matter can be transformed into energy, and energy itself has a structure, then matter, which is only another condition of energy, must be structured. And structured matter is informed matter, matter made up of forms. Matter becomes inertial substance and energy kinetic substance.

BIOC. This is all very abstract. J's night vision has just disappeared due to a decrease in arterial oxygen saturation depressing the function of the rods in the retina.

PHIL. But that is the point. We are concerned here with the survival of the forms, not the functioning of them. A circle is easier to draw than an eye. A diagram of a circle can be drawn, but what would the diagram of an eye be?

PHYS. I have just told you. The nine ratios will define

the stress at any given point. In certain special cases, the stress is completely determined by one ratio, rather than nine.

BIOC. During starvation the body preferentially uses carbohydrates rather than fat and protein, and fat rather than protein, thus sparing the vital organs. If J had 15 per cent body fat at the beginning of starvation—less since he had been eating sparingly for some time—all his fat reserves would have been gone in five weeks.

PHIL. But we are no longer dealing with matter at the level of gross common sense. J comprises, in addition to measurable solid matter in stress, both micro- and macro-levels of being. At the micro-level, J is not solid, but porous, containing more space than substance. At the macro-level he may be absent in space or in time, yet still be actual, as in remote, or at least possible, as in future or past. We could treat of J *in absentia*.

PHYS. J is not so remote. He is there. *(Points.)*

BIOC. Arterial oxygen saturation will probably remain around 90 per cent up to ten thousand feet. This represents a 4 per cent drop from sea level. J is at five thousand feet.

PHIL. But now we have instruments to extend the senses and mathematics to formulate findings. What we call J stands revealed as more subtle and much more complex than supposed. All of the properties which we were inclined to deny J—J as a heat reservoir, or a mechanical object, or a life-support system— can from a philosophical point of view be returned to J. J represents nothing less than the repository of all being, both what is and could be, as well as what was and will be.

BIOC. *(peering through the field glasses)* J is down! Soon he will sink into a comatose state, and then freeze.

PHYS. By freezing I presume you mean that the system approaches thermal equilibrium with its surroundings.

BIOC. The process of feeding off the protein in one's vital organs goes into abeyance as freezing sets in.

PHYS. The system, when it reaches mechanical, thermal, and chemical equilibrium with its environment, is no longer thermodynamic. It becomes thermostatic. The quasistatic heat flow in that case differs only infinitesimally from a reversible process.

PHIL. The properties to be returned to J are of two kinds: the forms and the qualities. The forms, such as two, as in two arms and two legs, defy the ravages of time and cold; and the same may be said of J's qualities, his courage and his will to survive.

BIOC. J is a function of many finely tuned and nicely balanced biochemical systems, but they are nearly all dysfunctional.

PHIL. It may not be too late for J, given his monomaniacal drive, to adapt to his environment. If we understand learning as the ability to elicit from responses the capacity to respond, and man as the animal who consistently over-responds, then the stimuli available to J are of three types: nonhuman nature, artifacts, and other human beings.

BIOC. But consciousness depends on a particular area of the brain, namely, the midbrain section of the upper brain stem reticular formation. In J's case only the macro-molecules with long sidechains are fully oxygenated. A condition not unlike senility—I call it stupor—has seized him.

PHYS. Let's face it. J is fast approaching a state of thermal equilibrium with his environment when no work can be done. Around J's fingers and toes, his nose and ears, and to a lesser extent his arms, and his feet—not his legs though—the surface area in contact with the surroundings being larger, the heat loss is proportionately greater, with the result that his fingers and toes, his nose and his ears, and even his feet up to the ankles and his hands up to the wrists, are numbed, chilled, incapable of feeling and thus of working except as spatial extensions of the larger units which drive them. In his movement from ordered to disordered molecular energy output, and from work to wastage, J has switched from a work reservoir to a heat reservoir. In order to restore J to his initial state, heat would have to be removed from the low-temperature environment and delivered to the high-temperature J. But heat will not flow in this direction. A quantity of heat could be removed from the low-temperature surroundings, or from bodies in which heat has been stored—animal, vegetable, or mineral—thus restoring J to his original state. But the heat flowing into the high-temperature reservoir would need to be greater than the heat which has left it, by an amount equal to the work done by J. But this work J is no longer capable of performing, and a disordered molecule state does not return to an ordered one without producing outstanding changes in still other systems. The original process, so far as J is concerned, was irreversible. Of that there can be no doubt.

BIOC. No doubt at all. It's curtains for J.

PHIL. I can imagine Johnson in a meditative trance, encased in rock wool, on a mountaintop.

PHYS. The process might conceivably be retarded, but not reversed, by enclosing the system in a thick layer of some thermal insulator. We would then have an adiabatic, or no-work, situation—but that is ideal, as ideal as the frictionless surface J would have to climb.

BIOC. Drowsiness, lassitude, mental fatigue—effects of hypoxia as he gains altitude—headache, euphoria, nausea...

PHYS. No, J's entropy inventory has so increased that, from a molecular point of view, his final uniform state is more disordered than his initial state, in which parts of his system were at different temperatures. And this increase in disorder results in an increase in entropy. Regarded not as a coherent system, but as a collection of parts, J has now reached the zeroth law of thermodynamics: when any two parts are in thermal equivalence with a third, they are also in thermal equivalence with each other.

BIOC. It's game over for J.

PHIL. It is easy to assume that the name is the thing, but the name is not the thing. What do we mean by

"J"? Do we mean this dying bundle of organ and tissue needs staggering and crawling across a mountain range? Or do we refer, rather, to the indomitable will of an individual, doomed, of the genus man, failed, of the species human, dead-ended, engaged in an eternal quest of the spirit, the goal of which is freedom? It is not only personal ruin that we bequeath to the future, but also the will to exceed ourselves. Surely anything as small as that black speck down there can serve as no more than an example.

PHYS. I'm glad you agree.

BIOC. *(taking a long last look through the binoculars)* I can see them! I can make out the blotches! Now he's retching. *(Offers the glasses to the* PHILOSOPHER. *The* PHILOSOPHER *declines.)*

PHYS. Shall we go then?

BIOC. Nausea is not usually seen below twelve thousand feet. *(The* BIOCHEMIST, *the* PHYSICIST, *and the* PHILOSOPHER *pick up their instruments and depart from the mountain, leaving Johnson alone, an inert black speck on the horizon.)*

THE THIRD DAY

He was suffocating. A man struggling for breath knows what work is. The tides of breath permit work, and the dying know how little they keep and how hard they work for that little. His breath was a thin inner blade, a bayonet from his brain to his bowels around which he writhed and edged forward, painful step after step, against the saber-toothed wind which slashed viciously at him and kept the breath within him vibrating. Air: the only free thing in civilization, and now it too was against him. The men who had tried to kill him had stirred up the wind against him. They had brought in machines and confused the wind, upsetting air currents. Faceless, nameless teeth from all sides snapped and barked at him: "Haha! We've got you surrounded! We know where you are. We know who you are. We know where you're heading. Haha!" He had nothing, next to nothing, but even the little he had, when threatened with extinction, was something. Greedily he sucked in air and with each breath gasped he groped forward. Behind him the wind was abolished. In its place lay a vacuum, a darkening bruise with a thin little trail of white puffs, his exhalations, which *they* would be forced to follow, to swallow, and drop dead like flies from inhaling. Ahead of him was all space to breathe in; behind him was nothing, no air, he had swallowed it all: thousands of needles of ice and steel shavings twisting within him, transfixed. His bitter breath continued to sparkle.

425

The ice crystals trapped in his nose, throat, and lungs, released steam which would blister and kill.

All nature around him had died. The earth's surface was hard, flat, and black; a granite pall covered the earth. This hard darkness passed into him, and he into it. The air around him was porous and grainy, and porous and grainy he was. His outer perimeter was solid darkness, a wedge-shaped core of darkness marked him. There was an aperture leading out, but he was locked in. Alone in the gigantic dark. Not entirely alone, though, for there were two of him: one of him slept while the other stayed wakeful and worked. Only when the working part of him slept did the sleeping part wake. The now waking part of him labored on, ignoring the now sleeping part, stepping around it so as not to disturb it. Then that part of him went back to sleep, and it was the turn of the other. The two parts never spoke to each other, one never knew when the other was wakeful. One part never asked the other, Who are you? They knew each other only by their works.

One by one the voices ceased. The voices stopped whenever he spoke, or threatened to speak. Their words were slain by his words. When he ceased to speak they rose up around him, deafening him with their uproar, their "Why" and "Why not" and "Because" and "What if," suggesting courses of action, advising plans of inaction, undermining all action with words, squads of words, regiments, armies of words. "But what if...?" one would begin, "Do you ever...?" another would say, commencing statements for him to conclude, recommending conclusions to him, not speaking aloud but repeating, incessantly in a loud buzz, the commands and questions they hurled at him by the thousands, garbled but distinct, wearing him down with what *they* chose to say, menacing him like the thousands of eyes that watched him from above.

A completely different starry sky had suddenly sprung into view. In the gigantic dark he was a star, fallen and glowing feebly but not yet extinguished, not yet cooled down. His head was filled with stars, but not yet arranged into constellations. The stars overhead, attracted to him, dripped thoughts on his head like tallow, endangering themselves. On nights when the stars dripped too many thoughts, with a radiant energy of ten billion suns, he feared for the universe. The death and decay of thousands of stars every night was directly attributable to him, to his thoughts, and to the stars' attraction for him. On one occasion Venus had to be given up, and Cassiopeia had to draw together into a single sun; of the old constellations he saw with alarm that only Orion and the Pleiades could be saved. Nightly he longed for the world as it was before The Destroyer, man, had been created. He yearned to be standing among animals who would not know, and not fear, their slaughter and extinction. He wanted to hang from the stars as they were before they began to fall and drop thoughts on his head. He wanted to be coldness, not cold, a star, not a corpse. He could comprehend that all people had died, and that he was the only one left alive, but he could not get used to the thought that he was the last, not the first, man.

The voices had ceased within him, but their place had been taken by thoughts: brooding thoughts, bitter thoughts, vengeful thoughts stuck like burrs to his mind and sucked at his brain like leeches. He was the last living man on the earth's surface. The earth was so dangerous that no living creature dared show itself anymore. Below its surface the earth teemed with life, millions of dwarves stumbling into each other, shuffling stooped through air-heated corridors between mazes of tunnels and shafts, wearing box-respirators, with precise knowledge of dangerous gases. But the crust of the earth was as deserted as the moon's rind. Even puffs of snow might be lethal. He had to keep vigilant for the pack with gas masks who pursued him. They were supplied from below and now that their mouths were covered their eyes were all around him, spying on him— through binoculars, periscopes, gunsights; from the rocks, from the stars, in the wind—eyes everywhere tracking and searching for him, and their search was murderous. They hated him for being the last man alive.

It occurred to him suddenly that the voices around

him had not ceased, nor were they outshouted by
thoughts. He was deaf! To be deaf was more dangerous
than to be blind. The blind were blind in only one direction; the deaf were deaf in every direction: to the
rear, on both flanks, and in front. This was the work
of a special nerve gas which penetrated the ears. Another nerve gas, aimed at the eyes, would soon be
launched against him—what had they to lose? They
had abandoned the earth's crust already. The gases were
pumped up from hidden mine shafts which sappers were
constantly digging—he had heard their shovels at work.
They could not leave a single human being alive on the
earth. The whole earth, once he was annihilated, they
would use as a graveyard. He began to see, for he was
not blind, in the shadows around him the vague forms
and shapes of thousands of corpses, all animal corpses
that he recognized as the animals he had trapped and
killed: beaver, ermine, muskrat, foxes, wolverines,
lynxes, otter, bear, caribou, moose, wolves, rabbits,
mink—a tremendous carnage. He, the only man left
alive, was wading through, walking on, climbing over
the slaughter. They lay all around him with glowing
eyes, some flayed, some gutted, some with their hides
on and bloated, some with ears cut off, some with paws
gnawed off, some strangled by choke-wires, some with
spines broken, their carcasses lifeless but their eyes
fiercely glowing—mountains of corpses with eyes, claws,
and teeth—the wolverines and the bears and the lynxes
and wolves with teeth bared and ready to bite, rend,
and tear. He could feel his own bones crunching and
being sucked clean and the wind whistling through his
clean bones.

The thought came to him that some of his victims,
and the parasites from his victims, had attached themselves to him and were writhing and wriggling inside
him. Lungworms from the caribou and blowfly larvae
from the moose had got into his lungs and intestines.
A weasel had wriggled in through his navel and eaten
most of his stomach. There was a cavity there. If he
were to eat, as he sometimes considered eating the sun
like a hunk of meat, it would simply pour through his

abdominal cavity and lodge heavily in his thighs. His throat and gullet had been slashed and pierced by the claws of a lynx, and a bear had smashed all his ribs. Worst, he felt his spine ready to snap from the weight of dead flesh both within and without, all the more so because millions of blackflies, swarming inside his clothes, were constantly feeding off him. A special worm had bored up through his feet to pump out his spinal cord. It was the fluid from his spinal cord which, when he breathed, issued from his mouth in little clouds, and, as he gasped away his spinal fluid, he could feel his whole skull become thinner and the delicate membrane between him and the world stretch to the point of splitting. Walking, standing, sitting, lying down, all were equally impossible because of the pain in both legs and in his coccyx. Only his sight had not yet been affected, but as he mounted, carcass by slippery carcass, the mountain of corpses, he found himself, as the winter sun sank, going progressively blind as well as deaf. It was then, in the gathering dusk of the third day, deaf and blind from nerve gas, dumb from terror, numb with cold, and nerveless, that he spotted the airplane.

The low winter sun was sinking behind him and he was watching his shadow disappear and, with it, his ability to see anything but coarse, grainy darkness. The sun from behind him on the winter horizon, a dull light from below, cast his shadow larger than life and made it loom over him and the glacis before him, a long disappearing shadow. He was leaning on his rifle, its butt stuck in the snow, enhaustion evident in every angle and line of his lengthening shadow. The shadow did not lie. He was dying. The brutish torpor of sleep, the brutish toil of climbing. Shorter intervals between them, briefer periods of both. In sleep he was climbing, while climbing he slept. There was now no distinction between them. Lying, standing, walking, sitting, all had become equally painful. Forward motion had stopped and he dreamed of flying, of finding the pass and crossing the mountains as if they did not exist, as if he could not prove to himself that they did by the simple expedient of holding up his two hands—the shadow mimicking him—and saying, or thinking of saying, as he held up one hand, "Here is one hand," then adding as he held up the other, "And here is another." The shadow had held up its hand too, as a hand raised against him, barring his way. But now the shadow was fading, or his vision, or both; the sun was sinking behind mountains of men with binoculars, animals with eyes, armies with gunsights—leaving him alone with the stars dripping thoughts on his head and the wind with its voices, taunting.

It was then that he saw the plane, a high-wing monoplane, Bellanca CH300, cruising at about 125 mph at 450 to 500 feet, casting a sharply etched shadow and droning distinctly. He quailed beneath it, watching as it passed out of range, out of sight, out of hearing, 'An airplane,' he thought. "An airplane," he said. "A bloody plane!" he shouted.

With a lurch he started to climb, the first step, then the second, the third like the first, the fourth like the second. And climbing, using his rifle like a ski pole, between gasps for breath, he hummed, then sang: "Th' bells...of hell...go...ting-a...ling-a...ling....For you ... but not ... for meee.... And th' little devils how ...they sing-a...ling-a-ling....For you but...not for meee...O Death where is thy...sting-a-ling-a-ling, O...Grave they victoree?...Th' bells of hell go ting-...a-ling-a-ling for you...but not for mee...." As he sang, the voices in the wind around him ceased, the glo-eyes were extinguished in darkness.

WHITEOUT

Snow falling, floating, feathering down like the down from torn pillows. Snowflakes, crystals of snow: one-legged, two-headed, twinned, polyhedron. Wet snow, porous snow, grainy snow, sodden snow. A skiff of snow, hummocks of snow, snow mounds, a snowscape...

The occipital lobes, enabling sight, and the frontal lobes, maintaining a balance between caution and concerted action, are suffused with blood and still function. The speech system—brain, larynx, tongue, mouth, and ears—still intact. Facial musculature, despite severe freezing, damaged but still differentiated, especially around eyes and mouth. From the eyes and mouth and out of the nostrils and ears, which are lobed and set close to the head, moisture seeps, freezing immediately.

...Persist. Consciousness at all costs. The costs are high. The mountains a mile high. The sun and moon and stars have been blotted and the blizzard will bury the pass. Persist...

Snow swirling, snow drifting, snow sculpting creations enduring a moment, an age. Snow layers, ages of snow. Snow formations: a skirmish, a hedgehog, a tunnel, a parapet, a revetment, a trenchwork of snow...

The enlarged brain makes for a high forehead and flat face, except for the snubbed, up-turned nose which extends the nasal cavity and warms incoming air. The jaws are recessed, the tooth row short. The dental arcade is rounded in front, the canines incisiform. In the upper left jaw, the third molar and wisdom teeth have been extracted. There is a silver filling in the second molar and a gold filling in the second incisor. In the upper right jaw, the first and third molars and wisdom teeth are missing. In the lower left jaw, a gold bridge extends from the bicuspid to the third molar, both of which are gold crowned. More teeth are loose, and the hair on top of the skull has begun to fall out.

...Enter the snow trench. The concave front line with the pillboxes useless and bulged, poking out. There begin burrowing. A deep and almost encircling front, but to the south a pass gouged out—The Gap!...

Snow towering, pressing, compressing. Snow melting under the pressure, compressing itself into ice. Layers of ice, ice ages. Encased in ice, crushed by ice, icebound. Burrowing snow-blind forever through aeons of ice...

The body is fully and continuously balanced on two legs. It is also, in climbing, almost continuously leaning forward. This places stress on the backbone. The backbone is no longer a single curve, but S-shaped. The thoracic curve may have developed in the delta, the cervical in the foothills, but the lumbar only under extreme compression once the mountains were entered. This vertebral compression alters entirely all transverse struts and ties.

...Penetrate the crawl space. Trenches for the duration. Eyes film over, teeth replace. Dig, or be massacred in no-man's-land. Dig deeper...

Snow swirling and sifting and drifting in strange shapes, strange sculptures. It is the great cold, the night. Gunmetal gray, the greatcoat of darkness. Snow is falling, and snow will fall...

The weight of the head is balanced on the backbone. The viscera are suspended from the thorax as from a bracket. The abdominal muscles carry the weight of the viscera. The back muscles act as ties of the vertebral girder. No long neural spines or large transverse processes develop, since the girder is not cantilever. The girder is one unit, with bending stresses along its whole length.

...staggering up to the summit of Vulture's Peak, a lump of flesh flying through air, with crows, ravens, hawks following hard, tearing at it, pulling it to pieces, while it uttered cries of distress... This lump was Johnson...

Snow sifting and stinging and turning in dark clouds. It is the great cold of night, it is the dark. Deathly blue, sable, the pall of the great cold. The crows are flying. The man must be moving...

Balancing the body involves many stresses. The muscles around the hip joint achieve balance by changes affecting the gluteal muscles and the ilium and sacrum to which they are attached, these being the extensor and abductor muscles, which raise the body and prevent it from falling. The buttocks are central, the center of gravity, but the heavy pack places more stress on the backbone and occasions a greater lean forward. New requirements are made of the legs.

...crawling up the glacis of Symmetry Mountain, a man with hair like needles falling through space. The needles piercing his head came out through his mouth, piercing his mouth they came out through his chest, piercing his chest they came out his stomach, piercing his stomach they came out his thighs, piercing his thighs they came out his legs, from his legs they came out his feet, while he uttered cries of distress... This pierced thing was Johnson...

Snow stinging and burning and twisting. The animal runs, it is dying. Snow follows it, meets it, outflanks it, surrounds it. Snow maddens. The snow swarms with millions of maggots, feasting and flying. The maggoty snow...

In climbing, the snowshoes have been removed. The propulsive thrust is obtained mainly from the calf muscles. The knees remain bent, due to the backpack. The thigh muscles come under great pressure, serving to keep the knees extended both while the calf muscles develop their thrust and, as a check to toppling forward, when the foot touches the ground. The whole foot, from the ankle joint down through the tarsus and digits, has been converted into an arched system. In walking, when the foot is raised by the calf muscles, the toes remain on the ground to prevent slipping forward. This stress is accentuated in climbing.

...this tarn of water, cool water, sweet water, pure water, this lake is frozen. And yet the water is blazing. It seethes and sweats and bubbles, snow falling on it turns to steam... This boiling thing is Johnson...

Snow flailing and beating and clawing. A hand gropes forward, the digital pads badly damaged. The hand is immediately covered with snow, transfers this snow to the mouth. The hand disappears in a pocket, gropes among names, shapes, items; withdraws a compass, wipes it, holds it, returns it to the pocket. The hand swings forward and dangles...

The arms act mainly as balance against the backpack, one hand grasping the rifle which functions as a third leg, the rifle butt touching the ground. The chest of the man is lightly constructed, thirty-four inches around the pectorals, and the deltoid muscles of the shoulder and the flexor muscles of the elbow, wrist, and hand are relatively small, as are the ridges to which they are attached. The arms, though numbed due to the blood supply being depressed by the pack straps, are mobile, and the hands, especially the thumbs and forefingers, though desensitized due to frostbite, are still capable of grasping and handling.

Like the open end of a gun barrel, like the cocked teeth
of a steel trap,
Like the sun blurred and blotted by whiteout,
the stars by a frenzy of snow,
Death is before the man now, like a shadow that never
leaves him...

(The two ravens, who have waited the blizzard out,
croak)
Death, Death, come and feed us!

THE EIGHTH DAY

Fire. Fire on the mountain. The peak was ablaze with the low winter sun, at the western edge of its circuit, as Johnson toiled up the east glacis. Behind him the mountains, an arcade of flame, curved round and stood on a level with him above the rubble of shadows, frozen and gray, he had crossed. Three-tiered the vista: to his rear and on both flanks the mountains, tongues of flame; in the spaces between them glowed foothills like coals; beneath the foothills an ashen scrub line. Far in the distance the delta of the Rat where it meandered down out of the mountains was a lavalike maze of streams and lagoons, and on the distant horizon, dusky and vague, lay the Mackenzie River and delta, from which he had viewed only last summer the mountains he stood near the top of. Long chains of mountains—he was breaking out.

The sun lulled, and shadows confused him. Snow-bearing clouds cast long shadows over the mountains, so that some of the mountains seemed covered in smoke, others with flame. A few paces more and he stood in the sunlight, his shadow against the summit. Just short of the world's top he stood and looked back: eyes, blood-shot, glaring out through eye slits; lids, lashes, parka trim frosted over like armor; face blackened with multiple frostbite; cracked lips in a lopsided leer. It had all been too easy. His pursuers were lost and could not track him here. A desert of snow lay between him and them: new snow, fresh snow, trackless snow. How he had come here and where he was heading no trace in the snow testified. He stood near the top of the world and looked down, and his pursuers to him were as snowflakes. Against him they would not rise again. How much could a man do without, and for how long? He had done without, and was done with them.

Quickly he took inventory. He still had his .30-30 Savage with the homemade brass foresight, his Winchester .22 with the stock blown off, ammunition for both rifles and for the shotgun, his ax with a bullet hole through the haft. He had crossed the mountains with his lard tin and lid, bullet holes through them both, a rag containing some pepper, a sack containing some salt. He had his pearls and his gold teeth and gold dust and money. He still had his compass, some fishhooks. He still had his knife made from a spring trap, his three-cornered file, his awl made from a three-cornered file, and his chisel made from a nail. He still had some nails wrapped in tinfoil, some matches wrapped in tinfoil, a .30-30 cartridge box containing two dozen liver pills and a wax candle stub. He still had his moosehide pouch containing sailmaker's needle and thread, a small steel spring, and spare snowshoe lacing. He still had his carved wooden bowl: it had come with him to Canada and it would leave with him, though little use he had had of it lately. His stomach muscles were knotted in seizure, and had been, for days. Also he was stupid with tiredness. The inventory was a way of defining himself to himself. He still had his nose and his fingers, his toes, both his ears, and his mind, he still had his mind, though his sight went blurry after dark and in shadow, and he had to rely on peripheral vision for objects close up, or dark objects. He still had his sawed-off shotgun, loaded, for sudden marauders or a patrol in ambush or a surprise posse from the Yukon.

He scaled the last summit up to the world's edge and, squinting, peered into the sun. The sun was a dying star which he saw double: a wounded ball awash in the sky and a wake of blood on the mountains. Stretching westward as far as he could make out, and

he could see for at least fifty miles, lay the Yukon side
of the mountains: their dusky backs like so many whales'
humps, quick-frozen while spouting and stranded forever when the world's summer ended and the waters
receded. He too had been caught, but he had burst free
and would stride on their spines all the way to Alaska,
to freedom. Alaska!—the word had a magical sound.
Far to the southwest, rising from a vast plain, stood a
solitary conical mountain, snow-dusted, with a necklace of ice around it. The necklace stood out from the
throat of the cone and gleamed emerald green in the
distance—limestone—as if slung by a god, or a grief
of gods, at the world's submergence. The emerald mountain would be his lodestone to steer by, the bleeding
sun his polestar. He peered down the slope of the mountain he stood on: its western slope less steep, more covered with snow, deeper snow, snowshoeing snow. The
pit of his stomach began to unknot, his cracked lips to
part in a grin. He was laughing, laughing as he scanned
the mountains stranded forever, laughing as he stared
at the sun doomed to circle, laughing as he stood at the
top of the world and prepared to stride down its backbone: his pursuers behind him like last summer's blackflies, like slate shattered into a million pieces, like
snowflakes scattered and mashed underfoot...from here
it would all be downhill....Far away in a valley, four
or five miles distant, a stand of trees clung to the banks
of a frozen streambed. Tiny sticks, gnarled spruce, several hundred years old, having attained to a height of
three or four feet. He could boil up there, make tea,
find a break from the wind...but would the heat ex-
pended in the walk down be worth the warmth gained?
He wondered. Pausing briefly as an animal pauses, he
instinctively veered toward the trees....

　(As Johnson stoops to lace on his snowshoes and start
downhill, a shadow moves across his path, blocking his
way. In the lee of the shadow, he is unable to rise. The
shadow is thinner, taller than Johnson. Johnson raises
his hand, the shadow's hand goes up. He raises his other
hand, the shadow's other hand is raised. He drops both
hands, hesitating with one. The shadow drops both hands

without hesitation. The sun burns on the snow. The
snow sweats. Johnson's shadow stands between him
and the sweating wall of mountain. The shadow does
not sweat and has ceased mimicking Johnson. The
shadow squats down beside Johnson.)

—Suppose a fire were to burn in front of you, Johnson. Would you be aware that a fire was burning?

—If a fire were to burn in front of me, I would be
aware of it.

—And if a fire were burning in front of you, what
would you do?

—Warm my hands, then boil up.

—But suppose someone were to ask you, "On what
does this fire burning in front of you depend?" What
would you answer?

—I would answer, "On fuel. Grass and wood."

—But there is no grass. There is no wood. The fire
which depends on fuel, when that fuel has all gone and
it can get no other, lacking nutriment, dies.

—I have not had a fire for eight days, and I have not
eaten for six. There is fuel down there....(Points.)

—The fire inside you is going out, Johnson. Your
fuel is used up.

—You're blocking me. (He makes an effort to get up,
but falls back and sprawls in the snow.)

—You don't have the strength left to reach that valley...

—I only have to get started. I can crawl down.

—...much less to break branches, find a match, strike
it, find another, strike it, gather snow in your lard pail,
the one with a hole, boil water, break more branches,
keep feeding the fire—you don't have the strength left.

(Johnson glares, makes another effort to rise; gets
to his knees and, with the aid of his gun, to his feet.
With his free hand he makes a gesture, as if to brush
away flies.) Everything will burn!

—*Et in Arcadia, ego*...

—Even the stars...

—Die and decay...

—...melt and drip thoughts like fat tallow.

—*Stella, stella, parva nova*...

—No fat. (Johnson sinks down and convulsively weeps.) No fat!

—(Shadow) You have burnt up all unskill, it is true, but have you profited from your efforts? Of what use to you is this evil and difficult life? Evil, in that you have been hounded, plagued, persecuted more than your own folly warrants, harassed beyond reason and driven to this extreme for no cause, to no purpose. Difficult, as when the fingers freeze, the toes freeze, the hands go numb, the feet go numb, when both hands and feet have grown useless; when the ears are frozen, the nose is frozen, when both ears and nose will fall off. Because of this evil and difficult life, wouldn't death be a relief?

(Johnson tries again and again to get up, turning in circles on the ground, weeping angrily.)

—(Shadow) As a bird tied to a string flutters every which way, then finally returns to the place where it is tied, so you, Johnson...

(Johnson, panting from his exertions and slobbering like a dog, tries to vomit in the snow, but nothing comes.)

—(Shadow) The line of your horizon grows thin. Your shadow shrinks.

JOHNSON: Where were you at Stuff Trench? I looked for you there—in the three-foot-deep trenches, corpses underfoot, corpses on the parapet, shell after shell shaking the ground...

DEATH (singing): The bells of hell go tingalingaling, for you but not for me, and the little devils how they singalingaling...

JOHNSON: Then the retreat: waves forming, men shouting, changing direction in the dark, in broken and entangled ground, under crumps of shellfire and sweeping gunfire. Where were you in the retreat?

DEATH: ...for you but not for me. O Death, where is thy stingalingaling, O grave...

JOHNSON: And at Schwaben Redoubt: bodies, bodies, heaped with their useless gear on the ground, twitching and jumping as each new bullet struck them. I looked for you then. You weren't there—just your

shell holes, your slimy track, and proof that you'd
been there.

DEATH: On a day in the merry month of May, a half-
million soldiers were swept away...

JOHNSON: I crawled out, barely alive, stunned and unhinged, but alive...

DEATH: And then in the jolly month of June, another
half million danced to my tune...

JOHNSON: Maybe I died then...

DEATH: In July of that summer it was polly-wolly-doodle, polly-wolly-doodle all day, as all her lovers with
Sweet Fanny Adams, with Sweet Fanny Adams they
lay...

JOHNSON (*a grin slowly spreading over his face*): Death,
you don't know my name. You have what you *think*
is my name, what *they* think is...

DEATH: I have it.

JOHNSON: My real name....

DEATH: Not the one you left on a corpse in Stuff Trench,
just before you deserted. I have your real name.

JOHNSON: ?

DEATH: Bishop Geddes gave it to me.

    (JOHNSON *lunges. They grapple. A gruesome dance
ensues.* JOHNSON *shambles.* DEATH *shuffles. They
grotesquely embrace.* JOHNSON *struggles free, draws
back, lifts his rifle and fires twice, kills* DEATH.)

DEATH (*in the guise of Millen*): Very good, very good,
more food for my ravens. They circle, they wait for
you, Johnson.

    (JOHNSON *fires at a raven overhead, misses.*)

DEATH: Not so good. Your night vision, remember? It
wasn't that way when you shot through the door.

    (JOHNSON *fires again, wounds* DEATH.)

DEATH (*in the guise of King*): Not bad, considering the
door between us.

    (JOHNSON, *grimacing, holds* DEATH *at bay with the
gun.*)

DEATH (*in the guise of Eames*): You sympathize with
me, Johnson, admit it. We understand one another.
We've experienced similar treatment—the same
shabby evasions, the same transparent shufflings,

the same sinister weakness—from women. Perhaps
from the same woman. Is that why you spare me,
Johnson? You do me a favor. One favor deserves
another. In sparing me, you condemn me to this evil
and difficult life, this life complicated by...

MILDRED URQUHART *(stands before them, wistful, recep-
tive, on a frozen riverbank. The foxfur trim on her
parka, around the throat, waves gently back and forth
with her warm breath. Her face is not fearful, but
childlike. She turns to face* DEATH, *and says)*: I saw
Johnson in a vision and I said to him, Albert, I saw
you today in a vision. He answered me, Don't be
afraid, Millie. He is a good man really. A good man
misunderstood.

DEATH: One of your well-wishers, Johnson. What do you
say to her now?

(JOHNSON *aims quickly from the hip and blows her
head off.)*

DEATH: Tch! Tch! Imagine that! And she believed in
you, Johnson, believed! Now look who's coming...
(Enter the RIGHT REVEREND THOMAS MURRAY, BISHOP
OF ATHABASCA, *and the* RIGHT REVEREND W. A. GEDDES,
BISHOP OF THE ARCTIC. *His Holiness,* DEATH, *sits as
judge.)*

1st BISHOP: As spiritual head of this diocese, I demand
that this creature, commonly known as the Mad
Trapper of Rat River, a slayer of men and a threat
to society, a corrupter of innocence also, and no res-
pecter of women, be denied burial in consecrated
ground.

2nd BISHOP: I knew the deceased, and I think we shall
find—history will comfirm it—that Albert Johnson,
alias the Mad Trapper, was not a criminal, and he
was not mad.

1st BISHOP: There is no offense against God or man, and
he is not answerable for the crimes he committed, if
he repents, or is mad, or retarded, or in extreme pain
such as would vitiate reason, or a child under twelve
years of age. If one or more of these states describes
him, then there is no offense.

2nd BISHOP: But what if he was provoked beyond reason,
harassed beyond endurance, badgered to a state of
temporary madness, so that, setting aside both the
law and the gospel...

1st BISHOP: No man can set aside both. Even God cannot. If a man is not under the law, he is living by
grace. But as soon as he commits a sin, or what is
called sin, he comes under judgment.

2nd BISHOP: What is sin? The Savior said, There is no
sin, but it is you who make sin when you commit
such acts as adultery, or murder, or robbery, or rape,
which are called sins. That is why the Sinless One
came into our midst, to restore the corrupted nature
of man to its root. The root...

1st BISHOP: Man is the root of the problem, the radix.
The sin of man is radical, against nature. That is
why we sicken and die. Matter gave birth to a passion
contrary to nature. The wages of sin is death, and
death...

DEATH: Did I hear my name mentioned?

1st BISHOP: ...shall die.

DEATH *(flinches)*: Gentlemen, Gentlemen! This semi-
narians' debate is no way to resolve the problem
before us. The specific problem before us is the disposition of the deceased, his body and what is called
"soul." "Earth to earth, ashes to ashes, dust to dust,"
as the saying goes. But how precisely? By cremation?
By burial? Drowning seems to be out. Shall we simply abandon his frozen body to birds and beasts of
prey? Or does outraged society require some com-
pensation, and if so, what kind and how much?

1st BISHOP: I have here a petition signed by residents
of Aklavik and the surrounding district requesting
that the remains of Albert Johnson, murderer, be
denied burial in consecrated ground and interred
without ceremony outside the settlement's confines,
available clergy having justly refused to officiate at
any form of Christian funeral. The petition is signed
by E.F. Hersey, Knud Lang, R.F. Riddell, Mr. and
Mrs. Noel Verville, Frank Carmichael, Cal Main,

John Parsons, N. MacLeod, Kenneth Stewart, A. Johnston, Lazarus Sittichiulis, James Edward, Olaf Jensen, and A. N. Eames.

DEATH *(to 2nd* BISHOP): Have you any objections?

2nd BISHOP: I would be available to conduct a small ceremony provided the residents of the parish wished it.

1st BISHOP: Aklavik is my See.

2nd BISHOP: Perhaps later, when Johnson's identity has been determined and his family located. A memorial service, perhaps.

MILDRED URQUHART *(headless at her husband's side)*: I will visit the grave, wherever it is. I will place on it flowers in summer, and read over it words from the Scriptures. A clergyman is not needed. Love is.

DEATH *(to the doctor)*: Stifle that woman. Are there any organs worth salvaging for donation? Eyes, liver, heart, kidneys?

DR. URQUHART: None, Your Eminence. All vital organs were damaged beyond repair on receipt of the body. The body, you might say, was burnt up from inside. No fat.

DEATH: And was a positive identification possible?

DR. URQUHART: That is Inspector Eames's department, Your Eminence.

DEATH: Inspector?

EAMES: We are still working on it. The Coroner's Jury, taking statements from each of the members of the posse, have ruled that the deceased is indeed the man who was called Johnson, the same man who shot Constables King and Millen and in the final skirmish Constable Hersey, and who terrorized the district from December 26th, 1931, until February 17th, 1932. He was identified by the peculiarity of his left snowshoe track.

DEATH: February 17th? Today is the 12th. Perhaps we are getting ahead of ourselves.

JOHNSON: You mean I'm not dead yet?

DEATH: You're as good as dead. Your body is spoken for, your burial is arranged, and you're five days from certain destruction.

JOHNSON: Alive is not dead. Alive is alive.

DEATH: 120 hours of dragging a dying body toward a violent end. 7,200 minutes of painful awareness, semi-awareness, half-stupor, half-sleep. 432,000 seconds in which to make errors, feel pain, know remorse, sense danger, fight madness. A final ordeal in which to make more mistakes and struggle against the snarling fit which is life. A last skirmish with the inevitable. Wouldn't you rather die now? You have your rifle. Why wait for Eames and his group to dispatch you? A wounded animal...

JOHNSON: Fights or hides. I've done both. I'll keep on doing both: hiding for as long as I can, fighting when I have to. My body goes on, but I am not with it. I'm outside it, behind it, watching it stumble, hearing it curse. See, there it blunders into a snowbank, falls down, recovers itself, gazes dully about, staggers on. Here I'm hiding and watching, I'm laughing...

DEATH: Your little joke, eh? You *will* have your little joke, Johnson.

JOHNSON: It's curious, being divorced from your body, watching it die, knowing already the truth which your body through trial and error, mainly error, is learning. Have you ever watched yourself die?

DEATH: Many times.

JOHNSON: It goes before me, doing its Charlie Chaplin walk over the top, and it remains behind me, twitching and jumping...I feel no pain.

DEATH: This detachment, this morbid interest is boring, it's...Christian. You disappoint me, Johnson.

JOHNSON: It's all downhill from here. Down there I see trees, fuel for fire, a windbreak...

(As JOHNSON *staggers down the western slope of the mountain, the sun sinks below the horizon. On the mountain both the illusion of fire and the shadow of* DEATH *disappear. Stars become visible in the night sky, and in the southwestern quarter, over the emerald mountain, the seven stars of Orion appear. As* JOHNSON'S *body continues its journey downhill, two ravens, flying back to their crag, remark a strange sight:)*

1st RAVEN: Why is this night different from all other nights?

2nd RAVEN: On all other nights we eat whatever Death leaves us.

1st RAVEN: Why on this night are we deprived of a meal?

2nd RAVEN: On all other nights we eat what has been killed.

1st RAVEN: Why on this night must we go hungry?

2nd RAVEN: On all other nights something has died.

1st RAVEN: Why on this night does the body go on while the spirit goes up?

2nd RAVEN: On all other nights when the spirit goes up the body remains.

1st RAVEN: Why on this night does Death not reward us, remember us, feed us?

2nd RAVEN: On all other nights our watch would be rewarded, our fast ended, our bellies filled.

1st & 2nd RAVENS: This night is different from all other nights!

(As the ravens remark JOHNSON'S *ascent toward the stars above the emerald mountain, the* INTELLIGENT TRIO *from their eyrie on an adjacent mountain try with the aid of a powerful telescope to locate J and chart his progress:)*

PHYS. There are two sides to the mountain.

PHIL. At least two.

PHYS. J was here when we last observed him. *(The* PHYSICIST *trains the telescope on the east slope of the mountain. The* PHILOSOPHER *and the* BIOCHEMIST *look through it, nodding assent.)* At the rate he was traveling, in the time elapsed, taking account of his deterioration and the bad weather, he should be approximately here. *(The* PHYSICIST *aims the telescope on a spot further up the east glacis. The* PHILOSOPHER *and the* BIOCHEMIST *look through it, nodding assent.)* But he is not there. Before we can chart his movement, we need to locate him. Any suggestions?

PHIL. I have one. If to his being on this side of the mountain we assign a number, 1; and to his being on the other side of the mountain we assign a number, 0; then the sum of the numbers, defining where he is on the mountain, must equal a unity, 1.

PHYS. Other values are possible. If he were partway up the mountain, three fourths of the way up, he would have to be one fourth on the other side; and if he were nine tenths here, he would have to be one tenth there; just as, if he were all the way over, he would be fully there and not here, as earlier he was fully here and not there.

PHIL. The sum of the two values must equal a unity, 1—as I said.

BIOC. So where he is at any given moment on this side of the mountain complements where he is not on the other side, and vice versa?

PHIL. That's right. We can say that he is on the mountain, but where he is on the mountain remains undecided. We can make predictions regarding specific locations, with probability quotients for each.

PHYS. Not that where he is is unknown. It is known generally, but not precisely.

PHIL. Presumably J knows precisely.

BIOC. If J knows anything. J may be dead. He probably is dead.

PHIL. Dead or alive, we can say, "He is on this side of the mountain," but we cannot say, "It is true that he is on this side of the mountain." Not with certainty, for we have not seen him, only his tracks.

BIOC. I haven't seen his tracks. He hasn't made any, or else they're buried in snow. He's probably buried in snow...*(Peers through the infrared telescope at the east glacis. Moves the telescope around.)*

PHIL. From our point of view, the correctness or incorrectness of the first statement—"He is on this side of the mountain"—implies the correctness or incorrectness of the second statement—"It is true that he is on this side of the mountain." But the incorrectness of the second statement does not imply the incorrectness of the first. If the second statement proves incorrect, it may be undecided whether he is on this side. He need not necessarily be on the other side.

PHYS. So there is equivalence with respect to correctness, but not with respect to incorrectness.

PHIL. With respect to incorrectness, there is doubt.

BIOC. How can he be on both sides at once? Either J died on this side of the mountain, or he crossed over and died. What does it matter which side he's on, if he's dead?

PHYS. Whether he's dead or alive is not our problem. Where the body is, that's where we'll gather. (PHILOSOPHER *begins to dismantle the telescope, and to pack up equipment.)*

BIOC. If he's dead, biochemically speaking, we can say he's neither on this side nor that side. As a life-support system he has ceased to be. J is not; therefore, he is nowhere.

PHIL. In that case, J's body would be in one place, his soul in another. Does J have a soul? If there is any absolute truth it is that we do not know absolutely.

PHYS. Let's not get involved in semantics. J's body, dead or alive, will occupy a point in space for a measurable duration. The location of that mass called J is the aim of our inquiry. *(The* PHILOSOPHER *packs the dismantled telescope. Exeunt the* INTELLIGENT TRIO.)

(Far above the emerald mountain, the seven stars of Orion, which are the seven powers of wrath—Darkness, Desire, Ignorance, the Excitement of Death, the Kingdom of Flesh, the Foolish Wisdom of Flesh, and Wrathful Wisdom—ask in chorus:)

Whence do you come, O slayer of men, or where are you going, conqueror of space?

(Johnson, ascending, answers:)

What binds me has been slain, and what turns me about has been overcome, and my desire has been ended, and ignorance has died. I am released from the ordeal of life and the threat of death, from the details of living and the stages of dying. From this instant on I will attain to the rest of the time, of the season, of the aeon, in silence.

(The seven stars of Orion, in unison, ask:)

Who are you? And who has freed you?

(Johnson, far above the emerald mountain, answers:)
I am he who was within me. Myself.

(A chorus of voices within the cluster of stars, including the voices of Nimrod, Enkidu, Bolthorn, Arjuna, Beowulf, Cuchulain, and Hornby, replies:)

There you were capable of acting, but could not see yourself. Here you see yourself, but are powerless to act. Take your place among us, and watch with us.

(Johnson enters the constellation of the Hunter.)

PART SEVEN

The Oxbow

EDMONTON JOURNAL, February 12, 1932

FLEEING TRAPPER FALTERS, PATROL HARD ON HEELS
Shortened Tracks Indicate Johnson Becoming Groggy
Expert Mushers Pursuing

Northerners Now Doubt if Wanted Man Is Demented

Aeroplane Aids Posse
Police Close in on Slayer of Mountie

(Special to Edmonton Journal via
Radio Telegraph)

AKLAVIK, Feb. 12—Advancing ahead of the main patrol, Quartermaster Sergeant Riddell and Staff Sergeant Hersey, of the Royal Canadian Signals, Aklavik, today are believed to be closing in rapidly on Albert Johnson, wanted for slaying a Mountie.

Johnson's trail, viewed from the air, showed him to be somewhat "groggy," as his tracks were getting shorter and "wagging" back and forth. The radio men, who are two of the best trackers and mushers in the north country, are on foot and following the trail so quickly that it is thought they will catch up with Johnson within a few days.

Johnson is a trapper without a license. At first it was thought that he was demented, but those who have been out on patrol declare, "If he is demented we all ought to be."

The wanted man is a first-class trapper and bushman. His ability to cover his tracks has made tracing him difficult, but that part of his trail which has been found indicates that he knows his business and that he is not mad.

AEROPLANE AIDS

Captain W.R. "Wop" May, who piloted a Bellanca aircraft 3,000 miles from Edmonton, was brought in on the manhunt to airlift supplies to the posse and to track the fugitive from the air.

But storms have prevented Captain May from making an extensive aerial search. The wind at times has blown snow clouds to as high as a thousand feet.

Twice this past week Captain May flew out from Aklavik in an effort to make contact with the ground party. Once he was turned back by weather, and on the second occasion he was able to land but could not locate the posse.

TWO POLICEMEN IN POSSE

At the present time there are only two policemen in the posse. They are Inspector Eames and Constable Carter. Other members of the patrol include trappers Lang, Carmichael, Ethier, Sutherland, Gardlund, and Verville, Signal Corps Sergeants Hersey and Riddell, Special Constable Lazarus Sittichiulis, and the Rt. Rev. Thomas Murray, Bishop of Athabasca.

Aklavik radio station is sending all available

information to the posse, which is equipped with a portable radio.

EDMONTON JOURNAL, February 13, 1932

ALBERT JOHNSON ENTERS YUKON, POSSE CLOSE BEHIND

Yukon Trappers Join Pursuit of Man Wanted for Slaying Arctic Policeman—Natives Assist—Difficult Trail—Surprise Flight
(Special to Edmonton Journal via
Radio Telegraph)

AKLAVIK, Feb. 13—Albert Johnson, fleeing from a patrol which is pressing him hard, has crossed over the mountainous Divide and is now in the Yukon. He passed over the line Friday and the posse is still after him and believed to be not far behind.

Staff Sergeant Hersey, R.C.S., Noel Verville, an Aklavik trapper, and three white trappers who live just over the Yukon line are forming the patrol which is continuing the chase. They are being assisted by a number of natives.

JOHNSON'S TRAIL

Due to high winds, and the fact that the peaks are absolutely clear of snow in some places, Johnson's route across the Divide could not be traced exactly. In places, especially near the tops of the mountains, there are large gaps in the trail. For several days high winds have prevented the aeroplane from making contact with the posse, though large quantities of supplies have been dropped.

Meanwhile, the ground party has pieced together Johnson's trail bit by bit, under the most difficult conditions. It is now certain that Johnson crossed the highest pinnacle, going over at about 5,500 feet.

An alert has been sent out to all points in the Yukon to be on the lookout for Johnson's tracks on the west side of the mountains. The snow on the western side is soft and deep, and there should be no difficulty finding him.

SURPRISE FLIGHT

Since the aeroplane arrived, the matter of transporting men and supplies from Aklavik to the advance camp has been simplified. It has cut 100-mile journeys from 20 hours by dog team to 20 minutes by air.

Earlier today Captain May made a surprise flight to La Pierre House, Yukon Terr., 130 miles due west of where the posse is now operating. The purpose of the flight has not been divulged. Beyond confirming the above information, Supt. A.E. Ackland of the R.C.M.P. declined to make any comment.

EDMONTON JOURNAL, February 14, 1932

EYES OF THE WORLD ARE ON JOHNSON

Drama Played Out in Northland
Draws Worldwide Attention

Trapper Spotted Near La Pierre House, Yukon Johnson Joins Caribou Herd, Eludes Posse—Fog Foils Aeroplane

AKLAVIK, Feb. 14—The manhunt for Albert Johnson, which has occupied the R.C.M.P. since last Christmas, has attracted worldwide attention. The tale of his desperate bid to escape by crossing the Richardson Mountains in winter was carried yesterday by the Toronto Globe and Mail, the Toronto Star, the Vancouver Sun, the Calgary Herald, as well as by newspapers as far afield as the New York Times and the Times of London. Asked if the reputation of the R.C.M.P. had been put on the line by such widespread publicity, Supt. A.E. Ackland admitted it had. "No question about it," he said, "there's great pressure on Eames."

Inspector Eames is the officer in charge of the manhunt for Johnson. He is the man who has had to assess conflicting reports and make critical decisions. He is presently in the field with the posse, quarterbacking the search for the "Mad Trapper."

TRAPPER SPOTTED NEAR LA PIERRE HOUSE

On February 12th an Indian from La Pierre House in the Yukon arrived at Inspector Eames's base camp. The Indian had traveled three days without stopping to report strange snowshoe tracks on the Bell River. The Bell River is 130 miles due west of where the posse was operating. The tracks were believed to be Johnson's.

Inspector Eames immediately sent an advance patrol under Staff Sergeant Hersey across the Divide, to make certain Johnson did not backtrack. Another party led by Inspector Eames proceeded by air to La Pierre House to intercept Johnson.

TRAPPER'S TRACKS OBLITERATED

At 3:05 P.M., Pacific Time, Capt. "Wop" May took off from La Pierre House. In a matter of minutes he had located Johnson's trail two miles south of the trading post, and tracked him to the Bell River.

Capt. May was able to follow the snowshoe prints along the Bell River without any trouble, noting that Johnson seemed to be making no effort to deviate from a straight line. The tracks headed west, toward Alaska. Then Johnson's tracks were obliterated by thousands of caribou hoofprints. The fugitive had overtaken a caribou herd, and was traveling with it. At this point dense fog interrupted the search, and Capt. May returned to La Pierre House at 3:20 P.M.

FOG FOILS AEROPLANE

Dense fog continued to shroud the entire area, grounding the aeroplane. But Capt. May had accomplished in 15 minutes what would have taken the ground party days to achieve. Johnson's four-day advantage had been slashed to a matter of hours.

DIFFERENT TERRAIN

An entirely different set of conditions confronts Johnson and his pursuers on the western side of the Divide. Whereas on the Rat side pockets of packed snow and harsh winds played havoc with footprints, the western slopes leading down to the Bell are heavy with deep snow that retains snowshoe tracks. Inspector Eames is of the opinion that Johnson has made "his first grave mistake" in crossing over the mountains and entering the Yukon. But he added a grudging admiration for the man who, in blizzard conditions, traveled 90 miles in less than three days over a mountain pass thought to be impassable in winter. "It's incredible," the Inspector is quoted as saying. "The Indians have declared throughout the search that neither white man nor Indian could cross the Divide in winter."

In outfitting a party to follow Johnson's path over the mountains, Inspector Eames had Capt. May fly in eight pair of Ojibway-style snowshoes, suitable for soft snow. The snowshoes weighed ten pounds each.

The weather on the western slopes of the mountains is warmer, but dense fog presents much the same visibility problem that blizzards posed on the eastern side, hampering aeroplane activity.

EDMONTON JOURNAL, February 15, 1932

BLIZZARD SWEEPS ARCTIC, JOHNSON STILL AT LARGE

Storm Halts Aerial Hunt for Trapper
Whereabouts Believed Known

AKLAVIK, Feb. 15—Handicapping the police and giving Albert Johnson, trapper wanted for murder, a "break" which might enable him to evade his pursuers, an Arctic blizzard is sweeping the rough country in which he has taken refuge.

The aeroplane piloted by Capt. W.R. "Wop" May, Canadian Airways flier, has been "down" in the mountainous region near La Pierre House, Yukon Terr., since Saturday, when it left here to join in the pursuit of Johnson.

The ground party left La Pierre House this morning, and linked up with the patrol which followed Johnson over the Divide. The patrol carried ten days' provisions for men and dogs, and called the passage over the mountains "one hell of a trip." Both parties proceeded down the Bell River, where Johnson's tracks were last spotted from the air.

Meanwhile, the aeroplane had returned to Aklavik for refuelling. It is presumed to have been forced down by bad weather. The party pursuing Johnson on foot has left markers of spruce trees on the river and in the lakes, to enable the aeroplane to follow their trail when the fog clears. Johnson is judged to be about one and a half days ahead of the posse.

No anxiety concerning pilot May is felt here, as there are many places near La Pierre House which would serve in case of a forced landing. Capt. May is an experienced bush pilot, and a World War flying ace.

EDMONTON JOURNAL, February 16, 1932

ELUSIVE SLAYER TRAVELS RAPIDLY
TOWARD ALASKA

...Aeroplane Secures Fresh Fuel, Returns to Chase

AKLAVIK, Feb. 16—Making faster time than he has since he was driven from his rude fortress in the Rat River district, Albert Johnson, alleged Mountie slayer, is traveling through the Porcupine River country, about 30 miles southwest of La Pierre House and 175 miles from the Alaska boundary.

This was the report brought here Monday by Captain W.R. "Wop" May, Canadian Airways flier, who is assisting the R.C.M.P. in pursuing Johnson. Captain May, who had been forced down by weather, reached Aklavik yesterday and, after refuelling, took off for La Pierre House.

HAMPERED BY STORM

Although hampered by the blizzard which swept the district Sunday and Monday, the ground forces are still hot on Johnson's trail. Eight of the dog teams which left Aklavik to join in the manhunt have returned, their places being taken by fresh teams from La Pierre House.

Johnson is traveling on foot, but in country familiar to him, the searchers say, recalling the fact that he entered the Rat River delta last summer by way of the Peel, from the Yukon. The man wanted for slaying Constable E. Millen and wounding Constable A.W. King may still be counted on to use the most ingenious methods to throw his pursuers off his trail, and to put up a desperate fight when he is finally overtaken.

REMAINS ELUSIVE

The fugitive is making use of every wile known to the hunted, in addition to several new ones. His most recent ploy was to join a caribou herd where it crossed the Bell River, but the posse has successfully picked up Johnson's tracks among the caribou hoofprints, and judges him to be heading down the Eagle River. Unable to take time to make camp, or even to kill and cook food, the man must have tremendous endurance, otherwise he would have been forced to make a stand long ago.

Traveling light, he has managed to distance his relentless pursuers, despite the fact that he naturally has broken trail for them and their fast dog teams. Any food he managed to pack from his cabin on the lonely Rat River must have been exhausted days ago.

If he can manage to remain free until the coming of spring renders his tracks invisible, he may still escape. There is no doubt of his ability to live off the land. Even without ammunition for his deadly rifle, he could snare an abundance of game.

The Eagle River, where his tracks were last spotted, winds and twists through low rolling hills and surrounding timber. The banks are lined with a thick growth of willows.

WILL NOT SURRENDER

There is growing belief that Johnson will not submit to capture, and that if he is cornered he will fight to the last rather than surrender.

The spruce smell penetrated his nostrils, dizzying him. Where his hands gripped the bark, both were skinned. Spruce resin entered his scratches, and red stains appeared on the bark. Large scabs of bark fell on his feet where they dangled. With every heft upward, the dizzier he became, the more divorced from the tree he embraced. His whiskered face scraped the scaly bark of the spruce trunk, they scraped each other, he flinched. Hunching his shoulders he let go with one hand, gripped a higher branch, pulled himself up. One foot found a foothold, one armpit a perch. His bony buttocks straddled a crotch. He looked down on himself looking down.

A broad level plain sparsely treed with thin spruce, disorienting in terms of distance. Surfaces flat, angles sharp, trees black against the white snow. Meandering through this broad plain the Eagle, its banks thick with willows and poplar. On three, almost four sides, the river enclosed him. An island? He peered out through eye slits of bone and a lattice of branches, twisting himself around in the tree to sweep the whole countryside. The Eagle had gouged out an island, almost. An oxbow.

He had been on one tine of the hairpin curve when he heard them. They were still on the other tine, moving up toward the curve, about a half mile away. He had heard dogs yapping, men yelling, a plane's engine drone in the distance. He looked down on himself looking down on them, and could count them, names and shapes, numbers. There were many. Long lines of dogs with men attached to them pocking the river, which was already pockmarked with thousands of caribou hoofprints. The caribou had outdistanced him, but he had not outdistanced the dogs and the men. They would overtake him on the riverbed, but he would never overtake the caribou. He looked out over the tundra where the caribou had crossed. If he left the river and took to the tundra, there was the airplane to contend with. Except for the fringe of trees along the riverbank there was no cover out on the plain, a lone scraggly tree here and there. Any moving object would be sighted and brought down. No deep cuts or thick woods to hide in, no cover. He could not see the plane, but he could hear it, its drone unmistakably nearer. The dense fog had lifted entirely. Soon the sun would break through and shine on them all. Morning of the last day.

He rested his head against the spruce trunk, letting the smell dominate his senses. The spruce penetrated his sinuses, brain, nervous system, alerting each part of the dangling man to the hairpin situation. There was no rebellion from foot, hand, or stomach...

—Johnson...

—?

There was no debate, no one left to debate with.

Hacking, he spit into the wind to determine which side to go down on. If the spit fell on this side of the tree, he would enter the river on this side; if it fell on their side, he would go there. It mattered little which side of the oxbow he entered the riverbed on. He might as they turned the curve come behind them, but they were following his backtrack and would soon turn around, so that to go down the other side might put him behind them. It was difficult to assess at what point they would realize they were following a backtrack, at what point they would turn around. Hard to remember, too; maybe they had turned around? Also, there were many of them, they could split up, comb both sides of the oxbow at once. And there was the plane to contend with. . . .

It scarcely mattered which side he went down, but go down he must, one side or the other, as for days he had been going down, down, down. Worse for them to track him to where he was, treed, shoot him up the asshole, or worse yet, take him prisoner. Long days and nights in the South among people, thousands of pygmies, small hot rooms, crowded cells, sleepless nights, endless days, torment. Dead was dead, humiliation was extra. He had to move out, down and out. What he needed was a shot of fear, or of anger. But all anger had been burnt out, and what was there to fear? He had been killed before, and had recovered. The body lived on with a life of its own. All they could kill was his body, it was all there was left, and precious little of it. He lifted one leg and let his bony ass slip off the tree crotch.

As ripe fruit drops from a tree, he fell, not bothering to shinny down. At the base of the tree he crumpled, stood up, stepped into his snowshoes, leaned down to lace them, then hoisted his backpack onto his knee, slipping an arm through the frozen strap. With a lurch of his body he swung the pack to his back and pushed the other arm through, picked up his rifle and set off in his own tracks toward the river. When he neared the thick willows at the top of the bank, he put his free arm up over his face and punched through, not bothering to duck, veer, or sidestep. He came out on the bank overlooking the river and ran forward and down, not looking up- or downriver. When he reached the middle of the riverbed, hard packed by thousands of caribou hoofprints, he stooped down to unlace his snowshoes, stepped out of them onto the hard-packed snow, and jammed them through his pack lashings.

Then he stood for a moment gazing upriver at the curve around which, at any moment, the posse would come. He could hear the dogs plainly and, nearer now, the airplane. The curve was about half a mile distant, the river a quarter mile wide. He turned and started downriver, at a dogtrot, when his eye spotted signs he had not seen before. Slicing the rutted caribou tracks were four ski tracks, two skiers headed downriver as he was. The tracks had not been there when he crossed the river to climb the tree. They were fresh—an advance patrol for the posse—and he was between the two parties. He stopped in the middle of the river, hearing distinctly the shouts of the men close behind, the roar of the plane just above. Stooping quickly to lash on his snowshoes, he turned to face them as they turned the corner.

In the lead was the runner, the one with the fastest dog team. He was running behind his sled pulled by seven dogs, a huge silver brute the lead dog. As soon as they rounded the curve of the hairpin, cutting the inside corner, the runner saw him and jumped on his sled, struggling to pull out his rifle. The dogs barreled on without breaking stride, there was no stopping the dogs.

Two other dog teams with drivers and riders rounded the curve further back, on the outside. Then a fourth and a fifth team, a sixth—the curve was crawling with dark lines and dots, men and dogs yelling and yapping noiselessly, the O's of their mouths gaping and shutting but no sound came out. The roar of the plane struck them mute as it buzzed low—not that low, not low enough for strafing or a snipe-shot—and waggled its wings, signaling. Were there others, unseen, round the oxbow? The plane kept spotter distance, this first pass at least, leaving the kill to the ground crew. Like a gigantic wolf pack, or several wolf packs backed up by hunters, the posse was in position, and closing.

He found himself running, running on snowshoes for the opposite bank, over which thousands of caribou like a brown tide had flowed and disappeared into the tundra. He ran quickly, strongly. The pack on his back and the box of shells in his hip pocket burdened and banged him as he ran, but he was running as fast on snowshoes, straight-legged, as a man or a dog could run in snow. He had not known he had such speed in him, such stamina. It surprised him. He had not told himself to run. One instant he had been standing there stupidly gaping, watching the dogs bear down on him while the men grabbed their guns, hearing the plane's roar and seeing it signal, and the next instant he found himself running, running well and effortlessly and watching himself as he ran.

Now he was climbing the bank, still running as he leaned forward, legs pumping at the same rate, hands scrabbling in the loose snow and reaching upward and outward for willows to pull himself up and over the bank with ... The first shot hit the backpack and sent him tumbling, head over five-foot-long snowshoes, back down to the bottom of the bank he had just climbed. Not wasting an instant, but glancing quickly over his shoulder as he picked himself up, he saw the lead sled in the riverbed about a hundred yards off, its driver crouched down in the snow on one knee, his elbow propped on his other knee aiming what looked and felt like a Lee-Enfield. But even while sighting the sniper and noticing others leave their sleds and make for the banks on both sides of the river, he was scrambling on all fours up the same little hill the caribou had flowed over, his legs pumping pistonlike and hands clutching, scrabbling, groping to find a handhold ... The second shot struck the backpack again, knocking him off his feet, and he rolled headfirst down the hill.

The hill had grown slick now, but up he jumped and had again started up when the third shot again knocked him down. He felt his sight momentarily darken as though the brown tide had passed over him. It passed through and on—up and over the hill too steep, con-

trolled by the marksman too near. By now other shots
were being pumped into the hillside from numerous
angles by several marksmen. Johnson jumped up and
ran a few steps out onto the river. As he ran he reached
over his shoulder and pulled out his .30-30 Savage.
Without stopping he whirled on the five-foot-long
snowshoes and snapped off one shot at the sniper. The
sniper was blown back in the snow and ceased firing.
But now there was another man crouched in the river
and men moving up both banks to outflank him. He
ran dead out toward the center and diagonally downstream, away from the advancing posse. They had numbers and rifles and dogs and an airplane, but fear
hamstrung them, held them back. He felt no fear, only
freedom, speed, motion. Despite the heavy backpack
and ungainly snowshoes and the cartridge box in his
hip pocket, he began to draw away from the posse who
were running and firing at him. Across the river he
could see a cutbank, a feeder stream, trees, a crawl
space.

He was running, running, running toward the tree
cover, little riffles of snow springing up all around him—
some short, some long, some leading: splintering his
snowshoes, nicking his pack—still he ran. Running automatically, and well. Each stride a snowshoe length,
each snowshoe length five feet. A quarter mile across
and he was halfway. He was crossing the snow rift up
the center of the Eagle when in mid-stride something
hit him and he crumpled. Half his bony ass, his whole
right hip, was blown away. In the snow around him,
near his face, the burnt shreds of his cartridge box with
bits of bloody bone and blackened shell lay scattered,
the bloody pieces steaming, the empty casings smoking.
He regarded the debris with darkened sight. A wave of
nausea passed through him, then on. Instinctively he
slid himself around into the snow rift, facing his pursuers, presenting them with as little of himself as possible. Now they were shouting at him, and at one
another, shouting while snapping off shots. Wrestling
off his backpack, he positioned it in front of him and

heaped up snow around him and the pack. From this shallow trench he began, routinely and methodically, to locate his assailants on the banks and return fire...

Gardlund was staring behind him. His rifle was lowered and he had ceased firing, though his first shot had knocked Johnson down. Behind him the river snaked off in a long curve, before him the same—an S-turn. Johnson had picked himself up and was making a dash for the middle. The sixth letter was..."S. It's a goddamn *S*." Quickly he ran through the letters he'd crypted: *T, Y, H, E, L,* and now *S*. Six, he had all but one...six should be enough. Not twenty yards distant Hersey fired and hit Johnson. Gardlund went into a crouch. "HELP" wasn't the message, he'd decided that in the defile. Why couldn't he figure it out with six out of seven? *T, Y, H, E, L, S*...He stared downriver at Johnson as Johnson wheeled quickly and snapped off a shot. Hersey crumpled beside him. The plane buzzed overhead. As he lifted his rifle and squinted at Johnson making a dash for mid-river, and as he sighted him in, he saw Johnson in mid-stride glance over his shoulder and cast at him, Gardlund, the same baleful look as he had from the cabin when he'd had the gun and Gardlund held the flashlight. The look said, "No Mercy!" and yet Johnson had let him live. With his finger on the trigger and Johnson in his gunsights, Gardlund hesitated. Then Johnson exploded: one moment he was a figure in motion, the next he was a dark mound in the snow. A bullet whined near Gardlund's feet. The plane had turned and was roaring upriver. Johnson was shooting and being shot at, caught in a deadly cross fire and returning it. *T, H, Y, E, L, S*...*T, H, Y, S, E, L*...It was a code, a game for one, which none but its owner could crypt. Gardlund would sit this one out. He had gone this far, but no further. He'd been slow, but he wasn't stupid. The end of the game was at hand. Johnson was nearly finished, but he'd finish first—Gardlund. Emptying his weapon into the air, he sat down where he was in the snow.

* * *

Shoving his four-way stick to the right and dropping his left wing, May held the box camera up to the window and snapped two photographs of the oxbow. He set the box camera down in his copilot's seat and leveled his ailerons, passing over the action downriver at 1,200 feet, cruising. Casting a quick glance at the A/S indicator—it registered 80–90—he leaned his goggled head out the window and peered down at the river below him. Black dots of men and black lines of dogs were clearly grouped around one dot, the man in the middle. He hoped they were all in the picture. He sped on to the end of his run, went into a right bank and rudder, and started back against a head wind for another pass over the action. He could see the black dots now over the rotor, through the propeller.

Odd, how inevitable it all was from this vantage. It was only a matter of weeks since they had driven him out of the delta, a matter of days since they had tracked him over the mountains, now it was a matter of hours— if not of minutes—before they dispatched the man in the river. And he had been worried about this Wind-Jammer, Butt-Notcher, this Boche. Passing over again, he looked down on the man spread-eagled below, firing off rounds at the posse. The air was so cold he could hear the shots clearly above the roar of the engine— ping! ping!—like cash register sales. The Bellanca was high enough to be out of harm's way and there was no need to go lower. The posse was in control now. If the man wasn't exhausted, or his hip not blown out, he might make a run for it and the plane would have to track him and strafe him...but he was, it was, they were. It was merely a matter of time and of placement, relative placement. Two men on opposite sides of the river had climbed the high banks and were working their way downriver to get below Johnson, behind him. Soon they would cut through the bush to the banks overlooking the river and, having outflanked him, would have him in cross fire. Then it would be all over for

Johnson—Gone West, Trumpet Cleaning, Gone Phutt!

Oddly, May felt an impulse to warn the man who lay sprawled in the river, with his right flank, or what had been his right flank, exposed to the snipers. The man in mid-river looked so vulnerable, so small and helpless and handicapped, especially from this distance, so blind to the trap that was closing in on him. From 1,200 feet May could see what was happening, but could not influence events. The man in the river could act, but could not see the whole picture. Two half men— together they made one whole man. But the posse all together did not make a whole man, just a tangle of men and dogs churning and wheeling around the man in the middle, closing the circle on him. A matter of minutes now. Now.

He turned at the hairpin and began his third pass, depressing his rear elevators, descending to 800 feet. The two dots on the banks were men now, dark forms at the edge of the river slightly downstream of the figure sprawled in midstream. Further upstream two men were crouched in the river, and off to the side a third was laid out on a dark patch, a bedroll—a posse member who had been wounded. Another cluster of three on the right bank upstream were partially hidden in trees. Eight stick figures in all, each stick a man, bracketing the central figure from both banks and from up- and downriver. But it was the two men downstream who had him outflanked and in deadly cross fire. They were raking the river and the man exposed in it. Ping! Ping! went their little popguns. Ping! Ping! Ping! The cash register did a brisk business. But for all the puniness of the sound and the tininess of the stick figures, May knew they were laying down drenching enfilade fire.

The configuration as May roared down the river at a mere 400 feet was a double arrow, or X, with Johnson at the cross tie. This time as he flew over the shallow snow trench the fugitive spun over onto his back and leered up at the airplane. The upturned face was dark with frostbite except for the teeth, from which the lips curled back, and two tiny unreadable eye slits. May instinctively yanked off his goggles, fearful of a fluke shot and cursing himself for passing so low, so close to the desperate creature. For a moment it looked as if Johnson would fire, his rifle at the ready, his sights trained on the plane's underbelly. May held his breath and watched with terror the menacing sniper below him. A minute ago he had been feeling pity for the miserable creature, now he was at the man's mercy. Three seconds, four seconds, he was looking back now, almost out of range, though the rifle was still leading him. Then the creature holding the rifle jerked like a little rag doll and lay limp. Executing a short turn and swinging back, May waggled his wings to signal the posse and nosed the Bellanca down alongside the snow rift. As he flashed past, skis touching, he saw Johnson's face down in the snow, his right arm outflung grasping his rifle. As his tail-skid touched down and he turned in the river to taxi back, he knew that Johnson was dead.

The plane came to a stop and May jumped out and began walking toward Johnson. From every direction men were walking and running toward the small inert heap in mid-river that for months had dominated their lives, dictated their movements, determined their waking thoughts and nightmares, yet time and again held them at bay. Johnson was dead, May was alive. Never again would he menace May, or any man living. May would never again, from a riverbed or in bed asleep, be threatened by Johnson. Whenever he flew over snowy bush, delivering mail or diphtheria serum, he would know he had nothing to fear from below, no sniper to watch for, no madman to search and destroy. The dead were dead and the living were living. The living were crowding around the dead man, eager to view his face. May was first to the corpse and turned it over. The lips were curled back from the teeth in a sneer, the slits of eyes glazed and unseeing. Already two lice had crawled out of the hair and were frantically searching the beard. With a quick movement May picked and pinched the two lice, tossing them into the snow. Then he walked back to the plane for his box camera to snap a picture of the death mask. Johnson was dead and would stay that way, there was no getting around that.

EPILOGUE

From the foot of Orion, near the river Eridanus, Johnson looks down on himself being looked at: on May snapping pictures, Eames issuing orders, Hersey being lifted onto a stretcher and the stretcher lifted onto the airplane. He sees teams of dogs and clusters of men milling about the river. One group is around the corpse and May taking pictures, another around Riddell as he sets up his field radio, the trappers congregate around Lazarus as he builds a bonfire and boils up.

Johnson from the foot of Orion looks down and sees his corpse, having been photographed from all angles, sacked and shoved into the plane beside Hersey; the plane leaving the ground, the body airborne, flying back over the Eagle, the Bell, and Porcupine rivers, toward the raised ridge of the Richardson Mountains. As he looks down on the plane gathering loft to cross over the Barrier Pass and to enter the Rat River delta, he feels himself getting lighter and more luminous, farther away from the Arctic but with an ever more clear and commanding view of the mountains, the oceans, the planet…

He looks down on the inquest, on his own burial, on the men returning from the Eagle, the men spreading out as they return to Aklavik and disperse throughout the Arctic—to desk jobs, to small shacks and traplines, to wives and girl friends and partners. As he is lifted up into a broader and clearer perspective he laughs as he looks down on them looking back: Eames in a rest home in Burnaby, B.C., playing backgammon with the ghost of a dead man; Hersey an alderman in Barrie, Ontario, still granting interviews fifty years later to newspaper men, crouching on one knee on his living room rug to demonstrate how and where he got shot; May and Riddell getting together each year, drinking and reminiscing...

Johnson from his place in the brightest of all constellations, the blue-white star below the belt and below the Great Nebula, looks down on his pursuers—the first generation, who are dead or in rest homes; the second generation of newspaper men and journalists, book writers who try to prove his identity, movie script writers who know nothing about him; and even the author of this book, the readers of this book, and generations to come—and he laughs. He laughs mirthlessly and maniacally, without sound or substance.

Whenever anyone breaks free of himself and the herd and, looking up at the night sky in winter, aspires to the foot of the Hunter, Johnson will interrupt his mad laugh to chortle:

"I am he who was within me. Who are you?"

FLANAGAN'S RUN

TOM McNAB

The first and only Trans-America Race: 3,000 miles for $300,000. The press called Flanagan's race impossible. Crazy! But as Depression America cheered, two thousand hopefuls left Los Angeles running for New York City and their wildest dreams of riches!

Fifty miles a day. Day after day. It took more than raw courage. Five runners—a beautiful dancer and four determined men—pushed beyond physical exhaustion to the sheer exhilaration of a superhuman challenge. Until the miles became days, the pain became pure spirit, and their hearts became one in the magnificent drive for victory! 63149-0/$3.95

Tom McNab was Script Consultant/Technical Adviser of CHARIOTS OF FIRE

SELECTED BY THE LITERARY GUILD AND READER'S DIGEST CONDENSED BOOKS

Available wherever paperbacks are sold or directly from the publisher. Include 50¢ per copy for postage and handling; allow 6-8 weeks for delivery. Avon Books, Mail Order Dept., 224 W. 57th St., N.Y., N.Y. 10019

Flanagan 3-83

P.E.T.

PIERRE ELLIOTT TRUDEAU

and his unearthly adventures

Here is a collection of witty cartoons inspired by Canada's controversial Prime Minister, Pierre Elliott Trudeau. The man Canadians most love to hate is portrayed irreverently here, as an extra-terrestrial (P.E.T.) who is accidentally thrust into the earthly political arena. Using Trudeau's own words wherever possible, Jude Waples has created a satirical, funny—but never malicious—spoof of the Trudeau years. With black-and-white illustrations throughout.

<u>On philosophy:</u> "If you want to show up as an original thinker, you don't have to rely on turtlenecks or on sandals."

<u>On politics:</u> "I don't like Parliament. It's a place where men are shouting...and I find it vulgar. I am offended."

<u>On law and order:</u> "Well, there are a lot of bleeding hearts around who just don't like to see people with helmets and guns. All I can say is, go on and bleed, but it is more important to keep law and order in the society than to be worried about weakkneed people."

<u>Plus personal reflections:</u> "It's not a perfect job. But it sure beats working."

<u>And much, much more!</u>

An AVON Paperback   83543-6/$4.95

Available wherever paperbacks are sold or directly from the publisher. Include 50¢ per copy for postage and handling; allow 6-8 weeks for delivery. Avon Books, Mail Order Dept., 224 W. 57th St., N.Y., N.Y. 10019

P.E.T. 6-83